SYNOPSIS

This is about the author Harry's life from birth, a c̶ . . . . last world war. It covers the general conditions of ru . . . . 10 life in the bombed out towns and cities afterwards, t . . . . educational years, to the beginning of full time employment, at the . . . . just fifteen. It recalls his recreational pursuits, up to the time of the great reve........on, when he heard about the existence of the Royal Navy and the exotic life being led by the sailors who were part of it. He joined the R. N. at the age of seventeen years and six months, for an initial minimum period of nine and a half years. This is a requested recollection of times gone by and of things as they were, and not as people would have us believe they were. Plus a series of fascinating stories from the mess decks of various warships, and shore establishments, and tales from the deep and the supernatural. Told with fervent candour and sometimes enthusiastic euphemisms, just enough to make your balls strain, twinge and ache at the seams, – – – – that's if you are fortunate enough to be blessed with natures ultimate gift, and have got any!.,

So if you like a good fast flowing read, hang on to your hat, fasten your braces, settle your nuts and away we go.

The stories, tales and ditties, are told in true Naval style. Imagine yourself sitting around the mess deck table in the early 1960's. Its tot time andRums up, the Rum Fanny has just arrived at the mess deck table over flowing with the precious amber nectar, the drink of the Gods. The mess is cleared of sprogs, the ceremony is about to commence.

The Rum bosun is about to start the age old ritual of dishing up the rum with sippers for himself and the ticker off alike, or maybe swinging from the hammock bars in your Mick, a few inches down from the deck head, hanging on for grim death in rough weather, when its blowing a bastard up top, and the ships all over the place, were riding the big rollers, one minute were in, then out and above, we can see everything that's happening outboard through the scuttles (port holes) in the ships side in our mess deck, with ribald tales of our escapades ashore, the more coarse, smutty and salacious the better.

But if fiction is your forte and you really like to get yourself all emotionally mixed up and involved in the realms of drivel, lies, bullshit and fantasy I suggest you get yourself curled up with a copy of the Labour party manifesto and leave reading about the realties of life to real understanding people. However, if you want to be in the privileged position to earwig on the tittle-tattle around the rum Fanny on a mess deck table aboard one of Her Majesties Pussars warships in times gone by, get your hands in your pockets, loosen your shekels, and dip your bread in! Fuck the Pope and the one eyed Jock alike, sit back, relax, and enjoy the ride. Yee! Hah!

FOREWORD

I have known Harry Green now for five years and during this time he has become a friend. As a privateer cabbie he rescues me from the Beachcomber pub twice a week. We exchange stories from our time in the Royal Navy, the problem is that I can't compete as I only did six years ashore as a scab lifter (medical assistant) whereas as Harry served all over the world doing his time and can recount some cracking tales at the drop of a hat. These tales spring out of the life Harry has led and the friendships he formed during his time as a child, boy and young man in the North of England and then as a man in Her Majesty's Royal Navy.

The story of his early years is indeed a social history. The bitterness of Northern folk about the hypocrisies of those in power was fed to him with his mother's milk. Yet the dogged character of an old fashioned Englishman shows through always ready for a joke

You will laugh out loud at the antics he got up to as a youth. If there was trouble Harry would find it, Harry could walk into church during evensong and through no fault of his own it would end up in a punch up, if not worse. You will also be touched by the sensitive way in which he talks about his family, friends and the animals he loved. Harry then goes on to explain how and why he joined the Royal Navy as an electrician. As an ex R. N. medic I was totally enthralled with how he delivers the stories, from his first day at the training establishment, H. M. S. Raleigh (boot camp), through to the various shore and sea postings and to warships in the days when the R. N. had a fleet to be proud of.

As Harry's career progressed you will continue to laugh out loud at stories he recounts about his time as a young Matelot. You will love the story about the sick sailor playing darts in a Gosport pub wearing pyjama's with an intravenous drip in his arm!. I'll say no more other than now'a days this would be headlines and everyone would be outraged and demanding a public fucking enquiry.

You will also be shocked at the conditions these young men endured for their country and amazed at how these men dealt with levels of danger only now remembered in post W. W 2 movies. Post traumatic stress disorder, I don't think, not in them days.

Despite the considered language of the officer classes Harry enlisted as an ordinary seaman and his language belongs to that class. Do not think for a moment that he is swearing he has actually improved on the preferred method of communication which was generally an oath every other word. This book is an open, honest, and transparent account of Harry's life. No holds barred. Some people will be offended by the way men of Harry's generation describes people and their situations from different parts of the world and attitudes to them at that time.

Remember this– opinions and attitudes are based on real and true life experiences, such as Harry Green's before PC, so, whether you agree or not he has earned his right to form an opinion unlike so many people these days who have formed views and opinions that are based on absolutely fuck all. As this book progresses I hope that you will begin to understand why men of Harry's Generation talk and feel the way they do about things that now days we have been conditioned to tolerate. The reality is that Harry Green probably represents the true feelings of Mr. And Mrs. Middle England.

Harry Green is a man of integrity who has served his country.

I now invite you to sit back, feet up, read this book and enjoy!.

Alan Merry. Royal Navy Medical Assistant. 1975–1981

ACKNOWLEDGEMENTS

To Mother God bless, she'd have loved it
To our Beryl for the necessary
Rhian Kavanagh for original instigation
Boe Higgs for help with management and support
Chris Vine for patiently typing and transcribing
Amy Koller for grammar and typing etc
Guy Macdonald for overall spelling and layout
Vic Williams for being a big inspiration
Saz Vine for general support
Amanda Payne leading tech advice and support
LesleyHarvey17@hotmail. com for brilliant artwork
Thank you to Alan Merry for the Foreword.

HAVE A LAUGH BERYL AND THANKS
FOR A LIFETIME of SUPPORT.
LITTLE BROV.

MY COCK IS MY COMPASS

Harry Green

ANTONY ROWE
PUBLISHING

Published in 2010 by Antony Rowe Publishing
48-50 Birch Close
Eastbourne
East Sussex
BN23 6PE
arp@cpi-group.co.uk

A catalogue record for this book is available from the British Library

ISBN 9781905200993

Printed and Bound in Great Britain by
CPI Antony Rowe, Chippenham and Eastbourne

CHAPTERS

CHAPTER 1

The Halcyon days

Push, push … oogh! Push its coming that's it OOOOAAAGGGGHHH!, Push I can see the head. OOOOOOOAAAAGGGHHH … . Gasp! … its not a head … . Stone the crows! … Your not going to believe this … . It can't be … . It jolly well is … . "what is it, what is it?" … it's his cock, todger, chopper, what the hell, Jesus Christ! I was born with a lob you could hang your jacket on. Apparently mother said "bloody hell, he's going to break some hearts" "as well". So there I was a ten pound baby feeling a little light headed, with a slightly strange sense of humour, and half my body weight straining towards the future. Well if you are going to blow your own trumpet make sure it's a big one and that you blow it hard, loud and long because nobody else is going to blow it for you. " Not in them days at any rate" Little did I know where this fascinating appendage was going to lead me over the next few decades. I spent the first nine months of my life trying to get out, and the rest of it trying to get back in. I can't wait; I'm really going to enjoy this one off life. Right up to the hilt.

I was born 8–8–43 at number 2 School Terrace, Oughterside near Carlisle, about twenty miles south of Scotland. I have my parents to thank and be grateful for, for their fore sight and consideration to my future plight as a human being on this Planet. Another twenty miles north, and "I "would have had the terrible misfortune of being born a bloody jock, a malady from which it would be have been impossible to recover and which I could never hope to live down.

There were four of us Beryl, the eldest about nine years older than me, Margaret, three years older, myself, and then nineteen months later James. It must have been a hard life for mother and the girls. Father worked away as a Steel erector (reserved occupation during the war) putting up electricity pylons across Cumberland, in readiness to distribute power from the soon to be finished nuclear power station at Wind scale now (Sellafield). The Politicians changed its name after a devastating fire inside one of the chimneys spread deadly radioactive dust across the beautiful countryside, contaminating the whole area plus the Irish Sea with its discharge of contaminated cooling water even up to today.

Their instinctive moronic train of thought was to lie to the population, the people paying their wages to take care of their welfare, (Their employers) about the catastrophe, who were by the way ultimately responsible for paying for the project. The absolute totality of their sheer incompetence and ignorance is nothing short of miraculous and to think they are still trying to work to the same standards with a totally inferior education to their predecessors, and getting away with it is pathetic, and nothing short of criminal, for which they should be held accountable. The only infinitesimally redeeming factor for these obnoxious beings, is with the self recognition of their own inability to compete within society to fulfil a worthwhile and honourable occupation, and so putting themselves on a platform from where the rest of society can recognise them for what they are, parasites.

The war was still raging, and had another two years to run, food and clothing etc, was all on ration. Yet I think we did ok, being in the countryside and living about a stones throw away from the farm. Everyone looked after each other. Through thick and thin, they had too to survive. The cottage was tiny with one room downstairs plus a scullery which housed a couple of shelves but unfortunately no running water (this had to be carried by bucket from the wash house three cottages down the line.) and a back door leading on to the long rough back garden which was planted with veg. Among the weeds and way down at the bottom had the dilapidated toilet housing, just about on its last legs and still just managing to support the roof and door, inside was a raised wooden plank with a hole in it for the purpose of depositing the superfluous, of which their was pretty little in those days.

The tin bath hung on the wall outside the back door, and for all I cared it could stay there, it didn't hold any good memories for me. Once a week it would be man handled indoors, placed in front of the fire and filled with hot'ish water from the communal washing boiler three cottages away carried in buckets by Mother and Beryl, disinfected red washing (lifebuoy) soap was cut up and administered to discolour the water, and whether we needed one or not we all had a bath, the red peril was gradually worked into every orifice individually with much dedication and discomfort to us who couldn't fathom out the reason why, one by one the troops went about their ablutions gradually turning the now rapidly cooling mixture into an uninviting scum topped slimy mess, which was by now myself and our Jims destination. We were both plonked in the mire and stood there freezing and holding our breath, wee peckers and future ball bags, waiting for the scrubbing brush, I promised myself I'd never get dirty again, what a pallava.

Upstairs was one bedroom and a tiny attic space where Beryl Slept on the floor, along side jars of home done pickled eggs, emergency victuals so we wouldn't starve, the rest of us were in a small bed alongside Mothers, it brought a whole new meaning to the word cosy. Beryl reminds me that every morning she had to go to the farm to collect our milk in our half gallon aluminium container; she says the thin wire handle use to cut into her hands especially in winter when it was frozen and full of milk. One of my first memories is of chasing after the lid of the four pint pail, when the cold wind had blown it off, and it was rolling down the hill.

The sea was at Alonby which was about three miles away. Mother and the girls were taking me in the pram there one sunny afternoon; on the way they were collecting rosehips from the wild rose bushes in the hedge rows.

They were sold to help the war effort, they would be converted into rose hip syrup which was very high in vitamin 'C' and was prescribed by the doc's for the young children as a supplement to make up for the lack of goodness in their meagre rations which left a lot of kids with rickets, weak bones and consequently bowed legs and stunted growth a good percentage of the population were crips. in those days anyway.

An aeroplane flew overhead, as it circled they noticed a swastika on the wing mother instantly recognised it as an enemy machine, – German, a Fokker Wolf possibly, (but this Fokker was a Messerschmitt) it was about a mile ahead of us it straightened out and was in a dive coming towards us, Mother lifted me out of the pram and all four dived under the hedge for shelter luckily he didn't open fire or that could have been curtains for all of us.

Another time when I was about two or three, Mrs Oscal from across the lane came running to our house shouting for my mother, PEGGY!!! Come quick, your Harry's in the field with the carthorse, standing under its belly and pulling the long hair on his back legs, the horse must have known one kick would have killed me. It's a good job I didn't start trying to ring his bells or he definitely would have clogged me. They had to get Farmer James to call the horse away in order to retrieve me.

On another similar occasion on a lovely hot day, I had taken all my clothes off and was in the horse's drinking trough in James' field, cooling off, when Billy the big black bull came wandering over to see who this little squirt was who had the audacity to encroach on his patch. He was standing about four feet away eyeing me up, probably wondering whether or not to gore and toss me over the hedge and out of the field. They managed to extricate me again to while away the hot summer days on my little three wheeler bike.

What a brilliant start, heaven. I remember the men coming with the big steam roller to tarmac the lane going up to the farm. When they had finished for the day and retired, I rode my bike over it, by the tiny little school house and my wheels sank down into it as it wasn't yet set, having the hot sun shining down on it all day and by the time I'd freed myself from this glutinous mess I was absolutely covered in tar, as well as my bike, another Oh dear, come here lad what am I going to do with you and a big clean up job for mother. I still love the smell of boiling tar, it must be ingrained in my sub conscious some where, reminding me of those beautiful hot care free days of summer time, in those far distant days of bliss.

One night a week when we were all turned in, Beryl used to tune into this particular programme 'The Man in Black' on the accumulator powered wireless we had. He use to tell ghost stories, starting off with 'Make sure your windows are closed tight, you don't want any ghosts or skeletons coming through them to get you in the next half hour.'

Beryl now tells me that our windows wouldn't close properly – WOOOOOAAAAAAAH – that was it, straight under the army blankets and trench coats, talk about your imagination running riot. He used to frighten the lives out of Beryl and Margaret, when he'd finished they would then proceed to scare the shit out of me and Jim. "Typical" After the war was finally over, and the soldiers that were left alive, returned, the 'Land fit for Heroes' they had been promised, (they had been abroad enduring a living hell, watching their comrades being blown to bits, and the unlucky ones being badly mutilated, gassed and some blinded as well, but still managing to survive.) returned home, to find out all the promises the politicians had promised them was just that promises, another big pile of bullshit delivered from the safety of their hiding holes.

Sixty years on and hardly anything has changed still thieving lying bastards, they have just got better at it. (Politicians are the same the world over, they promise to build a bridge, even when there's no river,) "Nikita Khrushchev, " they promised the cannibals they would send missionaries, just to solicit their vote, (they won't even recognise that they are working, that's the wrong word, employed by us, and should do what we want, and not what they want. Anyway that's digressing more on those thieving bastards later on.). "Don't tell my mother I'm in politics – she thinks I play the piano in a whorehouse". (saying 1930's).

Billy Oscal across the lane was told when this strange bloke arrived at his house, "Billy, this is ya fatha', Billy says "That's not me fatha, he favors George Formby. " But it was, and it wasn't Billy's fault he'd never seen his father before, He'd had to leave for the war to help defend HIS country, our heritage and culture against being over run by foreigners before Billy was born, but not before he was conceived. (but as we can all see nowadays it was all in vain, the poor sods gave their lives at the asking of politicians and died in agony as we can see nowadays, for nothing. R. I. P. you were conned.)

Well our time in Cumberland was coming to an end, we needed larger accommodation, and there wasn't a lot of work going on in the area, and I think Mum's brother Bobby had put our names down for a council house in Rochdale, and our time had come. Little did I know the Halcyon days were over. All the farm yard animals that had been part of our lives through the summer, the chickens had given us their eggs, the ducks amused us with their comical language and funny antics on the pond, the cows gave us their milk, but the greatest sacrifice of all, came from the pig's, who, not knowingly, donated there tasty feet (trotters), along with their heads, livers, kidneys, ribs and especially their skin, which could be scorched into that lovely crackling that makes our digestive juices flow and allows us to enjoy devouring the whole unknowing benevolent animal. So kind !. The big cart horse recognised I was just a bairn, and did not hoof me over the hedge, Big Billy the bull knew it was a hot summers day and I was just a nipper cooling off in the mid. day sun, and he decided not to gore me to death

The haymaking was finished, the lane had been tarmac'd and the summer was just about finished, the war was over it was now time to pack up all our possessions, which didn't amount to much, but they were all we had, and begin a new life of so called progress, and negative democracy. In re-building our bombed out country with backbreaking toil for the minimum reward, setting up the Coop to feed ourselves and not be robbed of our hard earned coppers by those thieving bastards, who had manoeuvred themselves into a position to be able to do so, as so many Englishmen in our land were dying from preventable accidents, and unknown diseases brought home by our surviving troops, it was decided to set up a health service to take care of our brethren and their families (From the cradle to the grave), who happened to fall ill through no fault of their own and had no means of paying for the attention they required.

This was to be called the National Health Service, as the name implies set up to care for the people of the Nation whose contributions were paying for it, and not for some International Health Service being paid for by the toil and savings of the down trodden British Citizen, somehow manoeuvred into place by the totally incompetent efforts of the moronic M. P's which has left our once great Nation on the verge of bankruptcy.

Money was also put aside to pay for some of our population to be chosen to look after the welfare of our citizens and Called our Members of Parliament.

The idea being that people with a great love of their country and an overwhelming sense of Duty would put their names forward explaining their competence in life's great mysteries and how they could be a benefit to the progress of our society and our country.

Not the rest of the Fucking World, that's Gods job. If their sick and dying surely that's the will of Allah let him sort them out. The whole of society would then be given the opportunity to vote for, and thus select if in the majority, a trust worthy, reliable and honourable citizen to represent them and their wishes in the parliament which was set up for them just for that purpose, its called DEMOCRACY, if unelected by the main populace and elevated to power by their own weasel cronies its called DICTATORSHIP, and should be instantly overthrown as has been the case for generations and the culprits beheaded as is the case in the rest of the civilised World to restore Democracy.

To pay for our new set up, it was agreed that everyone should be working and paid a fair days pay for a fair days toil, out of their wage to belong to this society everyone should make a fair contribution to the communal purse. Tax. As it was inevitable members would at various times find themselves between jobs and therefore with no funds to feed their families, under such circumstances it was decided to make a reparation for the unfortunate family to buy food and maintain their dignity until a change in circumstances saw them in work again. If I'm wrong I apologise but that's the line we've all been fed since the last World War over sixty years ago. So let the bastards perish by their own swords.

CHAPTER 2

A Rude Awakening

A local chap who owned an open back truck had been coerced into taking us the one hundred and eighty miles or so south to Rochdale, where father had secured a job in the local hospital stoking up a big old boiler, (no? not the matron). – – – – come to think of it, – – – no!, I remember it was an absolutely foul night on our journey south, and by the time we arrived at Waithlands rd. Rochdale, everything and everybody was soaking wet through. We arrived at midnight in the middle of a great storm. Uncle Bobby was eventually summoned from his house a couple of miles away with the key to let us in, there was no electricity switched on, and in any case the house hadn't quite been finished and was being fitted out with the essentials needed to make it reasonably habitable, floorboards, windows, doors etc. so it was decided we'd all sleep on the floor at uncle Bobby's house.

Aunty Emily put us up for the night it must have been a traumatic experience for everyone, instead of four people, she now had ten, God only knows how she fed us all. And with what. Well this was it, I was now in Rochdale, and much to my detriment, I was about to find out what it was like to belong to the human race, in war torn England, and what a race, mother earth would have done herself a favour if she hadn't allowed these self centred, indulgent, illiberal, degenerate, cretins to evolve in the first place and to further descend into the mire to allow politicians the chance to foul up the life giving air she so graciously provides for the rest of the living creatures living on her beautiful surface.

I could not comprehend what was going on around me, my new diet was bread and milk (pobs) or porridge oats. Mother, as always was the best, she had a way of putting a Christmas day into every week. Each Sunday we had milk AND sugar on our porridge, I'll have to stop this I'm breaking my own heart here. 54 Waithlands Rd, an ultra modern semi-detached, central heated house with a garden front and back, a pre-fab. Just what the politicians had dreamed up for us – TIN TOWN! Gas and water worked, but the supposedly new back boiler and its connecting pipe work to the radiators (the ultra modern central heating system, never been heard of before) had been connected up wrongly and never worked, plus the electricity was off. We had arrived alright, to us hell.

Father had his job, in the boiler house, Mother worked at the tea factory, tea arrived from India in tea chests, and the women's job was to repack it for sale in the shops. We didn't seem to see father much, which was a good thing really, he just shouted at us, probably pissed off with being stuck with a trouble and strife, and four pan lids to support, and a mere pittance of a wage on which to do it. we were never beaten at home, only at school. By the perverted sexual deviants, with whom it was our misfortune to have to attend their so called instructional classes. I certainly thought I'd arrived in hell, comparing it with what I had known in Cumberland.

Looking on the brighter side (of the cowpat) for awhile, at home we had an upright piano and a grandfather clock which was great when it came to hide n seek. When I was hiding I'd open the clock door and get in with the big winding weights, at least we could make our own entertainment and have a laugh. The morning wake up started at about six, when the knocker up (not what it sounds like) he was a bloke with a long pole who would knock on peoples bedroom windows to wake them up, who paid the man about a penny for the service. The next thing was the incessant noise of iron shod clogs clattering over the cobble stoned streets. that went on for about half an hour.

Then the milk cart would come clip clopping down the street, his big shoes making one hell of a racket. The horse knew just which houses to stop at for the milkman to make his deliveries, he didn't have to be told, as soon as the milky took the bottles off the back of the cart the horse was off to the next house on the round. The horse's deposits (especially reserved for the residents of Tin town, being the only houses in the area with gardens) came in handy for fertilizing the rhubarb, no sooner had the horse done a pile and the shovels were busy, it had found its resting place around the rhubarb while it was still steaming. horseshit a penny a ball, bullshit free.

I was starting school at Newbold Infants, Newbold being the voting Ward in which tin town was situated, with Rochdale Hornets rugby club situated just behind the ghetto, and the railway shunting yard the other side of that. Both of which would have a large influence on anyone unfortunate enough to have to live in the area. September 1948, was the most terrifying experience of my short life.

Beryl was taking me to school for the first time, or halfway as it turned out, as we arrived at the senior school playground which was Beryl's destination, she told me to follow this group of younger kids, who she assumed were going to the infants school playground, which was situated next door, part of the same building, wrong, unbeknown to us I was tagged on behind a bunch of other kids going to the junior school, which was about a quarter of a mile away. We arrived at the school and entered the playground, to my complete bemusement as to what was going on. The next thing somebody blew this whistle, very loudly, then started ringing this hand bell for all they were worth. Every one froze, and there was complete silence.

This big battleaxe of a woman, dressed in thick wartime tweed attire, and looked for all intents and purposes like a German torturers Madame. Started screaming for all she was worth for everyone to form a straight line and start entering this foreboding building, the first thing I noticed was this horrible dry dusty, musty smell and a seemingly dire shortage of air (the place had been locked up for weeks during the summer holidays). As we arrived in the large assessment hall, the sphincter in my arsehole had developed a mind of its own. I was terrified, we were told to sit down on this dusty smelly floor in orderly lines and keep quiet. The teachers came out and began calling out the names on their particular list, when complete they marched their assortment of bodies off for further interrogation, eventually I was the only bemused sod left sitting on the floor in the middle of this great big assembly hall, on my own, frightened stiff, not knowing what the hell was going on, or what I was supposed to be doing.

By this time I was sitting in the biggest pile of shit this side of the Okefenokee Swamps, deep down in the Everglades. 'What is your name boy? PHWWWW! Even more shit, Harry I reply, 'No your second name' PHWWWW! even more of the stuff, 'Green' I replied, 'Any brothers or sisters?' PHWWWW! They managed to get our

Beryl's name out of me as well as anything left remaining inside me, they contacted her at Newbold senior's and summoned her to St. Peters junior school, to extricate me and this foul smelling matter in which I was now nearly buried, she arrived and to her total embarrassment the state of me, being my sister and so undeniably connected, she took the flack and proceeded to drag me off home, enjoying our own clear area around us all the way, on arrival she ran a bath (freezing water) and upended me into it calling me all the explicit names for a dirty smelly little beggar under the sun, without swearing because in those days people of a certain breeding didn't lower and belittle themselves into the use of foul language, obviously foul pants was a different story.

She got me to where I was suppose to be, Newbold infants, joining a class of even more strangers, half way through the morning, everybody wanted to know where I had been. The only good thing about my new situation was that there was absolutely nothing left inside me, no solids, not even a thimble full of gas. As from now on, this place they called school, punished me with a big leather strap wielded across my hands and wrists for just about anything I did, or more likely, didn't do. My biggest problem was communicating, to me, these morons could have come straight from the moon. I spoke with a very broad Cumbrian dialect (accent), and the enemy spoke with a very broad local Lancastrian accent, and never the twain shall meet. We couldn't understand each other, which of course was my fault, which in their eyes justified some educational correction, delivered to the seat of my short pants with a wide strap until I learned to master their method of communication.

Anyway, there I was, just started school and hating these bastards, just as I thought things couldn't get any worse, unbelievably they started to try and poison me school dinners! I'd seen the pigs getting better swill than this back in heaven on the farm in Cumberland, with figs, sago, or tapioca pudding (big frogspawn) and which tasted like what I imagined spider's webs would taste like, it was soon my vomit going faster than shit off a shovel or corn through a goose.

We had to sit there until we'd eaten it all, of which there was no chance of me doing, after half a spoonful of the cold puke it made me wretch, wretch and wretch again, I stopped heaving just in time as I felt a little brown ring coming up, thanking my lucky stars it was my arse hole, another wretch and I would have flopped on the floor inside out. or until the bell went half an hour later for the afternoon classroom torture session to commence. Mrs Westerman was the dinner lady using the term extremely loosely, she used to scream at us to eat up (sod that she'd only give us some more) and smack us on the top of our heads with a big table spoon.

Well I managed to survive somehow. When I was about seven 1950, Father must have had a day off work mid-week, out of the blue, he took me out of school at dinnertime. We took the local bus into town and then the No 90. express to Manchester, about 11 miles away. He informed me we were going to watch Jack Pye wrestling at Bellevue Zoo. When we got off the bus, I stood gauping at the strangest sight I had ever seen in my life a black man. Father said "Don't stare at him, he's got a big knife under his coat and he'll cut your throat. " That was enough for me, the black man was not going to have to endure the indignation of me looking at him any more.

In Manchester I saw so many blind and disfigured ex-service men begging selling matches from a homemade tray round their necks and big queues of starving tramps lining up outside Yates Wine Lodge for a cheap bowl of soup and a piece of bread. Everywhere smelt of toilet plus horseshit everywhere. Which had a rather sweeter aroma, than the stuff that was dropping out of the tramps trollies at a great rate of knots. So this was the place the mentally crippled politicians called a 'Land fit for Heroes'.

There certainly weren't any of those parasites outside the wine lodge knee deep in horse shit seeking sustenance from the only countrymen of theirs benevolent enough to care about them, all after giving and ruining their lives in the first place to secure the safety and potentially happy lives of the bums who now couldn't give a monkey's fuck for them. Well you arse holes some of us didn't forget your actions or lack of them.

Anyway, Jack Pye sporting his long black tights won, before the fight started all the crowds were shouting 'Dirty Pye' wheel him in, 'Dirty Pye' "Dirty Pye" the fanfare started, the spotlight was trained on the pugalists entrance lobby into the arena, the curtains parted and the showmen began to emerge all dressed up in their finery. The opponent made his entrance to the crowds obvious delight, then to an even bigger fanfare they announced the devil incarnate "Jack Pye" Through the curtains came this enormous cartwheel with Lucifer Pye crucified to it. The crowd went absolutely crazy screaming what they wanted done to him, he certainly looked the part with his big pot belly long black tights, a black tight hood over his head with holes for his eyes nose and mouth and bright red streamers flowing from the cartwheel.

They began rolling the cartwheel down towards the arena, the Master was strapped to his transport revolving with the wheel, the noise by now was deafening! "Wheel him in, Dirty Pye, Wheel him in" "Dirty Pye" This was all fantastic, unbelievable I was so exited, I hadn't even known anything like this even existed, and they weren't even in the ring yet, I enjoyed that. They climbed into the ring and Pye started chasing the referee around and round the ring, this was the best, if I had have been old enough I would have shot my bolt. The Ref. eventually took charge and got them to their corners when the bell sounded for battle to commence. It wasn't long before they were throwing each other out of the ring, when it was Pye's turn he landed on the laps of the people in the front row then fell onto the floor.

Not missing this golden opportunity a little old lady was up and trying to beat the living shit out of his brains with her umbrella and calling him all the names under the sun to everyone's delight. Later on half way through the bout, Pye was winding the crowd up even more in between rounds, he had his big fat belly and these long black tights on, he had the water bottle in his hand, he took a big swig and pulling a gurning face squirted the water into the crowd, brilliant, by this time the crowd were baying for his blood. He walked over to his opponents corner and put the water bottle upside down, down the other fella's trunks, all the spectators rose to their feet screaming at the referee "Hang him" "Hang him" don't forget Albert Pierpoint who lived in Manchester was the countries official hangman at the time and could well have been in the audience, to Pye's delight the two hundred strong mob wanted to see Alberts expertise in use now.

The bout finished and Jack was declared the winner to the deafening roar of Boo's from all the miscreant's present, followed by an even louder crescendo of Hang im, Hang im, Hang im. Jack had the lot of them in the palm of his hand. Which made him roar and insult them even more, pulling faces and gesticulating. I'd never been so excited in my whole life, that was brilliant. Lucifer Pye would be the talk of Tin town for years to come. I couldn't get over it.

We had a walk around the Zoo afterwards I was shocked, I had never seen anything like this before not having seen any animals other than what lived on the farm this was a real eye opener for me, the lions in small cages pacing up and down had big patches of bald skin where they had rubbed all the fur off against the cell walls, tigers in similar conditions with no where to go, a polar bear facing a wall moving its now shiny baldhead from side to side, not even having the memory of life on the ice to comfort him to his dying days, years later he was still there, obviously deranged by now but still swaying from side to side. Well it turned out to be an enjoyable as well as an educationally eye opening and enhancing day out. Although I left feeling sorry for the animals, locked up, with there lives destroyed and the big sleep in future unfortunately being their only inevitable escape.

Around about this time Father changed his job for a while. He got employment as the Caretaker and Verger at the C of E church and school at Balderstone parish about two miles away from Tin town, it was a beautiful old church with a big spire which was home to a large belfry with six of the best ancient bells installed in there. It was part of his job to ring the bells on a Sunday for the services, and on any other v special occasion. The vicar Mr. Coe. was a large stern and foreboding man, rather portly, with thin gold framed spectacles perched precariously on his huge hooked nose, long black vestments, and a huge brown leather belt with a large brass buckle on it slung about his midriff and a large gold cross swinging from his big fat leathery neck on which I would have been much happier if he had been fastened to it, he looked more of an advocate for the Marquis de Sade than Jesus Christ.

Definitely the kind of mortal to be given a wide berth he ruled the whole shebang with an iron fist and as he was father's boss, he had consequently manoeuvred all four of us into his choir, which entailed choir practise in the week and attendance at every service plus Sunday school it had taken over our lives, We did have some fun though, once father had got the hang of ringing the bells he proceeded to teach me so I could be his second dickie.

There were two ways of ringing the bells, the first was to have a ringer on the end of each bell rope situated in the church lobby at the base the steeple, then when the rope was pulled it got the whole bell swinging requiring six ringers (campanologists, that sounded about right when you saw what was swinging on the end of what seemed like extremely large toggles) Or secondly from up in the belfry where one person could pull towards him the control ropes which operated separate small hammers to strike the bells. The ropes were numbered 1 to 8 each operating different hammers ringing out the scale, the tunes were written in different no. sequences, Piece of piss, pick out your tune on a card, pull the relevant numbers and out goes the melodious message or tune over the parish, be it a call to prayer, Wedding bells or the hilarious ringing in of the new year. Good stuff,

It was a marvellous feeling first thing on a Sunday morning standing way up in the belfry, looking through the slats right at the top of the bell tower, especially when it had been snowing, casting ones eye over the whole of the sleeping community deep in their weekend slumber. Then pulling the bell ropes for all one was worth and delivering a religious calling to the whole Parish, knowing it was me sending out this raucous peal of bells right across the parish waking every fucker up and giving them the shits, I'm up every bastards up. They should ring them louder and longer these days and drown out that bloody wailing racket coming from the ever encroaching infidels minarets and their alien Mosque's thrust upon the ever down trodden indigenous law abiding English Christian society. M. P. 's !. I've shit better, now we can see what the Crusades were all about when the Country was run by leaders who weren't afraid to fucking well lead, and not these spineless kowtowing scrapings from the worst pig sty's .

Father was up there in the belfry at midnight on new years eve. giving it what for! Melodiously ringing in the new year (or so he thought) when the not too happy portly vicar tapped him on the shoulder way up in the belfry and way out of breath after struggling up the mountainous steps all the way to the top. "Are you alright Mr. Green, " Father with a big smile on his face and the bells ringing in his ears nodded in the affirmative, having been down the wine lodge earlier and was now having a whale of a time pulling all the right ropes but unfortunately in the wrong order. Mr. Coe got the gist of the situation and said "I thought there was something peculiar, he relieved father of his pleasure and continued pulling all the right ropes in the right order.

I Happy New Year (spoil sport). The three of us (Jimmy was too young) had to walk the two miles to church and be there for morning Sunday school at half past nine which was held in the school assembly hall, Father was busy in the church boiler house lighting the ancient old boiler, on completion we were turfed out into the cold at about 1000, to await the opening of the vestry doors at around 1030, when we would be allowed in to get our lagging on ready for the morning service, which commenced at 1045. After that was over we'd gallop home for dinner on our sturdy mustangs which we had just borrowed from yesterday afternoons western's hero's at the local three penny rush cinema. I was winning because I was on Roy Rogers Palomino horse Trigger, and nobody beats him,

We'd have to be back for afternoon Sunday school at 1400, then back home for tea, only to return again to the church for 1845 for evensong. Talk about having it rammed down your throat, it had the opposite effect than what was intended. We hated the place, and everyone in it and all that we could understand it stood for. It seems hard to believe these days but in the early 1950's I received a small prayer book as first prize for attendance at the end of the year, I hadn't missed any of the painful sessions every Sunday plus choir practise one night in the week. On another year one evening mid week, there was a knock at the front door and to every ones shock and horror, It was the vicar. I think he had called just to satisfy his curiosity as to what Tin town was all about, but he arrived on the pretence of being concerned about my welfare.

I hadn't been to church for the last two weeks, now master Green are you feeling better you certainly don't seem very sick to me. Why haven't you been to church we've missed you in the choir. "I haven't got any shoes" Father was pulling his hair out in the corner. "Oh! We'll see if we can do some thing about that" after finding out what he wanted to know and poking his extremely large bugle into everyone's personal affairs he said his good byes and left, saying he would see me in church on Sunday. Father said what did I say that for, I said because I haven't got any shoes leave it at that. Shortly after Christmas it had been snowing hard and we were outside after morning Sunday school awaiting to be let into the church for morning service, so we were occupying ourselves trying to keep warm by running about and snowballing each other.

When I noticed a soldiers head moving along the other side of the vicarage wall. I couldn't resist it I made up a big snowball and took aim at his cap and let fly. It was a beauty smack right in his ear, for some strange reason he wasn't amused. He jumped up and was over the wall in a flash, I was up and running going like a hare with a long dog in hot pursuit, but the Pongo (old smelly man of the jungle) was closing in, I was around the grounds a couple of times and just slipped his grasp over the wall into the vicarage garden which was about six inches deep in snow I slipped and the trooper nailed me. He grabbed the back of my hair and plunged my head into this mound of snow, unbeknown to him there was a white rockery underneath. My forehead just above my left eye exploded and blood was cascading all over the snow it was a really good contrast the poor old roughy toughy pongo was in a panic, he would have to call an ambulance and then explain that he did it and why to a nine year old little lad. The nurse at the infirmary sat me in the chair and said grip the arms then produced a large curved needle and threaded it with cat gut and proceeded to put six stitches in the open flesh above my eye without anaesthetic, they didn't want to waste what little they had, in those days there would be a more deserving case on its way in shortly, which was probably fates way of saying "what goes around comes around" serves you right.

At least I missed the morning service but had to be back in the afternoon for the nailing up on the cross of this apparently marvellously good young Jewish fella who had the audacity and gall to help the poor and infirm to manage the trauma's of a miserable life, without a permit or permission, to die in agony with all the rest of the thieves and murderers, condemned by the politicians of the day for doing what they should have been doing but didn't have the brains or the know how, but were only too happy to live off the sheckles they had purloined in taxes from the poor unfortunates who had no choice in their antics. (nothing changes). Funny old business I thought, I never could understand what the hell was going on. If the politicians hadn't cocked it up no one would ever have heard of the Jewish Bloke.

Who would have been lost in the realms of time with the rest of the would be Messiah's plying for fame and fortune, which was a particularly prevalent ambition at the time, which is conveniently not broadcast these days as it obviously doesn't fit in with the modern toe'rags ambitions.

We used to play cowboys and Indians going too and fro. from the church where our heads were being filled with all sorts of rubbish, which we didn't like or understand. I must have been going for a good couple of years, and I'd had enough. One Sunday morning the choir was lined up in the vestry, waiting to file out for morning service I was having a bit of a giggle with one of the others when I thought my head had imploded. The vicar with three huge religious books in his hands (psalm, prayer and hymn) brought them crashing down right on the top of my head from behind. My loaf (of bread) just about disappeared between my shoulders and when I came to my senses

I realised just what had happened to me, fuming I ripped off the choirs paraphernalia, ruff, cassock and serplus threw it on the vestry floor told them that they'd never see me again and was off. I was the singing cowboy galloping my horse all the way home smacking my rump which was really the horses, full of the joys of spring, until Father arrived home from church to put me well and truly in the dog box for weeks. I only ever to set foot in Balderstone church once again and that was when our Beryl got married.

I must have moved to St Peter's Junior School without any hitches as I don't recall any significant events. As kids we didn't have any money of our own at all so we used our brains and didn't ever let an opportunity pass by, if we found a beer or lemonade bottle we'd return it to the shop and pick up the penny deposit which had been left on it to ensure its safe return. Consequently we had to make our own amusement. Mine was bird watching and egg collecting very interesting and it didn't cost a penny, and depending on your skill you'd finished up with a collection that was worth having, plus it was all yours you owned it. About the only thing you did own.

In winter time after it had been snowing we use to borrow a large coke shovel from the boiler house of one of the cotton mills which were abundant in that area, make our way over the fields to a particularly good sledging field which boasted a large bomb crater at one end plus an exiting down hill run into it at the other. We'd see the young knobs from better places with there up to the minute posh sledges (just if they were the right shape and made by their dads) But I think we had more fun sitting cross legged on a big coke shovel with the handle rearing up in front of us and getting ready to push off, with not a clue as to what was going to happen when we hit the bottom, as you picked up speed at a terrifying pace, with no means of controlling the accelerating projectile, of which you were now part. The means of steering were very limited and braking non existent.

When the journey finally came to an end, at the bottom of the hill we were in hysterics, and if we were still serviceable we would brush the snow off, return to the top and start again. We always put the shovels back, that way we could always go back and borrow them again next time.

The Rochdale to Manchester canal passed the end of our road and sometimes froze over in winter time, on one such occasion I was walking down the tow path at the side of the canal kicking the snow about when a playful small dog appeared out of nowhere, being exactly what I wanted a friendly companion, but wasn't allowed any pets, not through any kind of malice but food for us was as rare as rocking horse shit anyway let alone trying to supply any super numeries as well, I had him rolling in the snow whilst I tickled his tummy, he was up and jumping about with a great big happy expression on his little chops.

I think he was probably a Border terrier cross a bitsa (this and a bitsa that) just what I wanted, I was trying to think of a way I could keep him without Father finding out, maybe keep him in the outhouse with the coal, .

I could make a little kennel and have it in the far corner. Father would never know, we hardly ever saw him anyway and it was me who lit the fire and brought the coal in, I could picture it, I had it all worked out when all of a sudden little scruff ran onto the ice playfully skidding about and trying to stand up when, Oh no! the ice gave way, right in the middle where it was thinnest Scruff found himself having a freezing cold bath in the hole in the ice. He was paddling away and trying to get out but the sides were too thin and slippery and kept breaking off as he tried to get a purchase with his claws.

I was trying to find a way to get him out but as soon as I put my foot on the ice it cracked and that was at the side which was the thickest part but he was out in the middle I thought of lying on my belly to spread the load and bellying out but the ice was now cracked with water above it, the ice was now definitely too unstable to support my weight, he was looking at me obviously wondering why I wasn't helping him, what could I do I wasn't up for drowning, not just yet anyway, water started to come down his nose I was by now getting so agitated trying to find a way to get him out it was so painful, especially with his pleading looks I could see he was getting weaker buy the second, his pleading eyes as he paddled lifting himself nearly out of the water to my shouts of my encouragement but as he was getting weaker he just slipped back in the water and went under, I was going frantic.

He came up again with water by now pouring down both his nostrils but he kept paddling not giving up!, how am I going to get him out, I was going to belly flop onto the ice hoping it would break it all up but if that didn't work it would be curtains for me as well, while I was contemplating my actions he went under again then I saw his little face under the ice for a short while, this really was to much and broke me, I banged on the ice while calling his would be knew name but he disappeared. That upset me quite a lot actually its not bloody fair, poor little sod. Bye Scruff, at least you went with a name.

Bonfire night was what all us kids looked forward too and was about the best thing that happened for us!, well second best after Christmas, the build up and sense of anticipation overtook everyone, the collecting of the firewood was something else if it wasn't nailed down and secured the lads would have it on top of the pile, there was so much old Victorian furniture stacked up and burned, people just wanted to modernise. There was so much ancient craftsmanship destroyed it doesn't bare thinking about. All for the sake of the modern plywood and Formica. The fire would be lit to the total enthralment of everyone involved, and also anyone else who happened to see the fire and wanted to join in, no one would be turned away.

All the mums would bring out their contributions to the over excitement of all the kids, Potatoes to go on the edge of the fire for baking, homemade parkin (treacle or ginger cake) black peas, boiled in a pan indoors, and served out to everyone in their own personal mugs, and seasoned with salt pepper and vinegar, MMMH, I can taste it all now, and for the finale' out would come big trays of treacle toffee, to be broken up with a small hammer on completion of which all the kids would dive in after the biggest bits. That stopped all the noise for a while, in the meantime they struggled with this glutinous sticky black mess in their mouths trying to masticate and manoeuvre it around which was very difficult as it held their gums shut tight and clamped in a vice like grip, but the job had to be done fast and the nectar extracted had to be swallowed in double quick time to get the next lot in while there was still some left. Which wouldn't be long, by the way the rest of the hungry little bastards were devouring the stuff. The operation had suddenly taken away any self control! (If they ever had any), of their mouths and facial features.

This was also the demise of many of their milk teeth which after chewing on such an ecstatic mouthful of heaven and swallowing rapidly left them wondering, why the blood and where the fuck their missing molars had gone, not to mention the slight pain in the morning while having a right old time trying to evacuate these new teeth baring Richard the thirds from their rear end.

As the fire was getting hotter, a back window would crack which would lead to the obvious question, did we build the fire a little too close to the house?. Many a house burnt down in those days due to this slight error, leaving the street with big problems, as practically no one had any insurance. Still look on the bright side and get the kettle on the embers, the firemen will want a brew and some toast, when they've put this lot out, we've got to see them alright!. Saturday nights were always good. The local pub the Vavisour would chuck out at closing time, and about half the regulars were Irish Navvies, who lived on tin town, they would make their way down Grafton St. which joined Tin town at the bottom of the road by the gas lamp, under next doors window. Where they all gathered and would begin their rendition of all the Irish songs they could remember, Molly Malone (cockles and mussels) followed by their rip roaring interpretation of Danny boy, then that was it!, Time for the fight, it was the same every Fri. and Sat. night. I used to pull the curtain behind me so I couldn't be seen, I was full of anticipation I wasn't going to miss this.

I'd been waiting all week to see who was going to get it this time it was Flagherty again, from across the road, he always seemed to get it. I could never understand it, his clothes were in tatters, yet he still went away on extended holidays for three months at a time, sometimes even six months. His wife had left him ages ago, he had a teenage son and daughter who would leave as soon as possible, but also little Robert who was about two years old and had a deformed right side, but could still walk after a fashion. Soon there was just Robert and his dad left. I think the old man used to put the young un to bed at about half past six every night then go out drinking. We would be playing out in the road, hopscotch, guessing film stars names from their initials and running up and down with arms outstretched like an aeroplane, shouting bombs over Berlin, great fun, but Robert was always present.

I think he just used to wait until his dad had gone out then got up and joined in the fun on the road outside. All he ever had on was a dirty old vest that barely covered his belly button, no matter what the weather not even anything on his feet. When the weather got bad and all the rest of the kids went indoors one of the other kids mother would sometimes take him indoors out of the cold. Flagherty would arrive home at all hours of the night then proceed to wake all the other house holds up by walking up and down the road shouting Robert.

Robert over and overagain until whoever was sheltering him gave up and handed him over to his dad. When at last we could all get some sleep. Peggy was a big friendly rough coated mongrel who had the misfortune of residing at the same address.

Flaghery's front garden was about twelve feet square not very big, the local council had just had planted lots of saplings in all the front gardens which were held securely upright by a sturdy stake in the ground, Flagherty took this as an opportunity to make a bit off extra cash. unbelievably he turned up with a pony and trap, attached was a single metal step at the rear on which to alight and three seats either side in the open conveyance, he had been running the kids up and down the road all afternoon to let his one horse business venture be noticed, to the obvious distress of the now thirsty over heated and well knackered hack.

On completion at about 1600 he released the pony from the trap and secured the poor animal to the newly installed stake and sapling in his front garden to fend for himself on whatever meagre forage lay beneath his feet and left the trap parked in the road. The following day when I returned home after school, in the heat of the afternoon He was standing on the rear step trotting the pony up and down the road again, as he was passing I noticed the pony in distress and shouted at him "give him a break you cruel bastard" his head shot round, he gave me a filthy look and was just about to have a go at me when he lost his foothold and fell off the back end with a super bone cracking thump. I cheered and shouted that serves you right. The pony was off up the road going at a fair old lick making his bid for freedom. Flagherty was shouting I'll have you, as he lay in the gutter with a broken leg awaiting the some one to come to his assistance and sadly contemplating the end of his two day equine career. I had to keep well out of his way for months. But it was worth it.

One Saturday night they were all having a right old knees up in the Vavy it must have been a special occasion (an unforeseen wake or something), as the whole pub was slaughtered, it came to closing time and Flagherty's next door neighbour was flaked out in the pub and they couldn't wake him up, they soon found a solution on how to get him home, "Seamus go get the wheelbarrow", on arrival with his own personal conveyance he was loaded into the barrow and transported down Grafton St. to the accompaniment of the by now well tanked and well versed Sat. midnight Irish Tin Town choir belting out Nelly Dean to all and sundry on their way to his abode on the road right opposite our house (where I was observing and wondering what was going on from my bedroom window), on arrival they turned him in on the makeshift sofa indoors, when the kids found him in the morning and tried to wake him, he was stone cold, stiff as a board and as dead as doornail.

Mam what's wrong with Dad he's freezing and he won't wake up, some night out that was. They later found out he was already brown bread in the pub, the wake had started without anybody even knowing. So that was now the topic of conversation. Rolling down Grafton St. after midnight on a Sat. night singing their nuts off and pushing a not quite stiff in a wheelbarrow to the tune of Nelly Dean, You'll have to try it sometime. Its good for the soul, a couple of doors up from them another Irish family not long off the Bog had a couple of clapped out motorbikes which they seemed to spend most of their time trying to get running, once running being revved up and back firing for hours on end.

The semi feral dogs used to terrify every one by running around the estate in packs chasing any unfortunate bitch that had come on heat, after they had sated themselves and left the bitch for near dead they would them concentrate on trying to catch these near lunatics riding up and down the road on their motorbikes.

The dogs snapping at their legs, to counter this they would catch the offending hound, tie it to the rear end of the bike with a length of rope, lift the bike onto its rear stand start it up then proceed to rev. the bike up to near destruction, on lifting the compression lever and wanking the accelerator up this would facilitate the back firing even more, as the unburned fuel in the manifold came into contact with the red hot exhaust valves and exploded, all the time the dogs head was tied to the bike frame about a foot away from the end of the exhaust pipes noise and flames, during clinic it would be howling and wailing like a Banshee, after a couple of sessions of this treatment the patient was usually cured but often developed minor side effects like the violent shakes and the oscillating of protruding eyeballs on getting the slightest hint of any mechanical sound, after that at the first sound of a motorcycle starting up.

The now cured hound would take off at speed in the opposite direction howling and leaving a trail of steaming shit behind it as a piece offering whilst heading for the distant Main road or maybe the hills and away, on his cautious return to the now more peaceful neighbourhood he could retake his place in the wandering pack and concentrate on the more enjoyable things in life.

His education now complete on that particular part of his behaviour society's next step was to find some correctional means of curing him of his anti social habit of trying to bone all comers legs when there wasn't a bitch on heat to hand or paw as was the case maybe . Where do these Liberal minded Prats get the idea that a deterrent doesn't work. They should have their offenders take a course of the Bog trotters therapy's and witness the near instant miracles of success.

With the arrival of a really cold spell the unfortunate council houses took an immediate hit from their knew inhabitants from overseas, usually it was the internal doors that first fell to the axe, if the spell was prolonged they were quickly followed by the floorboards from the periphery of the smallest bedroom first until the boards and joists had nearly all gone, now leaving the lesser members of the household with a hell of a job parking their motorbikes in the hallway, one advantage they did find however was the repairing of the 650 twin engine in the lounge without the hindrance of floorboards to stifle the drainage of the sump oil into the footings below. It did seem a weird way of living and was obviously what they were used to, and must have had its unseen advantages although we couldn't work out just what they could be.

I wasn't allowed any pets at this stage but I had a little white mouse I secretly kept in my bedroom, I could smell it though musky I just hoped no one else could, I was worried at the time as it had escaped and I hadn't seen it for a week. There was an almighty scream and shout in the middle of the night Father had awoken to go to the toilet and in the dark had stood on the mouse on the landing just outside my bedroom door, that was good night nurse and curtains for Oscar now deceased. I was back to no pets again I can't win.

I think about once a month the local slaughter house was in operation just a couple of hundred yards from our house they would kill the cows with a humane killer gun, a big drill would be fired through its forehead into its brain killing it instantly. After a couple of dozen had been dispensed with humanely then skinned and processed The place was then awash with blood and all the once contents of their stomachs. The floor was then hosed down and swept out making it very slippery indeed, like an ice rink, the sheep would arrive next and be unloaded off the lorry in a state of great agitation. they had to be manoeuvred towards a small gate at the end of the pen through which they would be driven to meet there fate. When there were only three or four left down at the other end of the pen, us kids would crouch behind them grabbing a handful of wool on either side.

The sheep would be off running for all they were worth, round and round the pen, dragging us along behind them, while we were trying to steer them towards the executioners gate! Shit ski'ng, Great fun for us, but unfortunately not for the sheep. The countries toff's had to travel by aeroplane to engage in there winter sports, but us kids had sorted out our own, open all year, budget ski'ing programme. It was good having no or very few restraints as a seven or eight year old, and developing as nature intended, it was sure good fun. We must have smelt a bit sweet and been a bit minty afterwards, because we would go and jump into the canal (cut) to try and rid ourselves of all the big fresh lumpy bits that we thought was giving us our newly acquired odour.

Which it never did, it just distributed it more evenly, into our hair and all the other unseen nooks and crannies, Crannies Crannies as it was far too powerful to be dispensed with using such little effort.

When Mother arrived home from work she'd take one look at me and go "phwuuuh, you've been over them damn fields again haven't you, you smell as though you've been Rolling in that damn cow muck, go outside and shake yourself. What the hell are you getting up too, I don't know!", I would roll my eyes upwards, if only you did. Next time I'll come back with a crusty cow Pat on my ead as a cap, that'll show her.

CHAPTER 3

The explorers – outward bound

I can't recollect much that went on at Junior school most of it is what would happen after school the fighting. It must have been the name calling I got from living on Tin town. The headmaster (Mr. Jones) would send me to round up the truants who lived on Tin town, and physically bring them into school. I didn't question at the time, when instructed by God one obeyed without thinking, it was becoming a ghetto, we just didn't know of them. The school board (the councils inspector for retrieving truants, miscreants and the like) obviously did, because he wasn't setting foot there if he could possibly help it.

As a consequence of all this activity, my status was rising. I didn't know why, but increasingly after school, there would be a crowd waiting for me, on the cinder common outside the church (St. Peter's), as soon as I appeared up would go the shouts of fight, fight. Someone at the front would be goading me on. All I wanted to do was go home, but before I could proceed there was an obstacle in front of me that had to be dealt with, which I always did to the cries of Harry's the cock. I've often wondered why I didn't know what was going on, and I have now realised, I was in the third year and not the fourth, where all the senior bods were, and I shouldn't have stood a cat in hells chance of beating them, and so the topic wouldn't have arisen. But that just shows the power of humiliation.

I gradually cleared all comers, including the mouthy bastard who I had just beaten in a marathon scrap, my right eye was completely shut and my left wasn't far behind. I was lifted onto their shoulders and heralded the new cock of the school. They were all cheering and running me around the common. There was barely any skin left on me, rolling around on all those abrasive cinders didn't actually do anything for my complexion. At home I cleaned myself up the best I could, but when Mother arrived home she said "my God lad not again" this was a phrase she would get fed up with using in the future, but what has to be, Has to be. and as there were always plenty of pretenders, I made sure that was the way they stayed, – Pretenders.

It turned out to be a very good education for me that would stand me in good stead through thick and thin for the rest of my life. Don't take any crap from anybody, sort them out, – – – Proper. ! I was ten years of age by now and had spent quite some time in the cubs first and then the church choir, and boys brigade at St. Peters. The two were kept very separate, a harvest festival was organised to take place in the church, and all the school was to attend. Apparently when the schooly's were ushering the riff raff into the church, they were looking for me thinking I'd done a runner. The organ flashed up and the vicar led the choir out of the vestry towards the alter, I was in the second row back, hair combed, cassock and surplice on, a ruff around my neck. I looked like a cherub, a picture of serenity.

The following Monday in school, they said they couldn't understand it, "what caused the transformation when I went to school". The powers that be, persuaded me to join the boys brigade, (The vicar later hanged himself, leaving a wife and four small children, we could only guess at what that was all about.) where we all learned the essential things an outward looking young lad was liable to need, while learning to survive in the extreme environment of Tin town, like morse code, how to make and cook in a biscuit tin oven, catch and skin rabbits, tickle trout, light a fire with two sticks, boil all stream-river water before drinking or cooking, sling a hammock, pitch a tent, beat a drum and sing your nuts off.

Not wishing to let this valuable knowledge go to waste, three of us decided to go on an outward bound camping expedition to lake Windermere, about a hundred miles north of Rochdale. We started collecting our camping equipment with a vengeance, beg, borrow and any odd jobs, birthday, Christmas presents, were all put to good use, I even sent away for a canvas water bucket, which I have still got after 55 years, you never know, it might come in handy! School holidays were approaching in the summer of 1953, and the anticipation was unbearable. We just couldn't wait. I felt like Davy Crocket about to explore the unknown frontiers of the wild west, all I needed was a coon hat with the big stripey tail.

The time had come and we were packing and repacking our gear. We didn't have any rucksacks, just some old army holdalls we'd managed to purloin from somewhere. We were up at first light ready to go, we said goodbye to mothers and set off for the station about a mile and a half away. We had return tickets and not much money, but that wouldn't be a problem as we were going to live off the land and our wits, which would be tested to the extreme. We must have looked a right sight clanking down the road, billy cans, pans, torches etc. all tied securely about our persons. plus tent, old army sleeping bags, all weighed down with tins of beans, corned beef, carrots, a few Bonio dog biscuits always a hunger pang reliever and anything else we got our hands on at the last minute. We were approaching the station and could hear the train but better still smell the steam. We had our tickets punched and the next minute we were in the carriage slamming the big door shut. We had both windows open, and had our heads hanging out, we wasn't going to miss a thing. The driver had given us a wink and a nod as we got on the train, he knew where we were going. He gave a big long ear piercing whistle followed by three short ones by releasing the engines high pressure steam through the same instrument and we were off. Chuff, chuff chuff chuff- – – – – -I Chuff, chuff chuff chuff you couldn't beat this, the smell of hot coals and damp air from the steam, it wasn't long before we were racing through the beautiful Lancashire countryside, approaching the trough of Bowland, which boasts some of the best scenery in the land. (Or it did in those days) into a tunnel we go pitch black, the noise increases smoke and steam filling the carriage through the open windows, we can hardly breath, but it doesn't stop us laughing, then flying out of the other end into the open countryside, what a landscape.

What a feeling, all new to us, heaven, the train terminated at Bownesss – Windamere, which wasn't so much tourist orientated in those days. (more a destination for young would be trappers, I said trappers!.). We had a cup of tea by the waters edge while surveying the landscape. Across the lake appeared to be the most natural and wild forest, and so we decided that would be our destination. It was a hot day and it took us most of the afternoon to trek around to the other side. When we arrived absolutely exhausted, I'm sure our arms were a couple of inches longer than when we set off, the army holdalls weren't, exactly the right kit. We left the road and made our way to the waters edge, where after a while we eventually found a clearing we deemed suitable for our needs.

We pitched the tent stowed our gear, and got some water from the lake, and made a well earned brew of tea. we scouted the area collecting firewood etc. which we stockpiled and covered, for when it rained. By this time we were absolutely cream crackered, we had some beans, then got turned in. we were awakened in the middle of the night by a really violent thunder storm. The rain was coming down in sheets forcing a spray of water through the not quite waterproof tent, we were soaking wet in next to no time at all, This is the life!.

What we wouldn't have given to be in our own beds right now, by morning it had cleared up and we went about surviving the best we could, by mid afternoon we had dried most of our belongings and were on the look out for food, I was at the waters edge and noticed two glass spherical floats, about twenty yards offshore and decided they needed investigating, I manhandled a large log into the water and rafted myself out to the said floats. I took hold of the securing rope and lifted, low and behold it held underneath a wire fish trap which was half full, including some large perch, which I transferred into my canvas bucket avoiding their spines. I replaced the trap for a steady supply of food for the rest of the week.

We worked out the trap was probably part of a scientific survey checking the numbers and species of fish in the lake. Whatever it was, it was spot on, well done scientists, keep it up. We had an educational week, enjoyable at times, when the weather bucked up and we had something in our stomachs, the time had come to leave, so this was our last night. We'd packed what we could and was nearly ready for the off, but we were dreading the trip around the lake carrying all our stuff in the morning. I went to sleep thinking about it. We awoke in the morning and had some breakfast, cleaned up our site, and was packing the rest of our gear when I had a brain wave, the penny had dropped.

We pooled what money we had left, I said "you two finish packing the gear, take it down to the waters edge and wait for me", "and where are you going?". Aha! I'll take a stroll around the lake to Bowness, hire a rowing boat, row across the lake, load our gear into the boat, then row back with minimum effort. Touche, a piece of piss, brilliant. and that's what we did, initiative!. That's what the cubs taught us. Use your brains, that's why you've got them, we slept most of the journey back, struggled from the station and I never ever thought I'd be glad to see Tin town. But knowing my bed, food, warmth and safety were there, made it the most desirable place on earth, for that night.

On another such occasion Ernie Greenwood and my self, took off with our little tent to see his Aunty in Tamworth. Another good hundred miles south this time, just north of Birmingham. We set up camp and H. Q. in a farmer's field, next to the main England/ Scotland railway line. We couldn't believe our luck when the big cross country express trains went thundering past, pulled by big famous blinkered and named engines, we used to save train numbers and mark them down in our spotters guide.

We just couldn't believe what we were seeing, every day, we were in a schoolboys heaven. One day we saw the Flying Scotsman go up the line, his next stop was probably

Scotland and that stretched our imagination to the limit, it was in a different world as far as we were concerned, the next day we'd wait for our Hero's to return back down the line heading for London, somewhere else we weren't even sure really existed. We were on the railway fence waving to the driver and fireman. The next time they went past there was a huge whistle and the fireman threw over shovels full of coal out of the tender for our fire, which we eagerly collected off the embankment, and continued to do so each day until we left. Brilliant and it didn't cost us a penny.

CHAPTER 4

Tech. School

I absolutely hated school; we were coming up to take the eleven plus exam to see if we had the common dog to go to the Grammar or technical school. No one gave me a cat in hell's chance, I couldn't blame them because neither did I. Father promised me a velocipede if I passed, the results came in and low and behold strike a light, the unbelievable, I passed. Needless to say no chariot, I learned a good lesson that day, take everything said with a pinch of salt no matter who they are , there all full of shit if you set your heart on something work hard and get it for yourself. I didn't go empty handed mind instead I got fathers second hand automatic 30 ruby's Swiss watch, very rare in those days in our neck of the woods at any rate.

What an awaking I was to get in the next three years when I came into contact with the Real sadistic bastards who went under the codename of school teachers. I had to go for an interview to see which sort of education would suit me best, basically do you want to work with your head or your hands. I knew I wouldn't be any good at knocking nails in with my head so I went for the other option. I knew that the Grammar school taught Latin and German not exactly Tin Town lingo, Technical school taught French etc … but what interested me was the practical side, wood, metal work and technical drawing which was taught at the Tech. If I was going to have to learn something I might as well learn something that was practical and useful, and would stand me in good stead for a trade in the future. It must of caused mother some hardship, all of a sudden she had to fit me out in a posh school uniform, (plus a couple of pairs of skidders, first time ever) and a satchel to boot. To start with I felt a right prat leaving Tin town in the morning passing all the lads who were off to the local school while I was poncing off down town in a posh uniform. It was like starting school all over again. I was the only one from St Peter's the rest were from other schools all over Rochdale and four lads from the neighbouring town of Oldham. These lads were all from the same school and behaved like a mini gang it wasn't long before they started establishing their superiority by sticking together in numbers and started putting everyone in there places.

Soon it was my turn little did they know I had been cock of my old school. The leader started pushing me around in the alley way between the desks as inexperienced kids do. With a full barrage of both fists straight to his face blood everywhere he was soon on the floor where I finished him off with a couple more good punches to his mince pies, surrender! At this point the teacher turns up takes one look at the situation and 'out here Green, hand out' six vicious strokes of the cane on both hands. I don't think I had ever felt pain like it, I couldn't open my hands. I shouldn't have worried though, plenty more to come from where that lot came from, and plenty more from where they didn't. I was soon to be well used to it.

Three of the lads and I had made arrangements to meet up after school on Tin Town. They were at the local school Newbold, and had to wait a good half an hour for me to get there; (the tech. was in the town) I must have been held up because by the time I had been home and changed, then mustered at rendezvous point, they were long gone. They had taken the gozzi, (a plank of wood set on four pram wheels and very much treasured, a billy cart), we were planning to go over the fields to this hill and have fun racing down the sides of this bomb crater. As they had left without me I was really hacked off I had been looking forward to the escapade all day.

I saw two of them after school the following day, 'Why didn't you wait for me?', the reply was 'Did you hear about Billy (Nailer) ?', 'No what?' I wasn't expecting what came next, he said 'he was cut in half by a train last night'. bloody hell, what happened?' he went on, 'we got chased by a gang of lads who were going to beat us up and take the gozzi, and Billy was escaping over the railway lines, he was running between the lines on the sleepers, we saw a train coming and were shouting to him but he couldn't hear us or the noise of the express train coming up behind him, he must have fallen across the line because the train went straight over him and cut him in half, " I replied 'Fucking hell!!! ... ... Is the Gozzi alright Have you still got it?. It couldn't quite have sunk in, poor Billy, but it was a rare prized possession.

It was around this time I got my first ever ferret. I built a hutch out of any spare timber I could find, and I kept her in the outhouse, a half storey alongside the end of the house. It was very useful it contained the outside toilet, coal bunker and another twelve feet of storage space, which I carpeted and we used as a den for all the planning of our future escapades. We had candles for light and to put our hands round for a bit of warmth when the outside was six inches deep in snow.

One day in the week we were in town during our lunch break from school, when the sharp reflection of the suns rays reflected off a car's wing mirror, and caught a certain spot in my eye and triggered something, because shortly afterwards I couldn't see properly, flashing lights etc ... In the afternoon during assembly I passed out, that was the start of my migraines. If I didn't throw up the headache wouldn't stop until I did. I had started in 1A, there was 1A, 1B etc ... Whatever knowledge I had in my head when I arrived, the perverts seemed hell bent that was all I was going to get in there, which apart from woodwork and technical drawing, which I liked, they were hugely successful at. I started the second year in 2B, I had begun my descent and there was not going to be any stopping it. Sure enough, 3B, Father wasn't amused. I just wanted out of that troubled place of distress.

At weekends and holidays I spent most of my time either bird watching in the countryside or out with my ferrets. I was in pursuit of anything interesting, mostly rabbits and rats on the farms. I was on my own, about four miles into the unknown, on a sunny Sunday morning. I came across a slaughter house all very quiet. I saw a couple of rats, great let's get at 'em. I was well immersed in the job in hand I had the ferret down one hole, when all of a sudden there were rats bolting out all over the place, I was trying to grab them with my hands, but they were in such a panic, they were beating me, but my adrenalin was up, and I was so engrossed in what I was doing, when all of a sudden. – PHRRRRRRRRRRRRRRRRRRRRRRRRRRRRRRRRRRGGGGH What the hell was that – – – – PHRRRRRRRRRRRRRRRRRGGGGH. I quickly hid in an old pig sty I didn't want to get caught trespassing or poaching, There it goes again, I couldn't leg it because my ferret was down a rat hole. PHRRRRRRRRRRRAGGGGH what the hell was it. I was now keeping as quiet as possible hoping I wouldn't be discovered, crapping myself waiting for the ferret to come out of the hole, it sounded like an old farmer who must have finished off a pan load of sprouts PHRRRRRRRRRRRRRRGH bollocks to this I was off to have a look then plan my escape PHRR ... I peered over the wall and behind it, was about a 3ft high pile of cow bones, fresh'ish with most of the meat removed, and thrown on top was a dead cow. There must have been something wrong with it or the meat would have been removed the same as the rest. The sun had been beating down on it, and all the gas inside was expanding PHRRR ... . GH. it was letting off the biggest smelly'ist Farts this side of the Elephant house in Belle Vue Zoo Manchester fourteen miles away.

If it had been alive it would have cleared the whole farmyard, pigs and all. Some to be really proud of. Gaseous Extrordinairious. That was ok, relieved I could now carry on ratting, with the dead cow blowing off to its dead hearts content every few minutes.

Back at school the 6ft rugby playing, piece of Irish pig shit, Mr O'Connor was about to mark my English book, one of those thick blue ones. The cretin would only mark it when it was full, about nine months work. 'Look at the state of this handwriting' he gave me six of the best on each hand with his four foot long vicious cane, he was shaking and drooling at the same time, he couldn't have laid on it any harder if he had tried, I now realise the perverted Irish bastard was getting himself off by beating me. He issued me with a new book and said re-write by morning or else.

I started when I arrived home from school and finished at three in the morning. It was just about intelligible. I handed it in to the Fen'ian moron on arrival at school first thing in the morning, he selected my homework right away above anyone else's, after a couple of minutes the veins in his neck were bursting, he must have been waiting all night for this moment, He came out with this vicious diatribe and the rest of the class were more frightened thanking their lucky stars it was me and not them who was about to get it. . I knew exactly what was coming next from this sadistic bog trotting pervert. I wouldn't cry I just looked determined, you wont crack me slimeball, another six on either hand, I was in so much pain but I wouldn't let go, l just gave him a look that confirmed what a piece of worthless dog shit he really was.

Although that would have been elevating the scumbag, miscreant way above his true worth. I couldn't open my hands now and I hadn't done my History homework (different teacher), 'Hand out', I couldn't, open it, so it was 'Bend over, ' six across my arse and same again in the Maths class. The dye was cast I was going to get out of this den of sadistic perverts as soon as possible.

I had money to buy myself a second hand airgun by now, a '22 Airsporter I was the proudest lad alive, rabbits and pigeons for the pot was the objective. My pal Ernie Greenwood had one as well, everything was a competition between us, who was the best at whatever we were doing. I had two or three ferrets by now I was breeding and selling them, I fed them on bread and milk (purloined from the kitchen) and for protein I was shooting stray pigeons (strags) off the mill windows sills along the canal bank also popping them of the house roof tops. They were in abundance when we started say no more, when we arrived home with to many for the ferrets we would give ourselves a treat and cook a couple each, they tasted pretty good to us with a crust of dry bread. For a bit of extra fun we would shoot to the side of each other's ear from about thirty yards missing it by an inch or two. It was a great sound that of a pellet rushing past your head. For an even greater effect one of us would stand behind one of the concrete pillars holding up the canal road bridge. The other would take up position where he could just see the others ear, move so it was just out of sight and than fire. It was literally a hair's breadth away, we would ping it off the concrete next to the ear, ace. An old chap came cycling past on his bike on his way home from work; he had an old army gas mask bag on his back, used as a lunch bag for his flask and sandwiches. He hadn't seen us and was cycling along the tow path of the canal. I took aim at the back of his head moved it a foot to one side and fired, he had the barbed wire to the field on one side, and the canal on the other, the pellet went whistling away then zipped passed right his ear, the front wheel of his steed took on a mind of its own wobbling all over the place but it was no good, he'd lost control, and he finished up in the canal, it was just like an old silent film we were rolled up.

Great fun. "for us" The canal must have been his best option rather than the barbed wire next to the field. Clutching his Velocipede for all he was worth he disappeared into the overgrown reed bed and was now covered in a thick black smelly slime, as he got out struggling to retrieve his now not so trusty steed he was looking around him and had no idea what had happened, he was trying to wipe this thick black smelly ungent off himself probably feeling a right Walter, I bet he thought that must have been one hell of a big fucking dragon fly it must have been doing at least two hundred miles an hour. He got back on his bone shaker with much trepidation and carried on his way with a big squelching arse that would be red raw by the time he got home. I'll bet he had a right tale to tell his wife on arrival, smelling more aromatic than a wheelbarrow full of pig shit. Really minty, she would have been throwing a few fucks into him while she cleaned him up and with a clothes peg on her nose, he wouldn't live that down for the rest of his life, and would still die wondering at the size of that dragonfly. "Come here darling and give me a kiss"?. "Fuck off you smelly twat". "I guess a shags out of the question then, – – – you can't win". Bloody women, even THEY don't know what they want.

Our heroes were the blokes ten years our senior, who had progressed from birding to air guns to shot guns, there were about four of them who lived on Tin Town, or in the area. Three had shot guns, and George a lurcher (a greyhound crossed with an intelligent dog for out thinking and catching hares) the main man, who was about six foot tall, gangling with a long skull like head, George Shannon. The ugliest bloke I'd ever seen, but with a heart of gold he lived on my road about fifty yards towards the canal and the open fields, with his wife and little girl. It was our dream to go out with them real hunting in our eyes. George had the best lurcher in the county, Russ, who was kept on a chain in a kennel under George's back bedroom window. There was a knock at the our front door one afternoon during the Christmas holidays, .

I opened the door and couldn't believe my eyes, Big George was standing there with Russ looking down on me, what's this big celebrity doing at my door?, 'were going to a secret rabbit warren tomorrow I need to borrow your ferret and nets', 'My ferrets don't go anywhere without me, ' they were my pride and joy and that was that. No problem young un, be at my house at three o'clock tomorrow morning and we'll be gone all day, I couldn't believe my luck, I was in with the big boys like professionals. It was a cold night with a heavy frost and a big bright moon, we didn't take the dog, he was whining and crying when he realised we weren't taking him, but it was all for his own good we didn't want him shot by the farmer.

We walked for about three hours, me constantly struggling to keep up. The fields were surrounded by dry stone walls which we had to climb over, we arrived at this farm at the foot of the Pennines. Shss. 'Keep very quiet we don't want to wake the dogs. ' About a hundred yards from the farm house was this pond, about the size of a tennis court. It had banks going down to it, and it was probably a large bomb crater originally. (fucking Krauts) Anyway the banks were strewn with rabbit holes, which the farmer guarded jealously as it was also a bit of a local sight seeing spot on a Sunday afternoon, dads taking the kids to see the bunnies. "Watership down type thing and all that bollocks" Well I had netted all the holes around one end then slipped the ferret in down wind, 2–6 that woke the fuckers up, there was panic underground, (as soon as the rabbits got the strong scent of the ferrets) they were thumping warnings with their back legs and then they started coming out. Faster than M. P. 's picking up expenses, some hit the nets and some missed. I pulled their necks and squeezed the piss out of them! Otherwise they would leak in my poachers pocket making my aroma even sweeter.

We heard a loud cough we thought it was the Farmer with his shot gun we laid low but couldn't hide very well because of the bright moonlight. I was looking around crapping myself as a cloud moved over and the moon shone through I could then just make out the shape of a cow's head looking at us over the dry stone wall, it coughed again, it was coughing out of one end and I was coughing out of the other it must have been wondering what the fuck was going on. The dog tethered in the farmyard started barking, we've got to get out of here and quick. It was a good job it was chained up to its kennel behind the house, the bedroom light came on, quick get the ferret and nets, luckily the ferret came sniffing out of one of the holes.

The farm door opened, we gathered the nets and our catch in a near panic, we were up and running going like long dogs. (greyhounds) The farmer fired two shots the pellets came whistling over our heads we were laughing our nuts off whilst legging it at speed, what a feeling. I had to carry all the rabbits as George's Mrs wouldn't have game in the house. I arrived home totally whacked I skinned and gutted the rabbits, quartered and washed them, placed them in a big pan with onions and seasoning, left the pan on the stove top and went to bed. I felt elated. I then realised I was frozen my feet were like blocks of ice I had had the best time in my life this was for me, I slept like a log. Dreaming of the farmers shotgun pellets whistling over our heads, Daisy the confused cow, with a bit of a cough. Brilliant. I can't wait to go again.

One of the lads in my class at the Tech., Adrian Drake, lived on a farm out on the other side of town. I use to go over there at weekends and holidays over the period of about a year. I learned a lot going there it was a small dairy farm, the cows were brought in twice a day for milking. The milking machines didn't extract all the milk so we had to finish them off by hand, that made my hands and arms ache a hell of a lot while the muscles built up. No wonder all the old milk maids had such a reputation for being so good at it, say no more.

All the cows were in three quarters of the big field, an electric fence was separating the other quarter which held the bull. One of the cows started calving trying to squeeze a big one out letting all and sundry know about it, this overexcited the bull by which time he was now running up and down the electrified wire fence determined to get through snorting and creating havoc with his massive pair of bollocks banging about between his back legs and making him all the more determined to put them to the good use they were designed for and he had them for. All the other cows formed a circle around the berthing cow with their heads and horns facing outwards to protect her. By this time the bull had run through the electric fence and was circling all the ladies at speed with the biggest hard on anyone could ever imagine, but they wouldn't let him in. Bastards. She gave birth and everything calmed down again. Leaving poor old Billy to slink away wondering what the fuck to do with his big aching prize coco-nuts.

There was big grey cart horse "Samson "that was used for general farm work, in conjunction with an old tractor and to deliver the milk locally one sunny afternoon someone had a camera and they got me mounted on this huge animal my legs astride his massive back, I was doing the splits they took a snapshot. To my surprise Adrian lashed his back end with a large cane, at the sudden shock he was off, me bareback galloping up the field going like a train, I'd never been on a horse before I thought I was dead.

The horse had gone from standing day dreaming in the summer sun to belting up the field at a full gallop wondering what the fuck had happened, he must have thought he'd been stung with a bird sized wasp, Whinnying and Neighing, Bellowing and snorting with me hanging on to the rope bridle for dear life.

Talk about ripe plums more like rotten oranges I couldn't walk half properly for a week. In the Autumn it was time to start ploughing and harrowing the fields ready to sow the seed to be grown for next year's hay as feed for the cattle. During the following winter Adrian taught me all the ropes, how to start up the tractor drive it, reverse up to and connect up to all the various machines towed by the tractor, and I slowly learned how to plough. This was absolute heaven for a thirteen year old, reversing onto a trailer, dropping in the pin, driving off then learning to reverse the trailer onto a second trailer just like a train. Not easy. But I persevered and cracked it.

I was leading Samson to the trough for a drink one boiling Sunday afternoon but its like they say, you can lead a horse to water, but you can't make it drink, I was pulling on his halter trying to get his head down to the water, . He wasn't having any of it, he then changed his mind and brought his left leg forward and put his massive hoof down right on top of my right foot, all his weight came forward as he bent down to the trough to get a drink, . I was shouting and thumping his leg, I had plimsoll's on. He took his time finished his drink then took his hoof off my foot, he then looked me straight in the eye as if to say 'that'll learn ya, ya little squirt. ' Cheers I was now hobbling around with one foot bigger than the other. Like a circus clown. – – -bastard.

It was coming up to Christmas and it was time to prepare the free range chickens for sale. We were chasing them around and around the farmyard having a right old laugh, eventually cornering and catching one every now and again, Adrian was demonstrating how to pull their necks. Head and neck between the first and second finger, pull and twist, snap, neck broken, piece of piss. My turn, all in position I didn't want to hurt it, I pulled alright, I pulled its fucking head right off! It was flapping around like a headless chicken there was blood and shit everywhere I was covered, I was alright with the next one though. When we'd necked them all, we took up the role as chicken pluckers, when plucking chickens just wasn't what us chicken pluckers wanted to pluck.

Adrian could just about manage the ducks with there much bigger and tougher necks, it must be said though, they harboured a lot more shit to cover us in. Especially with Adrian holding one tight, aiming it at me and using like an automatic duck shit gun. No wonder Mrs. Drake insisted on hosing us down in the farmyard before she'd let us indoors for tea. It took huge Mr Drake to do the geese he was six foot four and wielded a frightening pair of size sixteen clogs which had irons on the bottom of them (corkers) not much smaller than Samsons massive blacksmith fitted shoes he used to tell us to behave or he would be unleashing one of them in the direction of our arses. He would put a spade handle across its neck on the ground, stand on it a clog either side of its neck then yanked its head skyward, that broke it they've got some neck on them alright mighty powerful.

All good knowledge for me which I wasn't going to get anywhere else. Mind you I'm still keeping my eye out for the odd goose that wants its neck pulling! It wood be like asking Turkeys to vote for Christmas (sounds like P. M's. question time, all those years of training and all they finish up with is a marvellous grasp of the fucking obvious and are actually proud of it, only because they don't know any deferent). It was snowing hard and freezing outside but it was always quite warm in the hay and straw barn.

There were hundreds of straw bails on one side and hay on the other with about a fifteen foot gap in the middle to separate them and give access to the tractor and trailer for there removal, chickens clucking away everywhere, we would find eggs all over the place. We had some terrific fun in there. All of a sudden Arnold, Adrian's younger brother started shouting from somewhere at the top and back of the barn.

He'd fallen into a homemade den about 7ft. x 3ft. and 4ft deep. It had old blankets, army overcoats and beer bottles, someone was living rough in there. Probably an ex serviceman still looking for this land fit for hero's, he would have had to move on now though, it put the wind up us for a while thinking there had been someone strange watching us without us knowing. I think Adrian's dad cleared the den out. Somewhere over the back of the farm about four fields away from the house lived an old tramp in an abandoned old corrugated iron shepherd's hut on wheels. He even had a little stove and at times we could see the smoke coming out of the thin pipe chimney on the top.

He was probably another ex-serviceman living off the land and surviving as best he could, we kept well away though we weren't putting ourselves up for any thick ears or anything else we might be liable too for nosing around. A couple of years later when I was on leave from the navy, I learnt that Mr Drake had been killed on the farm when the tractor he was driving rolled over on top of him while he was going up and over a bank. Poor family, it was the loss of a very good family man, farmer and farm. Mrs. Drake had to leave the farm and eke out an existence somewhere else the best she could to try and feed and keep the family together. That put an end to young Arnolds ambition to take over the farm from his dad. Its now a housing estate full of foreigners.

I decided I needed some sort of income so I got myself a paper round. Last in, worst job, the bastards gave me the farms in the middle of winter twice a day morning and night. There were blizzards and very big snow drifts in the late 50's. I got to one lane and the snow had drifted level to the top of the hedges, totally impassable. On the radio news there were lots of sheep buried on the isolated farms. I didn't mind a joke but not a pantomime. I decided to look for a better job, work one day Saturday, rather than ruin the whole week. So Saturday morning I went down town, and started enquiring for work in the small shops. I came across this rather cheap shop (and that's giving it a status it didn't deserve), selling second hand suits.

Cheap suits on hangers, on hooks over the window outside, everything in the window had a hand written red Sale sign. I went inside talk about a right old mess. I asked the bloke (Danny, 30 years old ish) if he needed anybody, you would have thought I was heaven sent start now 25 shillings. Top money in those days over double the paper round money, 'tidy up and refold all the trousers, re-hang the sports jackets, sweep up and make the tea'and anything else Danny ordered. I couldn't believe it, I arrived home well chuffed with 25 bob (£1–25p) in my pocket. The following week when I'd cleaned and tided up and got rid of all the shit (clutter) Danny had been living in for the last week, he started to show me how to sell. Each item had a coded price on it, AY- was 25- shillings.

Therefore if the customers looked prosperous , ie. Shoes instead of clogs or wellies or really had his mind set on the item (by this time the price was irrelevant), when he enquired about the price, I could say 35 shillings or up to whatever I thought he could afford, or what I could extract from him. Thanks Danny, the better at selling I got the less hungry I became say no more nudge, nudge, wink, wink. Anything that fitted me and suited me to some extent went home with me, he had no idea what was in the shop. I worked my own bonus, and expenses.

Sounds familiar the M. P. 's. motto. I was the ripe old age of fourteen years beginning the last year at school. The tech school was separated into two, the girls and the boys. We didn't see the girls unless we were in the science lab. on the forth floor, which overlooked their playground I got their attention one afternoon.

There must have been about twenty girls skylarking about in a circle, I lobbed a Quink bottle of ink from the science lab. and it splattered right in the middle of the circle. Loads of girlie screams and they scattered in all directions, I hadn't thought, but it wouldn't take Sherlock homes to work out where the missile had come from. 'Green assume the position, hand out' with me it was always six on each hand, if they wanted to increase my cuts, they would deliver the extra six across my arse, there was an endless array of possibilities, that was from the science master.

He was a big tall fit bloke with sandy hair, very stern and wore rimless gold framed glasses, his left eye used to go wandering off doing its own thing, I used to watch it thinking I could stabilize that for him. Knock a sharpened pencil right in through the pupil to the back of his fucking head that would put paid to its wandering about and slow down the perverted Europeans gallop, that's for sure, I used to hang the bastard on my desk top. Mr Linsky, he looked the epitome of evil, I thought he was one of Hitler's bods. It seemed to me all these foreign bastards hated the true Englishman, but didn't have the backbone to confront him or do anything about it to his face, so the perverted spineless yellow bastards did the next best thing open to that kind of coward, They beat the living shit out of his children. We'll see about you tomorrow mister.

The following day I brought a large potato to school in my satchel. Mr Linsky had a small car which he parked at the top of the hill outside the school, across the road from the park. I couldn't wait for the end of the day I was so excited. It was going dark when the final bell went, great stuff. When the coast was clear I took the massive potato and lined the exhaust pipe up to the middle of the spud, and pushed it right over the pipe than pulled it off. This left me with a spud with a big hole in it, the middle implanted firmly in the exhaust pipe mission accomplished. I was into the park and hid under a rhododendron bush waiting for the fun to begin; I think there were three of us. Here comes the German looking bastard, he got into his car, turned the ignition key, it started then stopped. RRRRRRRRRRRRRRRRRRRRRRRRRRRGGH. It turned over four or five times, the pressure was building up. RRRRRRRRRRRRRRRRRRRRRRRRRRGGH – – – – – – – – – – – – – – – – – BANG! ! ! – – – – – FUCKING HELL! ! ! – – – There was an almighty explosion as the three inch long bung of potato was blown out and disappeared towards the town. All the unburned fuel and gas had exploded in the manifold causing the biggest back fire ever SUPERB. A flame about three foot long shot out the exhaust pipe what a noise!

It lit up the whole area just outside the staff room, at precisely the same moment the science master shot out of the car thanking his lucky stars he was still alive. The terrified fucking kraut with one eyeball oscillating to near destruction was standing in the middle of the road looking at his car and shaking to the point of mild convulsions, while at the same time trying to control his trembling body and wondering what the fuck had happened and if it could possibly be safe to approach his still unbelievably intact conveyance, whilst thanking his God he still had one. Well, we couldn't stand up we were laughing and farting so hard I thought I was going to do a pile. He heard us, bollocks! we were off at a gallop anyhow. Going like the clappers, we kept going over and over it, and we just couldn't stop laughing, it was getting worse. I hadn't had so much fun since the old king died.

The following morning with much trepidation I arrived at school, they were waiting for me. 'Green, Headmaster's study (In the shit! big time) '. He didn't throw the book it was the whole fucking library, he started to quieten down just before his head blew up. So what, this time it was more than worth it.

We use to meet up with the girls in the park at lunchtime. I was chasing Sandra with the big tits round and round this park bench, we were all having a laugh when my right blazer pocket slipped over the arm of the bench and as I was still in hot pursuit. It ripped my new blazer from arsehole to breakfast time, from the buttons at the front and down, across the top of the pocket to the seam at the back. Half my jacket was hanging down, just a big flap. Fuck my luck, I was the talk of the school again. At home however, 'mother I've ripped my school jacket' (mother was a time served dress maker, but with no money about she had to take what was going and weaving in the mill paid best). 'don't worry son bring it here, I'll sew it up. Hell fire you haven't torn it, you've damn near pulled it apart. ' She did a good job, but it was in a right state a few months later, I wasn't getting another one though, not until the coop Divi'd up next year.

To get away from school midday I use to go up to the Besco Mill where mother worked, for my dinner. There must have been over two hundred weaving looms in that one shed which must have been about half the size of a football pitch. The noise hurt my ears, as loud as you could shout no one could hear you. They had all learned to lip read. If they could see you they could communicate. The women worked either two big six foot looms, or four three foot looms, getting paid for their output (piece work) and the women got half as much as the men. That was because the man was the main breadwinner and his wage was the mainstay of the family's existence. There was a good canteen and mother put me down and pay for tomorrow's lunch each day. I used to leave with a half hour of lunchtime left. Just round the corner from school lived Ernie Greenwoods Aunty, she lived in an ancient back to back terrace house.

She lived in the one room with bed, stone sink, fireplace, coal if she could afford it etc. . It was below street level was damp, cold and had a small coal cellar. She never went out, never left her miserable abode, she was always wrapped up to the eyeballs with old woollen jumpers, cardigans, and shawls everyone said she was a witch she was more than a bit wiffy, she certainly looked the part as the freezing cold water from her tap wasn't used to remove any of the dirt and grime she was encased in, she always had a big runny nose on the go and a huge snot rag clutch'd in her tiny claw like to service it with. She was always terrified. The local kids used to harass her calling names through her letter box throwing stones and banging on her door and window, I use to call in to bring the coal up for her from the tiny coal hole, not really a cellar when she had any that is, she said that is where they lived, down the cold black stone steps, when I arrived each day she was so pleased to see me, she would close door and then she would start poking her walking stick in the 3 inch gap under the bed and start fishing about, 'Come out, come out, I know you are under there' Harrys here now so you can get back down the cellar where you belong and leave me alone. I hated leaving her like that but there was no option, she hated Fridays because I wouldn't be back round again till Monday, poor old sods. I would say half the old population lived like that, always hungry and on the bones of their arses. Still no use digressing, my turn would come soon enough so it was back to the park for me for more desert, a bit of slap and tickle while its there, then back to school to get the rest of the day out of the way.

It's indescribable just how much I hated that place and loathed the imbeciles in it. Halfway up Grafton street about a hundred yards from our house, there lived an old man with one good eye.

He used to stand on his doorstep first thing in the morning and ask anyone passing if they could put his glass eye in for him, just to see him through the week, because he couldn't see it he couldn't do it for himself, he was a sight in himself tatty filthy dirty old clothes on his body needing a shave with an open weeping blood red eye socket seeking attention from the few and far between who would give it some, the majority crossed the road to avoid embarrassment feeling sure some one else would tend his needs.

The butcher's shop at the top of the road use to sell horse meat, and just about every part of the particular animal he was chopping up was for sale. We would ask him for a sheep's eye, and take it to school wrapped up in my pocket. We'd be skylarking with the girls in the park, I would pretend to take a knock, aarrrrrrghhhh look, look, and have the eye ball in my hand, screams all round. Harry's knocked his eyeball out.

At that time everywhere was burning coal, all the houses, mills, hospitals, and schools. There was so much pollution in the air when Autumn arrived, as the air was damp wet even, the water particles pulled all the unburned coal particles together and formed a thick dense yellow sulphur smog. It used to burn the back of your throat and lungs, you couldn't see your hand in front of your face in the middle of the afternoon during a pea souper. On one such occasion the farmer had been taking his cows to the slaughter house, the smog came down and the cows couldn't see, well nobody could see, they were make a hell of a lot of noise, mother was feeling her way down Grafton street, house wall to house wall, door to door, when suddenly the commotion started heading her way.

All the cows snorting and bellowing coming closer, in those days the cows weren't de-horned, you could quite easily get impaled on the lethal weapons poking out of the top of their heads, petrified she started trying each door to escape, until luckily one opened. She was standing in someone's front room and all she could say was 'sorry, sorry but the cows, the cows are coming, I can't see, I can't see'. Soon afterwards they made everywhere smokeless zones, so you couldn't burn coal on your fire, only smokeless fuels. It had to be done, gradually the air quality improved and people stopped dying in so many numbers as their breathing got better.

That year, all the Hungarian refugees came over, they were very unpopular, that was the first lot I was aware of (immigrants) after the Irish that is. This was about the time of the start of the Teddy boys, rock n roll etc., 1956 or there about's. before that it was Grandad hats, Trillby's", three piece suits, and cowboy music, Frankie Lanes Jezebel, or George Formby's when I'm cleaning windows the real start of the rave scene, you could go all night to that. The Teds. soon developed a bad reputation, as flick knives and bicycle chains soon became part of their accessories. It soon came up to boiling point when it was perceived that the town was being over run with bloody foreigners, therefore things had to be sorted, locals verses invaders. The stuff of the Crusades Two double decker buses used to leave the town centre every Sunday afternoon, to take visitors to Birch hill hospital.

This particular Sunday there was a showdown organised in a field behind the hospital an apt venue. The first bus left with the Teds, the second with the Hungarians all tooled up. They lined up in the field behind the hospital, battle lines drawn, shouting abuse. Then battle commenced, one row was straight in to the other.

Both sides had all sorts of weapons, flick knives, wood chisels, bicycle chains, mortise chains, hammers if you could swing it hard and it was dangerous, it was there.

Apparently there were wounded everywhere, the local paper had a hey day, bodies lying all over the place, with knives still sticking out of them, bicycle chains wrapped around their unwanted heads. That was the first of many such encounters. Fucking Moronic Politicians, never ever had an inkling what would be the outcome of their pig ignorant meddling. (Oh Yeah, just let em in, our lot won't mind paying for em, they pay for us and don't complain, work it right into em.) our fore fathers had been fighting wars and dying for generations to stop this happening, just for these mostly home grown lame brained imbeciles to demolish in no time at all and not even understand what the concern was all about, unbelievable.

Father was a stoker at the hospital at this time. He shovelled coke into the boilers for the hot water etc. and our Beryl was a trainee nurse there. I use to hear Beryl telling mother about all the things she saw, she was crying as she spoke about it. One of her friends an Irish nurse had been found floating in the pond behind the hospital, one of many. Funny end for being pregnant, they didn't realise in those days you were supposed to hold the pill between your knees and don't bend over.

Beryl was saying she was in theatre and the surgeon sawed a fellow's leg off above the knee and handed the severed limb to her. She remarked how heavy it was then the artery opened up spurting and covering her in blood. In maternity it broke her heart seeing some of the babies born, one was covered in black hair like monkey. I think they used to smother them and present them as still born.

Father worked at Wolstenholm on a Friday, it was situated out of town on the moors to supply fresh air for its inmates TB patients. It was a late shift for him, he finished at 9pm. There were just the two fellas on duty a porter and the stoker. They used to take it in turns to go down to the pub for a couple of pints, to clear their head of the smell of death? or just to have a couple of bevies anyway father had just returned from the rub a dub dub and the porter had gone for he's bevies when the nurse informed him that another patient had died and they had to get him to the morgue, which was out in the grounds well away from the main buildings. Father said 'push the trolley up to the window Ill go outside and pull him through, that will save the long walk around the hospital, and I'll carry him over my shoulder to the morgue, which they did. He said it was a moonlit night and he was making his way along the dark path, past the rhododendrons bushes when something grabbed his arm.

He wasn't one for being frightened but he froze that night, he said he involuntarily called for a damp and nearly followed through, he was standing there petrified not knowing what to do with something gripping his arm, when a voice whispered in his ear, 'Do you want a hand with him, Harry?' It was the porter who'd crept up on him. You Bastard! quick check of trousers, they got to the morgue and put him on a slab. The porter than proceeded to put him on the correct slab, father said he got hold of his feet and pulled him off the slab. 3 feet high, There was an almighty crack as his head hit the stone floor, father cringed Ooh! The porter said 'what's up with you, he can't feel it!'

They use to breed guinea pigs up there for experiments trying to find a cure for the T. B. . Dad brought a couple home for us, no not for dinner, a stay of execution for them our first legal pets. It was a good thing really because I could progress to a lurcher later on for hunting hares.

When Beryl finished her midwifery course they gave her a velocipede to do her rounds on. She couldn't ride a bike but that was to be no excuse for not getting around her part of Manchester. Apparently the off duty nurses were determined to get her riding the bike, and were holding her on to it nearly all morning outside the nurses home, before she semi got the hang of it.

On her first outing she was careering down a hill, in Manchester totally out of control, and finished up in a big pile of arms, legs and push bike at the bottom. Feeling rather embarrassed by the spectacle, the passers by saw she was ok and helped her back on to the death trap. She wasn't having anymore of that so she dismounted and continued on foot to complete her rounds pushing her bicycle.

I had been working at Danny's on a Saturday for nearly a year now. I absolutely hated school. I hadn't grasped the basics in the first year, and every subject was moving on so quickly. I hadn't a clue what they were talking about. Maths, science, history, geography, English (not too bad), French, metalwork, woodwork and technical drawing (pretty good). Music (imagine, they gave me a violin). I was contracted to the Tech. school until I was sixteen, although the legal age for leaving school was fifteen. We had our end of term exams, and it had gone way beyond a joke. Maths, arithmetic 3/100, Algebra 0/100, Geometry 6/100, nine out of three hundred, my mind was made up. I couldn't tell anybody, but the more I thought about it, the more I liked the prospect, to be free of these sadistic perverts.

I had an offer from Danny to work for him full time. It wasn't what I wanted but it would be work with good money coming in. I could find something more suitable later on at my leisure. The main objective was to get out of the clutches of those sick perverts. End of term was coming up, during the last few days of July. Last day of term Friday, the final bell went, school was over. I went and stood outside the Headmaster's study. I had to wait there ¾ of an hour as they were having a staff meeting. "What are you still doing here Green?" "I have just come to inform you that I am leaving school so don't expect me back next term. " I insisted. "Don't talk stupid Green. You are only fourteen you've got another year to go. " "I'm fifteen in just over a week 8–8–43. I'm legally allowed to leave school. " So this was my final day. "What do your parent's say about this?" "They don't know. " "I will be writing to them forthwith. " The real fun was about to begin. "Well I have told you now, so you won't be seeing me again.

What a brilliant feeling when I finally got out of there. I broke the news to mother who was not too pleased, but when I said they would beat me no more she understood. I told her how I was to start at Danny's. The next thing on the list was to face father they would have to find ten pounds to get me released, my dad's wages for a week in those days. I offered to put forward some of my wages. They received a letter from the school and they continued to try and persuade me, but I was not going to budge. I spent the rest of August up at Drakes farm. Helping with the harvest mowing the hay, stacking the bails in the barn, threshing the barley, wheat, corn etc. and bailing the straw for the animal bedding in the winter. I really enjoyed helping out up there, it was hard work and tiring but that does not count when you enjoy it. Mrs Drake always had a big dinner for us followed by a tasty duff.

CHAPTER 5

Full time work – Danny's

I started full time at Danny's at the beginning of September I was fifteen years and one month old exactly, nine till six five days a week and a half day Wednesday. He paid me four pounds ten shilling a week, which was exceptional money considering my age. By this time I was quite a dab hand at selling. We had a really good day and there was very little stock left. A little old fella came in the shop and said he wanted a suit for five pounds. Well!! Danny must of thought no chance, and retired behind the curtain and left me to get rid of him. I put a jacket on him, I could see he didn't like it, but I kept pushing it, I eventually took it off him and put on the next option the one he said he liked. The trouble was it was the last one in stock and a good couple of sizes too big. I put the jacket on him and took a great handful of jacket at the back, held it tight, standing next to him and just behind, I showed him in the mirror, how it accentuated his shoulders and slim waist. Well that was it, wrap it up. I took the five pound ten shillings and sent him on his way rejoicing.

Danny came out not being able to believe his own eyes, 'I couldn't have sold him that suit, not in a hundred years'. Danny loved me, he thought I was brilliant. We made sure with the next delivery there would be the same suit two sizes smaller for when he returned. Sure enough Monday came round and the little guy's missus came in and had the suit under her arm shouting, 'Who the hell sold him this bloody suit! He's not fit to be let out on his own. ' I replied 'Problem Madam, too big?' She replied 'Too bloody big, it would fit fatty Arbuckle with plenty to spare. ' We took plenty of stick, we gave her a cover note and told her the new stock would be in later that week. she took the note and left muttering into her beard.

During the week there was never much business, I had never been so bored in all my life, waiting all day everyday for six o'clock to arrive. The lads from the tech. would come up some lunch times, and invariably take the piss, for having such a lowly job. The writing was well and truly on the wall. I arrived for work one Monday morning and there was no Danny, actually he left early on Saturday saying he'd be back, but he didn't return. He'd been gone nearly a week by the time it got to Friday, we had a delivery of more stock. Come the following Wednesday the shop was nearly empty I had just about sold up. I had all the money bundled up and hidden, I was really chuffed I thought he was going to be over the moon. I hadn't had the full set of keys to properly lock up, so I had managed with a padlock on the outside.

Well he went berserk he took me outside put the padlock on the door than proceeded to shoulder charge the door and break it open. He was calling me all the names under the sun, asking why I hadn't called the police, 'Anybody could have broken in!' I just stood there thinking that's it you have just killed any loyalty I had for you Mr. I had made up my mind, I wanted to be an apprentice carpenter and joiner. I wasn't going to be stuck in a dead end job especially with this fucking lunatic. He didn't even say where he'd been for over a week, I reckoned he'd been locked up, it just seemed par. for the course.

Every Wednesday afternoon after that, I started at our end of the town, going into all the carpenters workshops enquiring about an apprenticeship. all to no avail, one afternoon I walked into Jack Crabtree's shop, a family firm of Carpenters and Joiners for over a hundred and fifty years, as I walked in the main front door it opened straight into the joiners shop, there were benches for about ten joiners, and big head (his nick name.) the foreman joiner was on the front bench.

He asked me what I wanted, I said an apprenticeship then went on to give my spiel; been to the tech, good at technical drawing, woodwork. He asked where I lived, 'Newbold the other side of town', he thought about it for a little while and then replied No, I lived to far away, there was no way I could get to work for half past seven. I was on my way out past the little office whose door was open, and Jack Crabtree was sitting there, he'd been listening with the door slightly ajar he asked me in, he then asked me how would I get here, 'well, on my bike' I replied 'only three to four miles', he then asked a few more questions, to my total delight he asked me, "when could I start". At the end of the following week, in order to work out my notice at Danny's,

I really dreaded telling Danny. I told him late Saturday afternoon just before we shut up shop. He went banzai, he had come to rely on me running that place, he could disappear all he wanted and know everything was okay and safe plus I was a good salesman, and he didn't want to lose that. The following week he offered to double my pay, as the week dragged on the more agitated he got, he was opening another shop in Bury about eight miles away, and he wanted me to manage this one. But there was no going back, I could never have been happy there, I could have made a lot of money, but what the Hell is money if you are miserable and bored stiff all your working life, not on your Nelly.

My final day had arrived he kept on at me all day for me to change my mind, but no chance. He finally asked 'whose the better salesmen him or me' I just wanted out, so I said him, wrong answer, he started raising his voice again. 'Never ever say that, you are always the best. ' I took my wages and said goodbye and thanked him for what he taught me. That was it Danny was history, I had worked there full time for eight weeks, all good knowledge stored away to be called upon anytime in the future. I was away up the road with a spring and skip in my step. It felt like a massive load had been lifted off my shoulders. I was really looking forward to the future. I couldn't wait, for the following Monday morning to start at Jack Crabtree's carpenters and Joiners shop, to be working and actually being taught by tradesmen who actually knew what they were talking about, and were damn good at it.

CHAPTER 6

A proper job

It was about the beginning of November 1958 when I started at Jack Crabtree's as an apprentice carpenter and joiner on Spotland road Rochdale. I was very apprehensive on that first day, the foreman joiner (big head) had turned me down and was overruled by Jack, the owner. and I had a feeling that big head would be resenting the fact of having had his nose put slightly out of joint. I was expecting to take it on the chin, and I was not to be disappointed. Straight away he treated me like something off the bottom of his shoe.

He set me to work clearing up the yard in the rain, and when it rained in those days it could rain for weeks, because of the smog brought on by the sooty smoke constantly belching out of all the big mill chimneys. he kept me outside in the yard working in all the bad weather either clearing up or starting to repair the numerous supply of painters ladders, step ladders and trestles, of which there was a constant supply of broken ones arriving from the big painting firm opposite. Every time I looked up from the yard he would be at the window a floor up at the end of his bench watching me, we didn't have foul weather clothing consequently I was soaked to the skin for the best part of a month.

I had two pair of overalls so I could dry one pair out overnight and at least start the day dry sweeping out the shops which I would make last as long as possible before he pinged what I was up to and sent me outside again He was obviously trying to crack me, what he didn't know was that I had now got my pride I was an apprentice carpenter and joiner and proud of it, so I wasn't going anywhere. Big head must have realised I was not going to be giving in and leaving, and began sending me out on the jobs that needed an extra paid of hands. Big Cyril Mansley took me with him to repair and renew the wooden trough (guttering) at the front of a set of terraced houses, just up the road from our workshop. We had just manoeuvred the new replacement trough in position when a little black citron car pulled up at the bottom of my ladder, I know that car I thought when I spotted O'Conner, I collected a big handful of mud out the old guttering, and as the asshole got out the car, I let fly. The mud pat splattered on his shoes, he looked up and saw it was me and began to shake violently, it was the sadistic Irish pervert who attempted to teach English at the tech, and use to beat the shit out of me for his own pathetic pleasure.

With the most insolent look I could muster, I stuck two fingers up to him and carried on with my business. Big Cyril said what the hell was that all about, and was well chuffed when I told him the reason why. When he came back out of his house after his lunch, big Cyril gave him a thunderous look as though he was about to go down and rip his sadistic head off, that's it Cyril make the bastard have it. The bog trotter couldn't get into his car quick enough, and was off like the slime ball he was, no doubt to vent his anger on some other helpless child down at the Tech.

I had one full day release from work to go to college, and I had to go to night school two nights a week as well. The more I learnt the more I liked it, the satisfaction of looking at a good job well done, and admiring the praise, which wasn't handed out that often. Mind you it was well bad when I made a cock up, but that's how I was to improve, making the mistakes, then learning how to rectify them. The pay wasn't much just over two pounds a week for a forty eight and half hour week, about a third of the money I would have got at Danny's emporium, but I was under instruction and I loved it, and in five years time I would be on full pay as a fully qualified carpenter and joiner, how's about that then.

When I was just turned sixteen, I had managed to save up enough money for the deposit of a motor bike. Mother signed the contract for the hire purchase and that was it, I was the proud owner of a 197CC Francis Barnet two stroke motor cycle, what a difference it was going to make for work. I could now be sent out on small jobs on my own, with my tool bag fastened on the back seat.

One particular job I was sent too just before Christmas 1959 was right in the middle of Rochdale cemetery WHHOOOOAH! WHHOOOOOOAAAAAH!!!!! I hadn't met Alan Martin before, he was an advanced apprentice an improver with less than a year to go before he finished his five year apprenticeship. Well he had started work on this hundreds of years old registry office, which was absolutely riddled with dry rot, which is a creeping fungus that gets everywhere and looks like thick white spiders webs. The only way to get rid of it, is to remove all infected timbers (pretty much everything) and burn with a blow lamp all affected brickwork. then soak with cuprinol, chemicals made especially for the job. Just before lunch break one day we were exploring the rest of the place.

There wasn't any electricity and the only light we had was from the paraffin blow lamps. There was a door with a latched handle for securing it with, we opened it and went down into the cellar below which was pitch black. There seemed to be no air no ventilation from the outside and it smelt very musky as we entered we both went very cold and the hairs on the back of our necks developed a mind of there own for no apparent reason the pair of us were trembling, but we carried on down the stone steps to the cellar floor. The air was so dry still and dank there wasn't anything down there as far as we could see by the dim light of our blow lamps.

We looked up and there was an old vaulted ceiling in ancient brick work by now we were so uncomfortable we just had to get out of there, it was a relief to get back onto the stone steps and be on our way out of that foreboding place, I remember trying not to be the last one out but Martin was a lot bigger than me so I was left struggling behind him frightened of what the Hell was behind me, we struggled through the door together and couldn't wait to get that door back on its latch. I don't think we said anything but it was obvious we were both very uneasy. Work continued well into the afternoon, I had removed the window frame and was scorching the brick work in the cavity wall burning the fungus.

At about quarter past four being that time of year it was dark when we saw some lights coming through the cemetery, it turned out to be big head in the open back works truck. He had a quick look at how the job was going the bald headed big fat miserable twat used to get right under my skin, he never gave any praise just bollockings whenever he could you could always tell how you were faring by the size of your bollocking. He told Martin that an old dear was locked out of her house, and as she lived on route to his house, he should leave early and gain entrance and let her in. Big head left at about half past four, Martin took off right afterwards, he collected his tools, flashed up his motorbike, and was gone like a shot.

Looking towards the main road everything was pitch black I could just see the street lights about a hundred yards away, I was nervous and was dying for half past five to arrive and finish. I was sitting in the window space.

The only sound I could hear was that of the roaring flame from the blowlamp which was comforting and the wind blowing through the tree's, there was a bright moon shining in between the clouds scudding across the black sky, All of a sudden the silence was broken with three massive BANG ... . BANG, BANGS. I froze petrified. The door to the cellar was thrown open and slammed as hard as possible then stopped dead, half open. Fucking hell fire, to say I was terrified was the understatement of the century.

I started shaking violently I held the blow lamp out in front of me trying to keep a grip and walked towards the now open cellar door, with only the roaring flame for a light in front of me and wondering what the hell was down there I nervously got hold of the door handle – latch and closed the door. Making sure that the latch was in place, I double checked to make sure the door was secure I went back to the window ensuring the lamp was well pumped up, the last thing I wanted was the light going out the state I was in. After about ten minutes BANG ... . BANG, BANG. Jesus Christ!! I held the blow lamp at arms length again and the light was everywhere as I was now palpitating shaking and just short of defecating, I closed the cellar door again looked at my watch it was just about five to five half an hour left. The half hour ahead was beginning to seem like a week. I had been burning for about three or four minutes when BANG ... . BANG, BANG. It went again, by this time I was in one hell of a state there was no way I would survive another half hour of this, fuck the consequences I thought I am off. I put the door back on the latch and proceeded with increasing haste with the blowtorch in front of me through the outside door. I shut the outer door kick started my bike, put my headlights on and leaned through the window space put the blow lamp on the floor let the air out extinguishing the flame, got on my bike and was off like a bat out of hell.

I came out of that cemetery like shit off a shovel. It was such a feeling of relief to be racing down that road with the wind and rain in my face. I don't know what the hell it was that was performing with that door, but if its intention was to put the shits up me it should have been awarded a gold medal for over achievement. I turned up in the morning but I didn't say a thing, I didn't want to appear a big girls blouse so I carried on as normal. At eleven o'clock Big head turned up and asked where I was last night at ten past five , I quickly saved my bacon by telling him that I had a half hour dinner break so that was why I had left early. He blatantly didn't believe me but he left it at that.

We started talking to the other blokes that were working in the cemetery, the grave diggers who were casual workers sort of semi-tramps, when they had a bit of luck every so often, they might get a bit of work sweeping the roads, cleaning the drains, emptying the bins or digging graves, anything that their war medals qualified them for, and sleep where they could under the hedgerows, or in old barns, haystacks were always particular good places as they generated their own heat as well as multitudes of blood sucking parasites, which once acquired were permanent lodgers and were the bane of their lives, although they had some slight benefit as the constant scratching they necessitated helped to stop them from freezing to death in winter if a hedgerow was their only refuge.

There was a Salvation Army hostel in town opposite Danny's shop, in Winter time it was always full as there could be a foot of snow on the ground outside. I think it was three pence for the luxury to actually lie down and sleep on the freezing stone flagged floor and at the other end there was a thick rope slung right across the dark morbid shelter, and for a penny they could lean over it for the night.

The men would stand in a big long line crammed tight and leaning over the tight rope for support and sharing their own generated body heat they would stand there dozing all night, swapping fleas, body lice, crabs and lots of other numerous exotic unwanted lodgers. trying to get warm and nodding in and out of sleep.

At least they were inside out of the bitter cold blizzard blowing outside and as there were no such things as toilets in these places, the steaming turds dropping out of the bottom of their ragged pants and the communal efforts of all participants in the maximum production of methane gas, would lift the temperature slightly.

At least if they were caught in a slight draft it might be a warm one, even though a bit smelly. Beggars can't be choosers one night late on, after midnight the hostelry was full when a tramp knocked on the door. The disgruntled Captain after being hailed from his warm bed in the small isolated room at the rear answered the door but he wouldn't permit entrance because the poor chap didn't have the minimum amount of money necessary, a penny. (That will teach him, he'll come earlier next time) The man curled up in the door way to shelter from the weather, rest and attempt to secure some sleep when they opened the door at about five in the morning they found the young tramp curled up, covered in snow and frozen solid, as dead as a door nail a sorry casualty of the horrendous blizzard.

At the subsequent enquiry and afterwards reported in the local newspaper. The Captain said, 'What a shame the poor man made it all the way to our door if only he had the strength to have knocked and let us know he was here we could have let him in and given him some warmth and sustenance, he would have still been alive today". (to continue tramping the countryside prolonging his miserable existence, while observing the antics of society's well placed, taking advantage of their positions of trust and fattening up off the privileged gravy train they had created for themselves.) Most of these unfortunates were crippled ex-servicemen abandoned when no longer of any military use after the war.

A Land fit for heroes. (Their M. P. s had promised. them.) Lying, thieving, yellow I bellied, parasitic, self-serving bastards, didn't do a thing for these destitute down and outs, who's demise they had caused by forcing them to save their own pathetic skins for them, their own countrymen. While opening the doors to all sorts of foreigners who wouldn't fight to defend our country, but accept housing and maintenance, way above the servicemen who had been promised the same in exchange for their lives. These were the hero's back from the war, after being traumatised in the trenches doing the politicians dirty work for them. It stank then and it stinks even more today, what are these incompetents doing with the rest our money.

When I was at Danny's I watched this fella shuffling past the shop along the pavement, he stopped and stepped into the gutter, stood there for a couples of minutes, he then shook his right leg, a Richard the third (turd) fell out of the bottom of his pants into the gutter. He still had his dignity and manners, he didn't want anyone stepping in it. It hurts like hell having to remember all of this, but having told my very great young friends some of the stories, Rhian whose first inclinations was to be a politician to try to change things for the better, convinced me these stories had got to be told. So stand by your beds all you arsehole M. P. s I am going to tell it warts and all.   Now they are even trying to change the recorded history of what actually happened, by banning teachers from telling our youngsters what really happened, the truth. They have actually succeeded, as no modern teachers have got a clue as to the why's and wherefores of what really went on, as the educational system was steered in the direction it was, by the left wing perverts who were in charge, and that is why the country now finds itself with a growing population of educationally.

Bereft unemployables, instead of being the once green and pleasant land, for the future generations to enjoy. It is now quickly turning into a demoralised dustbin, that a lot of the original inhabitants are seeking to abandon, in search of better prospects elsewhere in the world. It would have been absolutely unthinkable to foresee what a catastrophic mess, these self serving, pig ignorant, unknowledgeable, moronic M. P. 's could do to this country in half my lifetime, unbelievable, and even more frightening they haven't the brains to see it.

They are still there making pathetic laws to cover everything they know fuck all about, merrily driving the train at full speed into a blind half finished tunnel. Goodbye cruel world.

An M. P. s lament.

If at first you don't succeed.
Pull your foreskin over your heed,
   and whistle down your tube.

Spot on. With expenses, ten fold. But woe betide anyone who dares to follow our example. – – – – We'll jail them. Do as we say ! not as we do.

I got a little side tracked there, but fuck em they deserve it. We started taking our lunch break with the grave diggers in their hut. It was the only semi-warm place available. They had a round metal stove fed from any fuel they could acquire, a nice warm fire with a big old sooty black kettle on top. The conversations would go in all directions. I asked if any of them believed in the supernatural, ghosts etc. They all laughed that's rubbish, but one of the older blokes said he didn't, but knew of a couple that did.

He said that just after the war he was digging a grave after work in the early evening during the wintertime for an old impoverished lady who's husband had died leaving her destitute and unable to afford his burial in Ashworth Valley Church yard (where my folks got married just before the war). It's a remote place but central to a few hamlets and farms. It was a dark moonlit night, and he was about three feet down into the grave he was digging. He had a candle standing on a slate base, and four other candles arranged around its sides to stop the wind blowing it out. He had the same arrangement three feet down in the black hole of the grave to be in order to see what he was doing. Some soil fell on the lower light and extinguished it. He was straightening up to re-light the candle, and unbeknown to him at the time, a courting couple were walking up the driveway towards the church, not knowing their amorous intentions were about to be devastated.

There were two blood curdling screams as they both turned tail at the sight of something slowly emerging from this moonlit grave, they beat a rapid retreat at an ever increasing pace towards the distant gates, helped along by the jet effect of the fast dropping pressure of the escaping methane gas, with our hero at least two lengths ahead of his date by now and approaching the exit and escape, the pair of them still vocalising to the extreme, to the point of terrifying the local wildlife, (you can imagine the local dog fox's hackles shooting straight up as he legged it thinking what the fucks that!, the bastard, that's my job) he was increasing his lead as they passed through the cemetery gates and heading off down the isolated moonlit valley to the floor below, to initiate new tales of the horrors taking place in Ashworth valley graveyard after dark on a chilly moonlit winters evening as the un dead arose from their cold resting places, to go about their sinister business in the dead of night.

Their screams put the wind up the lonely old grave digger, to such an extent it made him quite nervous about returning to the foreboding grave and wondering just how long it would be before it was his turn.

At the same time thinking about his unseen companions close by who had been residents of this undisturbed ground for many a bygone generation, the hairs on the back of his neck were by now standing up like Porcupine quills, with not a single thing he could do about it, to say he was not just the tiny'est wee bit, absolutely fucking terrified would have been more than a slight under statement, so back to the job in hand, the quicker he got it dug, the sooner he would be on his way home to bury his own bone into something a damn sight warmer than this old chaps uninviting future cold dismal Resting place.

I asked the guy who ran the crematorium if he could show me around the place, to which he agreed, much to my delight. It was really an old boiler house type of place with two "slide in" ovens side by side with a large coal fire burning below. At the time he was showing me it was all fired up as a he was burning a stiff. He swivelled a little metal cover which revealed a spy hole into the flames. He was taking a look to check the progress of the diminishing remains of the little old dear, when I asked if I could have a look, he refused saying 'you wouldn't like someone watching your recently deceased granny fry' I held back from informing him she was more or less roasting and not frying, but then thought don't be pedantic. It wouldn't have bothered me for someone else to see granny roast, but there you go it takes all sorts.

If he wasn't going to let me look he was going to have to explain the whole process, because once I get the bit between my teeth I don't give up easily, if nothing else I was a persistent little fucker. The first thing in the process, remove anything valuable or sellable off the coffin, brass handles, crosses etc, ready for resale. " Don't tell the family" The box is then slid into the oven and the door closed. The fire is lit, The temperature is built up high and the coffin (timber) starts to burn, it doesn't take long before the coffin is reduced to a fine ash along with any body hair, eye balls, low balls and any other loosely attached members. At this point an external flew is opened, and a large blower fan is started, which blows everything that has been reduced to ash up the chimney and away, to settle and fertilise the neighbouring gardens, and any operating lungs which happen to belong to anyone who unknowingly are breathing in the contaminated air in the immediate vicinity.

The cadaver is now sizzling like a barbeque chicken or sausage, at some stage shortly the corpse sits up, which could come as a bit of a shock to any first time viewer to the fascinating spectacle taking place in front of their very own eyes. All the sinew's are now shrinking quite rapidly and continue to do so until they can shrink no more, they then start snapping, the body having lost all the tension holding it up, lies down again to continue with its incineration. Once all the meat has been burned off, he ups the temperature to finish off the bones. On completion the bones are soft like chalk, and break up into all uneven pieces. He then rakes the bone clinkers through the grate into the ash pan below and removes it from the base of the oven. The clinkers are then fed into a large hand operated worm drive mincing machine (similar to the ones found in old fashioned butchers shops), with a metal funnel arrangement at the top to pour the remains into. Just prior to the worm wheel, there are two large bar magnets situated on opposite sides of the entrance shoot to catch any remaining metal work that might be included. Nails, tacks, etc. The handle would be turned, the clinkers fed in to the top, and the deceased would then receive a top quality first class mincing. The ashes dropping into the ash can would be of the late Mr or Mrs X and contain no extra unwanted foreign bodies.

The ashes would then be boxed up and labelled all ready for there final trip to fertilize some lucky rose bush or ornamental commemorative tree.

The oven is then all ready for the next crop. I thought at the time it would have been ever so easy to dispose of an extra stiff that was cluttering up the garden shed at the same time, and have learnt since in some circumstances that was certainly the case. When some destitute old tramp turned up with no funds for his desposal, the problem could be solved by fitting him twos up in the next box with plenty of room in it, mind you it must have appeared quite comical watching the pair of them sit up together.

The original two for one waste not, want not. Now you see it – now you don't. By having to go to day and night school, I made friends with lads of the same ilk. These lads were from other carpentry firms in Rochdale.

One such lad was John Walley who used to bum lifts everywhere on the back of my motorbike, he never had any money, I didn't have much, but John didn't have two pennies to scratch his arse with or a pot to piss in. One weekend we decided to go to Rhyl for a break, a seaside holiday town about eighty miles away. It had to have been a Saturday night as we were off work, we travelled down there on the coast road really enjoying our adventure, as we approached our destination, there was a small sea wall to my right and a large twelve foot high country estate wall to my left, with no pavement or road lighting. It turned out to be a foul night, pitch black and absolutely pouring down with rain, the tide wasn't coming in, it was coming down.

The road ahead was dead straight in front of me for about a mile, all of a sudden a pair of headlights appeared on full beam. It seemed to take ages before they were approaching close, John screamed in my ear 'LOOK OUT!' at the same time he threw the bike over to the left. I put my left arm up thinking that I would be colliding with the big country estate wall and wondering what the hell he was playing at, but actually we crossed back over the middle and returned to my side of the road, (there wasn't any road markings to guide me) a wagon and trailer shot past just where we would have been. I was riding towards him at sixty miles an hour slap bang between his headlights and head on with his radiator, we would have been chips, with the deluge of rain coming down I could hardly see through my goggles,

I must have been mesmerized. I stopped the bike, we got off, we couldn't speak, and was then taken over and consumed in a violent body reaction, every muscle in our bodies was shaking, trembling, shuddering you name it, it was doing it. We couldn't even contemplate saddling up for over half an hour until the tremors began to calm down. We eventually continued our journey at a sedate twenty five – thirty miles an hour. Having decided to get there in two pieces, myself and John, safe and sound.

We arrived just about ok, arranged bed and breakfast and fixed ourselves up with a couple of ravers from Warrington (they didn't realise they were a couple of ravers just yet), who were staying at the same place. Bobs your uncle, we dipped our bread in and had a really good weekend, before very cautiously wending our way back home late Sunday night.

For some reason I had stopped growing and everybody else was shooting up past me, which really began to hack me off. We had a new joiner start at the firm, and just to add insult to injury he was massive. A body builder who\ I worked with for a few weeks in the Summer, he was constantly taking the piss out of my scrawny body and couldn't see why I wasn't doing anything about it. In the end he said he would give me a bar and few weights so I could start training at home and get some meat on my bones. We finished work one Saturday lunch time at twelve thirty and I was to take him home on my motorbike, pick up the bar two collars and some weights, then drive the whole lot back to my house.

He was to sit on the back seat holding the bar and weights. He lived in a different part of town which I was not familiar with.

We picked up the weights and set off I was going a fair old lick along the road couldn't wait to get home. He was chatting to me and I turned my head to answer him when I shot straight across a main road junction, and went straight between two cars that were bombing along the main road at right angles to me. There was such a terrified, panicking scream from behind me, then 'STOP STOP let me off ya crazy little bastard!' I couldn't help it I burst into fits of laughter, I cracked up automatically, this massive hulk of solid muscle the object of hero worship was reduced to a quivering mess in two seconds flat, it was just like the key stone cops.

I think he had jacked himself up a couple of inches on the back seat. (it smelled like it anyway). I didn't think it was just the bikes exhaust fumes which were contaminating the air we were leaving behind, I now concentrated on getting home with my newly acquired weights, to start exercising and begin the process of getting some meat on these ere bones. I was so pleased and exited you'd have thought someone had just given me a bar and weights to train with.

Its been a particularly good day today Amy came round this afternoon 7/12/06 with her laptop computer so we could begin the mammoth task of recording this original manuscript. For just under the next two and half hours between me dictating, Amy correcting and recording we consumed pots of tea and enough profiteroles to make a little pig feel sick. By 1800 Amy had managed to get the first ten pages on record, brilliant the book now feels like its on its way. Well done Aimz.

One weekend John and I decided to take a trip to Blackpool about fifty miles away. John never wore a crash helmet but as we were going so far I got him to wear our Margaret's old corker helmet she used when riding her Lambretta scooter. It had a peak on the front, it was the same as the police helmets of the day, he thought he looked a right knob with it on, but there you go, he did, a right big cock, just like the policemen, he had a monster Bobbies helmet on his shoulders I tried not to let him see me laughing or he wouldn't have worn it, then half his brains would have been spread along the main road on Blackpool's Golden mile. mine was a half round bikers helmet, on the front of which I had painted a white skull and cross bones, .

I thought it looked really good, if the truth were known we probably both looked like a pair of mounted cocks tearing along on our super charged velocipede not giving a monkey's fuck for any one else!. As you do. We arrived in Blackpool and it was pissing down, it had just gone dark. I was doing about thirty miles an hour when suddenly in front of us appeared a parked car, I had to pull out to pass it, and on doing so I would have to cross the shiny wet slippery tram lines. I knew what was going to happen.

As soon as my front wheel touched the tram line it just slid away. The bike crashed to the ground on its right hand side. We went spinning off down the road gradually slowing down from thirty miles an hour. I kept a tight hold of the handle bars and held my head up off the road, John kept hold of me but his head was on the road bumping and scraping over every hump, bump, nook and cranny until we finally came to rest. I was alright if a little bruised, John was the same but all the right hand side of his helmet was worn away which could very easily have been his scull, imagine the mess that would have made. We picked up the bike, straightened out the handle bars and anything else that was bent, started up the bike, and carried on our merry way rejoicing.

Another time in Rochdale about ten of the lads decided to have a Sunday afternoon run out on their bikes over the Pennines to Rawtenstall in Yorkshire (The yocals would say "Yorkshire born, Yorkshire bred, strong in the arm", and we'd finish it off, "and thick in the head. ") That would set the tone for the afternoon.

We were all to make our way over the Pennines and meet up at this recently heard of café, which was the proud owner of this new fangled jukebox with all the latest records, and sold this new sought after American espresso coffee with the frothy milk on the top. On the way there we were climbing this winding "A" road up the Pennines, with the typical dry stone walls, on either side of the road, built to keep the sheep in, when the first bike caught up with a lorry struggling up the seemingly never ending hill. He pulled out took a quick look to see if it was clear to overtake, which it was and away he went.

All the bikes in front of me carried out this correct manoeuvre. I was on my new, new to me, much bigger bike a 350cc AJS, with a full size bike frame with lots of power. I overtook in the same manner and we all met up at the café. We got our coffee and played some records while chatting up the yokel fanny, then someone enquired "where is so and so", I didn't know half the lads but our ten had diminished to nine. We soon worked out that he had been at the rear, as he hadn't been in front of anyone else. We flashed up the bikes and took off back to look for him, what a mess. He had been at the rear all right, and must have observed the nine bikes in front pull out and overtake, he must have pulled straight out without taking the initial precautionary look to see if the road ahead was clear to overtake.

He was hit head on between the headlights of a lorry hurtling down the hill after the bang the lorry careered through the dry stone wall taking the bike and rider with it and onto the desolate moor. I didn't know the lad but his mates stayed there waiting for the police to arrive which could have been hours in those days, this was around 1960 the era of Heartbeat the television series after the carnage was removed the wrecked vehicles could have stayed there for days as there was no efficient recovery vehicles as is the case today. We carried on back down the Dale to Rochdale not exactly in the same vein or mood of mind that we had been expecting. It was becoming increasingly clear that these motorbikes were very dangerous machines and should be treated with the utmost respect, and if anyone didn't give the bikes and situations the respect they were due they certainly wouldn't be making old bones, just like this young lad most certainly didn't.

Unbeknown to me I was about to meet the most mentally unstable, deranged ex-con anyone could have the misfortunate to encounter, untethered and actually roaming free. To give an example he was on a par with, and unbelievably even worse than some MPs and as you know that's really saying something. George Shannon got in touch with me and said be at his house next Sunday morning at 0300 hrs. with the ferrets, we are going to head off onto the moors and go in the opposite direction to usual, and head towards Manchester 11 miles away, covering new ground. We were to play it by ear and see how it goes. I arrived at George's at 0300 hrs and Russ his big lurcher started going ballistic once he saw me. He knows we are going hunting I unleashed his collar from the chain of his kennel and he was off sprinting up and down the road, he couldn't wait he was whimpering in his excitement.

Good well trained dogs do not bark, that only let's the quarry know just how close the dog is and so take evasive action prolonging the chase. Wild dogs don't run around barking they wouldn't live long if they did, it's a trait forced on them by ignorant humans who keep them in a state of frustration from birth and so barking becomes its learned means of expression and only way of gaining attention, thus putting it on the road to making everyones life in earshot a misery. George's lights went on he's up and his wife is moaning, its dark and crisp outside with a heavy frost clear skies and bright moon ideal for the task in hand, the ground was frozen, poor Russ he's feet will be torn to shreds if he puts a hare up before the ground thaws.

But there is absolutely nothing on earth that would keep him from his job. He is shaking in anticipation, George comes out, 'How are ya young un'?' We've got to go pick up Bomer and his dog' He always called me young un. 'Who is Bomer?' a bloke I know, just out of Strangeways prison Manchester. Bomer lived with his mother in this old end of terrace house, another Irish family. George knocked on the front door, we could hear the dog's excitement in the backyard a light came on and about five minutes later out shot the dog a real mean looking fucker which was used to living on the streets and fending for itself.

Another big thick set lurcher the two dogs were obviously acquainted this was their nirvana. A killers heaven. Then out stumbled this unkempt Neanderthal about twenty five years of age, a right fucking Troglodyte, with a 32 inch double barrelled twelve bore shot gun slung over his shoulder. Fucking hell!, am I glad he is on our side. His whole body appeared to be square, he looked like he had been breaking rocks with his face for the past few years causing his nose to be in the state it was in. They whistled the dogs which returned at speed and we were off. We crossed the Rochdale canal which was built to bring coal and raw cotton in from Manchester, on barges towed by large cart horses along the tow paths at either side of the canal, to supply the cotton mills and the near slaves who were kept to operate them.

The co-op was formed in Rochdale, Toad lane, the original shop is still there now as a museum, with its little square windows and a spring bell on the door. Inside the big old weighing scales are still present, plus sacks of produce which used to be sold off at just over wholesale prices for the workers, who had the idea and formed it, so they could get more meagre rations for their families, with the pittance they received for their near slave labour they were grudgingly paid for. The idea was a none profit organisation owned and operated by the workers who set it up and used it. Two five double six eight, I can still remember Mother's co-op dividend number. At the end of the year depending on how much divi. (dividend) she had earned, from money spent there. that would be put towards our clothes (bought in the COOP shop) for the next year. We didn't have a choice of clothes, we were only too chuffed if we could find something that nearly fitted.

We crossed about five farms incorporating lots of fields attached and came to the beginning of the moorland. The hares were few and far between, they were fit, big and strong, weighing in at about nine pounds. It took a good strong dog to have a kill in about one in five chases. The dog could be on the chase for about three or four miles. If he killed, on top of being knackered, he would have to carry his quarry all the way back, retracing the exact path he took on his outward journey until he was back in view. It always baffled me how he could follow his own path in reverse, by scent presumably all the way back with a heavily scented Hare hanging from his chops. At which time George would whistle him to make contact, and when he first caught sight of us his tail would shoot straight up in the air with only the tip of it wagging.

He was really chuffed, we would sit down and wait for him to slowly make his way back to us, he would have to drop the hare and have a short rest every couple of hundred yards or so until he arrived back, when he would drop it at George's feet, his whole sides were covered with saliva, from his mouth to his tail. George would then holds the hare upright with its back to his right thigh, and and then depress its stomach, expressing all the urine, which the dog would thankfully drink. By doing this we kept ourselves dry when the relaxed quarry was placed in our Donkey jacket, poachers pocket.

We had been going all morning, the dogs had a couple of chases which hadn't concluded with a kill. We were now on a strange (new to us) farm on the way to Manchester, it was early afternoon when there was a loud bellow from the farmhouse, "Get off my Land!" it was coming from a big bloke well over six foot tall and about twenty eight years old roughly the same age as Bomer and George. He was probably the farmer's eldest son. Bomer told us to ignore him. He shouted again "Get off my land!!" "Ignore him" Bomer repeated. "Right you've asked for it" and with that he disappeared into the farm house and returned with a thirty two inch, single barrel twelve bore shot gun.

The three of us just stood there with the dogs at our feet. He slowly approached us, he was wearing the biggest pair of clogs I'd ever seen, they looked like canal barges. I would have been long gone if I had been on my own, I was now nearly crapping myself I didn't see how the hell we were going to get out of this one. "I'm telling you for the last time, GET OFF MY LAND!" Silence no one moved. "You've asked for this!" He stuck the business end of the shot gun to Bomer's dog's head, the dogs lips curled back baring his vicious looking fangs, and beginning to froth at the mouth. He was eyeballing his assailant and emitting a terrifying snarl, I was thinking he's going to attack, going straight for his throat he'll kill him. "NOW GET OFF MY LAND OR I WILL SHOOT THIS DOG. " Bomer calmly stuck the end of his double barrelled twelve bore shot gun right under the farmer's nose, "You shoot that dog and I will shoot you. "

He would have blown his head right off. Now it was Bomer's turn, he screamed "Unload that gun or I will blow your fucking head off". The farmer was now petrified, he unloaded and threw his cartridge to the ground, "and the ones in your pocket", another five appeared and he threw them to the ground. "You might be the farmer of this land, but I am the squire of these parts, and don't you forget it, now fuck off before I lose my temper. " He took Bomer's advice and fucked off back to the farm house with his tail between his legs. Bomer watched him go, then picked up the cartridges, placed them in his pocket, and signalled for us to come on, and we carried on as if nothing had happened.

We came across a small rabbit warren on some other farm. I netted about a dozen holes then put the ferret in, down wind, So as the rabbits did not catch scent of the ferret. If they had, they would have bolted instantly, in a mad panic before we were ready. . All of a sudden the ground starts shaking and thumping as the bunnies get a whiff of the ferret, sheer terror below as they know that lethal scent, then plop the first one to break cover gets caught and bagged up in the purse net. We caught about half a dozen, before the farm dog got wind and started barking aggressively, the bedroom light came on and very soon the farmhouse door opened, so that was the time for us to be off. I squeezed the piss out the bunnies, locked their legs together, put them on my stick, hung them over my shoulder, and then we headed for home at speed before the farmer had a chance to fill our arses with shotgun pellets.

As we neared home Bomer left with his dog to go to his place. George said to me "He's a bit of a lad with that gun isn't he" that was a slight understatement. Some weeks later I found out George had mated Russ with this really good lurcher bitch, and she was about to give birth. The owner of the stud dog (George) got either the pick of the litter, or a financial settlement for the lining of the bitch, and in this case, it had been agreed, he would have the pick of the litter, which George then told me I could have. I was over the moon. It was cleared at home that I could have the pup., so long as it was kept in a kennel outside. I built a kennel out of any old timber I could lay my hands on, and situated it in the back garden under my window.

So I could talk to and console him until he got used to being separated from his mum, whom he would never see again.

Beryl was now married which meant that Margaret moved into the small front bedroom, and Jim and I moved into the girl's bedroom at the rear of the house, I had made Rough's kennel and checked every night before I went to sleep, anticipating the time soon when it would be occupied. All these dogs were kept outside in kennels, as it was considered keeping them indoors would make them soft. Bomer's dog was the exception, when Bomer was inside for six months for GBH, his dog lived on the streets. He would take himself hunting.

I witnessed this later when I was out with my dog. I saw him burying a half eaten hare to save for later. When Bomer was inside, the dog knew, he use to bring a chicken or a duck from one of the farms and drop it on his mother's front door step. She would open the front door pick up the present say "Good dog" and close the door and off he'd go to get on with his own life. He must have rooted all the bitches in the area, it seemed like a good deal to me, it must have been inadvertently logged into my own brain (more of that later). Now I know where I got the saying from, when people used to phone me and ask, what I was up too, my reply was "my nuts, but that's got nothing to do with you, you nosey sod"

George was taking me to see the new born litter, he told me to pick the one with the biggest head, and make sure it was a fawn coloured one. I wanted a fawn coloured dog just like Russ. There were five pups in the litter three bitches and two dogs. The fawn dog was very small, the others were brindled (fawn with blackish inter-mingled colouring) but compared to the others, the brindled dog had a massive head and great big feet. The feet indicated he was going to be big and the head plenty of sense. That's the one I want, and named him Rough. Now I had to wait six weeks until I could take him home to his nice new kennel underneath my bedroom window. I picked him up when he was six weeks old, and I used to sit with him until bed time, telling him what a good life he was going to have.

About ten o'clock was my bed time, I put his chain on its little hook and placed him in his kennel which was furnished with as much straw as it could handle, and he was missing his mum. I spent the next couple of hours hanging out of my window trying to console him, he got fed up of whimpering after a few days and settled down. There were no injections for parvo virus or none that we knew about. If there were, I had no money anyway, Vets in those days were mostly used for farm animals. To start training the pup (Rough) I dried a rabbit's skin and wrapped it around a big cloth tied it around with string and used it as a lure (decoy rabbit). Every time I threw it I would exitedly repeat the word "Sithee, Sithee" whenever he heard me say that, he would be jumping up and down looking for the rabbit or hare, and as soon as I threw it he would be after it like a flash.

He used to love playing with it, and by now he was growing fast and I shortly had him retrieving it. The next stage of his training was very important, if he put up a big hare, of which he had no chance of catching, after a couple of miles out of frustration alone he could start yapping and this is the biggest no no, as a yapping dog will never catch a hare, as the hare then knows exactly where the dog is behind it and can take evasive action when appropriate. So the trick is to make sure the dog catches his quarry. To do that we need a live rabbit. So when we judge the dog is ready its off to the rabbit warren with the ferret and nets, we net the bolt holes and introduce the ferret, they come out like shit off a shovel into the purse nets. We select a medium sized rabbit, which now gets a stay of execution, while the rest get their necks pulled for the pot.

We now make our way to the beginning of the moor where rough will begin his life as a hunting lurcher. Initiated with his first blood. George took Russ a good way off, and Rough was going crazy, so I told him to sit and stay which he would no matter what, I walked about about twenty yards away, and released the rabbit excitedly shouting "Sithee Sithee" the bunny was going like a good un but it didn't know where, rough was up and running going like an express train, after about fifty yards Rough hit it and killed it instantly, he was playing with it, the joy on his face was a sight for sore eyes, he wasn't going to give this up easily, as far as he was concerned he caught it, it was he's.

I kept calling him and he eventually retrieved it. After much praise I held the rabbits back against my knee and pressed its stomach which evacuated its bladder and the dog gets a well earned drink every time. I was so pleased he'd passed his test, there would be no holding us from now on, well done Rough. It was late spring and rough was six months old now, we were still waiting for his first kill, when he put up a young hare he was on to it like a shot, he chased it for a good two big fields, he dived as the hare was turning then wallop, got him. We were so overjoyed it was untrue, and didn't Rough know it too. I whistled him, his tail was straight up with just the tip wagging, he picked up the hare although he was knackered and trotted back to me and lay the hare at my feet.

My heart was bursting I was so proud. I did the business with its bladder, he loved that, I put it in my poachers pocket and said go find them Rough, then he was off trying to pick up another scent. It took a good dog to catch one of these big strong Pennine hares, it was considered good to kill in one in five chases. On one occasion big Russ caught three in twenty minutes. Only ever that once but he was the best, the gypsies offered George big money for him but no chance the dogs are family. George came home from work one day and Russ was gone, off his chain. The gypsies had come back and stolen him, George was heartbroken. The word went around the town that everyone was to keep a lookout.

After about a month a bloke who worked for the electricity board burying cables, spotted Russ chained up on a gypo. site about twenty miles away. That was it, Bomer was fuming he got together about six big ex cons. They all boarded this old beaten up truck and headed for the thieving gypo's site, they all had their shotguns, they new where they were going alright, it was like the wild west. Apparently they arrived spotted big Russ. All six walking towards him, then Bomer lets go both barrels into the air and reloads. Just to let the fuckers know we mean business, they strode towards Russ, who by now was going crazy, George took the bolt croppers he had over his shoulder and cut the chain, Russ was up and running, pissing all over the place with excitement he couldn't believe his luck seeing George again, Bomer lets another one go to command attention and said. " If we have any cause to come back here again, it will be for you fucking lot first. So just think on. With that they boarded the truck with Russ and fucked off back home, with George and Russ over the moon. Pick the bones out of that one, thieving bastards.

It was the beginning of summer and we had got this job to fire and weather proof the mill roof that was just down the road from the joiner's shop. It was a massive job, it was going take us apprentices (cheap labour) about three months to complete. The roof area was about six hundred square yards and we had to fit, eight foot x four foot corrugated sheets of asbestos to the roof. We had first to unload them from the lorries than hoist them by hand via a pulley system up about five stories to the mill roof and re-stack them. I got to know the other two apprentices well and being relatively knew to the firm, and the youngest, I was everyone's dog's body.

I was asked one week by the boys if I wanted to go with them one Saturday afternoon to see Manchester United play. I said yes as I had never been to a professional league match before.

When we did finally go Alan Martin came with a few of his mates on their bikes, I was on the back of Martin's bike, United were playing Leeds both top clubs. This was shortly after the Munich air disaster when the Busby babes got killed. It was a terrible tragedy Manchester's manager Matt Busby had had most of his ever so young team killed in the crash. he had managed to form a young team like the world had never seen before.

The country was right behind them as they continually pummelled their opponents and were predicted to be one of the best teams in the world. Due to their youth they became fondly known as the Busby Babes. I think it was the winter of 1958 when United had an away game at Munich; everyone was getting revved up in anticipation. The plane on its descent into Munich crashed and burst into flames, Matt Busby, Bobby Charlton and a few others had survived the rest perishing in the flames. The whole football world was stunned beyond belief as the youngest talented players fell to such an unfortunate tragedy. Man U were trialling a new first team, the lads were pointing out to me Bobby Charlton who had survived the crash was in the line up for Manchester United and his brother Jack was on the starting line up for Leeds. The two of them went on to play in the England side who won the world cup in 1966. I enjoyed the afternoon out but it didn't convert me to a football turkey, dog and ferrets for me.

Back at the mill it was lunchtime and we came down off the roof, and had to walk through the stations were a lot of the mill girl's worked. They each had their private sections where they toiled although it was a big open floor. As we continued past I was embellishing their pop idols features, Elvis, Cliff, Buddy, George ! – – Formby with moustaches, windows and Big knobs, they'll never know who did it.

A couple of days later I was sent down off the roof to fetch something and had to walk through the same area but this time it was full of women working. This little old lady stood up and shouted "there he is!", fucking hell! Apparently, I found out later she had been hidden from view troughing her sandwiches, espying me doing the terrible deeds.

"After him Get the little bastard!!" About a dozen girls aged 18–25 were after me like a flight of screaming banshees, "Have his pants off, get the knife, chop his cock off. !" It was now my turn to cough in my rompers and I was off, going like a bat out of hell and heading back to the roof. Up the steps to the attic door, I had a good lead up the steps to the top room before the roof door, up the rest of the steps, try the latch, bollocks it had been locked. The bastards were in on it, that's why they sent me down there. Down the steps I shot and dived under the biggest bail of cotton waste ever, like a twenty foot square three foot thick Eider down, thank fuck they'll never find me under here. The first door opened to the sound of these hell cats "Where is he?" Strip the swine naked lets give him a good going over, come on, the bloody works.

They were searching and their voices getting closer, and I didn't know part of my foot was visible, here he is. "Fuck Me I'm dead" "Get his pants off" I managed to half escape. Next news we were on top of this enormous cotton waste sack, they were undoing my belt and tugging at my trolley's, I had to save face somehow, I managed to get a grip of this essence one hands on her bra and knickers, if mine were coming off, so was hers, and so it was, tits, fanny's, arses, cock, bollocks everywhere.

They were trying to smack my arse, and most of them were succeeding "that will teach you, you little fucker" It did that alright, I knew which side of the fence I was on, tits and fanny's fuck the arseholes. I had a hard on for a week, you could have prised a safe door open with it.

After the mill job was completed the firm was contracted to build a private bungalow. We didn't go to the site until the foundations and brick work had been laid and ready for the carpenters. Our first job was to put a roof on it. During our lunch breaks we all used to eat our sandwiches and drink our tea together. I was listening to this labourer who was in his forties talking about his son who was in the Royal Navy. I

asked what it was like, what did he do, where did he go. He gave me a right recruiting spiel, they got special cigarettes ten pence a hundred, blue liners. I later learned they called them coffin nails. They also got a tot of rum everyday consisting of three single measures of rum which had to be between 96 proof to 104 proof, mixed with six measures of water, now called Grog. After an old admiral who introduced the mixing with water so it couldn't be saved and stored. The old Jack Tars hated the miserable bastard for it. This was issued at eleven forty-five just before lunch. Tot time, the Pipe would be made over the tannoy" Up Spirits" to the chorus "Stand Fast the holy Ghost". From the messdecks, It was a tradition carried on from the sailing ships when after awhile at sea all the food gradually deteriorated and went rotten, so they got one tot each everyday.

Two when the KING or Queen said "splice the mainbrace" on whatever momentous occasion, the more the merrier as far as Jack was concerned, the toast was always "THE QUEEN" God bless her. Around the rum fanny on the messdeck table. They were also given six weeks leave a year, taught a trade, good pay packet and you got to sail around the world having a bloody good time leaving a trail of havoc behind you. The risk of imminent death was never mentioned, That was it I was hooked where do I sign? My decision was re-enforced by the fact all the joiners I was surrounded by were saying "look at me I am in my fifties and what have I got to show for it?" A powerful lot to think about for a young ambitious seventeen year old.

No one had travelled anywhere in those days, no one who was of the working classes anyway. All this talk about the Far East, Middle East, South Africa, South America, Canada this was the stuff even my fantasies didn't reach, only rich people and parasites went abroad in the early sixties, everyone from our neck of the woods went to Blackpool. It certainly made anything I had achieved up until then seem pretty tame that's for sure, and I thought I had been doing alright. From that moment onwards I could not get it out of my head. Imagine just to get the chance to keep sailing around the world visiting all these exiting countries and that's your job being paid as well, they took great care not to mention the chances of getting your head blown off. with a bee in my bonnet I set off to find out where to join. The recruiting office was in Manchester about eleven miles away but the recruiting officer visited the outlying towns once a week.

He was due in Rochdale in two weeks time so I made my appointment to see him, I was so excited it seemed to take forever. The day eventually came I made some excuse for skipping work and went to keep my appointment. He was a pleasant chap, he asked me what I did, he than asked me if I enjoyed my work. I said I loved it and that's what I wanted to do in the Royal Navy. He said they didn't have carpenter and joiners the nearest to that was an Artificer – Ship Wright, "That'll do I'll be one of those then" he then dropped the bombshell and told me I was too old. "We train all our own apprentices and an apprenticeship starts at sixteen, so you are too old. My advice to you is to go back, enjoy your job and have a good life. "

I left there thinking "you top drawer bastard, " He's just given me the bum's rush right you ignoramus I will fucking well show you, you twat. The Royal Navy is for me, now watch this space.

Later that week I phoned the recruiting office in Manchester and organised another interview. My heart missed a beat when I eventually went in for the interview; it was the same bloke as before. "Haven't I seen you somewhere before?" I replied "I don't think so". "What do you do for a living?" he enquired, "I work on a building site. " "And what do you do on the building site?" "I am an apprentice carpenter and joiner. " I could see the penny had dropped.

"Do you like your work?" "Not particularly. I don't like working outside in the freezing cold. " "Ok we'll let you take the entrance exam. You can go away to revise and then come back to sit it. " "Can't I do it now?" "If you think you can. " I did it there and then. He told me afterwards I had done very well, and than gave me my options; electrician, mechanic, sick bay tif., steward, chef, stores. "I would like to be an electrician". Well at least it was another trade. "Sounds like a good choice to me but first we have to fix you up with a medical. Take these forms to your own doctor, he'll perform the medical and then return the forms to me. " "And what happens then?" "If all goes well you will receive a letter from us telling you where to go?" "How long do I sign for?" "Nine years". "Can I get out before that if I don't like it?" "NO. "

1553 31/12/06 Just a few lines to reminisce its mid-afternoon New Year's Eve 2006 and I am writing this with my lovely new pen our Aimz got me for Christmas. I don't know how good it handles when I am pissed but there is no doubt that we will find out later. Notice said when not if.

Well I received my joining instructions sometime in December 1960. I was to report to the Manchester recruiting office 9th January 1961. I wasn't looking forward to telling my workplace "Jack Crabtree "I was leaving, it felt like a betrayal, but it was them who put it in my head in the first place. I can't remember telling my parents it was probably a blessing for them. Me, my motorbike, my ferrets, my dog all gone in one foul swoop. The only thing that worried me was my dog. His kennel was below my window I use to sit there and talk to him, say good night, we thought the world of each other. He had knocked over his first young hare and he was just six months old, and going out hunting was heaven to us both, that is what we were bred for. George was pretty upset when I told him, we had become a good hunting team who enjoyed each others company.

I had decided what to do with Rough, I knew no one else would take him out every night and all weekend, and that is what he lived for. So I was going to have to have him put down. I was breaking my heart talking to him but I couldn't see any other way. At least he wouldn't know anything about it, I put my decision to George and he didn't go much on the idea. "This dog could and is in the making of being one of the greats. " He came up with this fella called Moran, he said he was a keen hunter who lived on the opposite side of town.

The pen is much better now, straighter lines. Back to the dog. After Moran promised me he would look after the dog, keep him hunting I was persuaded to sell him for five pounds. Two weeks wages. As he was taking him away on the lead, he looked at me and started howling and crying, he couldn't understand what was happening, We'd never been separated before. That night I went to bed and broke my heart. Kneeling on my bed as usual, I opened my window to say goodnight to Rough but he wasn't there, my tears were falling like raindrops on to his kennel roof, what have I done. I consoled myself by thinking after basic training, six weeks, we get two weeks leave, then I can go over and see him and take him out for the day. That's it Rough me old cock, I'll see you in six weeks time and we'll have a cracking day out. Roll on, can't wait.

CHAPTER 7

Life in a blue suit

9th January 1961 We all met up at the recruiting office in Manchester. One lad I teamed up with was Malcolm Pyrah, he was from Doncaster in Yorkshire. He had been in the Sea Cadets, and knew quite a lot about the navy, where I knew nothing at all. Sure enough I was about to find out. It was a long boring journey by steam train to Plymouth, it took fourteen hours in all. God only knows how many train changes we had to make. Shortly after arrival we boarded the Tor Point Ferry, which took us across to Cornwall where a couple of miles up the road was HMS Raleigh. Whilst crossing on the ferry I was asking Malcolm Pyrah about these big grey ships, with these massive guns I had never seen anything like it. "That is the Monitor HMS Lord Roberts, with something like a 20inch gun. " "And what's that?" "That's a cruiser" "What" " does that do go on cruises?" much laughter. "No it's the size of it, it is much bigger than a Frigate and Destroyer and then a massive Battle ship with 18inch guns. " I They sure were an awesome sight. We arrived at HMS Raleigh late on, they bedded us down in this great big wooden hut (One of many). It was a big dormitory with a row of double metal bunks one on top of each other, and a double locker in between each pair of bunks. There was a row of each side of the hut, there were about thirty of us ranging from 17 – 27 years of age. One lad about twenty years old had a big black eye, his name was Brefit. They started calling him Shiner and that name stuck with him all the years in the Navy "Shiner Brefit". If they could fit you up with a nick name they would. There were lots of standard one for surnames like Green all Greens were Jimmy, White's (Knocker), Brown (Buster), Bray (donkey), Miller (Dusty), one lad was called Humm (Stinky). Of course I didn't know all of this at the time. We had brought a small over night travelling bag each so we bedded down with a real feeling of desperation wondering what the hell tomorrow was going to bring. Well we soon found out.

We all awoke to this terrifyingly loud noise, of some deranged lunatic making this ear splitting raw nerve curdling, mind bending cacophony of sound by emptying his fucking lungs into some form of copper pipe that was probably a bugle, into a turned up Tannoy (loud speaker) system, and then screaming into the microphone "Wakey Wakey, Show a leg, show a leg, show a leg, Wakey, wakey? It's a bit late for that. My hair was already standing on end, and my eyes were standing out like racing dog's bollocks, wondering what the fucking hell had landed. So this was it, six o'clock in the morning, frightened out of my wits and freezing my nuts off. We had to get cold showered and dressed then they marched us through the snow to the dining hall for breakfast.

After breakfast we all congregated by the police office near the main gate. In a nice calm voice "you will be signing on in a minute this is your last chance to take a return ticket and return home to Mummy. Now who wants one?" "Yes I do" this big Teddy boy at the back came out with some apt. expletives, got his ticket home and was gone. Despite how bad I felt there was no way I was going to give up, we hadn't started yet, as I was about to find out. We filed through the office where they gave us an official number P/059814 was my new name. They could tell when you joined and who you were by that number. I signed on the dotted line, that was it, come hell or high water, I was in the Royal Navy for at least the next nine and half years. I was seventeen and a half, actual time served didn't start until your eighteenth birthday, so they would cleverly rob me of six months pension time later on, thieving bastards.

It all started to happen so quickly. "Ok you lot into the slop room" here we were kitted out with everything we needed and oodles of stuff we didn't. And most things nearly fitted, working clothes, underwear, studded boots for parade drill, unstudied for best, polish, shoe brushes, sewing kit etc. Then all your bedding. Back to the hut with that lot on your back, we must have looked like twenty nine deformed tortoises struggling back to the den, next, get changed into number eights; working gear. "Bag up all your civilian gear and report back here in fifteen minutes. You will collect your civvies in six weeks time, if you pass out, and are leaving. " (a veiled threat already to carry with you for the next part of the sentence).

The next thing was in to the barbers shop where the gags were flying thick and fast. How would Sir like it?, Like Tony Curtis please. Bzzzzz – Bzzzzzzzzzzh – Bzzzzzh. Look in the mirror, fucking hell, Tony Curtiss doesn't have his hair cut like this. – – – He does if he comes in here. He shaved everybody's heads, as if we weren't cold enough. Everyone had longish hair in the sixties. They had just stripped us of anything that made us unique, no one was suppose to have a personality. Everyone was so down it was untrue. What had we done! We were all dressed the same and looked like old time American convicts. All we needed were the chains, and they had even worked that one out, mental ones. That day seemed to last forever.

We were all hoping the next nine years wouldn't be as bad. The worst of it was we never knew what was going to happen next, no routine that we were aware of, every thing we did was on the spur of the moment, all because of what came spilling out of some mental cripples mouth. Eventually at about seven o'clock they left us to make up our beds, and store our hideous kit in our lockers. We were to polish our boots ready for inspection in the morning, well, once we were left alone in the mess to get on with it, the mood changed to frivolity. Shiner started cavorting up and down the mess as if it were a catwalk and he was the star, which at that moment he was, his attire was this ludicrous last war underwear, underpants down to his knee's with an open fly, vest, worn just above the knee, finished off with a big pair of daisy roots to balance on.

We just had to make the best of it. We started having a laugh, imitating these seemingly demented Hitler type morons who had just completely taken over our lives. If we hadn't laughed we'd have cried. Ten o'clock came, lights out, completely knackered, freezing cold, bed time, I can't believe it took so long to get here, at least we didn't have nine and a half years to do anymore – – – – only nine and a half, – – minus 1 day.

Once again we were woken by this prick on the end of a bugle with "Wakey Wakey" only this time the mess door burst open and in and came this deranged lunatic dressed like one of Hitler's bods. He literally came in screaming "GET DRESSED, GET DRESSED, FALL IN OUTSIDE, FALL IN OUTSIDE! COME ON, COME ON, WHATS WRONG WITH YOU, CHOP CHOP, MOVE YOURSELVES. What the fucking hell is going on. I thought he was about to have a seizure. He got us all fell in outside, after a fashion, and took us for a quiet morning run (Double march) around the snow covered parade ground, round and round and round until our lungs were bursting. When we got back just about everyone had burst blisters on their heels and feet, running with these brand new boots on that didn't fit. The sadistic bastards knew exactly what would happen and were just establishing their authority. Now shower and shave no such thing as heated water, I'm sure there were icicles hanging from my bollocks, dry off and round to the sinks en masse, finishing up with a lacerated face from scraping an old fashioned blunt razor across it quickly, before it froze to your chin, then unbelievably, clean and polish the mess.

That meant six troops on their hands and knees laying thick polish, another half dozen following up rubbing it in, then a relay of operators frantically swinging this Bumper, a big heavy oblong weight of an object covered in dusters, connected to a six foot long broom handle by a swivel pin. this lethal piece of apparatus was sent flying up one end of the mess and then returned at speed threatening to break any legs not quick enough to out manoeuvre the fucking thing. This seemed to be the objective of the exercise more and more now of the now demented operators, who by now were so hungry they could eat a scabby dead rabid dog with mange, but not yet, not before you can see your face in the polished wooden floorboards.

For the first week we weren't allowed out of the mess on our own, only as a group and even then we were marched everywhere in a tight knit block, presumably to kill any notion in our now defunct brains of anyone making a break for it. It was one long visitation to purgatory. Kit musters, inspections, window cleaning, learning to march, first aid for our feet, trying to get warm, evading the semi lethal bumper. One lad twenty year old blondy O'Hara, who had an eighteen month old little girl couldn't take it anymore, and hung himself in the drying room from the metal dhobi rails. Luckily or not depending on your point of view, Medway the six foot odd class leader walked in there and found him (dancing on thin air suspended by a rope around his neck choking trying to get a grip of anything, but everything was just out of reach, to lift himself up with,) just in time and lifted him up taking the weight off the stricture and screamed for help. They cut him down and carted him off to sick bay. We didn't see him again after that, obviously a mental case and (bad influence) he would be sent to R. N. H. Nettley to weave baskets until his brain returned to normal, when he would be given another chance to complete his basic training with a bit more close supervision and encouragement the second time around just to make sure there weren't to be any more unfortunate incidents. Another lad Goddard who had been brought up on a remote farm by his grandmother and had, had very little human contact in his entire life. he was so soiled and his skin was so engrained with dirt he looked yellow, he was covered in blackheads, whiteheads, ripeheads, and not so ripeheads and was quite adverse to the thought of soap and water touching his skin or what there was left of it. One of the most important things about having sailors living together in close proximity on ships is cleanliness.

As he wouldn't wash our instructor told us to take him down to the Dhobi room strip him off and scrub him raw, which is what happened, he was dumped in one of the big clothes washing sinks and with long and short handled thick bristled floor scrubbers. He was scrubbed alright! raw, he didn't get the message straight away he just thought he was being picked on for some unknown reason, but after a couple of weeks of the same, he started to wash his clothes and shower with the rest of us. Problem solved, as he was such a scale'y individual he was awarded the unenviable task of becoming the keeper of "CLIVE "the camps ceremonial mascot, he was for the next six weeks to be the sole keeper of a big horny Billy goat with a massive pair of horns and a cock to match, he had a pair of bollocks a buffalo would have been proud of, and he knew it, the way he lorded it around showing them off. "just take a look at the size and quality of these bastards then" He knew it all right. He had a sexual preference for anything with a pulse that moved and sometimes not even that fussy. I had heard of the famous Mountain Goats, but Clive was supreme as the top mounting Goat, he was up everything, he even fancied the Blue jacket bands big base drummer, or was it his drum. Goddard wouldn't be dropping his soap with Clive in the vicinity that's for sure. If he did he would have been top of the list for a sore arse for certain.

We were beginning to get quite fit, marching and double marching (running in step) as a squad everywhere. Our class instructional petty officer, began to warm to his class, as every ones personalities began to emerge. It was hell when we were handed over to the drill instructors on the parade ground. Any single mistake by anyone and the whole squad was doubling around the parade ground with a nine pound .303 rifle at the shoulder, until it felt as though our lungs would burst. They had us so terrified we never knew when or if it was going to stop. They would just say okay you orrible lot round again, it was only when someone was obviously going to collapse the drill was relaxed to something slower to allow our breathing to almost return to normal.

We were doing the "fix bayonet" drill, I was in line next to this big older twenty-seven year old fella, half way through the routine by numbers, everyone's a quarter bent over doing the drill removing the bayonet from its scabbard. I was looking down and I noticed the water coming out of the top of his boot, I thought "how can that be, he's fucking sinking "he was so terrified, and shaking in his boots he was pissing himself, as soon as the GI's (gunnery instructors) saw this big puddle forming they started on him. It was a good job we all had a gaiters on (the bottoms of the trousers are held in tight by them) because the next lot he jettisoned had us all gasping for air. He had to stay like that for the next hour transporting the mess around in the bottom of his trollies, spreading his own particular aroma around, as we marched around the parade ground, until we were fell out for lunch, talk about making your own mark, his nickname was smelly after that lot "Be back in one hour all emptied out and cleaned up. " O. K. Chief, "We'll be looking forward to it". Yeah alright.

Some of the lads had joined the navy as boy sailors at sixteen, a lot of orphans and ner do well's. They had been together for a year and worked as a unit to intimidate all the others and stamp their authority so they could rule the roost. At HMS St Vincents they had been through the mill, where they still birched them for any misdemeanour. No one could touch them on the snooker table, they had been playing each other every day for a year. Everything with them was for money or smokes. I learned my first good lesson, don't gamble. Navy cigarettes were about sixty pence for 300, well I didn't smoke and we were playing Brag for smokes. Anyway I had Ace, King, Queen which was a bloody good hand, and he had Jack, Queen, King of hearts. He was blind all the way but his cronies had been moving around looking at all the cards plus his as well.

He won thousands of cigs and that put me right off, if they could cheat that blatantly then anyone could. January is slowly passing and the class is beginning to gel, I cant stop thinking of the dog, I hope Moran is looking after him ok, taking him out and treating him well. I expect I'm just a distant memory, and he's having the time of his life hunting and chasing hares, I keep looking forward to receiving a letter from home, its not much but at least its contact with the outside world. One of the lads I was pals with was Bogey Knight (John). He was a bit younger than me, he was the next to sign on after me, so his official number was one greater than mine, he lived with his folks in Portsmouth, who'm I met later on. Unbeknown to us then, years later Bogey would be my boss. Now there's a story worth waiting for.

After about three or four weeks we were granted night leave, chance for beer. I was on duty on the Friday when most of them went ashore. Shore establishments are treated as ships, nothing really changes. Lights out 2200. I was turning in, in my top bunk, pyjamas you could never get warm in. We were all awakened at about at 2330 by the St Vincent boys, all had obviously had a few wets and were pretending to be more pissed than they actually were.

They had come in put the lights on and were making a right old racket no fucking consideration. Ginge Gaunt, slept in the bunk under mine He came over started taunting me, when I didn't rise to the bait he was saying "Green outside I am gonna fucking have you". Not forgetting this lot were fully dressed and with a big pair of daisy roots on. It soon became obvious that I had to do something he wasn't going to let up, so I hopped out of bed and started to put my boots on. He said "What are you doing?" I said "You want outside, well outside, I am gonna kick your miserable ginger fucking head in. "

His attitude changed he punched my head there and then, my temper blew I flew at this prick with both fists pumping, I used all my power from the soles of my feet upwards, you want violence you tosser right up my street. I finished him off sharpish. The rest of the mob stood there not believing what had just happened, one of there leaders had just been battered and he was a lot bigger than me, but obviously not as useful. There was blood all over him and his bed, I grabbed my wash bag and towel and went for a shower. Ten minutes later when I returned, all the lights were out and all was quiet. I was thinking what a way to live. In the morning Reveille (Call the hands) I hopped out of bed and saw Gaunt with encrusted blood all over his face and bed. He had the audacity to say to me "Hey Green your blood is all over my white front, you'd better dhobi it. " I said "Any more threats from you, you fucking wanker, and they will be washing the rest of your blood away with a fucking hosepipe. " Now wind your fucking neck in and zip it, or I'll zip it for you.

As he was one of the leaders, the rest kept quiet, with all the other mess members looking on in disbelief, with that, my status rose and they kept well clear of me and left me alone. Sunday mornings was ceremonial divisions, our no. 1 uniforms had to be immaculate and our boots polished to gleaming so you could see your face in them. We would be fell in on the parade ground in classes, inspected by the divisional officer, then up would strike the blue jacket band, who would lead the guard and the rest of the parade around the parade ground and finally past the captain, who took the salute on the rostrum, of each class in turn, as they eye's right, as they passed the dias.

Goddard was right behind the band with Clive held in on a short lead, in his ceremonial dark blue jacket en'blazon'd with insig'nia, I didn't know what it was that set him off, but every Sunday as soon as the band flashed up, Clive went cross eyed and produced this enormous erection that put the fear of God up Goddard. I think he was praying that, that was all he was going to get up him, It might have been the big base drum or the bugles, but every time, right on cue, Clive would produce his third horn. as they came past us, I'm sure he was eyeing up Goddard. We were all hoping he could break free, then we would really find out who Clive was in love with, I could just imagine the big base drummer high tailing it over the parade ground, with his tiger skin and big base drum bouncing all over the place and a rampant Billy goat in horney hot pursuit. I wouldn't have liked to be in his boots if Clive had caught him.

Well we had a couple of runs ashore when we weren't part of duty watch, and the final week gradually came to a close and we took the last exams, we then had a passing out parade. Clive gave us another spectacular show to the sound of the big bass drum, he sure was some horny old goat, in more ways than one. The next class would be starting on Monday, so Clive could sort his tackle out, ready to frighten the life out of his next unsuspecting keeper. I think Goddard had grown quite attached to Clive over the last six weeks, so he said goodbye to him nuts and all, with another bag of sweets, It was now time to leave Raleigh for the last time and join our individual parent establishments, depending on which branch of the navy we joined.

As I was electrical branch I would be heading for H. M. S. Collingwood the royal navy's electrical school in Fareham Hants. Which I would join on numerous occasions as my career progressed over the coming years. Our transport turned up, not even a bus, but an old covered navy wagon, with practically no springs, we threw all the kit bags in the back, then joined them for the most horrendous journey yet, from Cornwall to Hampshire, in the boneshaker of all boneshakers. We arrived in Collingwood nearly dead but were impressed with what we saw. It is three miles in circumference, and at that time had the biggest parade ground in Europe which I would circumnavigate much to the distress of my lungs on innumerable occasions with a nine pound .303 rifle on my shoulder in the many years to come.

They drove us to the new entry block which consisted of about twelve big wooden accommodation huts, each capable of housing forty bodies. The accommodation was situated six either side of the road, and a big wooden walkway joining all six huts together at the rear for entry into the heads (toilets) showers, big washrooms and drying room. When we had unloaded we were given a locker each in the end hut, and told to stow our kit, on completion we were to draw our bedding from the bedding store, then do a joining routine, have some supper, get turned in and pipe down. I was thinking of Rough even more now as I new we would be going on leave shortly. I dropped off to sleep absolutely worn out, to dream about seeing Rough soon and going hunting on the moors.

We were awakened by the usual din. and during the course of the day we were told that we were being allowed seventeen days privileged leave, commencing midday

Friday, and don't drop yourselves in the shit. Because if you do, you won't be going. Friday came at last I couldn't wait till noon. They gave us a return travel warrant, and told us enjoy your leave but don't be late back or else. There always had to be a threat involved. Who cares we're out of the main gate. Whooppee. We're on our way I couldn't wait to get home, it seemed like I had been away for years. I looked George up straight away, I wanted to see my dog. I met him in the bar of the Kingsway Hotel by the canal where we used to set off hunting with the dogs,

I was so excited, Great to see you George, you too, my you've shot up, what have they been putting in your shoes – horse muck. "Where does Moran live", "I'm going to see Rough, he'll be over the moon to see me" I'm taking him out, can't wait, we'll have a great time together, were going over the moors again, you know how he used to love it, with a bit of luck he'll knock over a hare for the pot, mum will be chuffed, I've been waiting six weeks to see him, that's what kept me going when I was really down, come on where does he live. "Harry sit down" I don't want to sit down, stop pissing me about where does Moran live, come here and sit down, come on what's wrong, I want to see Rough, you can't, what do you mean I can't, is it that Moran being awkward. what's wrong? – – – – – – – – -

"He's dead" were the only words he used to describe that awful blow. "What do you mean he's fucking dead?!" Moran had a firewood business out of town, they use to sell bundles of firewood (kindling) for lighting your coal fires with. Apparently he kept a few pigs as well, a bit like a Steptoe's yard, they had locked my dog up there and expected him to be a guard dog. Moran had told George that the dog just sat down and wouldn't eat and just cried and howled for about a week, pining for me and then died. " To say I was upset was a bit of an understatement I felt like I had lost half of myself. I just couldn't get over it. anyway George said "come round tomorrow morning about four o'clock and we will take Russ out. " Of course I had not got any ferrets now, so we were on the hunt, just for hares. I turned up at about four o'clock and Russ was going absolutely bananas, I hadn't seen him for about eight weeks.

I let him off his chain he was all over me, he was up and down looking for Rough, he knew where ever I was, Rough was, he also knew where we were going. What an exhilarating feeling crossing those moors again, after being constrained to that camp. I hadn't realised how much I missed it until I got back there, I hadn't appreciated that this had been my whole life, as we made our way over the fields, there was an icy cold easterly wind blowing, probably originating on the Russian Stepps causing our eyes to run, the floods streaming from my eyes were nothing to do with the wind. I could see Rough in my minds eye running up ahead with Russ having the time of his life and keep coming back to me with a big smile on his face to check.

I was alright. It was all I could do to stop myself letting go and completely breaking down, but I couldn't let George see that, but knowing what I know today George would have seen but was just being very discreet about it. (Cheers George) We had a great day out and Russ caught a couple of hares to boot. I skinned and cleaned them and put them in the pot, mother was chuffed 'Harry's home'. I don't think I would like hare now it's a very dark and strong meat, tough, blood almost black. I always imagined that is exactly what dog would taste like, plus were not so hungry these days. The tears I secretly wept out of my bedroom window onto Rough's kennel roof that night, weren't like raindrops anymore, more like a torrent, the tide wasn't coming in it was coming down as I broke my heart, I'm so sorry Rough, I didn't know. What have I done?. I would have given anything to turn the clock back. I eventually sobbed myself to sleep not caring about being embarrassed I was just too upset.

The following Saturday after a few beers I was talking to some of the lads I had known at the tech. school. They were having a collection for Allen Kenyon's funeral, he was this lad who was sent to escort me home when I had my first migraine starting in the town. I couldn't see at first my vision disappeared behind a blurred mess. It cleared up after about an hour and so instead of going home we went birds nesting in Carr wood the other side of town, all the other bods were stuck into their text books on this boiling hot summers day, whilst we were gallivanting across the countryside enjoying ourselves big time. We were outside the Carlton (local dancehall) I had a few bevy's in me from the Bath's hotel, a small pub which I had been using on dance night for over a year and I still wasn't eighteen still I was about to go in and shake a wicked leg jiving, as I was on my own it was often difficult to get a dance, as the girls hung about in pairs and wanted two lads to ask them so they wouldn't leave one on the side on her own, so I went about it my way.

I would look for two girls dancing together one of which I had to fancy, because the other would soon be getting the Bums rush when the opportunity arose and the time was right, I would wait for the two girls to start a fast jive. when one spun the other round, momentarily letting go of her hand I would step in and catch the pair of them, taking advantage of them both being a bit dizzy and not quite sure what the flying fuck was going on anyway, with my legs going like the clappers and spinning them both around to the hot music jiving with the best of them. – all good fun, in next to no time at all a couple jives were up, and I'd slipped the Growler to get on with the main task of trombone'ing the looker. "Well, what happened to Kenyon?" "He was riding pillion on the back of his mates motorbike. It was pissing down and they were behind a flat back truck which was carrying some sheet metal which was over hanging the back of the truck, and unfortunately for Alan it didn't have a red flag on the overhang to indicate it was there The bike was a bit close, the truck did an emergency stop for some reason, the bike rider couldn't stop and went skidding towards the truck, as the bike went under the back of the truck he ducked under the metal sheet.

Allan who was sitting behind him, hadn't seen it and the sheet metal sliced his head straight off. Apparently it went rolling along the metal to the front of the truck and banged against the cab, blood and snot everywhere, " poor sod, that had to be worth five shillings of anybodies money towards his flowers, so I coughed up then entered the Carlton, on my mission to bury the bone.

After my leave expired I returned to HMS Collingwood the Royal Naval electrical school. This is where I was to receive my six months worth of basic electrical knowledge. We started off with a week of maths then basic electrics with an exam at the end of each week, which I find to be the most effective way of learning, as you gradually learn how to store and then recall all relevant information, and having done this become adept at exam techniques, also the info. Is now permanently stored.

About half way through our course we were doing marching drills on the parade ground, we were called to attention and visiting dignitaries who were being shown around the camp, decided to come and give us an inspection (good of them). They were General Montgomery, and Margaret Lockwood (1950s film star) I noticed she had a mouthful of dimps (fag ends) remains of bad teeth, through smoking her way around Hollywood. I couldn't believe what a short arse Montgomery was, he was about knee high to a grasshopper, mind you he tried to make up for it with the size of his cap, it looked more like a funnel cover for the Ark Royal, or an African Missionary cooking cauldron. On another occasion I was detailed off to be part of a car door opening party, when Princess Margaret was visiting, she inspected the workshops and as she was leaving it was my job to open the door of the limo. So she could board the motor with minimum effort, she was tiny.

She jumped in this big Rolls Royce and landed half way back on the huge rear seat, legs in akimbo, flashing her light blue knickers. I gave her a big smile and a wink, she already had that look on her face, there's something about being on a ship or establishment, in the presence of all those sailors in uniform that puts the ladies half way to another planet, or onto their backs, strange really. I was duty watch on another occasion and hadn't been given a particular job to do, as I was a spare hand we were on call for the rest of the night and were allowed into the cinema, we were watching Tarzan and was just about to find put how he got his ape call (Jane was in a pool in the clearing, with croc's going in for the kill, "Jane grab the bottom of my vine as I swing past" – – – – – – – – - AAAAHHGGG AAAHHHGGG) the film stopped and a notice came up all spare hands muster at the main gate. Bollocks.

We made our way down there and they fell in about a dozen of us, this was about nine o'clock in the evening., and proceeded to inform us that a lot of the young pigs (squealers) had escaped from the piggery – a money making scheme to make use of the vast quantities of food waste that was produced by the camp, and to make life even more comfortable in the other piggery (the wardroom) They sent us off in all directions as they had no idea where the little grunters were, I was sent up the main road with its manicured lawns, flower beds and rhododendron bushes, normally out bounds. (keep off the grass, different connotations these days) I was on this lawn peering into the bushes when an officer startled me, he said "You are a suspicious looking character, what are you doing?" "I am looking for a pig sir". He really went into one "Right fall in here, left right, left right, left right" he marched me down to the police office at the main gate. "This insolent little so and so, when I asked him what he was doing he said he was looking for a pig!" "That's correct sir they have escaped from the piggery. " "Carry on Green. " At least "I" found one, We finished up having a right old laugh as little pigs aren't all that easy to catch, the squealing only heightens the fun.

Wakey – Wakey was done by the duty leading hand, he would scream his way through about a dozen huts, banging a big stick, like a truncheon with a metal end, on every metal bed end, making one hell of a racket. On completion at 0630 he would return to the first hut, and anyone still in bed was told to get your boots on, plus your gas mask and roll up your bedding, and fall in outside, mattress, blankets, pillow the lot and then told, get it on your back and over the six air raid shelters, which were about twelve feet high and covered in grass, Before you hit the third one you thought your lungs would burst, as there was not enough air coming in through the gasmask. You only did that the once. Your body would get out of bed automatically when the poisoned dwarf started banging the beds in future.

One day they marched us outside the air raid shelters, we were ordered 'on gas masks!' Then we were ushered inside, and the door was locked, and canisters of Cs gas was let off (tear gas). Any exposed skin started to irritate and burn. After about five minutes they ordered off gas masks! I thought my eyes and lungs were disintegrating. They kept us like that for 30 seconds the screams hit a maximum. They then kindly opened the door, the gas had penetrated our clothes. As we all ran out, it seemed that everyone had their own personal gas cloud surrounding them. The instructor told us that was to prove to us that our gas masks really worked, decent bastard. I replied 'you could have just told us, we would have believed you. '

The next was the swimming test, 2 lengths of the pool, get out, put on a pair of overalls and plimsols, and then back in for another length, than tread water for another minute. This was extremely difficult as you can imagine. For those who went under with the weight of the wet overalls, the instructor, who was standing on the side with a big long pole which he would plunge in front of them, but only once there lungs were half full of water and it looked as if they were about to drown. Those who failed the test, had to practice in their own time until they were competent enough to complete the task. Luckily I was a strong swimmer, but I was holding on by a hair's breadth.

I managed to get through the basic training finding it difficult to understand what exactly was going on with the electrics. I did not find any of it in the slightest bit interesting, but I finished it all the same.

We passed out, then moved on over to defiance division the wooden huts on the far side of the camp, which was under the ships company, and not under training. We felt as though we were now in the navy as our initial training had been completed. The ships company work force was a big pool of labour, to be used to carry out all the tasks necessary to have the establishment running as smoothly as possible, any job could come your way, like in a kabuts, galley slave, messman, landscape garden Wallah, Skirmisher, General dogs body, but the best of all was on the bins the dust cart, start early finish early plus they got a trip into the normally out of bounds fenced in wren'ry and a chance to ogle all the fanny in there and exchange all the lewrid banter.

Giving them all what for and getting twice as much back, only to be interrupted by the truncheon / cosh wielding big bull dike of a chief wren, at least I think it was a truncheon / cosh, it was certainly a weapon you could do some serious damage with, especially with that big pair of cocoa nuts dangling from one end (who was not very happy with all the racket going on disturbing her, especially when being only half way through her morning shave and still being hung over from last nights darts and curry supper) looking after her darling little chickens and trying to make sure little boy blue didn't stand a chance when he turned up looking for one of her young wrn's to come blow up his horn, who told us in no uncertain terms to pick up the rubbish and fuck off quick before she got angry and sorted us out.

Just imagining what that could entail with that fucking thing she had swinging from her wrists, we picked up the rubbish telling her there was plenty of room on the back of the cart for her and her lethal looking oppo, and fucked of out of the gates quick with all the troops hanging from the sides of the cart and laughing their nuts off looking forward to an even better encounter next week as everyone was getting the hang of the routine. - – – -Happy days!- – – – -Fuck em all. Fuck all the bloody lot of em. Singing Bell bottom trousers, coats of navy blue, let him climb the rigging like his daddy used to do.

Another time I was sent to work in the wardroom as a general dog's body. Things began to get a bit easier and more pleasant, as we were given a little more freedom ie. Being able to walk around the camp on your own, to carry out your duty, and not being marched around in a squad all the time, plus the added bonus of not having to get up so early.

emember one Saturday morning when the duty leading hand came round calling the 'hands'. He just walked through the mess and turned the radio full on and then marched on to the next mess, (no horrendous banging on the end of your bed) this privilege was granted because we were no longer under training, one of the older able seaman with a hangover, jumped out of bed and turned it off. The hookey (leading hand) came back and switched it full on again and marched off to check the other messes, the same A. B. leapt out of bed and switched it off again. This is getting interesting. The hookey came back turned it on again and stood there. Again the A. B. leapt out of bed but this time he picked up the radio which was plugged in and blaring away, and threw it straight through the window. There was a hell of a smash as it made its way through the window and an even bigger one as it disintegrated on the path below. Hook'y said 'get your lid (hat) main gate'. That meant he would be marched down to the main gate, halted in front of the head policeman, with another crusher bellowing in his ear" OFF CAPS"

Which was known as lifting your lid. Then the charge would be read and the appropriate punishment awarded. It wasn't a case of am I in the shit. Just how deep.

I had cushy job in the wardroom helping this old guy, a civilian caretaker. I was to work there for a couple of months while I awaited a draught order to post me to a ship. I was disappointed when it finally arrived, as it was to HMS Torquay, a frigate that was under going a massive refit in drydock. That meant that the ships company would be victualled in HMS Victory (Royal Naval barracks Portsmouth), R. N. B. and have to march back and forth between the two. Each ship in drydock had its own skeleton crew, (not anorexic matlots) just not a full crew. R. N. B. was separated from Portsmouth dockyard by a huge wall.

It had three gates all policed to try and stop Jack from smuggling contraband out of the dockyard. There was the big main gate down on "the hard" by the ferries, unicorn gate which was the working gate through which all the stores, were brought in by rail, and multitudes of dockyard matey's poured in and out every day, literally thousands of them on their pushbikes, and the ships companies were marched up and down three or four times a day. (for dinner and supper etc.) and a third small gate inside the barracks to which was attached the Detention quarters (D. Q's) the sailors jail, fenced off and guarded by vicious alsatian dogs and lobotomised crushers.

The thought of D. Q. 's put the fear of god into the sailors hearts, the severity of the place was the deterrent. That's what these mindless morons wandering our streets these days could do with, and that's just the policemen. As lots of major machinery had been removed from the ship for repair and maintenance, and all structural work being carried out by the dockyard matey's.

Our main duties consisted of fire watching for the welders, keeping the ship clean and clear of rubbish, sleeping onboard when duty watch as fire and emergency party, the safety of the ship being paramount, It was not the most pleasant place to be in the middle of winter, with snow everywhere for weeks on end. The ship was in drydock without heating and power for tempary lights only.

We were constantly frozen. Where our mess was in barracks was on the first floor and it was huge, it was separated off into four quarters, housing about three hundred sailors from four different ships, a lot of the old sailors left over from the last war, were scrumpy addicts, Consequently the mattress's had been soiled so many times, the acid had burnt away the fabric so that the horse hair on the inside was hanging out and stunk to high heaven. There was one big communal wardrobe at the end of each mess, there were so many people coming and going it was a real job trying to hang on to your kit. If the alch'ies were broke, they would nick a raincoat or a suit and take it ashore to a hock shop, what a life. Still not to worry just another nine years to go,

CHAPTER 8

First ship

On the 2nd July 1962 I flew out to Singapore, on a Bristol Britannia Turbo Prop aircraft (4 propellers). It took nearly two days to get out there, we landed first in Istanbul for refuelling the next stop was Bombay. We disembarked in the middle of the runway I think it was about midnight – I thought these engines are hot. About a hundred yards nearer the terminal I found out it wasn't the engines, but the heat of the tropical night. This was a strange feeling, it was my first time on a plane, and the first time abroad, and I was off to meet my new ship HMS Hartland Point. This was named after a place in Devon. A point of high land jutting out into the sea. I had no idea how long I was going for, or what this place was going to look like.

I had no idea what lay ahead and I was going with much trepidation. We re'boarded the aircraft and carried on with the journey. We arrived in Singapore and the heat and humidity was stifling. They took about a dozen of us to the dockyard in a big covered wagon, and dropped us all at the Quayside. A cutter (motorboat) was waiting to take us out to the ship, which was anchored in the middle of the River. Singapore was an absolute shit hole, dangerous, dirty, and wild, we were not wanted there but that was something I was to experience where ever we went in the world.

This was my first time on a fully operational ship, It was good, it was alive, you could smell the steam from the boilers all through the ship, food was being prepared and cooked in the galley by the cooks in there immaculate whites, overseen by the petty officer cook with his big tall hat on and his mouth full of foul but opportune language, all ready at the drop of a sausage to let rip into his galley full of piss taking reprobates it didn't matter how smart they all were, there was only one boss and he ruled with a rod of iron. The laundry was busy, busy, busy, all the noises of a very active ship board life.

A Chinese Goffer wallah would stand by the gangway selling goffers (soft drinks) out of a very large half wooden barrel, filled with ice to the ever thirsty ships company. the metal upper deck was wooden boarded to keep the temperature down and make it possible to walk on. I saw a big rat run behind his barrel, and so did he, his knife was out in a flash, he'd thrown it and pinned the rat to the deck, where it was squealing like a stuck pig. Its killing wasn't in vain as it would have joined the rest of the scraps he would have gathered during the day to go in his curry that night joining the odd chit chat (lizard) that had succomed to his crafty traps. Inside the ship was roasting as there wasn't any air conditioning in those days.

All the mess decks were on the accommodation deck (unusual for a warship) and there were about half a dozen portable hurricane fans to circulate the air , the senior mess member always had the air flow directed to his bunk (privilege). After the evening vindaloo for supper, the sound of up to three hundred sailors blowing off at leisure, reminded me of the salvation army brass band back home playing the Trumpet Volountary, and unless you needed your sinus's clearing, the option of sleeping on a camp bed on the upper deck was heaven. Sleep was possible once you got used to the to the sound of the tropical night life performing, I was unceremoniously awakened one night by a huge flying beetle the size of a small bird, which had crashed into ships superstructure and had chosen to land on my bare chest, as it was scratching around recovering my terrified screams had the rest of the lads awakened with there eye's popping out of there sockets wondering what terrible catastrophe had happened and would we live.

I was about as popular as a pork chop in a synagogue. On another occasion we were abruptly awakened by this massive clap of thunder, right above our heads, followed by sheets of lightning flying all over the night sky, illuminating the whole area for a couple of minutes at a time, the tropical vegetation on the river banks was made visible and the whole of Singapore dockyard it was a sight to behold, at the same time a blanket of water descended from the night sky it was like the tide was coming down rather than in, the air was then turning blue from the streams of invectives coming from the mouths of about a dozen irate, hairy arsed sailors in the bollicky buff, clutching there now rain sodden camp beds and bedding, arms and legs everywhere, bollocks swinging in the breeze, heading at speed for some sort of shelter under the awning.

The ship was a fleet a maintenance vessel. It was the mother ship to all the frigates and destroyers operating in the south China seas, and down off Indonesia and Borneo where the royal marines were operating ashore. There was conflict at the time to the South between Britain and Indonesia, and Vietnam to the North, where the Americans were well and truly bogged down. We were slap bang in the middle of a war zone. It was a wake up call, a long way from life with the dogs and ferrets. Come to think of it I could have some fun with the ferrets, with these rats onboard, they board ship via the securing ropes when the ship is alongside, round metal discs (rat guards) are secured to the ropes to try and deter them. The older lads used to tell the sprogs that it was a good job being a rat guard, standing on the focs'le with a loaded .303 rifle shooting them off the ropes. Then they would persuade them to put a request in to be a rat guard.

Our first trip in to Singapore ripped my eyes wide open. We were informed not to go anywhere alone, preferably 3 or more to a group, otherwise you were likely to be found in the gutter with a knife in your back. There was at least one sailor a week found dead killed by the chokies some had had their toggle and two sliced off and sewn up in their mouths before the fatal blow was delivered, they had a certain way about them the evil bastards. We landed by boat onto the jetty nearest to our ship in the dockyard. We then made our way to the dockyard gate – all establishments were surrounding by huge twelve foot walls – the town was about 18 miles away so we would wait for a pick up taxis to come along. The fair was a dollar each. The driver would go flat out stopping to pick up anyone who flagged him down. There would be old crones with three or four live chickens being held by their feet squawking their heads off, heading for the street markets in Singaore. The cab was full to the roof, and as many hanging on to the outside as possible, it was a hair raising trip going through all these remote and poverty stricken villages.

There was certainly a sense that we weren't safe. The locals hated all white men, so we automatically reciprocated by hating the murdering slant eyed yellow bastards. What an introduction to foreigners. By the time it was my turn to go home, the hating of these yellow fiends was complete. We will leave that there, times have changed and I too have moved forward although some feelings are hard to eradicate.

We got out of the pick up taxi and were heading for downtown Singapore. It was absolutely filthy and stunk to high heaven. We turned a corner on the street and walked into the overhang of a butchers shop, all the meat was hanging the whole way up to the roadside. I was nearly sick with the stench of the semi rotten meat and roadside sewerage, we disturbed thousands of black flies which had been infesting all the raw meat, We were in the middle of a big cloud of them and had to cover our mouths as not to breath them in.

We soon legged it out of there before we threw up. We were ashore in – half number six uniform (tropical rig) i. e. white front, white bellbottom trousers, white socks, white shoes. After a few beers we started exploring the nightlife around Boogie street, commenting on the good looking lassies who were all done up and obviously on the game. After talking to some other Matlots we found out that these were the Kai Tai's, at the first glance they were beautiful specimens they all had a lovely big pair of tits but the frightening down side was they had an even bigger pair of bollocks to match swinging low, fuck that. We steered well clear of them. The last thing we wanted to be tapping up some bird expecting a handful of sprats, and finishing up with a handful of nuts and bolts. We carried on up Boogie street visiting all the bars and having a really good eye opening run ashore enjoying all the street vendors and all the bar girls trying to rip Jack off with their sticky greens (sugar water drinks).

Later on we were making our way back to the departing area to look for a fast black, when all of a sudden all hell breaks loose, what looked like a Chinese bird came flying through a plate glass window of one of the bars followed through the door by about half a dozen big old hairy arsed matlots with a crowd of Kai Tai's who were then involved in one of the best melee' scraps I'd ever seen, the matlots were all well pissed and one of them had been lashing this bar girl up to her sticky greens all afternoon and was now ready for the pay off, away for short time or even all night in. He had apparently slipped his hand down the "Y" to explore the hot silk purse in great anticipation of the night of pleasure now coming his way, but encountered a big set of knar'ld hairy old bollocks instead, to say he was non to pleased was the biggest understatement of all, he was well pissed off, mostly for having been taken in but now for the ribbing he was getting from all his oppo's, there were about a dozen brown owls with claws bared and more arriving all the time, brilliant.

They were into all the vegetable barrows and anything else to hand, the produce was all over the road nothing was spared, one of the hatters took a huge pine apple to the side of his boat race, sending his Irish Jig flying down the road, his make up was really fucked by this time and he had the starboard side of his face enblazened with a superb pattern of holes left by the now defunct tropical fruit (not the only one) visited upon him by one of the irate steaming Tars who were by now giving it their all. The scene was one of total havoc with the Kai Tai's in a state of undress, some with wigs still attached chong sams and stockings ripped to arse holes trying to embed their stiletto heels into Jacks skull while the rest of them were being over run by an ever growing number of the opposition, soon there was the noise of bells ringing gradually increasing in volume, we soon found out it was coming from the paddy wagon fast approaching the scene bursting at the seems with R, N. Crushers. The shore patrol led by a fully qualified lame brained Leading patrolman who had long since had his head blown just before qualifying from the police school, he soon had all the wrong people arrested and locked up in the meat wagon. So long as his mobile prison was full as far as he was concerned that was a top job well done.

The prisoners would be locked up for the night, then released in the morning to make their own way back to their individual ships to report and explain why they were adrift, and why they had been locked up overnight and that a charge with a patrol report would be arriving on the ship just as soon as the duty bonehead could string together enough complete sentences to fulfil the requirements of the incident report sheet. They would then be put on automatic stoppage of leave until the completion of the first lieutenants defaulters. This was a classic case for a near sods opera (Naval Pantomime.) as you could get.

The scene is set, the first lieutenant at his lectern to preside over the proceedings, the prosecuting officer trying to convict the prisoner, the defending officer endeavouring to clear the defendants name, the defendant, off caps answering the charges, and all the witnesses to recall the events of the afternoon terminating in the defendant sliding his hand inside the bar girls frillies to examine her particulars only to be presented with a scaly pair of nuts and bolts that would have been more at home in an iron mongers drawers and to say they were just nest eggs would not placate the defendant.

You have to picture it all, everyone dressed in No. 1 suits, all proceedings being transcribed by the Captains secretary, the case could easily go all the way to a court marshal. The case had to be carried out with the same professionalism as in a court room – – – ish. The witnesses for the defence would be laying down the sequence of events with the Kai Tai's with a trowel, in favour of their oppo. and making it as comical as possible to try to secure his freedom. Where did he put his hand ?, why did he put his hand ?, what did his hand discover in the nether regions, but Sir, after playing with the most gorgeous pair of tits for most of the afternoon and being a little bit pissed I finally got around to slipping my hand into the vicinity of the silken money box. Instead of fulfilling my expectations I certainly wasn't prepared for what I found. Prosecuting officer "and what pray did you find lad " "Well Sir, I found what felt like a pair of cricket balls, backed up with this huge fucking truncheon "All the troops fold up in hysterics all vying to back up his version of events. Master at arms, "Calm down, calm down just answer the questions "Jimmy the One, " Do you expect me to believe, Boy, that this was the sole cause of the plaintiff! exit'ing the Bar "John Thomas "through the plate glass window, and the start of the riot on Boogie street which was the cause of so much havoc and destruction last Saturday night "– – – – – – – – – – "yes Sir ".

Egg banjos became our favourite roadside food. It was savoury fried eggs in a French style stick. Cheap but tasty. We were well pissed by now 2200, our leave expired at 2359 in the dockyard eighteen miles away. So we were now searching for a taxi to get us back in time for the last liberty boat back to the ship at midnight. As we waited we reminisced the days events, the Kai tai's were definitely the highlight, none of us had ever heard of such abnormalities, let alone seen them with our own eyes, weird man !. After awhile we finally managed to get a taxi back with four other Matlots and we were all just nodding off, when this ball and chain rating opened up with his horrendous rendition of Waltzing Ma Fucking tilda. Fucking hell, we couldn't shut this spring loaded prick up. All the way to the dockyard, eighteen nerve grating miles listening to this obnoxious Australian Twat, all we could think about was what we wanted to do with his fucking billycans, while he was shagging his bedroll (Matilda).

It was strange when we arrived back in Singapore dockyard, it being nearly midnight so hot and humid and there we were standing on a jetty listening to all the sounds of the wildlife in the middle of the night, waiting for a liberty boat to come and pick us up, and take us out to our ship moored midstream. In the cutter on the way back I was looking at the moon, hardly believing that just over the horizon people at home, could be looking at the same object, at the same time. But in reality it could be months if not years possibly never before we saw our families and friends again.

On the really humid nights I use to take a camp bed up on deck and sleep under the stars. That was all well and good until every now and then a tropical storm would break in the middle of the night, being awakened by sheets and sheets of water flooding down.

Matlots by the dozen were then scrambling for cover dragging camp beds and whatever else with them. It was great though, when you woke up after a nights sleep on the upper deck, having been breathing fresh air all night and not the high percentage methane gas abundant in the mess decks down below it was the most rejuvenated I think I have ever been in the morning.

After a few months we were being treated to a couple of weeks in Hong Kong. It took us a week to sail up there. The ship literally being the slow boat to China. I was amazed as we sailed in to Hong Kong Harbour, it was so much cooler than Singapore, as my prickly heat was healing up. At the weekend we were granted a weekend leave pass. It was good to get off the ship. We hired a couple of rooms in the China Fleet Club, somewhere to haul up over the weekend. We were off boozing down wanshi, the Red Light District. There were plenty of American sailors on leave from Vietnam, wherever the Yanks went you could guarantee the pox wasn't far behind.

The Yanks had a stupid policy of informing the Next of Kin when a sailor reported sick with V. D., consequently they would not report sick, and spread the disease everywhere. Our blokes tended to keep it in their pockets when Elma was about. After a good dinnertime sesh, down wanshi we were ready to get our heads down for a couple of hours in the Fleet club, ready for Saturday night. In order to get back we decided to both hire a rickshaw and race them back to the club. That was it we were off, with the two Coolies between the shafts running flat out. After about half a mile they slowed right down and my Coolie was falling behind, I was clipping him round the ear shouting faster, faster! He didn't like that, he stopped and put the shafts down ranting and raving in chinese (which was fair enough really).

I leapt out of the seat lifted him into it, then I was right in between those shafts and was off. I soon caught up the other guy who was exhausted, I passed him just before the fleet club, and won the bet. Jan. Pack didn't want to pay up, he accused me of cheating. Well it was worth it for the laugh. The locals couldn't believe there eye's, seeing a

Matlot running like the clappers between the shafts of a rickshaw, with the Coolie in the back. They were rolled up laughing we'd had a good afternoon, we'll see what tonight brings.

n those days Wanshi used to stink to high heaven. All the refugees from China used to live on the rooftops above all the shops and bars, behind the billboards, using tarpaulins for shelter. They used to use the empty five gallon gee cooking oil cans as toilets. When they were full, they use to empty them off the rooftops, straight onto the road below. We soon learned to walk in the middle of the road, the last thing you wanted was to cop a bucket load over your head. One afternoon we decided to take a trip around to Repulse bay and go for a swim, there was a shallow beach area, which after a few beers, we didn't bother to inspect too closely, after skylarking in the water for a few minutes, we noticed we were going a rusty colour. On closer inspection we recognised it as sewage.

The cause of the problem seemed to be Aberdeen city, a massive floating platform, made up of San pans (small family boats) all tied together in a big raft (space for all the people being the problem) the small boats were filled to over capacity, consequently it wasn't unusual to see dead babies floating about in the harbour as there wasn't any room for any more onboard, so as they were born they would hold them over the side probably at night and drown them and let them go. Times have changed. Probably just at weekends now. Nearby was the famous floating restaurant, where you could point out to the cook, which particular fish swimming in the aquarium you would like for your meal.

After which it would be caught and cooked to your liking. Another time we took a trip up to the tiger balm gardens on top of the rock that is Hong Kong, huge stone statues of dragons all set in classical Chinese gardens, it was brilliant. The view looking down over Hong Kong which at that time had less than a dozen small skyscrapers, Kai Tak airport in the harbour, with its runway jutting out into the sea, and on to Kowloon and the new territories which was part of mainland China to be seen in the far distance, was breathtaking. It was a lovely sight in the ornamental gardens looking down over Happy Valley, where we played hockey on the local sports field.

That is probably the Hong Kong racetrack now, some of the most valuable real estate in the world. I played hockey down there on Happy Valley sports field, running around hacking into each other, true sportsman style. Amidst all the mayhem of hockey sticks and tackles my plimsolls managed to tear clean off at the end. Leaving the rubber sole flapping in the breeze. That was it barefoot for the rest of the game, which with much determination we won. We decided we couldn't come all this way and not visit mainland China, all be it the new territories which could be reached by taking the Kowloon ferry.

On one occasion that's exactly what we did. The trip over was grand, but was surprised at the hostile reception that we received when we got there. We later learned that lots of servicemen had been found in the back street gutters with there throats cut. We had a quick walk around but the hatred they felt towards us was obvious and so we decided that discretion was the better part than valour, and made a quick exit (fucked off sharpish) on the next ferry out of there with our heads in tact. We were just young lads of eighteen, no one told us anything, we had to learn it the hard way, find out for ourselves, we were just canon fodder really.

We had no idea of the seriousness of the situation that was going on all around us, with Vietnam close by, Cambodia, China up here, like one big boiling pot, no one new what the hell was going to happen. China wanting Hong Kong back, threats coming from everywhere all pulsating away. and down south in the stinking, humid Singapore, a near uprising, we were hated everywhere we went. All the people wanting the Brits out. Who could blame them? our troops were fighting in Indonesia, we had troops and Royal Marines in the jungles of Borneo and Navy war ships as back up all over the South China seas. We sailed from Hong Kong into a big war exercise that lasted nearly the whole week. There wasn't any satellites for communication in those days, and radar picket ships could detect a ship for about fifty to hundred fifty miles.

With mock friends and foe, we enacted mock battles between the enemies, all the ships at action stations and blacked out at night, with lots of American and British aircraft carriers flying their aircraft searching the South China Seas looking to destroy the opposition. Things were hectic to say the least. So what happened next was particularly embarrassing for our lot, especially for our Captain. It was in the middle of the night and all the ships were at action stations, all hatches battened down and all lighting on the upper decks of all vessels extinguished the only illumination on the bridge were very dim red night lights which couldn't be seen from off the ship. Jets were flying all around searching for enemy vessels to attack and destroy on contact, the chief engineer on watch down the engine room phoned the electrical switched board situated in the electrical control room, manned twenty four hours a day, at this time manned by Paddy Murphy. Paddy had an incredibly strong Irish accent and had difficulty making himself understood or for that matter understanding anyone else, especially on the inter compartment sound powered telephones which weren't much improvement on the original two cans and a length of cord.

The Chief Engineer phoned the sw/ bd and asked for the electrical feeder breaker no. woppity wop wop, to be closed to put power through to the emergency fire pump in the engine room. So Paddy replies 'What number breaker?' He repeats, but Paddy still not sure closes the breaker he thinks he has heard. Power to the emergency fire pump! no way, he'd only gone and put the power onto the Ceremonial and upper deck lightning and the funnel floods. From pitch black to Blackpool illumination, lit up like Blackpool tower miles from anywhere in the vastness of the South China seas.

The captain, navigation and gunnery radar crews were closed up on the bridge you can only imagine what it was like, one minute incognito everyone in anti flash gear, noise to a minimum, whisper, whisper, discreet darkness than bam Paddy strikes! Jet planes attacking us from all angles at least their eyes must have been hurting from the brightness of the lights but it was too late, that was it, we were sunk. Our captain was left pulling his hair out, now having to make his excuses to the Admiral of the Fleet – utter humiliation, and there's seamus down the sw/bd wondering what the fuck all the panic's about.

The working head of the electrical departments was chief electrical artificer Dunstan. his Uniform on a hot day was a pair of shorts, and Chief Dunstan was an awkward shape, he was tall, thin chest, body and legs but with a pot belly that hung over is shorts at the front, thus his nickname Saggy Dunstan, which he wasn't best pleased about. His lair was the EMR (Electronics Maintenance Room), if anyone in the department fell foul of him, they would get a message to report the EMR Saggy wants to see you, he's gonna read your horoscope'. Blokes of the same rank would quiver in their boots. That was always guaranteed to strike fear into their hearts, he could deliver the most fearful bollocking, without raising his voice at whoever his victim was when he finished they'd come away feeling like the lowest form of low life shaking like a leaf. I was just trying to think what state Paddy Murphy would have been in when Saggy Dunstan finished with him, oh to have beeen a fly on the wall on that day. Saggy use to say 'what a chap had to do in life to have it good was, ride a horse, play the piano and take a ladies knickers down' Its always seemed just about right to me.

We arrived back in Singapore to carry on with fleet maintenance. I was now seconded to the over the side maintenance team (previously I was part of the onboard maintenance team) it was so much more interesting, as we got to visit other war ships, and hear the tales of what our lads were going through down south in Indonesia and Borneo. It just goes to show, I did not have a clue what the fighting was all about, it was probably to do with independence, it usually was.

I was working in the engine room of HMS Cavalier (now on show in Chatham dockyard). We were out at sea testing equipment and the lads were telling me how they had captured these 'Indons' (Indonesians) and had them shackled to the guard rails on the quarter deck, apparently this lot had done some serious damage to the landing party, off the ship. So consequently their mates weren't treating the prisoners with kid gloves. I seem to recall talk of rifle butts. There you go. It was great rushing up and down on the river on a Destroyer, sailing at twenty five knots twice what our ship would do. Our ship was like a big comfortable old lady, taking her time to get where she was going, and didn't care for anyone else's point of view, so long as she arrived in good spirit, which was always the case. After completing all outstanding maintenance and the ships deployed back down south, it was now our turn for a break. we were allotted time, to go on a jolly to Ceylon.

I was so looking forward to this. Our destination was Trincomalee, on the east coast of the now renamed island "Sri Lanka", it was a slow crossing, as the ship would only do ten to twelve knots. We sailed up the Strait of Malacca then right across the Indian Ocean. They were long hot days, we spent as much time as possible on the upper deck taking advantage of any breeze, lying on our stomachs looking over the bows of the ship breaking through the water. After dark the bow wave would glow a phos-fourescent light blue, and fairly regularly there would be a school of dolphins swimming in the bow wave. You could make out their shape by the glow they made in the water. Early in the morning just before sun up, we would see these giant manta rays come flying out of the water, about twenty feet into the air, than flip over and land on their backs making one hell of a splash.

We assumed they were doing this to dislodge any parasites like barnacles etc, living on their backs. Another marvellous sight was being in the middle of the Indian Ocean with a tremendous electrical storm in operation all around us. The noise was deafening, and the sky seemed to be permanently alight, with all kinds of different lighting flying about in all directions all over and lighting up the humid tropical night sky, with all shades of colours, from brilliant whites through the blues to orange and reds. It must have taken us about two weeks before we arrived, and what a sight to behold when we awoke that morning, Instead of just blue sea and sky, there was the white sands, and behind that the lush green of the tropical forest, fading to the magical blues then greys towards the cloud topped mountains in the far distance. wow eeee! Lets be getting ashore, this is what it is all about.

The whole point of the visit was to give us some time off as they put it to us and asked for volunteers to go camping in the jungle for a few days. I was up for that and my name went straight down. They dropped us off with all the camping equipment and our victuals plus numerous cases of beer, together with our rum ration to cover the time we would be camping for all the G (Grog) members, which was everyone over twenty years old.

That was what all the young lads dreamed of. All the u. a's (under age) were kicked out of the mess at tot time. Oh to be allowed to stay in the mess when you could smell the rum fanny with its precious contents arriving, and being able to actually join in the age old ceremony that the tars had been carrying out since before lord Nelsons time. Sippers, wets, gulpers, half a tot, and see it off if you dare.

All seated around the big mess deck table, with the rum bosun at the head, carefully I measuring out each matlots ration, with two fingers in the measure to make sure there would be some of the nectar left in the fanny (now called queens) to be passed around the table with the words "The Queen God bless her" as he offered each tar his tot they would say "have a wet" which wasn't quite a sippers, then the ticker off sitting next to the rum bosun would be offered a wet and woe betide them if they took a sipper.

These two were normally the most senior able rates in the mess, i. e. not having a rank to lose as this job could get very hairy at times, especially if "God forbid" the bosun dropped the fanny he could well easily get lynched. As soon as the fanny was empty it was off for dinner, all come back from the galley with a tin tray with your dinner on one side and your duff on the other sit back around the messdeck table and proceed to burble all over each other until the effects off the rum began to wear off, then it was head down on your bunk for the last ten minutes, before the bosuns mate made the pipe over the tannoy "hands turn too" off to work in the afternoon looking forward to tomorrows tot.

We were landed at a river estuary so we wouldn't have any trouble finding drinking water and were told to be back at the same place in seven days time to be picked up at 1200 hours. That was it – we shouldered all the equipment and set off into the jungle, looking for a good camp site. After a few miles we came across an abandoned village, with had quite a few fallen down buildings which the jungle was retaking. There was this very large troupe of monkeys who had colonised these buildings and they were making one hell of a racket and running all over the place. We were obviously novelty intruders to them, their order of the day was now flashing big red arses at us, and enthusiastic wanking gestures, little shits.

We found a good clearing near a source of fresh water and divided the group up, some erecting the big tent (a big old Army one), some preparing a meal and three of us were detailed off to go looking for firewood, dead brushwood etc. which, looking back, was good. We didn't seem to be worried about all the snakes, spiders, scorpions etc. but that must have been part of the fun.

We built the camp fire early evening and had a meal and then we started on a few crates of beer and a matelot's sing-song. We all turned in and were soon sound asleep when we were unceremoniously awakened in the middle of the night by a loud crashing through the trees, followed by some extremely loud heavy breathing. What the fucking hell is that? We were all coughing in our rompers by this time, whatever it was wasn't going away so we kept as quiet as possible and tried to get some sleep.

Easier said than done when you've got King Kong sitting outside your tent picking his nose with one hand and scratching his nuts with the other wondering what to do with a fucking great lob on in the middle of the night. One thing was for sure there were no volunteers to open the tent flaps and find out. Somebody should have checked on the local horny wildlife long before we left the ship, it was a bit late now, there was much nervous trepidation as no one wanted to wake up in the morning with a sore arse, especially with that fucking big dodgy steward who was in his seventh heaven mincing around the tent, "Uhmm, All that meat and only two potatoes" "Fuck off you bent bastard" ready to blame his perverted antics on Kong outside. Anyway I was so tired I was off to sleep and the next thing it was early morning and we were all awake wondering who was going to be the first out of the tent, hoping like hell that Kong had fucked off!

We were all whispering and listening around the walls of the tent for any heavy breathing. Birds were beginning to sing so we took that as a good sign. Whoever was volunteered to open the tent flap and stick his neck out, hoping his head wouldn't be ripped off, did so with much trepidation. He undid the flap with us all in deadly silence and stuck his head out. A couple of minutes later, whoopee, it was still on his shoulders and we all lined up to come out to a beautiful dawn. Our eyeballs were standing out like chapel hat pegs, low and behold our big clearing was covered in great piles of elephant shit. At least we weren't the only ones to do our bit for global warming.

We got the fire going and the cook started a massive breakfast which we just couldn't wait for as we were so hungry and the smell of the breakfast cooking was heaven sent. After breakfast everything was cleaned and tidied away. A couple of lads were detailed to stay in camp all day, making sure everything was safe and to gather more firewood and keep the fire burning, prepare all the veg. Etc. and get all the makings into a big stew pot on the fire, ready for when the rest of us returned later on after exploring the local area and swimming in the river to cool off.

The derelict buildings we had seen the day before now seemed to be old colonial places.

I think the monkeys were Macacs that over run India. In some places they are treated as sacred but they sure made a racket whilst we were mooching around. We saw what appeared to be a derelict cellar about the size of a small room, no walls above ground but full of water to within three feet of the top. Floating in the middle was a large fifty gallon empty oil drum and resting on the top of it was a massive lizard which was about five feet long, with a dangerous looking set of chompers at the sharp end. The walls were sheer and it obviously couldn't get out and there wasn't any food in there for it so it was doomed. We searched the area and found something to make a basic ramp for it to climb up, two big old dead tree branches. On completion we didn't hang around just in case it decided we could be its next meal. So we carried on our way rejoicing.

We carried on in the same vein for the rest of the week and then met the Pinnace (large sea boat) at 1200 hours as arranged to take us back to our ship. We were well chuffed to get back and have a good hot shower, clean clothes and a good, hot meal from the galley but it had been a good experience, especially King Kong frightening the life out of us, who turned out to be dumpers the Elephants, as it happened the last of their kind.

The following Sunday, myself and my run ashore oppo Jan (Janner – nick name for West a Country man) Pack, got the first liberty boat off the ship at about 0900 hours. We landed ashore then walked about three miles to a beautiful isolated beach, where the local fishermen had large dug-out tree's as boats. We communicated using the international sign language for wanting a drink (mouth open with finger pointing down it and grunting) we were looking for some sort of drinking house and they sent us up this jungle track where we came upon this old style colonial hotel, it was really run down it looked as if it had been derelict for years, a ragged waiter arrived after we had been making a racket for about ten minutes. All they had to drink was Ceylon gin and for two nip's they wanted half the money we had. We didn't take that up but decided to find out what the locals drank and finished up in this very dark shack, where the locals were drinking the local brew, Arrack.

We sent one of the locals to find us an empty bottle which we then proceeded get them to fill up with a pint of Arrack from this oil drum which was standing on the makeshift bar, (another oil drum.) Feeling 'over the moon' we headed off for the beach. We were communicating with a local fisherman who was working on his nets by the side of the dug out boat on the beach, I had a mouthful of this Arrack, fucking hell, it nearly blew my head off. My oppo took a mouthful and that was it. He wouldn't have any more but I know what I'm like and as we had bought it I wasn't going to throw it away. !

This decision nearly brought an end to my short, but eventful life. The next thing I remember was waking up and feeling like there was axe in the back of my head. The ship was rolling over the waves and I felt violently sick so I rushed to the heads and was trying to be sick but there was nothing there to bring up. .

We were at sea, on our way back to Singapore via Penang (in Malaya) I had been comatose for three days and had had a medical watch on me. Talk about being in the shit, the whole ships' company were talking about me and not in the least, the Captain, who would have been working out what punishment to bestow upon me. Thank fuck they had done away with flogging and keel hauling but no doubt they were dreaming up the next best thing! "This little Northern twat – he's as good as gold when working and sporting, but let him off the lead and anything can happen" and usually does.

The discipline in the Forces in those days was so strict that the Courts convicting young criminals gave them the option of months and years in jail, or join the Army or Royal navy where they soon had any unto old unacceptable behaviour corrected and surlyness knocked out of them. It was a good system, and sorted out most people, so I wasn't such a bad lad after all, just liked to escape now and then, now and then, now and then! The best thing about the Forces is that you could usually rise to fulfil your ambitions and achieve your early promise (rank wise) but we all started out at the bottom and we've all been there and we all know the ropes, but the youngsters think they have just discovered everything and don't realise they were being pointed in those directions by their superiors in the first place, don't seem to get it.

My oppo. began filling me in on the missing three days. He had had to leave me unconscious on the beach and walk the couple of miles to our liberty boat pick up point, and wait for the next liberty boat and inform the coxswain that I was spaced out, and they needed a body carrying party to transport me from the beach, a couple of miles away, to the liberty boat which would transport me to the ship and into Sick Bay. I don't know whether they pumped out my stomach but I would have thought so. I certainly wasn't going to bring the subject up again, I was keeping a very low profile and keeping my head well down.

I would have been too ashamed to talk about any of it as I had done the dastardly deed, and I would have just wanted to be awarded my punishment, do it and then forget all about it. That was one good thing, you were only the scallywag until the next port of call and run ashore, when you could be dead certain that there would be another crop of defaulters, slinking up to the first leutenants table to be weighed off, and become the next rash of men under punishment. This was the navies way of having a small group of working hands, to be available for any unforeseen tasks that crop up outside of working hours, which could lighten the load on the duty watch.

I did manage to get a run ashore in Trincomalee before the fateful last one. I bought a pair of ebony and ivory carved elephants for my Mother. She absolutely loved them "my elephants" she would say. It used to transport her to wherever I was in the world for the rest of her life, another forty one years. They had been in front of her chair be it on the mantelpiece or in front of the television for all those years until she died in September 2004, aged ninety three and was still living in her own flat until then. "Well done, Mother, we were all proud of you".

I must have completed whatever punishment I received at sea on the way back to Singapore because we called in at Penang, Malaya, for a few days and I got a run ashore there. I remember travelling across the town in a tri-shaw which was a bicycle type taxi with two candles on the mudguards for vehicle illumination. The whole place was very original, bamboo huts etc. There hadn't been any structural development in Malaya or indeed any part of that area. It was good to see it in its original raw state before the skyscrapers arrived. When I awoke the following morning onboard to the usual splitting head, I found I had an additional pain, my right forearm up by the elbow had a two and a half inch blister where I must have leaned on the candle powered traffic light, on the mudguard. will I ever learn – sadly – – – -no.

We arrived back in Singapore to enter the dry dock for a small maintenance period over Christmas of 1962. The ships' company was moved up to HMS Terror, the local shore establishment for the duration of the ship's incapacity which was probably three or four weeks. The accommodation for the troops was a two storey extremely long dormitory, each with bed space containing a single bunk bed and locker.

There were twin veranda doors leading to an old colonial type veranda, the length of the building, overlooking the parade ground. It was really reminiscent of times gone by, and we felt privileged to be barracked there before it disappeared off the face of the earth into the annals of history

It was really good sitting out there of an evening, especially when the breeze gradually got stronger and brought in the torrential monsoon rains. Although there were three foot deep monsoon ditches around the parade ground, within minutes of the rain starting the temperature took a dive and the ditches were full and the parade ground three inches deep in water. We were on the first floor overlooking the parade ground.

It was good sitting out there with our Tiger beer, playing cards with the lightening flashing all around us and the constant clapping of thunder right above us – we were alright for bevy. We used to go down to the NAAFI canteen after supper at around 1900 hours, have a sing-song down there until closing time which was about 2230 hours and then take back with us three or four buckets full of draught Tiger beer and while away our time on the veranda listening to the tropical nightlife and generally spinning the shit until it was all gone, then bed time. What more did we want? It makes me smile when I think back, we were nearer to Navana then, than we'd ever be again, and didn't know it.

At the bottom of the concrete stairwell, leading off the path and the parade ground and going up from the ground floor dormitories to our first floor, one of the local traders had permission to sell his wares to the troops. Shirts, shorts, briefs and lots of nick knacks – he would lay a couple of sarongs on the floor then arrange his goods on them and then proceed to harass everyone going up the steps.

Well, this particular evening, one of the junior seamen arrived in our dormitory with a new shirt. The guy had managed to sell to him.

Straight away.

The older able seaman, looking after his own, asked him how much he had paid for the shirt. When he told them they were fuming as apparently the chokey had charged him over double the going rate. Well I could see they were all up for revenge but I didn't know what they were going to do about it. There were about six of them in a huddle with the odd giggle coming from them. They made their way to the top of the stairwell and I thought "I'm not missing out on this" so I nipped out and onto our veranda over looking the parade ground, and waited with great trepidation at what was about to happen. All I could see below me was the parade ground as the stairwell was under cover below me.

was hanging on for about five minutes when all of a sudden there was this loud "yahoo!" and one of the lads was galloping off over the parade ground with three or four shirts tucked under his arm and with one certain chokey trader screaming after him in hot pursuit. Talk about laugh, when the able seaman reached the other side of the parade ground, he started scattering the shirts in different directions and the chokey was quite happily picking up his shirts, probably congratulating himself on getting one over on the white trash.

I watched him walk back over the parade ground and then he disappeared below me into the stairwell. Then there was this loud, heartbroken wailing and all the cursing and abuse imaginable. When the lad had taken off with the shirts across the parade ground the rest of the lads had gone down the stairs and lifted the rest of his stock and legged it, obviously hiding it in a safe place in anticipation of the regulating police officer (crushers. All brawn and no brains) coming round and doing a thorough mess and locker search.

I would have loved to have seen the chokies face when he realised all he had left were a few rescued shirts under his arm and a couple of sarongs. He must have been off whining down the police office because after about an hour (plenty of time to hide the evidence), there was the thumping of the crushers boots coming up the stairs "Stand by your beds, right where is his stock?" Silence. No chance, "open your lockers". A full search but they didn't find anything.

It was Christmas Eve 1962 and we had been down the NAAFI bar all evening drinking draught Tiger beer and having a communal sing-song. Just before the bar closed, we purchased two buckets full of draught Tiger. It was good as we were now sitting at the bamboo table on the balcony reminiscing, telling stories and listening to the tropical nightlife. We sat there until it was Christmas Day and we had run out of beer. I said "I'll open my Christmas present from Mother". Whatever it was, it was heavy. It was in a twelve inch cubed old biscuit tin and Mother had posted it two months earlier so it would arrive by Christmas. I opened the parcel and there were all sorts of goodies in there from home.

I was working my way down from the top: Christmas cake, Mars bars, sweets and anything else that would survive the journey, when all of a sudden I struck gold and I gave out a big cheer, good old Mother had come up trumps again, six big cans of long life beer. We sat there having a midnight feast and drinking the beer. At that time I don't think I had ever had anything that tasted so good. Well we sat there until we had had our fill and finished off the beer. I think that was just about the best start to a Christmas Day I have ever had.

Well shortly after Christmas our ship's overhaul and bottom scrape was completed and we moved back onboard and went and anchored out at our usual spot, to continue the maintenance of the frigates and destroyers on station. One day we noticed two of the Radar / radio blokes were missing Edmunson and Wilcox they were like brothers both big lads and about twenty four years of age and seemed ancient to us sprogs. It was reported they were in R. N. H. Singapore and so it wasn't long before a couple of their oppo's were despatched to visit and find out what was wrong, they located Wilcox first who was wearing a set of blue, brown hatters overalls (pyjama's), which indicated to all and sundry a non venereal complaint, ie. Leprosy, T. B. or some other such malady.

While skulking in the next ward they discovered Edmundson decked out in full bright green Brown hatters working gear, clap clap. Apparently Gonned up to the eyeballs literally, not only did he have a sick dick which would soon be undergoing the dreaded umberella treatment, but the Goner Cocci bird had also manifested itself in his Eyes as well which were by now discharging themselves of a thick yellow green Singaporean puss of which he thought he would never recover, of which he did, only to return onboard after about a month to be greeted by his mess mates with much jocularity and ringing of bells with the welcoming song of unclean, unclean, bring out your dead, bring out your dead. Back home at last, Tot time, have a wet bosun, and its back to communal cutlery, Yippee. After about a month we embarked on our final trip up to Hong Kong.

It didn't register with me the enormity of the Vietnam War that was going on and there we were sailing up the coast of Vietnam and not being aware of it. All the torture and killing that was happening and we were off on a jolly to Hong Kong.

We arrived in Hong Kong and went into holiday mode just working forenoons and if you weren't duty watch, it was off ashore straight after lunch. Things were very cheap then. I had a pair of handmade made-to- measure shoes made overnight and a hand sewn made-to-measure mohair overcoat which was completed in two days.

Together with a two piece suit. They were all very nice, but when I was to get home, I would find them all completely out of fashion, and I would have to re-lag myself in the big boppers gear. Drain pipe trousers and roll collar jacket and get with it.

There were lots of American sailors about, (their ships having been given a short break from the action) who absolutely hated us limeys for not joining in the War with them. I remember one group asking "Why haven't you limeys joined the War yet?" Our reply was that the Vietcong (opposition – enemy) hadn't asked us yet. Big punch-up. Broken Elma's all over the pavement.

Our leave expired at 0730 hours but the Yanks leave expired at midnight, we called it Cinderella leave which got right up their noses, so consequently they had spent the night feeding drinks to the bar girls but come half eleven they had to go and we would move in. They hated it. One night this big Yank was telling this group of matlot's how much he hated them but they were secretly topping his drink up with strong spirit until he was just about passing out. They then manhandled him to a tattoo artist's shop where they had a Union Jack tattooed on his chest. I would have loved to have seen his face when he came round the next day aboard his American warship. The stick he must have taken from the rest of the crew, especially every day when he went to the communial bathroom for a shower. Good stuff.

Well we finished our jolly in Hong Kong and headed back down to Singapore, which I wasn't looking forward to because it was so hot and humid and it would cause another flare up of prickly heat and Singapore ear, which was an infection inside both ears which swelled them up with pus which you couldn't get at. I couldn't open my jaw at one stage for about six weeks. All the sustenance I took in was soup sucked up a straw. I hated the place and the people and swore to myself that if ever the Navy drafted me out there again in the future, I would go AWOL (do a runner) and miraculously, over the next twenty two years, I was never sent out to the Far East again.

Well, we had some terrific news, the ships' company joined the ship on a running commission basis, that is to say that each individual joined the ship at different times and did their two and a half year's stint or so and then waited for a flight home but it was decided it would be more convenient to change the whole ship's company in three phases, therefore, all of us would be going home in the next three months. Brilliant! I was going home eighteen months early and I couldn't believe my luck. I decided to take advantage of my situation and requested to sit the PPE exam (Provisional Professional Examination), and if I passed, that would allow me to go to HMS Collingwood and do the six months Leading Electricians Course and if I passed all that, which would take about eighteen months to two years and had a good character, that would enable them to award me with my first rank of Leading Electrical Mechanic. That was, of course, if all went well and I kept my nose clean and had a lot of luck so the three of us got the books out and started boffing up for the next six weeks.

I bought Mother a pair of ebony elephants whilst I was in Ceylon, "she'll like those". I also sent her a dinner and tea service home by sea mail which I had bought in Singapore. I think she received it at Christmas. Contact with home was sparse as the mail took ages to reach us. Half the time, as it was Forces Mail, it had travelled around the Far East for a month but it eventually found you ie. The ship's mail would arrive in Ceylon the day after we sailed and so on.

Well the day came for the two hour written paper (exam), and thank my lucky stars I just scraped through, now we were really worried as the next thing was the oral exam, set up with officers from different ships, so there was no favouritism.

God knows how but I scraped through that too, but because I was only nineteen and the earliest I could pick up my hook (rate) was twenty and a half, they recommended I joined the Reserve Fleet in Portsmouth Dockyard for a period of time to gain more experience, so I would be more able to deal with the intense six month's course in Collingwood. That did me, I was over the moon.

The next stage was already planned and what a time I was going to have in the next few years. Well that will come later. I was just trying to recall how we managed for money when we went for the odd weekend run ashore in Singapore because money was what we had very little of. Then I remembered that we used to the Britannia Club, which was a Joint Services club that knocked out cheap meals and beer for the three services. We were sitting in the bar, with a pint of Tiger beer as we couldn't afford to go anywhere else, and Jan (Janner from the West Country) ups and go's to the Heads (toilet). He was gone about five minutes when I looked up and saw him coming out of the Heads, holding hands with this Chinese guy, I couldn't believe my eyes, what the fuck's going on?

Jan looked at me with a smirk on his face and they sat down at our table and as we got the story out of this Chinese brown hatter over the next half hour, I could see Jan was playing footsie with him under the table. It turned out he was a knob jockey, down from Hong Kong on holiday. He just fancied a couple of sailors for his tea (fancy eating you're here) well he can fuck off. He's got no fucking chance with me. Anyway things moved on and Jan says he wants to take us somewhere quiet. He's really well dressed and looks as though he's loaded. Well he gets a cab and proceeds to take us somewhere quiet.

It turns out to be somewhere quiet alright, Singapore Cemetery! This guy is an old hand at this. Well we were out of the cab and Jan is off walking in front of with me with the brown job. We must have arrived at this guy's special place when he's starts trying to interfere with Jan. Well Jan grabs him by the throat and smacks him one. He throws his wallet to me saying get all his money. I said "we can't leave him with no money, we'll take half", which we did, and we jumped in a cab and headed for the good life in town.

The bloke was lucky really, he'd only lost half of his money, when he could have faced years in jail for importuning if he had been caught, which would have been like heaven for him, being banged up with a couple of hundred convicted hairy arsed fairies.

You've got to laugh, if you let your imagination run riot, a two hundred strong daisy chain with the bloke at the front with a lob on shouting "FUCK MY LUCK, FORM A CIRCLE" "FORM A CIRCLE"

If any matelot was caught partaking in anything like that, they were busted down to the lowest rank, given ninety days In D. Q. 's (detention quarters) the sailor's jail, just the thought of going in there put the fear of God in every ones bones, where they were constantly humiliated for three months, and then in disgrace, were given a dishonourable discharge from the Navy and if uniform were the only clothes they had, all Navy badges etc were removed so that everyone who came in contact with them in Portsmouth, would know. They would have no money either. Whilst in jail, the Navy was forced to pay them something like five pence a day, because they were not allowed to keep slaves. It's amazing how much things have changed since I was a young fella These days it's almost compulsory to be 'bent' – unbelievable. – – especially when you see who made the rules in the first place. Dodgy M. P. 's

Well we arrived back in town, ready for a cracking night out and money no problem for the first time ever, we were going to enjoy ourselves big time.

We came across the old Raffles Hotel and what a place; air conditioned, indoor palm trees, fountains, waterfalls, blimey how the other half live. I'd never seen anything like it. Well we were smoking cigars and drinking G and T's we could hardly believe it. Hit the big time temporarily. Still, take the opportunities when they arise. I would never have gone in there otherwise. I think we used the quiet place quite a few times in the future to fund our runs ashore.

When we were sailing On the South China Sea off the coast of Vietnam, one of the American aircraft carriers was involved with one of ours on flying exercises, when one of their pilots decided to show his own (perceived) flying skills and shock the crew of our carrier. He came flying in at sea level, below the level of the flight deck and flipping up and skimming the flight deck before disappearing over the horizon, shocking everyone in the vicinity. A very dangerous and highly illegal manouver. The Yanks must have thought that was good, until two of our pilots decided to retaliate, and show them what good flying was all about. The squadron leader picked one of his best pilots to retaliate.

They were approaching the US carrier at a closing speed of 200 mph, one coming towards the bows of the carrier again below the height of the flight deck but upside down, with the other coming towards the stern of the carrier the right way up and below the height of the flight deck. That meant that when they passed each other just above the flight deck their closing speed to each other was 400 m. p. h. plus. You can imagine the Yanks thought this was it curtains. At the last second they flipped up and passed over the flight deck, one the right way up the other upside down. All the Yanks were diving for cover waiting for the explosion.

Well apparently all hell broke loose, signals flying about all around the fleet, the American Admiral demanding retribution for our two pilots from our Admiral. When the air finally cleared, they grounded our two pilots for a week as punishment, or so they said. One of the lads brum. Falkener my age, we used to weight train together on the funnel deck of the ship, had been aboard the ship for eighteen months and had been sending most of his pay home to his Mum in Birmingham, for her to bank for him so he could buy a car for himself when he got home.

I saw him again back in the UK about a year later and asked about his car. Well he arrived home and after the welcome etc his Mother broke down and couldn't stop crying. He asked her for his bank book and there was nothing in it. He went ape shit as she had been spending it as it arrived, hence, no car so the lesson learned, never trust anyone ever, with your money.

Well my turn had arrived and it was the best thing that happened to me. I couldn't wait to get home. We were flying home in a Bristol Britannia turbo propeller aircraft by courtesy of the RAF. We weighed in and my baggage was ten pounds overweight. The sergeant said "lose ten pounds". I opened my kit bag and the first things on top were Mother's heavy ebony and ivory elephants. I gave them to him and he must have seen the disappointment in my face as he gave them back and said "go on". We took off from Changi Airport late at night and flew right into a major tropical storm. We thought this is it, were doomed. We managed to survive the bouncing around for a couple of hours until the storm abated somewhat.

We had been having a rough ride for about twelve hours (forty eight to get home) when we were struck by lightening. After about half an hour the pilot announced over the tanoy that we had developed a serious fuel leak and that we wouldn't be able to make Bombay so we would be landing in Karachi for emergency repairs and to refuel, which we did and then again in Istanbul.

CHAPTER 9

A right Royal Welcome home

We eventually landed in the UK at RAF Stansted and I arrived at 54 Waithlands Road, Rochdale (Tin Town) home, knocked on the door expecting a right royal reception from Mother and all, who had no idea that I was coming home, when a stranger opened the door. I said, "Who are you? Where's my Mother?" He replied "They've moved".

"When? Where to?"

"6 William Street, Hursted. "

"Where's that?"

"On the other side of town near Birch Hill Hospital".

"Cheers".

I eventually found it after carting my kit bag on three bus trips. I knocked on the door and my Mother nearly fell through the floor. Mother's little Harry home from the sea, as brown as a berry and hair sun-bleached blonde, and grown quite a lot. We had a right old drink and it was great, then I had to get down the town to have some bevy with the lads. They couldn't believe the colour of me or how much I had grown. I had been weight training onboard all the time I was away. As well as the extra muscle I'd grown about six inches,

We had a right skin full of beer and God only knows how I found the new house, which was a small two bedroom mid-terrace so I had to get in bed with my brother. The next day he was telling me I woke up in the night, bursting for a pee but didn't know where I was so I opened the wardrobe door, whereupon Jim's best suit falls of the hanger and I proceed to relieve myself of about a gallon of piss all over our kid's new suit. "Welcome home 'H' we missed you".

I went round to see George Shannon and big Russ. He was really pleased to see me "Where's Russ?" I loved that dog. "He's dead". "Oh no, what happened?"

"We had been out all day and hadn't seen anything (hares) and we were heading for home and it was dusk. The light was fading fast when Russ put up a hare. He was after it and then he was on it for about five minutes when there was this sickening very loud howl. "

George found him after searching for about half an hour. Russ must have been right on the hare when it ran under a big metal field gate. Russ was travelling so fast and the light was bad, so Russ wouldn't have been able to stop and there wasn't enough room for him to go under the gate. The bottom bar of the gate caught Russ right between his eyes and lifted the top of his skull right up. Just like taking the top off a boiled egg. George was devastated. He sat cradling Russ for about an hour. He put him to one side whilst he set off home to get a spade to bury him. He said that he had never wept so many tears. Unbeknown to me at the time, this was going to be the last time I saw George. A couple of years later, when I had come home from abroad again, I went round to look up George only to be told that he had died about a year ago. I have no idea what caused his death, still he had had a good life, poor money wise, but rich in his way of life. He was only about twenty nine years old and it was tops knowing you George. You certainly weren't forgotten, here I am writing about you forty five years on.

Well after my leave expired on the 18th March 1963, I was sent down to Portsmouth to join the Reserve Fleet which consisted of an accommodation ship HMS Mull Of Galloway (sister ship to Hartland Point, so I knew my way around) and a big city class cruiser H. M. S. Sheffield (the shiney sheff. As she was known) and I was to find out later, my father-to-be-in-law Cecil Powell had served on during the Second World War on the Russian Convoys.

It was a sister ship to H. M. S. Belfast which is now moored on the river Thames by the houses of Parliament.

The whole Reserve Fleet went under the name HMS Belerophon which was accessed by going through the Royal Naval Gunnery School HMS Excellent, which was based on Whale Island, a small island a hundred yards off the island of Portsmouth, which had a small causeway adjoining the two together, the whole lot being about a couple of miles from Southsea where I was about to spend most of the evenings of 1963 enjoying myself.

On joining HMS Sheffield, I was designated a mess deck to which I would be living in. I was told to report to the leading hand (Killick Hookey) of the electrician's mess with my kit, where he designated me a kit locker, where I was to store all my personal belongings and I was asked if I had ever slept in a hammock or if I knew how to sling one. I gave the answer in the negative and was told to go about my joining routine, where in the process I would be issued with bedding, plus a hammock, which he would then proceed to instruct me on how to sling it, and more importantly how to get in it, which in itself was no mean feat, also, how to lash up and stow first thing in the morning, because it had a thin mattress in it. When it was lashed up it was about the same size as a body and they were all stowed away neatly in a hammock netting which was like a six foot square metal basket. The first hammocks were laid neatly alongside each other about eight in number and then the following eight were laid at right angles and so on until it was full then that was it all bedding stowed. Then you had lots of room to live in without beds everywhere.

The first night I slept in it was a joke for everyone but me. Trying to get in the thing was a right palaver, imagine, its bar taut about a foot below the deck head (ceiling). I had to get hold of the hammock bar, one of two of them between which it was slung and swing my body up in the air and try and land in it. When I eventually got in there with my weight pulling it down, it was like being trapped in a massive banana skin. I didn't have any hammock stretchers (two strong pieces of wood about 2" x 1" x 18") which were homemade by each person and placed one at the top and one at the bottom, and used to hold the hammock open so it didn't grip you. That was the first thing on my list of things to do for the next day! It was the worst night's sleep I had ever had, arms and legs gripped tight, I couldn't move. This was sure going to get some getting used too. I felt as though I had spent the night in a full body straight jacket. At least this ship was moored permanently in the harbour, so once in the hammock it was at least stationery. The moving experience was something else which I was to experience in another ship HMS Decoy in a few years time.

The regulating chief electrician, who was in charge of running the department was Ron Fayle, a six foot four rugby playing giant, who you would not want to get on the wrong side of. He was a good bloke, very fair, he would only punch your head if you deserved it, and I'm afraid I deserved it quite a few times. I enjoyed my time on the Sheffield. Reveille (call the hands) went at about 0630 with a "show a leg, show a leg, show a leg, hands off cocks on socks, wake up you sleepy heads, lash up and stow, cooks to the galley went long ago.

The sun has got a twat on and its pissing down again" over the main tannoy system, after which we would shower, get dressed, followed by half an hour cleaning stations, that way the ship was kept immaculate and on completion we would be more than ready for breakfast, which was always the best after being dished up by the cooks in the galley, and served up In the dining hall. There were lots of the chef's specials to look forward to like "Shit on a Raft" (devilled kidneys on toast), "Train Smash" (eggs, bacon, sausages, mushrooms all covered with tinned tomatoes, smothered with brown sauce), "Cackleberries" (boiled eggs), "Horse Cock" (polony), "Blazing Saddles" (beans on toast), "Shit Lids" (oxtail), "Spit Head Pheasant" (a big sausage with a feather stuck in it), "Haggis" (shot down with a porridge gun), "Underground Chicken" (rabbit), "Ban the Pom" (dried packet mashed potatoes), "Chinese Wedding Cake" (rice pudding), "Babies Heads" (steak and kidney puddings), "Afterbirth" (tripe and onions), "Gorilla Snot" (oysters), "Pickled Clitorie" (cockles), "Nigger's Dick" (black pudding), "snake and pygmy" (steak and kidney). Whatever they were talking about, Jack (Matelots) would give it a nickname.

After breakfast, everyone who worked over the side (off the ship) would make their way to whichever ship they had bee allocated to work on. My ship was HMS Volage, a World War Two mothballed frigate. We would carry out routine maintenance on the ship so if it was ever needed in the future, it would be brought out of mothballs in about a week and all the machinery guns etc would be in working order. At lunchtime we would make our way back to the Sheffield for lunch, then back to the Volage to work away the afternoon and that was the work routine. All through the summer we had to work until midday on a Saturday and you could apply for a long weekend about once a month. All leave and pay were a privilege so for any misdemeanour such as being late, lip to superiors, disobeying any orders, which anyone your senior could give you, potential loss of pay and leave was always imminent and always on your mind.

I had applied to the Chief Elec. for a LWE pass so I could go home to Rochdale to see my family. I had to apply a week in advance and they wouldn't confirm it had or hadn't been granted until the Friday lunchtime you were going. The Chief Elec. Stopped me on the preceding Tuesday, "Ah, young Green, what are like at running?"

"I'm okay, I always seem to catch the bus".

"Good, HMS Excellent (Gunnery School) on Whale Island are holding their Sports Day next Friday and you my bonnie lad are going to be representing HMS Sheffield in the one hundred yards sprint".

"Fucking hell, Chief, I can't do that".

"Can't you now, were you hoping for a long weekend?"

"Fucking hell, Chief, that's blackmail".

"Call it what you like lad, be at the sports field on Whale Island 1300 on Friday and you'd better have a rocket up your arse because we're expecting a good show, and we want to beat those poncing gunners".

"Bloody hell, okay Chief".

"Good, I knew you'd see it my way".

"What about my weekend?"

"We'll see about that Friday".

Well, that sure gave me something to think about. He said I had to do something else as well, once they've got you they pile it on. I looked down the list. Throwing the cricket ball – yes, I can do that.

Well I turned up on Friday afternoon in my blue working trousers and shirt, and the only sports gear I had, which was a pair of pumps. I took one look at the spectacle in front of me and it was like the Lord Mayor's show. The Captain of the Gunnery School and all his entourage, the Captain of HMS Sheffield and most of the wardroom and fucking hell, the Commander in Chief Portsmouth Admiral Woperty Wop Wop and all his supporters. Bollocks and I'm on the menu!

It was a massive summer event. I looked at the sequence of events and the cricket ball, shot, javelin etc were first, on the far edge of the field, good! I was well out of the way of the crowds. My turn arrived, I didn't look the part, but I had been playing cricket for most of my life, and had been weight training for five years on and off, and I knew I could throw a ball from the boundary to the stumps.

So here we go, I took up position, everyone wondering who this turkey was in his No. 8's working gear. I took a short run up and let fly with everything I had. I used so much forced I strained the ligaments in my shoulder. I looked up and the ball was going like a rocket. It passed everyone elses and was still going. It went out of the ground and bounced off a tree on the opposite side of the road. "Pick the bones out of that bastard!" They couldn't believe it. All these big hairy arsed gunners all ponced up with running spikes, flashy shorts and vests, who's job on the ship was to propel missiles (Shells) at the enemy, way over the horizon and were very proud of being able to do so, and in their own eyes the best there was. It all went quiet while they registered my name, they were all pissed right off as that wasn't supposed to happen. Beaten by some jumped up encroacher from the reserve fleet' and a lecky to boot, he comes to the Royal Naval Gunnery school Whale Island, whose job it is to teach gunners how to lob missiles accurately into the far distance. I hadn't realised the significance of this event, and why they were all so pissed off. Brilliant! I would have trained if I had known, and thrown it out of the camp.

I was well chuffed, that showed the stuck up fuckers. I made my way over to where the track events were taking place and chased up 'Big Ron Fayle', the Chief Elec. He asked how it had gone and was over the moon when I told him I'd pissed it.

"By the way you're not in the one hundred yards sprint now, we've got someone else. "'Brilliant, thanks a lot Chief, I've been worried sick about that all week.

"No problems, you're in the four forty yards instead".

"Fucking hell Chief, I can't even run that far let alone race it".

"Don't worry, put your best foot forward, you'll walk it. (never a truer word said in jest.) It's the last race and is in twenty minutes time, so go and get changed and be on the opposite side of the track at the start and in the blocks ready to go on time, don't be late" "you got to believe this Chief, but I am changed, this is it".

"Jesus Christ Jimmy, we've got all the top knobs from Portsmouth on the finishing line, and you're in your fucking overalls".

"Bollocks, it's too late to find you some kit now, you'll be alright so long as you put on a good show, away you go and don't let me down. " "okay chief I'll try my best" Talk about coughing in your rompers, I felt certain I was going to do a pile, never mind! chin up and go for it.

Well, you wouldn't believe it, the time had come for the big event. I registered and they gave me a number and stuck it on my back, you're running on the inside track. The other five were athletes with all the gear, spikes etc. . They were looking at me as though I was part of a working party cleaning the track, wrong, this was the shiny Sheff's secret weapon.

"On your marks!" I was on the inside lane and I couldn't see the rest. "Get set". … … … BANG!

We're off! I was in the lead for about three strides and felt the wind as they shot passed me, they were going like long dogs. They disappeared around the first bend and I was running hard but not so fast. By the time I was coming to the last bend, they had all finished. I don't think the crowd realised what was happening. They had just witnessed five athletes flash past the finishing line, then they looked down the track and saw me coming around the last bend with my working clothes (No. 8's) flapping in the breeze. The penny must have dropped that I was a competitor and in the race and not a skirmisher picking up fag ends in a bit of a rush, there was this almighty roar. All the lot of them started to cheer. I still had about a hundred yards to go and they were all going crazy, you'd think I'd just entered the arena winning a marathon. Well, I started laughing, the whole fucking chebang were taking the piss.

I was about twenty yards from the finishing line and was absolutely knackered when I collapsed, I knew I shouldn't have been on the piss the night before. The roar doubled.

"Finish! Finish!" Our side were shouting "we need the point for finishing". Well I got up, I couldn't breathe, I was laughing even more. I carried on and when I crossed the line the roar tripled. Big Ron was straight there for the glory, massaging my shoulders like a prize fighter in a title fight, well Jimmy me boy you sure didn't win but what a performance, that was the best of the day, well done son. The whole lot were still cheering and laughing even more than me. Apparently, that was more than anyone could have dreamed for as a finale' to the big reserve fleets contribution to H. M. S. Excellent's Sports Day on Whale Island on a beautiful sunny summer's afternoon in 1963, that day secured my place in Big Ron's heart forever, which I would find out when serving with him on ships to come in the future. Fortunately for me our paths were to cross quite a few times in the coming years.

"Oh by the way Jimmy, here's your weekend pass and travel warrant. Have a good one and don't be adrift on Monday, Oh and well done, that woke em up for sure and showed em what's what".

They told me later that I got a hero's mention in "The Navy News" they were now officially taking the piss big time, my weekend leave was all I was after.

About a month later I had been working on H. M. S. Volage on a Saturday morning we were to work on our designated moth balled ships until twelve noon and then secure and make our way back to the Sheffield for lunch, then shower, dhobi, tot and scran then off ashore for a dinner time session down the strip.

Well we had been gradually securing earlier each Sat. morning, making our way back to the Sheffield, going down the electrical switch board situated in the bowls of the ship and entered through a tight manhole in a bigger water tight hatch, keeping out of everybody's way so we wouldn't get caught loafing and thinking nobody would ever think of looking for us down here, and going down to the mess at twelve and being first in the tot and dinner queue which meant getting ashore on the piss quicker. Well someone had worked out what we were up to. The duty Petty Officer dropped down through the hatch into the switchboard and caught about five of us at roughly eleven thirty. He went banzai. I was well knackered from the Friday night run ashore. I was on my back in the corner, snoring my head off. I thought the bloke was going to drop a bollock, screaming and shouting. "You're all on Divisional Officer's Report, and you Green, sleeping, you're really for it". hat was it, our leave was automatically cancelled until Divisional Officers Defaulters on Monday morning.

Great, just fucking great, our whole weekend ruined, Monday morning arrived and they lined the five of us up and the charges were read out.

The prosecuting Petty Officer was laying it on thick. The five of them were skulking down the switchboard in working hours, but Green was on his back in the corner snoring like a pig and actually asleep I couldn't believe it, the nerve of him, We then gave reasons in our defence. We had completed the jobs we'd been given on our various ships and had come back to get an early dinner. The Div. Officer weighed up the evidence, then gave us all a prolonged bollocking, "well as for you Green, being asleep, during working hours as well, Pheew, the way I see it if you're skulking out of the way down the switchboard, well you might as well be asleep. Award them one day's stoppage of pay and leave. On caps! Left turn. Quick march!" We got out and then rolled up, good result.

About a month later I came off shore after a Friday night on the piss down Southsea in the early hours of Saturday morning and I'd just walked a couple of miles back to Whale Island and I was in no condition to find and sling my hammock in a blacked out mess deck with just a red night light on. There were a few hammocks in the netting belonging to blokes on weekend leave so I snuggled in between two rolled up hammocks and slept like a baby. I woke up in the morning "where the flying fucking hell am I?" I couldn't move and I could hardly breathe. I was buried alive! I could just see a glimmer of light about a foot away. "Help!" They couldn't hear me and it dawned on me, "fucking hell, I'm at the bottom of the hammock netting with about twenty four hammocks above me, about four feet high and weighing a ton. I could just make out the duty cooks of the mess as they were scrubbing out. I kept shouting for help but they couldn't hear me, as they had the music turned up as they scrubbed the dand cleaned the mess.

Now I know I'm late for work. "Bollocks, I'm in the shit again. " I was shouting for another hour when the cooks came to the hammock netting.

"It's coming from in here. Fucking hell, there's somebody in there, quick empty the netting. Fucking hell Jimmy what you doing down here? They've been piping for you all morning on all of the ships, bloody hell you're for it. The Chief Elec. 's going crazy he's got a search party out for you.

They knew I'd come back and was somewhere onboard because I'd collected by station card at the gangway from the Bosun's mate, who was on watch there at the time. the Chief gave me a bollocking and told me to be careful in future. "You could have died in there". Cheers chief, my sports day performance was paying dividends already.

I worked on the Volage with Willie Walker. He was the same rank as me but about three years older. His Mother and Father lived in Portsmouth so he was allowed to be R. A (rationed ashore) and go home every night except for when he was Duty Watch. We got on well and consequently became run ashore oppo's for the summer of 1963. Our leading hand at work was Tommo, a good looking stocky bloke who was as blind as a bat but was much too vain to wear his glasses, which is why I could palm him off with all the growlers. We'd be on the side of the dance floor of the Savoy opposite the pier in Southsea, and I would say "look at that cracking bird in the red dress dancing with the one in blue". He'd say "come on", rush out in front of me and grab the 'red dress', squint at her then mime back to me "you fucking twat", got him again.

I'd catch him out and nine times out of ten he'd finish up with the growler. One Friday night, Lulu came on stage with the group 'The Luvvers'. She got half way through her first song and was booed off the stage crying her head off. The place was jammed packed with matelots and Royal Marines, when the fights broke out there, it was for real.

All these blokes were killers or potential killers, no one took prisoners. There were constant naval patrols on foot and in meat wagons who got to any rucks as soon as possible and arrested if they could. A whistle would blow and if the participants could leg it they would. The others went in the box (cell) or Haslar (R. N. Hospital) but if the Yanks were in, Portsmouth and Southsea was one big arena. The atmosphere Friday and Saturday night was electric. The Savoy Dance Hall was on top of the Festival Bars (Fez Bar), which in itself was massive, about a forty foot long bar with a stage at one end and a small dance floor in front. The resident organist (that was an appropriate title) was John Garr, who was about sixty years of age and as bent as an Arab's dagger. After finishing playing his own organ, he seemed dead set on playing everyone else's. I think his ambition was to munch his way through the entire home fleet, then have the Royal Marine barracks Eastliegh for afters!

I remember standing at the bar early one evening when a group of WRENS came in. After a short while I asked the one in the yellow outfit for a dance. Her reply was "fuck off Jack". Later on when the place had filled up and John was playing requests, I wrote one out for the 'good looking young lady standing at the bar wearing the yellow outfit'. When he read this out her face was beaming, "the request is for, – – – – – Little Donkey". The place erupted, he started playing and about a hundred matelots joined in singing "Little Donkey, Little Donkey". The Wrens drank up and left blushing and farting to a big cheer from the rest of the troops.

It was around about this time I met Eileen, she worked Friday and Saturday night in a pub on route from Portsmouth to Southsea and we used about the same five pubs every night as we made our way to be Fez Bars. I'd seen her a couple of times and then

I made a date with her. It turned out she was nineteen and had a young nipper and her husband played in a band and hadn't been near her for a couple years, so it wasn't long before we were both enjoying a bit of 'how's your father'. It was good, it suited us both, no strings attached. It went on for about five years.

It was early summer and all the women had started to arrive, first the weekenders then the holidaymakers. Portsmouth and Southsea was swamped with birds, all up for it. They couldn't believe the good time the matelots gave them, and they got taken on to the ships where everything happened. They'd go home after their holidays and then even more would arrive, all promising to come back next year. Navy Days were the highlight of the summer. They went on over the bank holiday weekend, all the ships were spruced up, the dockyard all marked out, food stalls, bunting flying everywhere and thousands of people arriving in Portsmouth for the big event.

This was my first Navy Days on a ship in the dockyard and I'd heard lots of stories (ditties) about them. I couldn't wait!, for a young twenty year old it was heaven sent, birds everywhere, high heels, short skirts, some even had knickers on!, talk about be prepared. Well the big day arrived, the Volage had been freed from its moorings and towed over and secured to the south jetty in the dockyard. It wasn't the most spectacular attraction, like a fully fired up aircraft carrier or destroyer but we'd do our best. We were all done up in our No 1 suits ready to act as guides and to help any damsels in distress, which we made sure they would be. Well, by 1500 the ship was crawling with fanny, talk about "is that a gun in your pocket or are you just pleased to see me?! I'd fixed myself up for tonight, Southsea 2100 for leg over and chips. "Sorry, we're fresh out of chips!" Everyone had a great time.

It was a beautiful sunny summer afternoon, me and Whisky Walker were leaning on the guardrails watching all the crumpet go by on the jetty, when this bloke came up to him and whispered something in his ear. All of a sudden there's this might roar as Whisky was emptying his lungs "Brown owl, brown owl" and pointing to him.

Well this 'hatrack' couldn't believe it. He pulled his collar up trying to hide. He was pushing his way through the crowds trying to get to the gangway to get off the ship. By this time the rest of the matelots had joined in pointing at him, "Psst, psst, hatrack, hatrack, psst". We were killing ourselves laughing. I said to Whisky "what the hell did he say to you?"

"Take me down below and fuck me Jack".

We were rolling about, this geezers forcing his way down the gangway whilst everybody else is coming up it. When he reached the jetty he was off like a whore's drawers.

"Ok lads settle down, settle down, you've had your fun".

"Ok Chief".

It was around about this time that Churchill died. It was a mad panic on Whale Island (Gunnery School). It was the G'I's (gunnery instructors) they ruled the parade grounds everywhere. who were tasked with the job of training up two crews to pull the gun carriage, carrying Winston Churchill's body ceremoniously across London to his final resting place, which would be in about a week's time. They had to pull bodies from everywhere to get enough hands for the two crews. (Two crews to cover for replacements if required.) Plenty of man power in those days. I was detailed off to be in one of the crews.

We worked solidly all day and everyday on the parade ground perfecting the drill until the day before his funeral, which was to be a massive national event televised, etc. a National holiday to mourn his passing. The other crew were detailed off for the event and we were held back as spares. The crew did him proud and they were admired nationwide with the country glued to their televisions. On completion, the crew were told to make their own way back to Portsmouth and join their own perspective ships by lunchtime the next day. So they were dismissed and they all broke up and went their own ways.

Four of our lads went for a beer in a local London pub. They placed their order and were promptly told to "Fuck off you white honky pigs. This is the bruvvers pub". They hadn't realised the place was full of black immigrants. Bloody charming, they couldn't get a drink in a London pub whilst wearing the Queen's uniform, and after such a momentous occasion They left bloody disgusted. There was talk of sending up the field guns crew and sorting the bastards out. But I think that was as far as it got.

Our run ashore nearly every night in Portsmouth began in the Railway Carriers pub, about a hundred yards from the Guildhall, down the Station Slip road. It was a good scrumpy house which was nicknamed the Apple Tree. A middle aged black guy used to run a string of whores from there and the Sussex Hotel next door. We knew all the girls who were aged from about eighteen to the late thirties, culminating in the big hard girl herself, 'Big Silve'. She used to keep all the boots in line. Every couple of pubs from Portsmouth to Southsea had their own girls, 'Their patch' and they didn't encroach on each others territory or else.

One of the girls in the Apple Tree was Scots Ann. At a wild guess, she was aged somewhere between thirty and sixty five she had a face like a ploughed field and if the rumours were correct a fanny to match hanging down in bites.

They called her 'The bear'. I think she must have been about a twelve pinter and a few tots. One night the place was packed the whole Yankee fleet was in and literally thousands of sailors ashore, all nationalities, all in uniform. The whores were buzzing, 'the bear' waltzed out of the pub with this nearly legless Yank and was back in about ten minutes. I heard her telling her mate "I've just taken a hundred bucks off that fucking lemon, and given him a dose of crabs to boot. " They didn't take any prisoners that's for sure. We knew them all and they were okay really just trying to earn a crust. It was an education watching how they all operated, exactly the same as most women, except they were being totally honest about it, with them you knew exactly what you were getting and how much it would cost you with no hidden agenda and a lifetime of debt.

During the summer months we only stayed for the most, a couple of pints on our journey to Southsea where all our action was. We used to look forward to every single night down the seafront as it always carried the same degree of excitement never knowing what the night would bring. I finished off many a warm summers night under the pier or in some secluded spot on Southsea common, followed by a good forty minutes walk back to the ship on the other side of Portsmouth, no wonder I was always knackered in the morning.

CHAPTER 10

Back to school

Well that was the summer of 1963 gone. I really enjoyed it and my time on the reserve fleet H. M. S. Bellerophon and my billet on HMS Sheffield. My time had come to go back to the Electrical School, HMS Collingwood to set about my Leading Electrical Mechanics Course, which was intensive and lasted for about eight months and consisted of about seven hours s day under instruction, five days a week, with an exam at the end of either one, two, three or four weeks depending on the subject. They certainly knew how to keep you on your toes. The pressure was always on.

The first two weeks was serious Mathematics, culminating in calculus, which completely baffled me but I managed to scrape through with a bit of extra tuition in the dog watches (between 4 and 6pm) from my mates in the class who actually understood what was going on.

There were quite a few clever blokes in the class of 224 in late 1963. We had got this schooling weighed off by now. The idea was to pay attention during the instruction and question the instructor on anything we didn't understand, that way it did away with lots of revision at night, thus making sure we were the bar markers down the Collingwood Club at 1800 hours, waiting for the bar to open. That was the routine nearly every night, weekends were slightly different, Saturday lunchtime was secure (finish work), a quick shit, shower, shave and shampoo then tot time. I had my tot of rum which was three single measures and had to be between 96% and 104% proof spirit and six measures of water, when mixed was called grog, from the old sailing days when seamen got a pint every day which was to help the rotten food to go down.

There were no fridges so after a few weeks at sea, nearly everything was off, except the salt beef and salted herrings, hard tack biscuits full of weevils (small beetles) which the sailors would tap on the table to dislodge as many as possible. Originally, the rum ration was neat, but it must have been having a detrimental effect on the sailors probably flying off the topsails when pissed. Then along came Admiral Grogram Vernon, who had the bright idea of mixing the rum at the rate of two and one, two measures of water for every tot of rum. This meant it had to be drunk more or less there and then as the mixture would go flat if left for much more than an hour, and this also meant they couldn't store it up for a big piss up. The men hated this and called the mixture old grog after Admiral Vernon, and so it was, up until the end (end of tot). about 1970.

The junior ratings (those men below the rate of petty officer,) weren't to be trusted, so were given grog. Senior rates, petty officers and above got neat rum as they could be trusted! (to semi secretly store it up for a mess do, social) invites would go out to the nurses home and wrns quarters, when a mess social was organised in either the chiefs or petty officers mess and a jolly goodnight would be had by all.

Well back to Saturday lunchtime and I've had my tot, a little bit of lunch in the dining hall and now it's off to the main gate, hand in my station card so there's a record of who's ashore, and through the gate and down to the Bird in Hand for a couple of pints of rough scrumpy, while I wait for the bus down to the ferry at Gosport. It was always a good trip to the Ferry, anticipating how good a run ashore this would be, but also the sense of freedom at getting out of the camp, where there was always the potential of dropping oneself in the shit. I'd catch the ferry from Gosport which took about fifteen minutes over to Portsmouth, take a walk, have a pint in the King and Queen.

On 'The Hard' (the name of the waterfront strip outside the dockyard gate) then a hundred yards round the dockyard wall to the Royal Sailors Rest, where I would book a room for the night, then off down Southsea to meet the rest of the lads and go for it, there were just so many females came down on holiday, knowing that the place was awash with sailors, of all ages, only too willing to do their bidding for them, especially with more than a few wets down their throats. What a life, but I suppose somebody had to live it! That was life for the rest of 1963.

Christmas arrived and seventeen days leave granted. Well I was worn out and needed a rest. I arrived home in Rochdale where I met up with the lads and the partying started. It was happening all over Christmas and New Year and when it was time to go back I felt so ill it was untrue. Back in Collingwood we started the first day in the Engineering Workshop, which was to familiarise us with using all the machines and tools to be found in the workshops, on all the ships in the Fleet. I'd been on the bench for about an hour and I nearly flaked out. I felt so ill. The instructor said "sit down before you pass out".

After about half an hour, I was getting worse and he told me to report to the Sick Bay. They looked me over, and took my temperature. "104. 5 degrees, hospital for you. Here, go and do this drafting routine. "

Typical, I'm nearly dead and I've got to go round all these offices to get my card stamped up, and also go up to the mess and get my wash bag, plus two pairs of brown hatters overalls (pyjamas). I got back to the Sick Bay after collapsing in one office. They said "Change into pyjamas and get on that stretcher. The ambulance is coming". Then they told two young junior ratings, who were just sent to the Sick Bay as a working party to pick up the stretcher and take it to the ambulance. They tried to lift it up and nearly tipped me out. I said, "Sod this, I've just walked round Collingwood, so I'm sure I can walk to the ambulance", which I did and then got back on the stretcher because it was about eight days later, when I woke up in a hospital bed at RNH Haslar, the Naval Hospital at Gosport.

There was this big, fat bastard in the bed next to me. He'd been sent in for an emergency diet. I had double pneumonia and hadn't eaten for a week. Consequently, when they brought the food round I had a normal dinner and 'Billy Bunter' had egg on toast, which he wolfed down without it touching the sides, then the big, fat, hungry twat was trying to get my dinner. I was very weak but I fucked him right off. Apparently, I had nearly croaked a couple of times, so they had done a damn fine job and I was lucky to be eating a dinner. I asked the young student nurse for a pee bottle, when she brought it I whispered to her and she went back to the store room, the sister asked what she was doing, she said the one in the end bed asked for a bed pan, when I took it he asked for one with a bigger neck. The sister flew down the ward to give me a bollocking, the old bat.

I soon gained strength and in a couple of days, they had me out of bed and polishing the wooden flooring with a big heavy bumper, on a long broom handle. They didn't have cleaners the patients did it. They soon got you fit again.

Sunday afternoon I was reading in bed, beginning to feel better when there was a bit of a commotion at the other end of the ward. It was four of my class/messmates who had brought four of the new WRNs over to visit me. They'd had a dinner time session and were all burbling like rock apes (Gibraltar Barbary apes). They had smuggled in four bottles of beer and a half bottle of whisky, brilliant, "I'll have that in a couple of days".

We'd been having a laugh for a while, when the ward door opened and in walked this beautiful woman of about twenty seven years.

She had on a midnight blue outfit and an Ascot type hat to match. Everyone in the ward looked and the place fell silent. She spoke to the nurse then came down the middle of the ward as if she owned the place, a big smile on her face, she came to my bed space and planted a big kiss on my cheek. My visitors were stunned and I was over the moon. I said "this is our Beryl, my eldest sister".

She had popped down from Fleet in Hampshire where she had done very well and secured the job of matron of a hospital there. I was very proud of her and I'm sure it showed. Early one afternoon, the sister was getting onto one of the young nurses, "Well where is he? He can't just disappear. I leave you in charge of the ward and you lose a patient. " There was a matelot down the other end of the ward, I think he'd been in a car accident some time previous, and was well on the mend but he was still on a drip, and missing from his bed. No one had seen what had happened to him but he was gone alright. They searched the ward, the floor, the whole hospital but nothing. Some time later a SBA (Sick Berth Attendant, matelot male nurse) came running into the ward, shouting "I've found him, he's playing darts in the pub over the road. I told him to report back to the ward and he told me to fuck off. "

They sent the heavy gang round to bring him back. Apparently he was standing on the okky, with the drip stand next to him and was picking it up and walking about with it. His mates had come for him, whisked him out of the ward whilst everyone was snoozing and they had created a diversion for the old bloke looking after the main gate, and out he went and into the pub – ten out of ten for initiative.

I think I spent about two to three weeks there but they used to get you out as soon as possible to clear the bed, so they gave me two weeks convalescence leave – bad move, my mates at home couldn't believe it, I had just gone back and here I was back home on leave, back on the piss. After another two weeks at home topping myself up with Sam Smiths and Boddingtons Best Bitter, I returned to Collingwood to face the music.

My class had moved on so I was back classed into 227A, a newly formed class full of miscreants and misfits and ner do wells. I thought just the job, we'll have some fun here. I remember coming off shore late one night with my new found pals, topped up to the gunnels with rough cider. There were a couple of lorry loads of bricks stacked neatly at the top of the parade ground. I said lets build a battle ship, which we did about twenty feet long, I said "three funnels" my oppo said "two". I said three, two, three". By this time I was laughing hysterically. All of a sudden I'm about to crap myself so it's down trolleys and I cheese one down alongside the battleship. I tried wiping my arse with the corner of a house brick – that made my eyes water! We finished the three funnels then went on our way rejoicing. In the mess I went for a shower before turning in. I was laying their giggling to myself, "thinking what a commotion the battleship is going to cause in the morning on divisions. About fifty classes will be marching past the dais, with Collingwood's Captain taking the salute, then past the battleship with a little destroyer moored alongside.

At this point, I realised I hadn't checked that I still had my ID card, something I always did. To lose that was a definite no-no. I leaped out of bed and checked my pockets, "oh fucking hell, no ID card, where could it be?" On lagging and hot foot to the battleship, thank Christ alongside the battleship was the big brown destroyer, and right alongside that was my ID card. I would have been in it up to my neck in it if the police office had found that. It had dropped out of my back pocket as I launched the destroyer.

On another occasion, when we came offshore late at night, we took a short cut behind the galley, where someone had left a dinner trolley out, "I know, let's hoist it up the mast". Sacrilege, they'll near hang us if we're caught, and there are tin hat'ed, truncheon wielding, random security patrols about, but it had to be done. The trolley was a big heavy thing with about six big shelves for transporting the troops dinner from the galley to the dining hall. It made a hell of a racket when we were pushing it with dodgy wheels and all. We got it to the parade ground Jack Staff (flag pole), undid the Engle field clips on the flag rope, but instead of a Union flag, yes the big dinner trolley, it was so heavy it was taking four of us to pull it up. about three quarters of the way up, this was the point we were in the most danger because if the security turned up, we couldn't leg it and we didn't realise that what ever securing arrangement had been used at the top of the mast to secure the pulley, if that failed, the trolley would come crashing down and probably kill or maim the lot of us.

Fortunately everything held and we secured the ropes to the cleats and beat a hasty retreat back to the mess and bed. We couldn't wait to see it when we arose the next morning, but alas it wasn't there, someone must have reported it and had the security patrol take down the offending dinner trolley.

We were in one of the pubs in Fareham one night, when I went to the toilets. I went in the wrong door, down the steps and couldn't believe my luck, I was in the cellar, I put the light on and went up the wooden steps that they roll the barrels down, slid the bolt on the small door and low and behold, I was in the alleyway alongside the pub. Great, I lifted a crate of bottled beer up the steps, left it outside, shut the door, slid the bolt, down the steps, over to the stairs, up to the top, off light, out of the door then into the right one the toilet – magic! I got a round in right on last orders, that way making sure we would be the last ones out. Just before we left I told the rest. The pub was right opposite the police station, so I said one of us to look out, and the three of us to go up the alley and pocket the beer. "If anyone comes, pretend to be having a piss. " No one saw us, so it was fish and chips then a fast black (taxi) back to Collingwood where we collected our station cards, making sure the gate staff at the police office didn't hear any bottles rattling.

Then it was off up the main drag, heading for our mess with the bottles rattling away and us laughing like drains. I was already thinking this could be a weekly occurrence, which inevitably it became because after a few beers we'd just start eyeing the cellar door. Bingo! We had done it again. This went on for some weeks then one night I was going up the alley, just by the beer when this detective came out of hiding. "Gotcha!"

I was always full to the gunnels with beer when I left the pub, so on hearing that,

I wretched and spewed all over his shoes. I said "sorry about that, I've had too much to drink". I hadn't touched the bottles, so he said "Fuck off you bastard" which I did. Phew! That was a close shave, but good whilst it lasted.

It was during 1964 that Cassius Clay (later Mohamed Ali) was to fight Sonny Liston (the Bear) for the World Heavyweight Boxing title. Clay had won the Golden Gloves at the Olympics and I'd been following his progress since I was in Singapore. He was a rank outsider as Liston had had his jaw broken in a previous fight but carried on to win. So the 'Louisville Lip' as they nicknamed the extremely gobby Clay, wasn't given any sort of chance at all. The hype was massive. All the world was interested in this fight. The bets were flying around Collingwood like wild fire. I had a bet with one of the lads, and on top of the money, the loser had to crawl around the dance floor on dance night, in the middle of a dance to the jeers of everyone in the club.

Well the fight was on dance night, so we were watching it in the TV room next door in the Collingwood Club. Clay was going to float like a butterfly and sting like a bee. He danced his way through a few rounds and caught 'the Bear' with a few good ones in the seventh. End of round. Ding! Ding! Ding! Ding! ... ... No one could believe it, Liston stayed sat on his stool and didn't come out. We were all up and cheering, Cass had won! There was a lot of controversy at the time. Rumours were Liston had been told "if you win tonight, your wife gets it straight after the fight".

I collected my money, and the other guy took off around the dance floor on his hands and knees, to the rabid amusement of everyone in there, who were throwing beer and any other rubbish over him as he passed. The place looked as if a bomb had hit it. Still, it was a good night.

During the summer, if a big storm blew up we would, after secure say fancy a swim, then we would go for a run down to Lee-on-Solent near the Fleet Air Arm Base HMS Ariel, the bigger the storm, the better. We would get our lagging off in the bus shelter, then leg it down the beach, and dive into the massive waves that were coming up the Solent from the Channel, and crashing on the beach. The second wave would pick us up and roll us right back up the beach. We would do that three or four times before it started to sink in. This was a dodgy old game we were playing here, then, there was always just one more, then back to the bus shelter get dressed, then leg it back the couple of miles, on board for a quick bath and dhobi, on night lagging. A quick pint in the Collingwood Club, then down the road to the Bird in Hand, to see Sid the landlord and down as many pints of his rough cider as possible before closing time. Then a mutual sing-song on the way back to the mess, too knackered to get up to any mischief tonight. Turn in, sleep like a log.

I successfully completed the Leading Electrical Mechanics Professional Course on the fifth of January 1964 and I was made up to Acting Leading Hand on the twenty fifth of February, 1964. Now I had a hook on my arm, I would have to behave because with the responsibility came a big pay rise, and I wouldn't want to lose either. Now I had finished the training, I was moved to Ships Company, and given a full time job on the camp to await my draft order to my next ship.

My job was the leading hand of the instructional area of the camp, maintenance, anything that needed doing. I had about ten hands to detail off, and employ and I worked under the Chief Bosun's Mate, who was in charge.

The summer of 1964 was one of the magical ones everyone talks about. There must have been about a square mile, covered with workshops, vast amounts of one storey classrooms, built before the last war and an unknown amount of back to back classrooms in those big old fashioned wooden barrack room huts, and the whole lot was surrounded by lawns that had to be cut. The job was just up my street, outside in the sun all summer, brilliant!

One hot afternoon, we got a call from one of the classrooms, they were having a problem with wasps. I took one of the lads with me to have a look. Sure enough there was a loose slab for a door step, underneath was a wasps nest. Quick, think how to get rid of it. "I know" I said to the lad "go and get a can of paraffin" which we used for the lawn mowers. When he came back the wasps were coming and going in a steady stream. You just had to be a bit careful using the door. I poured a good half a gallon of paraffin down the hole then set fire to it. There was no other fuel to burn that was safe enough. About five minutes later "Fucking hell!" There were these black and yellow really angry little buggers everywhere.

I'd sorted the ones in the nest, but now all the troops were coming back with their pollen and they had no where to go.

There were wasps on the attack everywhere. They were zapping everyone in the classroom who were trying to cover up before running the gauntlet through the door. There were matelots running everywhere, the air was blue. By now some of the other classes were watching the onslaught and were in fits of laughter, cheering on the wasps. There was no doubt, the wasps were winning hands down. The instructor called it a day and told them to dismiss and go and get their wounds sorted out. I went back about an hour later with a bucket of sand . All was quiet, I removed the slab, put down the sand and relaid the slab. Everything would be okay for tomorrow. I kept well away for the next few days as I didn't want to be playing the main part in a lynching.

Late on Thursday night, we'd had a cracking night at the club with a load of the Wrens and I'd finished up walking 'little chubby Elsie' back to the WRNERY. She was not a looker, but so funny and with such a personality and great company. She was short, chubby and with extra long arms. The rest of the troops had christened her 'Gravel Rash' insinuating her knuckles were on the ground, which they weren't, not by a good couple of inches at least. She was about eight years older than me, and she must have been on duty earlier on in the evening as she was still wearing uniform. On the way back we finished up in the entrance to a blocked up air raid shelter, just outside the. WRNERY I'd been struggling with her finger snapping blackouts for what seemed like ages, when bingo they were finally keeping her ankles warm, her muff could well easily look after itself it felt more like a fucking sporran anyway. I could have sworn there was enough material in them there drawers to make me a great coat, with just enough left over to do me a bait bag to keep my sandwiches in. I was soon in there tickling her ribs with the kidney wiper, when all of a sudden we were illuminated by six bright torches.

"Bollocks" it was the security patrol with their steel ended wooden helves and tin hats. "Allo! Allo! Allo! And what are you up to young man?" I was about to say "my nuts" but thought better of it. There we were Elsie with her knickers at the dip, and me with old one eye standing proud. They were going on about marching us down to the main gate (police office), all Elsie needed was an agony bag, and we could have done a highland fling down to the cells on our own with a few jigs on the way just to piss them right off. They had their fun then told us to thin out, and don't get caught with our trousers down again. I saw Elsie to the WRNERY main gate, said goodnight having a right old laugh, and headed off to the mess feeling as if I'd been kicked in the nuts, and planning to introduce old one eye to the five fingered widow spider. I didn't see Elsie for a couple of weeks but when I did, we looked each other in the eye and just cracked up.

My draft order came through for my next ship, I was to join a tribal class frigate HMS Eskimo on the 28th July 1964. I was quite chuffed it being a fairly new ship with air conditioning fitted on board as they were purposely built to operate in the Persian Gulf which can be extremely hot. More of that later on. I still had another two months to serve in Collingwood. Now they had a fixed date, they could work me into some more regular and important employment which turned out to be main gate staff, effectively, policing the main gate, vetting everyone entering the camp and controlling all traffic. It was shift work doing about three days on, split into watches and two days off. I had to move all my kit from my old mess and into a special small mess on the quarterdeck where the main mast was and it was adjoining the Police Office and in the same hut as all the regulating staff (Navy Police).

I didn't know whether or not this was a random choice of occupation for me, or a means of getting me right under their noses and feet, where they could an eye on me. It certainly did that, my new working gear was a No 2 full sailors uniform with red badges as opposed to No 1 which was better cloth, with gold badges, a pair of highly polished boots, white gaiters, white belt, white gloves, a chain around my neck with a whistle on the end and we had to march ourselves to and from our posts, which were about forty yards away. Very smart indeed, but the outer guard was the first person any visiting dignitaries saw, from the Queen down through Admirals, Captains, foreign 'big wigs', pub landlords, teachers, taxi drivers, dustmen, rag and bone men, ex. Cons. tramps. roaming vagrants and politicians.

It was a really hot summer and I enjoyed the job being outside all the time, and with no brainwork involved at all, so long as you were able to recognise the obvious and act accordingly, just good police work. We had a laugh there. One afternoon, thousands of bee's were swarming around the police office and main gate. They had us all running for cover but I still had to come out of the sentry box to check the cars in and out, as and when.

One afternoon, a small old van was pulling out of Collingwood's approach road to turn right to go to Lee-on-Solent. When he was just about in the middle of the road there was this roar of a motorbike coming from Lee-on-Solent towards Fareham. It was opened right up, it sounded and looked as though he was doing about a ton, the biker had no chance, as the bike hit the side of the van, the biker shot straight over the top going like a javelin. As he came down still going like a rocket, his head was the first part that made contact with the ground. As he shot up the road his head was being worn away just leaving a big red line on the road, as the only evidence that he had ever had one. It was a very dangerous stretch of road, especially for speeding bikers, beware.

CHAPTER 11

Return to Sea

My draft order had come through and I joined my next ship, HMS Eskimo, a tribal class frigate which was one of the first Navy ships to be fully air-conditioned and fitted with a G6 turbo gas jet aero engine for an immediate start from cold to be at instant notice to flash up and give chase to the illegal Arab dhows that were running guns and ammunition up and down the Gulf to Pirate states. I was joining the ship in Portsmouth Dockyard. I was rather apprehensive as this was my first ship as a leading hand, so what ever section I was assigned too I would have hands working for me.

I was wondering what the Chief Electrician was going to be like, because if your face didn't fit he could make your life hell. Well for all my worrying I needn't have bothered. I reported to the Electrical Office and was greeted with a big smile. I couldn't believe my luck, it was Big Ron Fayle, who was my Chief Electrician on the Sheffield. "Welcome aboard Jimmy my boy Congratulations on getting your hook, do your joining routine and report to the Hookey of the Greenies mess, which is the big broadside mess down aft. There's about forty bodies living down there, then go and see Petty Officer Jones (Taff) who you will be working for on the Domestic Section to get you used to the ship. "

Cheers Chief really good to see you and to be on board, I'm looking forward to a good commission can't wait.

The domestic section involved all mess deck electrics, galley's, laundries, all lighting sea boats, batteries. So we worked all over the ship and we got to know almost everyone, and if they ever wanted things done, it's beneficial to be in with the domestic leckies. So it was turning out to be ideal. I was feeling quite chuffed and looking forward to the Commission.

It was the 28th July 1964, I didn't know how long I would be serving on board but it was estimated at about two years. I had been on board about three or four weeks and I really liked it. My work was good, I got on with everyone, the food was good as we had a team of Goanese (Indian) chefs on board who dished up some top class grub. Anyway I got a message about eleven thirty in the morning, to report to the chief elec. the Rum Bosuns were collecting their mess's rum fanny's from the rum tub, where the officer of the day was overseeing the issue of rum, making sure there was no cheating (getting too much, as if).

I went to the Elect. Office where Big Ron was waiting for me, "Right Jimmy, my boy, as from now you are the new Killick of the Electricians mess. Go and relieve the old one, and tell him he's been stood down and change the Rum bosun and ticker off. " These were all highly prized jobs and none of them had been informed of the changes. I looked at Big Ron – he was very stern and serious. "Right go and do it, don't take any shit from any of them. "

The Leading Hand of the mess is usually the most senior Leading Hand and this guy was my senior by about ten years. I was the most junior killick in the mess. I didn't have time to think about it, I went down to the mess where the Killick of the Mess was sitting at the mess deck table with all his cronies around him, and the Rum Bosun had just arrived with the mess's fanny full of rum, and were getting ready for the ritual of dishing it out to all grog members. When in comes me, this lot is in for one hell of a shock, "I have just come from the Div. Office. I am the new Killick of the mess.

Any complaints go and see the Chief Elec. Leading Hand move off the table, I am going to be dishing out the rum until I appoint another Rum Bosun. Rum Bosun you are relieved of your duty and so are you Ticker Off. "

As you can imagine, I wasn't the most popular young Killick around, but I knew I wasn't going to be taking any shit off anyone. I soon made it clear, that I only said what I meant, and meant what I said. I would put anyone in the Rattle. They all soon got used to the idea, "Don't fuck with Jimmy Green", and everything settled down to be a good well balanced mess and a very friendly one.

A couple of the older blokes had been provoking some of the younger lads. I soon put a stop to that, and so the majority of the mess was happy. I soon got to like being boss man. All the leading hands and presidents (senior rates) of all the messes on board (if you were doing the job right) were treated with a certain type of respect from the Captain down. If anyone wanted to visit another mess to see an oppo. For sippers, gulpers, half a tot or God forbid a whole tot, they had to seek out the LHOM and ask his permission before entering the mess, as the LHOM was held directly responsible for the actions of all mess members and their guests at all times, so if I was hauled down to the Jaunty's office (Head Policman) for a bollocking, the person who had caused my grief, really had to stand by his drains, because I would give him so much grief that he'd wish he hadn't been born.

Big Ron seemed ever so pleased how I had settled into the job under his veiled guidance. The other good thing, I managed to purloin a fridge from somewhere to which I fixed a hasp and staple and which allowed me to fit a padlock, then I filled the fridge with illegal beer, so every now and then when we'd saved up enough we'd have a late night party. The mess being right aft, it wasn't on any thoroughfare for us to upset anyone else so long as I kept the mess immaculate. The powers that be left us alone. Every Saturday morning just before tot time, the Captain would hold his rounds of galley's and mess decks, therefore every Saturday's the cooks of mess's spent all morning, cleaning and polishing the mess ready for rounds, there were about ten different messes on the ship, Greenies, Stokers, seamen, cook's and stewards, etc. also the senior rates C. P. O. 's and P. O. 's The best mess would be awarded the coveted cake by the captain, the killick of the mess had to report his mess cleaned and ready for your inspection Sir. Then follow him around and take notes of things picked up and rectify them before the next rounds.

Every week as I followed him around the mess with his enterage, he stopped at my illegal fridge that was full of beer, he always looked me in the eye, giving me one of those looks which said I know what your up to, so be bloody well careful or I'll have your guts for garters, but he never said anything. That way there's no record of it happening. (good man).

They all knew the score, but because I ran a good mess they left me alone, and we all had a ball.

The ship spent quite a lot of time in and out of Pompy and one night on my way to Southsea calling in at most pubs on the way, I met Eileen, a nineteen year old bar maid in one of the pubs. I took her out a couple of times and we got on really well, I found out her situation which just suited the pair of us, she'd fallen pregnant a couple of years previous and got married, She had her son, her husband was playing in a pop group and spent most of his time out doing what band members do, and left poor old Eileen alone. So luckily for us I was now on the scene to provide some much needed servicing which incidently was never a chore, our arrangement, I might add went on for some years quite casually, just what the Doctor ordered.

If the ship was in Portsmouth and I was ashore and hadn't pulled, I would contact Eileen and Bob's your uncle, you've got to get yourself organised (literally) it turned out to suit us both, it was good, if we hadn't seen each other for ages, it would be a quick bed and breakfast in the same boarding house in Southsea that I always used, I use'd to book in at about half eleven and the landlady would look me straight in the eye and say "that'll be a pound each, breakfast is at 0830 to 0930, clear the room by 1030,

Don't be late. "

There was never any breakfast anyway, we organised our own more interesting Pre – departure routine, I'd taken so many birds up there. There was an attic room above. One night one of the girls said "what's that squeaking?" I said,

"Rats in the attic" She dived right under the covers shaking and saying "oh no". I didn't let on it was a rum rat. It was some other matelot burying his bone in the rafters above. Dirty lucky sod, All good fun. That top room bed made a right old racket when under pressure, I know because I had nearly been embarrassed by it quite a few times in the past, on previous manoeuvre's.

At that time in the sixties, there was a frozen food firm called "Eskimo" which was situated up in the North East of England in Grimsby in close proximity and with easy access to the fish market and all the seasonal vegetables grown in the area, ready for freezing A. S. A. P. for the best results. They must have heard of this fairly new warship, HMS Eskimo and all the young ladies in their employment must have fancied taking on a couple of hundred hairy arsed horny matlots for an extended weekend (silly girls). Well they wrote to the ship to see if it was possible for the ship have a courtesy visit to Grimsby, with the idea of a tour of the factory in the forenoon, an afternoon of field sports, bath and dhobi, then back to the social club for a much appreciated Champagne reception followed by a first class dinner dance.

Everyone had an absolutely superb day finishing off with an even better evening, culminating in the ultimate marathon bedroom sports sessions. The ships company was in a right old state in the morning. We had to complete our duties before tot time, then it was off ashore again to play cricket. We were all but sapped, I think it must have been a cunning ploy to beat us at cricket, ha, ha, but it didn't work, little did they know this was part of what we did for a living. We were well used to it. I played football on the Saturday where I was in goal, and cricket on Sunday, with Saturday night's evolutions in the middle watches which was something else and really worth writing home about . All these horny young matelots, with a skin full ale under their belts, turning up at the social club dance, hell bent on sharing their affections with as many of the all too willing Eskimos as possible.

Which probably had more than a teeny weeny bit to do with the mini baby boom later on that year after the well established Gestation period.

The Captain of the ship had managed to fit the visit in on one of the not too many free weekends the ship managed once in a while. The weekend was a roaring success. After leaving, there was much correspondence between the ship and Grimsby for a while after that, with quite a few of the lads spending the odd weekend up there when possible. It would have been quite normal for the birth rate to go up not long after a visit. Different times then, after a couple of months rigorous sea exercises (war games, for the want of a better term), up and down the South coast our next visit was to attend the yearly regatta in Santander in Northern Spain in a couple of weeks time. Life's a bastard isn't it!

We were involved in some exercises in the North Sea on our way back to Portsmouth. Saturday night I had left the ship for a run ashore down Southsea.

It was a lovely summer evening. After closing time I met up with Eileen and we went for a stroll through the park as you do (Southsea common). We were about a hundred yards off the main road and we had good clear vision to it There were circles of ornamental bushes about ten to twenty feet across, scattered about the lawned area of the park / common, We lay down on the grass discreetly behind the bushes to take advantage of the beautiful summer evening, thinking ourselves to be so lucky being able to take advantage of and enjoy the blossom and mild fragrance of the summer flowers, also enjoying the ambience of the situation whilst all the time in the back of our minds hoping to avoid the dog shit, being well obscured from view in no time at all she was having her wicked way with me.

I was thinking what a wonderful conclusion to beautiful evening, we couldn't have been more relaxed. Then all of a sudden she let out a blood curdling scream right in my ear, Fucking hell, I nearly followed through, I wondered what the hell she was up to, I knew what I was, you don't normally get an ear piercing scream when your trundling along half way through, I was beginning to think I must have squashed her fucking kidneys or something. "Someone's just had hold of my leg". I said" for Fucks sake it was me, "No, no it wasn't I saw his face".

It must have been awful close to my bare arse, for it was fairly dark down there which says a lot for her eyesight. Well, I stood up with his lordship standing up as proud as a Canadian Totem pole and as hard as a chocolate frog to boot, wondering why the intermission, I shipped my trollies and went to look for this so called frotter. I walked around the bushes, there was no one in sight. I would have seen anyone leaving against the back ground of the road lights a couple of hundred feet away.

I said "there's no one here".

"I saw him" "He was touching my leg"

"Well, there's only one place he could be, that's in the bushes".

The bushes were about three feet high in a circle, I cleared them and was having a good poke around there, on the inside was just long uncut grass and I couldn't see very well as it was so dark. I just made out the appearance of a dark object which I thought was probably an old oil drum. I kicked it and low and behold it sprang into action shooting up in the air, with the whole weight of my body behind it, I unleashed a punch, a right fucking pile driving bone shaker, drawing on all my strength, combining all of it and a bit more, from the base of my feet to my shoulders and arms, it arrived landing flush into his chops. Such was the force he took off, the fucking pervert was airborne. He flew straight over the bushes and landed on the other side. I dived over after him and punched him again, before I could get any more in he was up and running going like a coolie with the shits, with me close behind in hot pursuit. Each time I caught up with him I unleashed another bomb into his head again from the side as I drew level. All of a sudden he jumped up in the air screaming "Aaaarrgh!" and landed facing me, arms and legs akimbo in a karate stance, perfect, my right foot went straight in, slowing down from a gallop, wallop, bulls eye, right in the bollocks. He went down like a lead fart. It was a perverted Chinese tosser. He wouldn't be molesting anyone else in a hurry, not while his bollocks were up keeping his tonsils company anyway. Rape wouldn't be on that slant eyed bastards mind for quite a while. I had a big gold American high school ring (which I'd found in the N. A. A. F. I. club) living on the little finger of my right hand, a little embarrassing but that was the only finger on which it would fit, and being a pauper, beggars can't be choosers. It had (Winterhaven High School) inscribed on it, around a gold devils head with horns set in the centre of a blue stone.

I don't believe in men wearing jewelry unless their very tiny with pointed ears, hat andshoes wings on their back and glittering dust sprinkled all over them so you know what's fucking what., but this was a bit different, it looked more like a very expensive knuckle duster, as it turned out it was a buster not duster. At some stage while re-arranging the chokey's features the gold ring had broken (shattered) my knuckle. As I was walking back to Eileen I struggled to get the ring off my finger before it was the cause of the onset of gangrene, I quickly lubricated it with saliva and just managed to remove it as my whole hand was swelling up rapidly, being pumped full of blood from the broken bones. (occupational hazard) It looked like a blown up rubber glove when I showed her. She couldn't stop herself from laughing. She said, "you'll never forget me now".

She was dead right, all these years later and I can still smell the delicate perfume she used to dab around her ears, neck and fanny. Fucking horrible, like cleaning fluid, but it sure did its job, as soon as I got a whiff of that the old kidney wiper was up and raring to go, but sadly, not tonight Josephene, it wasn't the only one with a big throb on, but the other was far too painful and took precedence. I turned too the next morning (started work) and I couldn't do anything with my right hand, and there's not much call for a cack handed electrician but I persevered hoping I suppose that things would improve, as I wasn't too keen on explaining how I came by the injury to all and sundry, as I didn't even know if the chokey had come round yet, I would have loved to see all the tiny devils heads imprinted all over his scull, still it served the perv. Right. Come the next day my hand was so swollen it looked as if it was going to burst, I decided to go up to the sick bay in barracks (HMS Victory) to have it x-rayed, which they did, and said you've made a good job of that one it's shattered. I enquired if they were going to plaster it. They said "no point, you've left it too long to do anything with it, the fragments of bone have started crystalising and desolving, we'll put on a stretch bandage if you want. "

"Okay if you say so".

By the time I got back down to the ship's berth, it was gone, they'd received an urgent signal, "Sail immediately and help a ship in distress off the Dorset Coast", Bollocks, fuck my luck. Here I am in working clothes and not much money on me, standing on the jetty, was just about to get my head down in my messdeck and low and behold the miserable bastards have upped and gone, fucked off and left me stranded.

They'd left a message for me with the Harbour Master. "Make your own way down to Portland, Dorset, a naval port, where we will pick you up as and when. I took a small advance of pay against my official number and set off. I got down there by early evening and got myself into the window of a pub, where I had a view out to sea to watch for the ship entering harbour.

Closing time came, three parts pissed and nowhere to go. I know, I got a taxi up to HMS Osprey the royal naval air station and told the Quartermaster on the main gate of my predicament. Right, I can call out the stores people to issue you with some bedding, or you can get your head down in the cell to save all the trouble. "

"Okay". I got my head down with the cell door ajar. I was unceremoniously awakened at about five o'clock in the morning. By some demented lunatic screaming "Who the hell are you and why isn't this cell door locked?"

"I haven't done anything. I'm just using the bed".

"Don't give me that old bollocks, they all say that mind your fingers. "

Clang! Lock. Lock. "Fucking hell, this is all I need".

He wouldn't listen, so I got my head down again. I was awakened again at about half past seven with some regulating petty officer (policeman) shouting at me, "Why is there no record of you in the duty log?"

I said, "Don't ask me, ask last night's QM, who by the way had changed watches at 0400 and omitted to inform his relief. What a palaver, they managed to contact the off watch QM, who confirmed my story, which finally managed to affect my release. Thank fuck. Bastards.

I made my way down to the Portland Dockyard to await the arrival of the Eskimo. It was early afternoon when I finally saw her coming in through the breakwater. She tied up and I went on board. They landed the mail and we sailed. We were due in Santander in Northern Spain the following weekend for a courtesy call. On this particular weekend each year, they held a Regatta in the harbour. It was a long standing tradition. They probably still hold it today. All the smalley boats with bunting flying everywhere, the harbour was packed. Bands playing lots of food and drink everyone was having a ball.

We arrived Friday and I was duty watch so I couldn't go ashore that night. Some of the lads were making their way back to the ship when a group of Diegos started taunting them. Apparently, it came to blows, one of our lads smacked one of the opposition and sent him flying into the road, when around the corner comes a fast moving car, which hits the guy In the road, our lot thin out leaving a melee in the road. I hadn't heard about all this when I went ashore the following afternoon. It was hot knowledge in the local community. I'm not sure how bad the injured Spanish bloke was. There were about four of us making our way to the nearest bar, through this road tunnel where the incident happened. Everyone seemed to be staring at us when we passed them and were obviously talking about us. The penny dropped later when I found out what had happened.

There's me with my right hand bandaged up. They must have thought it was me who laid him out. Well through the tunnel, turn right up a cobbled hill and into this bar. We had a detachment of Royal Marines on board, who had spent the last two years out in the jungles of Borneo, fighting and killing the so called terrorists. They were super fit, and three of them were in this bar with about twelve of us matlots.

We'd been in the bar a couple of hours when we noticed an angry mob building up outside the pub, apparently looking for revenge for the previous night. They locked the doors to keep them out. I was getting worried by now. How the hell were we going to get out of here? Two state policemen arrived with the black plastic looking hats with the flat backs to them, thank Christ for them, they'll get us out. They unlocked the doors and let them in. All of a sudden one of them started ranting and raving in Spanish and started poking one of the Royal Marines. It just happened to be Big Jock, a wild bootneck from Glasgow, the last person they should be provoking. Things were turning nasty. Jock screamed back and told the Diego bastard to keep his hands off him. He started poking Jock again, and that was it he lost his rag. He punched his head so hard I thought he had unshipped it. He knocked him out cold.

At this, the other one drew his sword. Fucking hell. Big Jock wrestled it off him and lifted it up, brought it down on his knee and snapped it in half and threw it to the ground and smacked him. It all happened so quickly. Someone shouted "Form a scrum and stick tight" which we did and forced our way out of the door and through the crowd. Then we were all legging it down to the hill when all of a sudden, Ping! Ping! Ping! "Fucking Hell! Heads down run faster they're shooting at us".

Bullets were ricocheting off the road and walls. Somehow we all made it to the bottom of the hill and round the corner and through the tunnel, were all going like long dogs. The Bosuns Mate guarding the gangway couldn't believe his eyes. Fifteen bodies flat out over the gangway and down the hatch. There certainly wasn't anything to be gained by continuing shore leave, just a pile of trouble. I think the Captain made his excuses to shoresides, that we had to go and assist some ship in difficulties, and in the small hours of the morning, slipped our moorings and sailed off over the horizon.

It wasn't long before I was out on another run ashore down Portsmouth and Southsea. After a good skinful, I found myself in bed with this nineteen year old from Coventry. We were in a particularly old house down Queen Street which she was telling me was haunted. It must have seen some action over the last hundred and fifty years being one of the big old terraces just opposite the dockyard. There must have been legions of matlots performing here, going back to the old sailing ships and Nelson's flagship, HMS Victory, which is in dry dock just up the road. I gave her a damn good service and overhaul then fell asleep.

I awoke the proudest man in Portsmouth with an hour to spare, so it was come on wakey-wakey you're on next. I was soon a rockin and a rollin and thought its getting a bit choppy, it felt as though we'd just gone through the breakwater and were shipping the big green bastards over the foc'stle. I suspected something was a bit different, I had a quick butchers, "Fucking Hell".

"I didn't know you were pregnant, when's it due?"

"I should have dropped it last week".

Fucking hell a load, time for offski., best I thin out quick before she starts bombing the deck.

As soon as I got back onboard I carried out my essential usual routine when playing the field, strip off, on towel and down to the bathroom for a bloody good inspection, soapy scrub down, shower and clean off. I rinsed off and was drying myself, when I looked down and saw a black speck, "Oh no! Mobile dandruff, shellfish, the dirty cow's given me a dose of the galloping Ab dabs".

Right opposite the bathroom was the sickbay and luckily the pox doctor's apprentice (nurse) was always there first thing in the morning to collect the samples. I knocked on the door and entered, just a towel around me.

"O. K. Jim, what have you been up to, , how can I help?. " For a start my nuts and second "You can start by prising these little bastards off. "

"I've just come offshore after all night in, and I think she's given me a dose of crabs. "

"Let me see. I can't see any your okay away you go. "

I have a look "Look here, – - there's one. "

"DON'T flick the fuckers around my sick bay you twat, here put this cream on and come back same time tomorrow with a sample. Best to check she hasn't given you any more surprises, they usually do".

As luck would have it she hadn't, I was all clear. Selfish whore taking advantage of me when I'm pissed. Have they no shame.

It was about September 1965 and it was coming up for all the play offs for the football world cup and it was time in our commission to do a nine month tour of duty in the Middle East. We were not looking forward to this as it was near a war situation in Aden, which was our first port of call on station. Well it was a Sunday in Portsmouth and I'd made my mind up, we were sailing for the Middle East at 0930 in the morning, so I was going ashore that night for a last skinfull of English draught beer and to get my end away.

Because I wouldn't be seeing any more white fanny for at least nine months or maybe never with the situation out there as it was. So it was all stops out, the bone had to be buried. Southsea was dead, I was having a good drink when I noticed this old boiler eyeing me up through the thickest pair of glasses possible, her magnified eyeballs seemed to be wandering around their sockets at will. I thought you've got no chance lady or whatever, after a few more bevies and a couple of double tots of 100 proof Woods rum, just to put things into the right perspective, I had another quick glance, I don't know, she not all that bad – considering!, I've had worse, I can't actually remember where and when but I'm pretty sure. Mind you she must have had fucking good eyesight to see through those glasses, they were like Guiness bottle bottoms. Bloody great magnifying glasses, her eyeballs looked to be standing out like a bull dogs bollocks and wandering about at will just as freely.

Next news she's standing right next to me confirming my views on her re-enforced double glazing, and running her fingernails up and down my back. I had another pint and a double Woods Rum just to secure my position. By this time, she's got her hand down the back of my strides, inside my shirt and running her finger nails up and down my spine. My knob's got a mind of its own by now it's pulsating and nearly lifting the bar top the big trombones got knack all on this. I looked over my shoulder and there was a young couple about my age watching the pantomime unfold. He was laughing like a drain. She's smiling and shaking her head at me and mouthing "No, no. " I looked her in the eye and nodded my head "Yes, yes" its gonna go up tonight, I had another pint and a couple more double 100 proof Woods's, I looked at her, head on, and thought she's Okay really, I almost couldn't see her tash by now, it was probably blending in with her mousy beard and well hidden in the tram lines, and I'm pretty sure that's a tooth and not a tusk hanging out a right old pickle stabber, well lets go for it. Any port in a storm, and its blowing fucking a hurricane.

She was down from Cardiff for a week and had hired a room just off the seafront for the deeds. Just before we left, I had another large rum as I felt I was going to need it. I waved and smiled at the young couple and left arm in arm with this fucking old Welsh boiler as soon as we were in the bedroom she stripped off.

Her tits hit the floor and the cheeks of her arse were hanging and swinging like a couple of old pussars hammocks in a storm, she stripped me off 2 – –6 threw me onto the bed, and got me in an upside down pin fall, with her knee's holding my shoulders down and proceeded to swallow my knob I'm sure she hadn't had any supper, then this huge fanny which resembled a bear rug descending on my face, it reminded me of an old world war two gas mask I'd seen in an army surplus store, but this one was covered in a thick black matting, and looked like it would have been more at home covering the nether regions of a Grizzly bear than a dubiously lonely Welsh damsel. I thought take a big deep breath Jimmy me boy your gonna be needing it. "Fucking hell, she's got piss flaps like John Waynes chaps or Gene Autrey's saddled bags, and a clit like a blind cobbler's thumb. I just knew I would be needing that extra Rum.

It went over my face like an old Galley fire blanket. It wasn't the fact I found myself yodelling up it that was amazing, more the fact I was getting a reply, although a trifle muffled excuse the pun. and I can assure you it was no fucking trifle, it tasted more like a three week old Finnister cod. It was no use, I had to come up for air, talk about a bearded clam, this was more like Beaver fucking Creek and I was fast disappearing up it. I was thinking there was less room in my pussars holdall when I was searching for my keys.

That was enough of a Welch blossom to last me a lifetime, now I know why most of the Welsh blokes spend half their lives down the pit and the of the rest of the time with their heads stuck up each others arses playing rugby.

I woke up in the morning and round two had no chance which was unusual for me , she's making the tea. I looked at my watch, "bollocks, I'm going to be adrift. I leapt out of bed to have a quick wash and I looked in the mirror. "Oh fucking hell – No, – urgh!" Retch, Retch, I had a big red ring around my chops. A big jam dough nut was looking back at me, Just at that moment she started pouring the milk into the tea, plop! Plop! Oh not more, Fucking hell one lump or two, the milk had curdled Retch! Retch! The milk wasn't the only thing that was curdled, she said "do you take sugar", "do I take sugar", I was getting dressed "I need a damn sight more than fucking sugar with you, I'm off, you dirty four eyed smelly Welsh Moose. . " Retching "and think yourself lucky, I don't normally dish out complements willy nilly". down the stairs making my way at speed towards the livening fresh sea air of Southsea, which wasn't the only thing that was fucking salty, just around the corner from the Pier which was itself disgorging all the emaciated horny remnants of the night before.

Was I glad to see the back of that particular Celtic beauty I wouldn't fancy having to rely on her to see me through the week. I'll put that one down to experience, about the only option left open to me. I was just hoping she hadn't loaded me up with any mysterious Welsh fucking lodgers. Time alone will tell. I'd heard a lot about Welsh lamb and mint sauce but fuck all about the big black Welsh hares I was pulling out of my teeth for a week. Fucking stroll on.

The ship was sailing in half an hour and I had three miles to run with a right hangover and retching every hundred yards, leaving a potent trail of rum fumes and Jack and Danny odour in my wake I sure my breath would have knocked over a marauding Rhino, I just made it as they were lifting the gangway, I was put on a charge for being an hour adrift while the ship was under sailing orders, that's double the punishment, and twice the heartache as the punishment also involved the stoppage of one's tot. "sacrilege". Never again.

As I'm writing this book, in between, I'm driving my taxi, and I've just run Old Mac home from the pub, the Beachcomber in Seaford, Sussex, and I've just told him that ditty, he's an old Sea Cadet and an Army Veteran from the war, laughing his head off as he got out of the cab at home. He said, "Harry, you were just fulfilling your duty as a sailor, and it was the Woods rum that made you go with the woman that was curdled, not only the milk. " Well that was the end of the white fanny for a while.

ext on the agenda will be the 'black ham' their all talking about in the middle east. We sailed on time, it was going to take us two or three days to reach our first port of call, Gibraltar. That turned out to be a good run ashore. From the dockyard side of the rock there's a tunnel going right through the rock to the beach on the opposite side, where they had built a rain catchment down the side of the rock, which filled the reservoir inside the rock. Also on the inside were massive store rooms to supply the ships with, which were sailing into the Mediterranean Sea during wartime. Also big Navel operations headquarters as the rock is so big and just about bomb proof.

We used to spend the afternoons having a swim, sunbathing then back through the tunnel, back onboard for supper, then it was shit, shave, shower and shampoo and on tiddley gear and off for a run ashore down Main Street, Gibraltar where everything was duty free and the beer was cheap but not the senorita's, senora's yes, so copper up. – Grand Senora's get your lagging off your on next.

We would end up in Sugar's Bar. That was always a good end to the night. Sugar was in his fifties and as bent as an Arab's dagger.

He used to say he was the 'Queen of the Rock', All the matelots would heckle him and say he was "Queen of the Cock, not the Rock". He loved the performance he'd say "I'm here for the needy, not the bloody greedy", then he'd get his lipstick out. As he turned the barrel, a huge lipstick cock came out, then he'd flutter his eyelids and pretend to be offended and hurt, pout his lips, get his mirror and start applying the lipstick with this massive cock, to the rapturous applause from all those present. Sugar wasn't daft though, the trade in all the pubs was dependent on how many warships were in. When it was quiet, if there was any trade to be had, Sugar had it. This was the life, all this, and getting well paid, fed and watered, and rum ration to boot. It had a good feeling to it, Gibraltar, relaxed, the ship's Captain was now in full control of his own ship, he wasn't constantly looking over his shoulder, as in Portsmouth or Plymouth where there was always some Admiral with fuck all else to do, sending signals bollocking the ship's captains for not quite getting it right.

When out of their way the captain could relax, the ships company felt the benefit and the ships routine would run smoothly, you scratch our backs and we'll scratch yours. This particular afternoon, the Admiral of Gibraltar was on board up in the Captain's cabin for drinky poos. There was a 'pipe' over the ship's tanoy, "LEM Green Gangway. " It was the Chief Elec. "Jimmy, get your tool bag and go and fix the Admiral's car, he can't start it. "I was gone for a good half hour. When I returned to the ship "I can't find it Chief I've searched everywhere, it's not on the jetty". "It is".

"All there is, is a ramshackle battered old mini that's full of rubbish. "

"That's it, the infamous rock relic. "

As each Admiral got relieved of his duty (job on the rock) he passed the keys on to his relief. The mobile dilapidated midden was even more recognisable on the rock than the Admirals official Rolls Royce which was used to ferry him about on naval duties and jollies. They used it as a private little run about when off duty and held it in high esteem, in their eyes they thought every one was saying "There goes the Admiral, a right jack the lad" The problem was, the battery! – – it needed one, a serviceable one . I was inwardly in fits of laughter, I would have been nearly ashamed to be seen in such a wreck, I was going to call it a Jalopy but that would be elevating it way above its station. I got it going what a heap. There must have been a good dustbin full of assorted rubbish in there from many commissions previous, leaving just about enough room to squeeze in a couple of not so very particular bodies. They informed the Admiral who had been pouring it down his neck all afternoon in the Captains cabin, and he came down to the jetty well oiled, dressed only in his shorts, shirt and sandals. I first caught sight of him trying to negotiate the gangway, his backbone was very reminiscent of a string of conkers and he was trying to get his legs to manoeuvre his frame in my direction, when he eventually arrived I assisted him in behind the wheel and from behind it, he gave me an inane grin and said "Cheers Hookey" and took off down the jetty all over the place, It looked for an instant as if he was trying to warm up his tyres, but that would have been ridiculous (Roasting Gibralter).

When you're the big boss on the Rock, you rule, full stop. No one is going to question anything you do. Situation normal, the rules are for the erks, minions, peons every one else bar them. "Fuck em all, we're alright" That's there attitude, It's the knobs so called right, and prerogative. Well fuck them too, if that's there altitude they can stop up there.

We sailed from Gib. leaving Sugar with his huge lipstick cock to carry on coining it in entertaining the troops while we sped on our way to the dreaded Persian Gulf. (sand flies, camel shit and bent Arabs, at the time the arsehole of the World and Bahrein a good hundred miles up it.)

We were informed our next port of call was Valetta in Malta, that was after a few days soaking up the sun sailing through the Med. We arrived and the first impression: a really dry and arid place but we'd heard lots of stories about 'The Gut' which was a local narrow street with cobbled stones on a steep incline, filled with all these brilliant drinking dens of ill repute. I think red lights had been mentioned for some reason.

Still, being sailors, we had to sample the local hospitality for ourselves. The local drink was Marcavin (the local hooch) and Seven Up, lemonade (together, Screech). The local grapevine had been working overtime and the gut was overflowing with all this essence fanny, a matlots heaven (for the time being anyway) what a night ! what an introduction to Malta, brilliant!. We awoke the following morning with the Mother of all hangovers, so after tot and lunch we decided to go swimming and the place to be was St. David's bay on the other side of the island, three of us had left the ship dressed in short sleeved shirts, shorts and sandals with our rolled up swimming gear under our arms.

We were making our way through the quiet streets in the hot sunshine enjoying our wash up on last nights run ashore having a right giggle, when we came under verble abuse from a gang of teddy boys standing on a street corner. We were ignoring them but as we got close the gang leader flicked his half smoked cigarette towards us and it landed in my hair setting it on fire, I was franticly trying to shake it free to the ecstatic jeering mob of teddy boy's. it fell to the ground and I extinguished myself picked up the butt and walked towards the toe rags. There was a deafening silence as I approached, I stood in front of the thug stared into his eyes and extinguished the cigarette on his forehead, right between his mother fucking eye's. He made no noise but what a grimace, having completed my task I returned to my oppo's picked up my swimming gear and we carried on our way to the beach. We were having a laugh imagining the teds. not going a bundle on the royal navy turning up out of the blue, then filleting all the local fanny, crabs and all. It would tend to go against the grain wouldn't it, but come on they were all on the batter anyway, a fair exchange is no robbery.

The beach was superb with a massive rock a couple of hundred yards off shore, which we had to have a race around, it was much further out than we first thought, we were feeling a lot better by now, after a time oggling the local flange on the beach, it was time for back onboard, bath and dhob's, supper, then off ashore again for another skinful of screech and burying the bone and hiding the sausage, just to keep the system in top form, ready for our next Port of call. we had just heard of a short cut to the top of the top of the Gut.

Just off the waterfront was this rickerty old cage, which went from the pavement straight up the cliff face to the top of the town, three of us got in which instantly overloaded it, there wasn't a door not even a securing bar to stop you falling out, half way up we thought the whole thing was going to collapse. still its got to be better than walking all the way up the big hill to commence our run ashore, we had better things in mind to expend our energy on. looking back it's hard to believe it's over forty five years ago, before the times of affordable foreign travel, and before the oil industry began to dismantle and change the World irreparably for ever, sending it on an irreversible decline for all time.

The local water taxis were called Dhiagso's. when we bartered over the fare, because we didn't want to buy the fucking boat only hire it to travel too and from the ship. The drivers would sing. "Not for me, but for my dhiagso", – – – - "why for you so fuckina piso (tight) ". Always trying to extract the maximum coin possible, from us near destitute sailors.

It was always good banter and they had to earn their pennies. All in all it was a good run ashore, Malta, although a few of the blokes had 'caught the boat up', Naval slang for a dose. Fuck our luck we should have checked!, the yanks had been in a couple of weeks previous spreading the pox everywhere, after about another three days to a week, the queue outside the sickbay in the morning, was growing like Pinnocio's nose. They all had to take the flak from the rest of the crew. "Ding! Ding! Unclean, Unclean, bring out your dead!" when in this situation there was definitely no hiding place – – -"Fuck Off you Bastards". Was there embarrassed reply. "it's your fucking turn next, you wait" T

he first port of call to welcome us on station (Middle East) on our journey to the gulf was going to be Aden, but first we would have to negotiate the Suez canal. We arrived and anchored in Port Said for the night, to prepare the ship for the passage through the canal.

I had to fit a big floodlight on the front of the bridge pointing forward and a convoy pinlight on the quarterdeck for the ship in line astern to line up on and follow. *regulations before being allowed to sail through the Canal. It seemed really weird, a ship sailing through the middle of the desert. There were Arabs on camels to both sides of the ship in the wilderness. We anchored that night in Port Said then all the bum boats arrived full of thieving Arabs, Ali Baba had fuck all on this lot. It was an all night job keeping them off the ship. It seemed they would swap their own granny for a fag end. If anything wasn't nailed down it was gone, we'd never seen anything like it.

We were off again next morning heading for the Red Sea where we were informed Masawa was our next stop. 'Halle Salasse' the outright ruler of Ethiopia and according to the Rastafarians, was the God King, a direct descendant from God. He was going to inspect the ship's armed guard, which I was now informed I was part of.

On the way through the Red Sea the designated guard bulled our boots, polished the brasses and blancoed our webbing pressed our No. 1 suits and practised our guard drill "Royal Salute Present … . Arms" which was a salute to the King with our three o-three rifles, bayonets fixed, to which he would return the salute.

The big day arrived and we were dressed in full whites tropical uniform, we fell in on the jetty absolutely roasting, awaiting the arrival of the King. The big car arrived and out got what appeared to be about a four foot tall cockerel. Talk about being a bit over dressed. His brightly coloured uniform was covered in medals, which he must have awarded to himself and his hat was something else, all colours of the rainbow feathers and plumes everywhere.

"Guard. Guard Ho! Royal Salute present … . arms. Crash! Crash! … Crash! Crash!" with the .303 rifles. Old fashioned but impressive.

We're at the present, he returns the salute, "Guard, shoulder, arms, crash! Crash! Guard Atten … … ion!" Then the King proceeds around the guard inspecting each rating in turn. He arrived in front of me looking me up and down, trying to find some part of my uniform not quite perfect and should he do so would result in me being put on a charge for turning out on guard being slovenly dressed, and I'm looking through the top of the feathers in his enormous hat wondering what he was harbouring in there. I've never seen a person so small before who wasn't a dwarf.

With all the ceremonial ritual out of the way, volunteers were piped *for to represent the ship and R. N. in the next days boat pulling event to be held from the river mouth up to the finishing line just forward of Eskimo. The occasion was the passing out of the first maritime students from their new university of Ethiopia.

They'd had a huge gold cup made which was going to be the centre piece in the big showcase of their new University. *apparently they had been training for months to make absolutely sure they would win the race. There were warships representing about eight countries. Britain, West Germany, East Germany, Russia, Holland, Italy, America, and France. We were all informed about the race the day before, so they weren't really giving us much of a chance. Come the start of the race the boats were all *vying for position at the mouth of the river, the Russians were highly noticeable by their absence. They couldn't be seen to lose. (explain context) It must have been about a five hundred yards course. They lined up, bang! They're off. The blacks were away like shit off a shovel, the Yanks caught a crab right away and were out of it, the rest are pulling up the river in identical boats, supplied by the Uni. In hot pursuit after the locals, They're coming up to the ship astern of us. It's so hot they're all knackered. The Ethiopians were in the lead by about a length, followed by Eskimo, France and West Germany pulling for all their worth.

We've got all our ships company on the upper deck shouting in unison, "Eskimo, Eskimo". As they were approaching our stern, I started the England football chant, "clap, clap, ... clap, clap, clap, – - clap, clap, – - clap, clap, clap. ... . England". Suddenly, the chant from the Eskimo was deafening. It was the final at Wembley, you could see the transformation in our lads and it seemed to break the hearts of the other crews. Clap, clap, "England!" They were pulling level at the front. Clap, clap, "England!" They were pulling ahead. Clap, clap, "England!" They were in front, clap, clap, "England!"–We've won! The cheers coming from our upper deck were just out of this world. The organisers were absolutely devastated. This just wasn't in the script.

The big celebrations at the University were cancelled, my run ashore oppo. Slinger, who was an ex. Field Gunner and as fit as a fiddle and didn't like losing, and the other two Royal Marines, Pete Hanly and Sam Gelbert were also part of the crew, we are going to have some massive piss ups on the strength of this. I can't recall anything of a presentation of the gold cup and I can't remember seeing it. They probably held it back, until they could organise an event which they would win.

As far as I remember there wasn't a town as such, just a few streets of ramshackle houses behind the dockland, which was just a wharf really, and later that afternoon, that's where me and Slinger found ourselves. We were ashore wandering around looking for some sort of bar.

All the rest of the ships had sailed after the boat race. We managed to find a bar of sorts and got us a beer each. We'd had a few when a bunch of girls came in. Word had soon spread on the jungle drums. I was eyeing one I sort of fancied. She came over and whispered in international language "Giggy gig". I looked at Slinger and we both burst out laughing.

"Too bloody right, let's go. Yee Ha!"

I had the breaking strain of a Kit Kat when it came to getting my end away. They took us to different houses or brothels. Where I was there was just a row of beds with six foot partitions between them. I did the business and paid her and as I was going out of the door onto the road when four black guys came up to me, one of them pulled out a big flick knife, flicked it and put the blade to my throat. "You've just fucked my sister. "

Fucking hell, how am I going to get out of this one? I don't know what he thought I was going to do, after all she worked in a brothel.

I held my hand out and said, "let me have a look at the knife. "

I couldn't believe it, he folded it and gave it to me. He must have thought I was going to buy it. I held the knife in front of me flicked it and held the huge blade under his nose, "right move in there" I ushered them into the brothel, closed the knife and threw it in after them. I then legged it down the road and away. I was looking for Slinger but I didn't know where he'd gone. I was having a beer in another little shed bar I found when I realised I'd left my hat in the brothel, I didn't want to be put on a charge for returning from shore improperly dressed. so (unbelievably now) I went back.

The four girls were sitting on the step, I asked them for my hat and they replied "no hat".

This went on for a while and they wouldn't let me through to search the place. By this time I was wound right up, I wanted away from here so I told them again to move.

"No way".

So I bent down, put my hands on the two outside heads and banged them all together . I was in. I shouted for my hat, no hat. So that was it. I turned the first bed over and started to rip down the partition. The second bed was now over and I was just starting on the second partition when low and behold! my hat turns up, marvellous what a bit of gentle persuasion can do. I put it on and I'm going through the door again when the four pimps stop me with the knife.

My brains going berserk, I'm surely dead this time I can't see how I'm going to get out of this one. I was trying to work out how to get minimum damage from the knife before legging it. Just at that precise moment it was like divine providence. Right at that second, Slinger came around the corner at the top of the road I screamed as loud as I could, "Slinger here, chop chop give me a hand and we'll have these bastards. "

Slinger came running down the road screaming like a banshee, the four of them turned tail and legged it.

"Bloody hell, cheers, Slings. You just don't know how close that was. "

Then we burst into hysterical laughter. We returned onboard fully booted and spurred and I was glad to be there still in one piece and not knee deep in the shit.

CHAPTER 12

Arrive on station

We sailed from Masawa first thing in the forenoon on passage to Aden, where we would officially begin our tour of duty in the middle east. In doing so we'd be relieving the ship already on station freeing her up for passage home and well earned leave for the crew. We would have a ceremonial parade on the jetty, where F. O. M. E. Flag Officer Middle East would welcome us on station.

*We arrived in Aden Friday night and the security situation was dire, so serious with Yasser Arafat and his P. L. O. cronies paying the local Arabs to throw hand grenades at all white trash where ever they could and generally stirring up as much trouble as possible , that caused the First Lieutenant to put the ship on top security alert, awkward state one that meant armed patrols patrolling the upper deck with sub machine guns and orders to shoot at any small boat coming too close, in case they were going to throw bombs onboard. Also the ships divers were in a state of top readiness to search the ships hull for any mines which they may have been able to plant, which would have had a minimum fuse time of twenty minuets. Pretty hairy, a bit of a change from leg over and chips down Southsea, still I suppose we'll get used to it. Tough luck if we don't.

T   e following morning Saturday we were working as normal and ten o'clock was stand easy (fifteen minutes tea break), I took my mug of tea out onto the quarter deck to get some fresh air and see a couple of my oppo's. Bungi Williamson and Red Rider who were working at their part of ship, the after four point five inch gun. We were sitting on a couple of bollards, enjoying the sun and discussing our situation, when there was this massive explosion, about forty yards from the ship, down the jetty. We felt the blast and saw a big black mushroom cloud rising. It turned out it was the open back wagon bringing the ship's supplies, fresh veg. etc. onboard with the intention of blowing the ship up, considering how much ammunition we carried on board we were very lucky. The driver must have got stuck in traffic and was an hour late which was to our good fortune and not to his as the timing device on the bomb that was onboard had been ticking away in traffic jams and not in the holds of our ship. After the explosion and the mushroom cloud cleared we could see all that was left of him was a bit of red meat pulsating against a wall in the morning sun probably his torso, the wreckage was strewn up and down the jetty the wheels had gone bouncing off all over the place. Welcome to the Middle East! Cheers.

This was all supposed to happen when we were on parade on the jetty with the Admiral inspecting us and welcoming us to the wonders of the Middle East. Slight change of plans somewhat. My first visit into Crater City in Aden about a mile from the dockyard, which is situated in the crater of a dead volcano – it was like the Wild West, lots of cripples getting about on home made crutches and you could tell all the thieves because they had had a hand chopped off, and persistent offenders both removed. Which would have made it extremely difficult to wipe ones duck run after completing no. 2's. It was really an intimidating place to be and everyone was really hostile to the white man. On the road leading into Crater, there was a diversion road branching off to the left which led to a causeway, which in turn led to Little Aden, about ten miles away. which was like a big sandy island, where 42 Commando were based. We were invited over there for a game of rugby followed by a social evening afterwards, which turned out to be a real treat for everyone concerned. A couple of days later, our Captain made Crater city out of bounds, as a run ashore destination because it had become just too dangerous.

Arafat was paying the locals the equivalent of a day's pay to throw one hand grenade at any white trash, their lingo. We could still go ashore but only to the army camp, which was out of the dockyard gate, turn right, and about half a mile around the dockyard wall. We'd had a few beers down the mess when myself and Shiner Wright a hilarious scouser one of my able rates, ie. We worked together, decided ashore was the best option available to us. We made our way to the dockyard gate we were well primed already but ready for more booze. There was a taxi just outside the gate,

"I don't fancy the army barracks, do you?"

"No fuck it, let's get the cab down to Crator and the night life".

We were having a laugh in the back of the cab, not paying attention to where we were going. All of a sudden the cab picks up speed and we were doing about seventy miles an hour. "Fucking hell Shiner, this isn't the way to Crator".

I shout, "stop, you bastard, turn round and take us to back".

At this, he floors the accelerator. "Oh no we're fucking dead". Its time for reaction and quick while we've still got the chance. We'll have no fucking chance soon we'll be ragged bagged and shagged then chopped up with these fucking bastards.

I leaned right forward, put my right forearm over the front seat, around his neck and across his Adam's apple, and I yanked back as hard as I possibly could. I nearly pulled his fucking bent Arab head off! The car was all over the road. I think we were on the causeway heading out into the blackness towards Little Aden. He was somehow managing to slow the car down although I now had him in a serious neck hold using both my arms. One good twist and I would have broke his worthless fucking neck. The car was now stopped across the highway as he couldn't possibly drive the thing from the position I had him dangling from, I am by now screaming in his ear.

"Turn around, turn around", which he had much difficulty doing as I had him pulled so far back, he had difficulty reaching the pedals. Plus I wasn't sitting directly behind him, I was diagonally opposite thus putting even more pressure bending his neck, it's a wonder it didn't crack anyway I kept him in the neck lock all the way back to Crator, easing it slightly every now and again just to let the minimum air possible passed his gullet to get us back to town

I said to Shiner when we had stopped, "Get out and open my door, I'm not letting go of this murdering toe rag until the last second. " I didn't know what the hell he had hidden in the car, Whatever he had I wasn't giving him the chance to blow us up anyway. I leapt from the car after giving the twat one final choke and twist of his neck then we legged it for our lives. We were in the centre of Crator city and nearly all the lights were out and the streets empty as there was a curfew on. It was really bad and eerie, somehow we were going to have to get the couple of miles or so back to the dockyard, at this point it looked highly unlikely we would make it. I saw this other car come kerb crawling towards us with the offside window opened and an arm came out.

"Get down Shiner, he's got a gun. "

We were running from parked car to parked car using them as a shield. He was trying to line up a good shot at us when we arrived at a T junction joining onto a major road, there was a covered Army wagon full of Pongos approaching us. The two A rabs in the car who were lining us up for potted wog meat spotted the potentially much greater prize of killing and maiming a wagon full of soldiers, so as the wagon passed on the major rd. the chicken livered scum bags with their car lights extinguished and unseen tagged on behind the Army wagon preparing to throw in a couple of hand grenades and slaughter as many as possible at the first available opportunity.

We couldn't believe our luck, I said "come on Shiner lets get our arses back onboard while we're still in one piece" taking no chances, and on foot we kept to the shadows all the way back to the dockyard gate, we played hide and seek with anything that moved, we were absolutely knackered and thankful for our lives. Shiner was saying I fucking hate these black bastards which was a bit of a turn up, him being a half caste himself. He used to say its not my fault my mother was locked in an air raid shelter with a nigger during the war. It was one hell of a relief once inside the safety of the dockyard wall, but more than double that once we were onboard down the mess, sitting around the mess deck table with a can of beer apiece reliving our terrifying ordeal, much to the amusement of the rest of our messmates who were taking the piss something chronic, Situation normal.

The following night we decided to stick to the rules and have a few pints around the corner in the Army's barracks and play it safe or so we thought. The two bootnecks, Slinger and me after a few wets onboard, made our way around to the barracks and into the bar. We weren't exactly welcome but we didn't care as long as we were being served in a bar. The squadies had been baiting us all night, after a couple of hours the shit began to fly.

"Hello sailor".

"Fuck off bone domes".

"Right, outside".

Too right, the four of us were up against six or seven brain dead Pongo's and we were stuck right into them. There were three out cold. It was going well. Word must have spread fast as it sounded like the cavalry was coming. Around the corner came a torrent of fully booted and spurred Pongos screaming like banshee's, we were now out numbered about four to one, discretion being the better part of valour we got in our last punches and were off up the road going like long dogs, being pursued by this baying mob of fired up clowns screaming for our guts. We were covered in blood but the adrenalin was so high we were laughing like drains. Out of the barracks around the dockyard wall in through the dockyard gates, absolutely pissing ourselves steaming up the jetty over the gangway and back on board to the safety of the mess and the inevitable questions "What the fuck happened to you lot", Another good run ashore was had by all. You couldn't make it up.

We sailed from Aden, thanking our lucky stars we were still in one piece with our injuries healing slowly and hoping not have to the misfortune of passing this way ever again. Whilst we were in Aden a blonde, sixteen year old RAF's sergeant's daughter was gang raped on a Saturday afternoon by half a dozen locals, next to a chip van with all the shopping crowds looking on. The Arabs didn't bat an eyelid anything bad for the white eye's was ok by them. Then during the following week the P, L, O, (the enemy) fired a rocket launched grenade into the white kid's junior school, killing and maiming thirty or forty youngsters. All this fired up by religion. Give a man a fish and he will eat for a day. Give a man religion and he will starve to death whilst praying for a fish.

"Don't talk to me about religion. " It stinks and all the death and destruction it has needlessly created. The world is 4,000 years old, for fucks sake who are these deranged wallies down the ladder. There are tree's older than that. Money and Power that's what that's all about.

Our next port of call Bahrain was to be our main base in the Gulf. If, as it was stated at the time the Lion's Jaw, the entrance to the Persian Gulf was the arsehole of the World, then Bahrain is four hundred miles up it. When we entered the Gulf through the Lions Jaw, we might just as well have been going through the gates of hell.

W thought the heat was unbearable sailing up from the gulf of Aden towards the lions jaw in the Indian ocean, but it got even hotter. When opening a door to the upper deck, and going out of the air conditioning citadel, it was like opening an oven door and going in, the temperature's could be extreme. First thing in the morning there could be ice on the deck and come midday, you could fry an egg on the same spot, which we did just to prove the fact. Well we had better get used to our situation pretty quick because were in this shit hole for the next six months before we get a break. Roll on.

After a couple of days we arrived in Bahrain. It was easy to see why no one wanted to be there. There was a jetty which was the longest in the world at the time, stretching about a mile into the sea. The big oil tankers used to berth on the end to load or discharge their rich cargo of crude oil. We would berth anywhere along it. The island itself seemed flat and barren like a huge sandbank covered in sand flies and camel shit, at the beginning of the jetty was a crane plus a few workshops, which was all incorporated inside a military compound with a periphery of about three miles. In which was located the army barracks, a football pitch and a fairly new army social club, the Royal Navies beer canteen, (a two storey wooden hut) various tin shacks in which the locals resided and a few other essential amenities to make life just about bearable.

Near the jetty was the Sailor's Social Club, a two storey wooden hut with stairs running up at one end to a serving hatch through which when manned we could gain access to our beloved nectar, ice cold beer, where we could buy as many cans as possible, to take down below and pour down our throats whilst digressing on the rough tables and benches provided, and once we had our systems well lubricated and got our vocal chords well oiled the barren arena at the side of the hut and at the corner of the football field would be transformed into a theatre of much merriment and enjoyment, a real sods opera. The sea shanties of old would be sung, stemming from the days of the sailing ships when all the not so jolly Jack tars whilst at work would sing in unison to keep good time whilst hoisting the sails or lifting the anchor with the use of the capstan or windlass, a careless mistake from loss of rhythm could result in everything going wrong and the instigator for whatever reason, being tied to the capstan with his torso bared, and lashed with the cat-o-nine-tails with as many cuts as was deemed necessary by the Captain, for him to get the notion into his head as not to do it again. If the man under punishment died whilst receiving his award and the flogging was stopped, the captain would say "flog that man" but he's dead sir "then flog his kit". and bury him.

Then so be it, his body would be sewn up in his hammock, a cannon ball placed in with him to give him a sure and quick way down to the seabed, and the last stitch would be skewered through his bottom lip to confirm he was truly dead and not just trying to escape the rest of his punishment, a short service would be held on the upper deck and performed in thanksgiving for his short life and loyal service to his country, then his body would be committed to the deep, so it could spend the rest of eternity in its watery grave wondering what the fucking hell happened and why. God bless ye Cap'n. I hope your ears turn into arseholes and shit all over your shoulders. Consequently the lyrics to the shanties have been slightly altered and updated over the years to reflect jolly jacks progressively morbid sense of humour and relentless mistrust of anyone wearing gold braid with a beating heart and still breathing. The main town Manamah was a mile or two from the military compound, I took a hike over there to have a look see. (a good shuftie around the town and Bazaar's).

There was no alcohol allowed, as in any of the Islamic States. So the chances of me having a good afternoon and getting my end away were definitely in the negative. Alcohol apparently is banned by the Koran and that's why all the Muslims come to England to do their drinking and debauchery, (the Korans commandments obviously don't apply world wide, very confusing for the non believer or infidel, in their terminology) but I had a superb hot curry in some eating house with very large fat prawns fresh out of the Persian gulf. I've never had one so good since, different spices I suppose.

There were Arabs trotting or meandering around everywhere their transport being Asses or camels, their parking arrangements were brilliant, they would arrive at their destination, dismount, tether their beasts front feet together (hobble), go about their business and when they returned hey presto! uncle splayfoot the foul mouthed spitting machine would still be there. We were playing football one afternoon on the army pitch, when we heard this commotion. There was this Arab running like the clappers with his white robes flapping away behind him and screaming like a demented banshee, chasing his donkey which was going like the wind towards the jetty with a matelot mounted astride his fleeting steed, Jack was in white uniform with his cap on the back of his head well pissed shouting "Yeehaw!" imagining he was on the home stretch of the Derby – his philosophy. "Fuck walking when you're pissed up. " Especially when there's local transport available. Use your initiative Jack. His nuts must have been a sight for sore eyes as there was no saddle on eeh auh.

He could hardly conceal his dirty deed as he winged his way up the totally deserted jetty on "Pegasus" the flying ears towards the ship. The officer of the day plus the duty hands, who had been watching Vasco de Garma making his bid for freedom were in hysterics, he was approaching the ship and big ears was absolutely knackered by now and had slowed right down, he was still blissfully unaware of his realistic predicament, he dismounted his braying nag and was negotiating the gangway, when much to his bewilderment, he was arrested as he stepped onto the ship. The exhausted Arab boarded his knackered quadruped for the unexpected return trip back down the seemingly endless jetty. To continue his original journey and tell his tale.

A lot of the legal legitimate trade being carried out in the Persian Gulf was between countries bordering on the Gulf, there was also plenty of illegal trade being carried out at sea ie. Currency manipulation would be carried out at sea with Dhows from different Gulf States exchanging gold reserves, ingots and nuggets for various currencies. stopping this was not included in our brief as a warship Policing the Gulf. Our job was to try and stop the highly illegal arms trade, which was being carried out between Dhows usually under the cover of darkness, trading Gold bullion for arms, or exchanging arms for arms. This duty was not exactly a stroll in the park. But in reality was quite dangerous.

We'd been patrolling the Gulf, stopping and searching the Arab dhows (locally designed boats) to catch the gun runners. We'd stop any suspect dhow, go alongside and send a five man boarding party onboard to search for contraband. We had two marines posted on the port side above the sea boat about twenty feet apart with loaded and cocked automatic machine guns, as once the boarding party was onboard, we had no idea what the Arabs would do. Some of these dhows just looked like sailing boats but down below they had twin Rolls Royce engines capable of high speeds and they could take off with the boarding party disposing with them at will. I said to Sam Jelbert on one of the machine guns "What would it take for you to open fire?"

"Any one of them makes a sudden move and they're all dead". We had an invite from an America company to visit one of their bases on Halloween. The invite was accepted.

Aramco! A large American oil company, had a huge base about twenty miles north of Abadan, which is situated right at the top of the Gulf in Southern Iraq. We were berthed on a dilapidated old jetty for the duration of our stay. The local Sheik and his entourage appeared arriving out of the desert on a camel train, observing local Protocol to welcome the Captain and his ship to their country.

They still wore traditional Arab desert clothing, and had numerous bodyguards, who just looked like big bundles of rags with black desert headdress, they also had an ancient rifle apiece, with bandoliers of ammunition over their shoulders, and big bent Arabian daggers alongside antique pistols on their belts, a magic carpet wouldn't have seemed out of place. It looked like something from an old "B" movie I didn't know about Ali Baba but they could surely pass for his forty thieves, but the nineteen sixties was the beginning of the big shift in World wealth, with the majority of the World's richest oilfields being discovered in the Middle East. At that time the building of the Middle East and the restructuring of the Global Pecking order was in its infancy. During the next few decades, the World order would change beyond recognition. The big Sheiks were slowly being accepted as the new Father Christmas's, and the overbearing Yanks would have to learn to swallow their pride and dance to the new tune, without ever admitting it.

A single Decker battered old bus arrived on the jetty, a pipe was made over the main broadcast, those "volunteers" visiting the American oil base for Halloween muster by the gangway in ten minuets time.

It was party time, and so the unknown in the desert had to be preferable to the known, sweltering onboard. So with all the players rounded up and with much anticipation we boarded the old bone shaking jalopy for our expedition out into the unknown, and the big question! Is it going to be trick or treat?.

We set off in the sweltering heat into the unknown. There was nothing to see, just this bumpy old track disappearing into the desert and rough scrub land all around. We must have gone about fifteen miles and by now we were really choking breathing in the clouds of fine sand, when all of a sudden appearing out of the desert like a mirage in a dream, there was this lush green oasis with Palm tree's, green hedges, lawns, flower gardens, bungalows, tennis courts, bowling alley, cinema. In general it was uncle Sams "the lot" it was a small American town, unbelievable, they dropped us at this cafeteria, dining hall which appeared to be the main feeding station for the whole base and said "we'll pick you up here at midnight, don't be late as the ship is under sailing orders". Have a good time We were taken into the self-serve dining hall and told to order whatever food we wanted and just sign for it. We had never seen a spread of food like it, not in our lives, I had a prawn and lobster starter followed by a 'T' bone steak you could have choked a tiger with, the Chef said how would you like it sir, blow its nose wipe its arse and serve it – ollehy. My steak arrived medium rare and it was well over an inch thick and was hanging off this massive plate all around, and the juices were dripping everywhere I had to get another plate for the chips etc., I have never had a meal as good anywhere, either before or since, and I've had some classics around the world. "Those Yanks sure know how to eat!" and look after themselves. After the feast we all split up and about five of us went wandering about the base looking for some prospective action.

It was by now early evening and the kids on the base were out 'trick or treating' around the accommodation area. I said to our lot, you'll never guess what "come with me".

I'd seen about half a dozen sexy young women go into a bungalow just up the road all dressed up, obviously for a Halloween party. I knocked on the door, one of them opened the door and I said "Trick or treat?" There were screams of delight. They couldn't believe their eyes, or luck. Here they were! stuck out in the middle of the desert on a poxy oil base, and from nowhere, or possibly heaven, on their doorstep appeared five bronzy bronzy, fit, young horny British matelots with big smiles on their faces, and bollocks down to their knees.

"Come in". Which we did – – – – - all afternoon. We played a few tricks, for which we were rewarded with the most pleasurable treats imaginable.

Now this is a Halloween worth celebrating I said later on "Is there anywhere where we can get a drink? "I'll call the boys, I'll see if we can go up there".

The boys had this six bedroom bungalow and in which, they all had a room each. They were the oil prospecting team, three would go out into the desert prospecting for oil for three weeks, after which they changed shifts and were relieved by the other three who continued the good work. We got our invite and an impromptu Halloween party was set up, we were all well chuffed, a good excuse to get slaughtered.

"Any of you like a drink? We don't have any beer, but as much home made hooch as you can put away. "

They brought out a gallon flagon of this dynamite, white mans fire water with mixers. Just what the doctor wouldn't have ordered, but we had. It was like rocket fuel, high octane, high proof, highly inflammable and even more highly illegal being in a dry Arab State. Talk about round the teeth round the gums watch out stomach here it comes. So be it, bring it on.

"Come and see the main operations room". They opened up this secret room behind a disguised doorway and wow! Two big copper boilers, the type used in households as hot water tanks, attached was all the necessary paraphernalia to complete the experiments, heaters, thermometers, copper pipes in abundance, funnels to transfer from the initial still to the experimental secondary arrangement with safety valves fitted, to double distil the heavenly nectar to reach the highest proof possible, without the whole shebang exploding and slightly giving the game away, copper pipes everywhere all highly polished just like the mad Professors laboratory, it was brilliant. Come on shake a leg lets get amongst it. They got the music on and we were up dancing and performing with the girls. We all loved it. We'd had one hell of an evening and now we were all so pissed and were flaking out. One of the lads starts bringing us round, "Come on, come on it's half past fucking one. "

"Oh no they'll have our guts for garters, we're in the shit again! We managed to talk one of the blokes into driving us back. We burbled our thanks to the girls for looking after us, as well, and for their hospitality and the whisky. They managed to bundle us into the back of this car, where we all promptly went comatose. How the guy managed to drive that car I'll never know, he was well out of his tree, although you must stand a reasonable chance of not hitting anything else if your manoeuvring your vehicle through the sight of one eye, all be it alternately through the desert. I woke up in the well, at the back of the car, jammed in and suffocating from the deadly gas seeping out of the detritus I was buried under. It was about three o'clock in the morning when we arrived on the jetty, and they were having a hell of job waking us up and pulling us out of the car, and into the much needed fresh air.

The quartermaster and Bosun's mate of the watch were on the gangway and couldn't believe what they were seeing. We'd gone ashore lunchtime into the desert in a dry country and arrived back in this state. Apparently the bus arrived back with the rest of them all sober and complaining of a really rubbish day out. They said "there's five adrift, fuck knows where "they" went. " "Who is it?" "Need we ask ?".

"Jimmy Green and troops".

The buzz flew around the ship the next day like shit from a Hippo. with a hard on, and we were held in the highest esteem for achieving the impossible. (returning onboard drunk from a dry state in the desert and being the recipients of the best treats imaginable from Halloween's trick or treat – – – – a sailors dream), and didn't we rub it in to the rest of the crew onboard – -Yee Haagh. We sailed from there straight into action stations and a damage control exercise to keep everyone on there toes, which is an ongoing practice for a combat situation, to guard against a gas attack and protect against nuclear fallout debris entering the ship.

All airtight doors are closed, all upper deck fan flaps are closed and the ventilation fans set to recirculate the onboard air. This made it safe for most of the ships company, in fact, all but two. The five hundred kilowatt emergency diesel generator was situated on the upper deck, outside the airtight citadel in its own compartment with its own switchboard, situated next to it, as it needed a killick stoker to start and maintain it, and a killick lecky to parallel with the internal generators and transfer its load for the safety of the ship.

That meant, myself and Nutty Bar were the only two crew members, closed up and locked outside the gas tight citadel, and if the situation should arise, on completion of our duty, we were expendable, and which may I add no one had had the decency to inform us. We knew the fact, Although it wasn't officially recognised. So fuck em all. Consequently myself and Nutty spent a hell of a lot of hours closed up at action stations together, totally amounting to days and weeks, special sea dutymen, action stations and all other tight situations in which the ship found itself. Together, we got on quite well, you've got to in these sorts of situations, it was our job. He was a stocky Glaswegian who thought of himself as a hard nut. He was about four years older than me and the thought of me being able to look after myself wouldn't have entered his head. He was a total ships bully but putting up with the like is part of life, looking after yourself learning to live with it.

We used to have a film in the dining hall some evenings, reel to reel projector. We'd swap the films all round the fleet as and when possible. Everyone would be seated up, or on the floor ready for the film to start, then he would turn up shouting the odds and throwing whoever was in the best seat out, so he could have it, and being one of the most senior leading hands onboard had the authority to back up his belligerent / bellicose behaviour he would have the film operator stop the film at his whim, just because he could do, thus spoiling everyone else's enjoyment of the film. It didn't particularly bother me as I'd got used to it since joining up, where ever you went there was always one of these arseholes would pop up, it was how the Navy was run in those days, as much lower deck self regulation as possible, and thus not creating extra work for the senior rates who were all up for as quiet a time as could be had

That's just a bit of background information as to what happened just before Christmas in Bahrain. We had been patrolling up and down the Gulf now for about four months. It was really boring and the crew had just about had enough, so the powers that be had granted us some time off before starting the patrols again. We were going down to Mombasa for a two week break, one week station leave for the port watch and on their return, one week's leave to the starboard watch.

This was brilliant, we got the maps out and planned what we could do and where to go. At that time there was a list for twenty volunteers to forego their trip to Mombasa and exchange jobs with twenty pongos, who were up in the Radfan mountains in the Yemen, who were engaged with the enemy, Yasser Arafat's murdering mob. I thought, "no chance, go up there and get your head blown off". But, surprisingly, the list was filled in no time and so we called in at Aden to exchange twenty matelots for twenty pongo's, who had won the raffle to be able to come with us, for some leave in Mombasa. It was to be a real eye opening experience for them, living on a ship and drawing a tot and seeing a different interpretation of discipline, and marvelling at the wonders of how a warship and her crew operates in general.

CHAPTER 13

Station leave

To make life on the ship workable, they cleared a small mess below the dining hall and victualed all the pongos down there to keep them all together, and try to keep all the simple fuckers reasonably safe and out of trouble, trying to find a functional brain amongst them was proving to be an evolution in itself. On the second day at sea, on our way down to Mombasa it was tot time, but there was no sign of the pongo's rum bosun at the rum tub, who's duty it was to collect that day's ration of twenty tots. They sent a runner, who shouted down the mess for them to chop, chop and get their rum fanny up to the run tub now. The reply cracked everyone.

"No, it's okay, we've still got some left from yesterday. "

From that moment on, they had an ongoing supply of friends, quite willing to give them any assistance required in drinking their daily rum ration. – – – - (Turkeys). We went to action stations the next day, practice makes perfect, and we were to have a live firing of our fwd and aft four point five inch guns. Everyone was closed up at action stations, wearing their anti flash hoods and gloves, so as not to have any bare skin exposed, thus avoiding explosion flash burns. They would have pooled all the pongo's near H. Q. to be used as extra hands where and when required. One of their no. was missing he must have been asleep sunbathing on top of one of the upper deck cabooses.

There wouldn't have been anyone else on the upper deck only A and Y guns crew and all the upper deck doors and hatches were battened down tight, so he wouldn't have been able to enter the ship's structure. He was walking down the starboard waist towards the foc'sle, probably a million miles away thinking how serene and beautiful the afternoon was and how lucky he was to have secured himself a billet on this miracle cruise, not a care in the world, not even another soul about, just the comforting sound of the ship's bow wave as she glided through the calm waters of the Indian Ocean, just off the E. African coast, this is heaven. The Fwd gun was locked on to its target on the starboard side of the ship and just about to open fire, a message from the operations room, "Alpha Guns crew". Two salvos – – - Engage. BANG! – – – – – – – BANG! The shockwave coming out of the end of the barrel is devastating, any woodwork ie. Bollard gratings in the vicinity that hadn't been stowed away would be blown away and shattered to pieces.

Our intrepid trooper was about fifteen feet away from the end of the barrel side on, when it opened fire. All the light fittings, fluorescent tubes, plastic shades, all shattered in the mess decks, bathroom and storerooms directly below the gun turret and the noise down there was unbearable. It must have nearly blown old Percy pongo's head to smithereens. What a rude awakening he must have got when he finally came round over half an hour later, ears and nose bleeding, bloodshot eyes, a splitting head and his pants – well – shit everywhere. (fucking snot gobbling matlots, bastards.)

Someone from the guns crew spotted him. "Check. Check. Check. Check. Stop firing, stop firing, casualty focs'le Stbd, waist, First Aid Party to the Focsle at the rush.

" They scraped him off the deck stretchered him down below and turned him in the sick bay for a couple of days. I think he was nearly back to normal in the end, his brain was just a tad mushier than usual, he still didn't know where the fuck he was, one thing's for sure, if everything is nice and quiet in the future and he's wandering about thinking this is a fucking good holiday, he wont be taking relaxation and serenity for granted as before.

He will be tightening his arsehole sphincter trying to make sure he's got as much control of his bowels as possible, never knowing when all hell was going to break loose again.

We arrived in Mombasa harbour a few days later. Sailing in there was well good. The brilliant sun, the pure white sands of the beaches, no wonder the holiday place was called Silver Sands. That's where the port watch were about to take seven days station leave, starting the next day. I couldn't wait to get ashore, the anticipation of what was going to happen is immense. I was ashore with Slinger down the Kilindini Road where two artificial elephants tusks form a bridge like structure over the main road. We were generally sight seeing as we made our way around the bars, and it soon became pretty obvious that that we were right in the middle of the red light district, familiarising ourselves with the area, just in case a rapid disappearing act was to be called for later on. Always have an escape route planned, be prepared.

Two local girls started trying to latch on to us, plying there trade, from what I could gather they had become of age and were sent down from the jungle to Mombasa, as knowledge of the ships visit circulated. They were aged about seventeen or eighteen it was going to be the spring chickens and not the old boilers who would get the worms and earn some money for the rest of the family, and that's how I found myself all night in with Rosie. Who was a real good looker and as fit as a butchers dog. Slinger had thinned out with her pal who was an even better looker, with first division Tits and a body to match.

We were in a room on the first floor of a small block. I locked the door and viewed the bed which was next to an open window type gap that just had metal bars running down, something woke me in the middle of the night and it wasn't just another Lob. It was a big black fellah's arm reaching in through the bars trying to get hold of my wallet or my throat, not my cock for fucks sake you never know with these midnight munchers there never on a diet. I shouted and he legged it. Pretty scary stuff. I wasn't staying there, I slipped Rosie a crippler paid her got dressed and was off. Walking down Killindini Road towards the jetties, just as the sun was coming up, I felt on top of the world, some Safari we'll have loads more of this before were finished.

The following night was okay, Rosie had found another place. Later in the week I said to Slinger, "let's swap".

He said, "no way", but he was duty watch on the Friday and I told the other killick seaman not to do him a stand in. So I was pulling his leg all day. On commencement of leave, I had my civvies on and was still ribbing Slinger, who by now was getting quite irate, as he was having to stay onboard. Especially as I was singing "Its gonna go up tonight, Its gonna go up tonight, inky pinky par les vous. Really pissing him off. Just the thing he would have done to me given half the chance. Sure enough Rosie was busy, so I was off with her mate, Mammaries.

Well they say a change is as good as a rest, and shiver me timbers this was some change. I awoke in the middle of the night to go to the toilet, I pulled the curtain back and there was her sister, if not even fitter lying on another makeshift bed, and in the raw as well, " it was quite warm though" I went for a pee as I came back she winked, a nods as good as a wink to a blind man, I was in to her like a rat up a drain pipe, all very amicable, suited us fine. First time I'd heard of buy one, get one free, I'd go two's up with these dollies add infinitum. Superb. That's probably why Slinger was against it and had a bastard on. Greedy sod. That'll teach him. When I saw him in the morning, he was waiting at the top of the gangway I said "share and share alike".

"You bastard". He said with a smirk on his face, Its no use crying over spilt milk. I cracked up, I Couldn't help laughing like a drain. The second week was coming up shortly and our turn for some leave, we were sussing out the possibilities of getting ourselves a railway warrant and spending our one weeks station leave up in Nairobi, a couple of hundred miles up country. There was a big game reserve there they were just getting going, I was looking forward to that. We were ashore again having a few pints when we got talking to this Scotsman who lived in Nairobi and worked away in Mombasa. His wife ran a small bar called the Dambusters, and lived in a bungalow to the rear of the pub. He told us that they would probably put us up somehow for our custom in the bar, he gave her a call and said to expect us the following week, to which she whole heartedly agreed to, as business had been very poor and our money was badly needed. Brilliant!

We got the address and telephone number, which we could give to the regulating office on board as a contact address in case of a re-call. Sweet as nut. Three of us got permission to go, we were issued with three return railway warrants. We just couldn't believe our good fortune, and could hardly wait. Nairobi at that time was like a garden city, the jewel in the crown of Southern Rhodesia which in itself was the envy of the rest of Africa. Which after the Mau-Mau terrorists had finished slaughtering the white man and then stopped him running the country, they installed Jomo Kenyata to run the show, who changed the name to Kenya, and the road downhill from the most prosperous country to the most destitute, had begun for them. Finishing up as one of the worst regimes, and places to try and survive in, on this Planet, Robert Mugwabes Zimbabwe. Totally shameful.

This was it. We were aboard a train from Mombasa to Nairobi, we couldn't believe the stunning countryside we were travelling through. Half way there the Puffing Billy was nearly stopped as it negotiated its way up the ever rising terrain, the railway track dog legged it upwards back and forth to negotiate its way to the top of the high plateau. It made us smile as it was prayer time for Muslims onboard the train. They had laid their prayer mats down facing Mecca and no sooner had they started, then the train would start turning around, so it was up mats and start again. We reckoned they were dizzy by the time we arrived at the top. It was late when we arrived in Nairobi so we stayed local for the night, bed and Breakfast and had a few wets in town, looking forward to what tomorrow would bring.

The following morning, after scran, we purloined a fast black, (taxi) and headed for the Dambuster pub. I think there must have been a dam but we didn't get to see it, We arrived at the pub to find the landlady waiting for us which was good. She said we could sleep on the floor in the lounge of the bungalow, just behind the pub. She was all ears wanting to know the news from the UK. She was all over us. They obviously didn't get many guests stuck out there. We had a good bevy up and then she served up a delicious bright red curry. This place was tops, we had really fallen on our feet here.

The following day we spent relaxing around the pool getting to know the locals. I noticed one young woman staring into the pool and appeared in great distressed, I asked her what the problem was. She said her engagement ring had come off her finger in the pool. "Don't worry, we'll find it".

We had two or three of us looking for it. I knew where to go, straight down to the mesh covering the drain, that's the deepest point. I dived in and swam straight to the grid, Bingo! I surfaced with it on the end of my little finger, the look on her face was a picture. That was it, they were all most impressed and we were in like Flynn.

We got talking to one of the farmers in the bar that night over a few beers and I asked him if he could tell us what big game was in the area.

"I'll do better than that, I'll show you. The day after tomorrow I'll pick you up at 0500 as we need an early start, and I'll take you into the game reserve and we'll see if we can find one of the rhinos if they happen to be in this area. " Apparently there were two of them roaming somewhere in the big local reserve.

That gave us something to look forward to. He turned up at five o'clock and there we were still half pissed, our newly adopted mum had made us up a big packed lunch, with a gallon of water each which turned out to be heaven sent. I got in the front of the Landrover and the other two in the back, big Jock the farmer alighted into the driving seat with this great big hunting rifle for safety's sake and we were off. I didn't usually get excited about anything, but this was something entirely different, I was so alert with anticipation, just great.

He pointed out various antelope, giraffe etc. and we were going flat out to cover as much ground as possible. We were going round this long bend in the road with trees either side when all of a sudden there was this large dark object coming towards us flat out going at a fair old lick.

"fucking hell" I though we were going to have a head on with a charging rhino, shit shoot, Braking hard we perceived a squadron of hairy arsed warthogs with vicious looking tusks tear arsing towards us flat out. At the last minuet they parted in the middle and shot down either side of the vehicle. Which was by now swerving all over the road trying to stay on it. "what colours blood? Thank fuck for that, I've shit myself". A short while later as we were regaining our composure, we came to a river and were approaching a shallow ford, the crossing point of the river, and I pointed out a warning sign which said, Beware of the Crocodiles. It was all adding to the exiting tension. I was dying for a crap, but no way, I'll bake it till later. I wasn't going to be lunch for some starving Croc.

Looking up the river where it widened and was deeper, were some hippo's flapping their dung around with their tails, shit all over the place they were really going for it, a territorial thing I think. We were now travelling at a crawling pace trying to navigate around all the obstacles, boulders etc both in the river and on the unmade track on the other side. The next thing that happened was really frightening.

When we emerged from the river, we had encroached on the territory of a very large troop of baboons, who literally didn't go fuck all on it at all. The big male boss man with about ten of his strike force, were all over the vehicle. There were about four or five of them on the bonnet, with their big three to four inch yellow canine fangs bared, lips curled back, not in a threatening gesture, but attacking mode, screaming the place down and thumping more like drumming on the bonnet and windscreen.

We all knew if the windscreen broke we were in deep shit, Probably dead. The thought of them tearing our throats out made us more than a little uneasy. We couldn't go any faster in case the axle broke, so we endured this for about twenty minutes, when we must have been coming to the edge of their territory. At last they seemed to be losing interest in us, realising they had scared the shit out of us, and they were the obvious victors. They started to leave the vehicle in a most triumphant manner, re-grouping behind the enormous alpha male, who was strutting his stuff, showing off his big red arse and mighty bollocks then fucked off. Thank Christ!. I was thinking what I wouldn't have given to have had an even bigger luminous red arse, with a brilliantly multi coloured cocoa nut sized pair of bollocks, and a cock like a huge stick of pink Blackpool rock. I could have leapt out of the truck and really given the fucking thing what for. Maybe next time, that was just a bit too hairy.

About a mile further on there was a carcass of a Hyena, being torn apart by countless other hyena's, jackals, Vultures, plus other scavengers and opportunistic parasites harassing the weak and infirm, all trying to be first to get their noses into the fast disappearing trough of goodies, and fill their bellies before even more of their unrelenting kind arrived to devour the pathetic remains, a complete free for all, look after number one, fuck the rest. Looking back it was an absolute dead ringer of the sycophantic M. P's. of today. (February 2009). Well, we'd had a most eventful day in the reserve, but were disappointed that we didn't get to see any of the rhinos, elephants, or big cats, but there you go.

We were on our way back completely knackered, overawed, and looking forward to some supper and an evening in the bar discussing the day's events. Later on in the bar, we got into a conversation with this guy whose hobby was collecting snakes, with the idea of opening a reptile type zoo in the future, which he was in the process of developing. We were having a real entertaining evening as he was telling us all the stories of his escapades and dices with death as he answered phone calls and went to various locations to pick up these deadly poisonous snakes from the general public, who were only too pleased to see him and be relieved of the predicament they found themselves in. Once he'd bagged up the offending snake, they would happily give him a big tip to help with the funding of his snake pit, which he could see was going to be a future Nairobi tourist attraction, and the best of luck to him.

Looks like being another good day tomorrow. As he gave us an invite around to his place to see his set up. The next day we got a lift from the pub and when we arrived there he was handling these deadly poisonous snakes. He was getting the most deadly ones out of the glass cages, and telling us with one bite and you'd have only a few minuets to live without the antidote, the nearest antidote was thousands of miles away in South Africa and he had them on the concrete floor entertaining us. His phone rang and it was some lady who was doing her housework, she moved an armchair and underneath it coiled up was a big back snake she described it to him and he said it sounds like a deadly black Mamba. Whatever you do don't touch it–"Don't touch it". – – Yeah alright! as if, I was just about to give it a bath. he took her address, jumped on his boneshaker of a scooter with a carrying box on the back, said I won't be long and was gone to collect yet another specimen for his prospective zoo.

e was back within half and hour, with a deadly poisonous black mamba, a large specimen which he was really pleased with. He was building a sunken snake pit about thirty feet across and about ten feet deep, with a waterfall going into a pool at the bottom, and various rockeries with natural vegetation in abundance, which was secure enough to hold the reptiles and still give the public a good viewing area.

It was a brilliant idea, thinning out the dangerous snakes from public places and making it safer for the population and at the same time stocking his zoo. Innovative people like this was just what the country needed, to contribute to Africa's prosperous future, brilliant. We must have had one hell of a last night at the Dam Busters celebrating with our ever so kind and friendly new pals of which by this time there were loads, as I can't remember leaving there the next morning, or the train journey back down to Mombasa. We were probably that knackered and still half pissed, we slept all the way back down to the coast. One thing was for sure, we had spent one hell of a good week with our new found friends, and one that has stayed vivid in my memory for nearly fifty years, and for little more than our beer money!. Since then, the white man and his innovative brilliance, common sense and shear dogmatic perseverance and quest for excellence has been eradicated.

The whole of that part of the country has been reduced to not much more than hell on Earth for the poor souls who's unfortunate lot is to try and survive there , – – Criminal.

We sailed from Mombasa for Aden, to drop the Pongos off, and pick up the rest of our crew on our way back to the Gulf, to continue with our patrol duties. The squaddies had just had the best experience of their lives and were just marvelling at life on a Royal Navy warship and didn't want to leave, and weren't looking forward to going back up into the mountains, where there was a good possibility of getting there heads blown off, and for what.

Our lads were soon telling us all the stories, they said it was a right eye opener, likening it to the wild west. Exchanging fire with the Arabs, they would see a raghead pop up amongst the rocks and bang they'd let fly, then trying to dodge the bullets coming back their way, shells ricocheting all around them. Apparently they got a huge adrenalin rush, with their lives on the line no wonder. They had some unusual photographs, one that stood out was an Arab on his knees, his head had just been severed with a big sword, wielded by one of his compatriots, his head had just left his shoulders and the sword hadn't yet reached the ground brilliant photo., definitely one for the album, but Grannies seen it all before, she won't be impressed. All in all it was an experience they wouldn't have missed or will ever forget. Not realising coming along in the pipeline are all these ignorant tossers who are going to convince the unsuspecting populace that it never happened. Or that their version is more acceptable.

CHAPTER 14

Trouble brewing

We arrived back in Bahrein about two weeks later, in the mean time one of the three able seamen, Halliwell had been promoted to acting Leading seamen. As quite often happens the newly acquired status and power went straight to his head and he was immediately ostracised, especially by the people he worked with, he was quickly becoming the big I am, hooray Henry style, being a right pain in the arse all round. Just prior to this there had been a few rumours going around the mess, which if proven to be true would be explosive and most devastating for those involved. In the far quiet corner of the mess, there were twelve bunks, six either side facing each other and the whole could be curtained off after pipe down. Because of its remoteness it had been affectionately nicknamed "the Gulch", an almost ideal place to live being out of the general noisy turmoil of the mess, and not on a general thoroughfare, a place of relative privacy, like gold dust on an overcrowded warship.

When we originally moved onboard it was decided to billet the young lads UA's (under age, too young for rum,) there to keep them out of the way of the older "G" members, and in the mean time it would teach them a few manners and stop them getting thick ears for upsetting more senior ratings, and teach them what respect is all about. Over time one of the occupants had gone on draft, leaving a vacant billet available in the gulch. When the three AB's joined our mess Halliwell had been allocated the only spare bunk left, which happened to be in the gulch, everything had been running smoothly up until now with big Ron being in charge of our department, unfortunately for us Ron's time onboard was up and he had gone on draft. His relief our new Chief Elec., was an entirely different character who was about to stamp his own mark on the department. unbeknown to me this was the beginning of my troubles.

I went ashore this particular night with the two bootneck's, for a few bevy's and we returned onboard well after pipe down and got turned in. I was awakened by "Call the hands" piped over the tannoy, first thing in the morning. Then about five minutes later, LEM Green, Able Seaman Rider, Able Seaman Williamson, regulating office (Police office) at the rush. I hadn't even had time for a shower, this situation is always trouble, I was trying to think, what happened "I didn't do anything last night, it was a quiet run, what the fuck do they want me for?" I reported to the police office.

I said to the Jossman, (chief crusher, bonehead.) "What's going on?" he screamed at me. "Mess change. 3G, Seaman Gunners Mess – – – -, a broadside mess, with the Royal marine barracks on the Port side and seaman gunners on the starboard side. " "No buts, pack your kit and move. Now!" He threw a locker key at me for 3G mess.

I'd never been so insulted in my whole life, from being in charge of the mess, to mess change, all within a couple of minuets. I didn't know what this was all about, but I was sure as fuck about to find out, big time. I was fuming and there was just short of steam coming out of my ears. I knew blood was going to flow, but what I didn't know was how soon. I packed my kit to untold questions of what's going on, I said "I don't know, but I'm just about to find out".

I got to the hatch going down to the gunners mess, I called down "Can I speak to the Killick of the Mess" (Pricky Price) who soon appeared at the bottom of the ladder, accompanied by Slinger, I told him I had just been given a mess change to this mess and could I have his permission to move in.

"Certainly, Jim, pass your kit bag down and welcome to the mess. "

There were just the two Killicks down there Pricky Price (LHOM), and Slingsby, plus about a dozen big surly able seamen, all a lot older than me. You could cut the atmosphere with a knife. Then it started.

"We don't want any fucking greenies (Electricians) down here so you can fuck off now. " I was trying to ignore them, but the tension was explosive. "Which is my bunk?" Pricky allocated me the only spare, a bottom bunk.

Big mangled faced Harry Roe. "Are you fucking deaf, you're not sleeping in this MESS let alone below me so you can FUCK OFF now while you still CAN. " as he rears up in front of me sticking his big broken nose in my face.

Slinger steps in "Ok, Ok, rap it in, give the bloke a chance".

Roe said, "FUCK OFF" as he gave me a violent shove, which sent me over the mess deck table. I was so fired up I had the strength of two or three blokes. I was into him like dose of salts. He wasn't expecting a violent response, not from a Killick. Bang! Bang! Bang! I had him, a few more and he wrapped his hand in. There was a big cheer, I wondered who could be cheering.

I looked around and it was all the bootnecks who were sticking their heads round from their mess next door to see what all the commotion was about. Next thing Pricky LHOM. told Roe to go and get cleaned up and keep his mouth shut, which thank my lucky stars he did, at least he was a man about it, I could have been busted for striking a junior rating, although he was older and much bigger than me, and looked much like a punch drunk brawler with a mangled face, left over from the days of the old time boxing booths. I said, "Cheers Pricky and Slinger". I really appreciated that.

So I stowed my kit and was now a fully fledged mess member, the third Killick in the Gunners Mess. It wasn't long before the dust settled, and as luck would have it, they all turned out to be a great bunch of miscreants and toe rags, I was totally accepted and we had some great piss ups down there, and ashore. It turned out in the end to be a really good mess, of which I was proud to be a member.

Red Rider moved into the Bootnecks barracks next door, and Bungy Williamson moved into the T. A. S (Torpedo Anti Submarine) Mess amidships. I organised a run ashore that night, so we could fill in the missing information. I wanted to know what the fuck had happened the previous night to cause all these eruptions. The Navy bar ashore, just off the football field was a wooden hut with steps running up at one end and a few wooden tables inside and out. It opened about 1800 and closed at 2200, if not before. There was a small serving hatch through which we could purchase cans of Tennants Anne Lager. (Anne was the swimsuit girl on the can). It was all very meagre, but there wasn't' a Naval base as such. If a ship came in, the bar might be opened for business, but about a mile away, the pongo's had a new social club with modern facilities, air conditioning, bar, small stage and a western style crapper to boot, no need to dangle your bollocks between the footpads and provide big eats for the sand flies and anything else that fancied a belly full of the white mans delicacies.

We took a wander over there to sus. out our chances of gaining an invite to use the soldiers recreational facilities, especially over the coming Christmas period. We didn't really think we stood much of a chance, but what the hell, we'll give it a go.

I approached the Duty Senior member of the club to see if there was any chance of us using their facilities, he said the normal routine for guests was for the host to sign them in, but in our case we didn't know anyone, so providing we were all well behaved, and as a concession.

As it was nearly Christmas, we could sign our names in the Guest Book on the way in, and as the Pongo's arrived in dribs and drabs, they would be kind enough to counter sign our names in the guest book, sorted! well organised.

Thank you very much, brilliant! We were in and had somewhere to go over Christmas. There was still only cans of Tenants lager available to drink, but at least we were seated around a table indoors, and had the luxury of an air conditioning unit switched on. Magic!. He signed us in and we were in our element, we got him a bevy, then sat down to sort out the outstanding problem.

"Right, what the hell went on last night?" Helliwell was duty leading hand and the prick started as soon as you had gone ashore, "All beer (3 cans per man) must be consumed by 2200, and lights out at pipe down 2230, as per ships standing orders, I'm in charge and were going by the book. Any drips see me, any trouble and you'll be lifting your lids". He started giving the two AB's a hard time for chuntering away behind his back, not a good idea where there is alcohol involved, but the pressure had been building up and they'd more than had enough, then right out of the blue the safety valves lifted, they were up and after him, around the Mess deck table then around and round the mess, the tosser was going like a bat out of hell, with a couple of normally quiet and restrained hairy arse'd deck apes in hot pursuit, snapping at his heels and expelling hot breath down the back of his lily livered neck, their intention was to re-arrange his bollocks giving him a suitable pair of ear rings, he was up the ladder and burning round the upper deck in no time. His sphincter going like a football rattle.

The Midnight Muncher was still going like a train, with the pair of them still in contention, when right at the last minuet the Yellow Bellied Gobbler made his escape. He banged on the wardroom door, clearly in some form of distress, asking for the Officer of the Day (OOD), as best he could with what little breath he could still muster from his now nearly defunct lungs, then he reported he was frightened. What's the problem hookey?

"There's a gang down the mess, and they are after me. "

"Who is it?"

"LEM Green, AB Rider, AB Williamson. " – – – !, and I was ashore. The pervert was now trying to divert attention from his now rumbled highly illegal sexual activities as is the usual practise, carried out during the witching hours in the gulch. Which now, to all the residents dismay and embarrassment, had been re'named Gobblers Gulch. Which now didn't have the mysterious ring to it, and certainly wasn't a sought after address, on the contrary. All down to Halliwell the Porker, plus corrupting all the young lads, who wouldn't be mentioning this when they wrote home to mumsy.

Our fate was sealed, the bastard. I was warned by the coxswain not to think about any reprisals. In my frame of mind, I thought "we'll see about that. The Muncher is going to be stigmatized by the rest of the ships company, and for the rest of his time in the Navy. Too right!" It wasn't Minnie the moocher anymore, it was Millie the muncher, the Laird of gobblers gulch.

We'd been patrolling the Gulf again. It was very monotonous, stopping and searching dhows for illegal arms. Sometimes the Captain would take us in and anchor just off shore so we could do a spot of fishing. We'd catch all sorts of weird things. Groupers, which could be massive, parrot fish and even small sharks, which always caused a commotion, but the best laugh was whipping the sea snakes into the crowd on the quarterdeck and watching everyone scatter, me included because we didn't know which ones were venomous.

The AB's in the moored seaboats down on the boom, which were illuminated by a yardarm group of lights, which in turn would attract dozens of snakes from the depths, which the Dabtoes (AB's) would flick up from the side of their boat with the boathook, (an S shaped metal hook on the end of a six foot pole ued for controlling ropes, boats ETC.) into everyone leaning over the ships side fishing. They'd roar as we scattered. One of the bootnecks pulled in a four foot sand shark which was flapping about in the port waist. None of the roughy toughy Royal Marines would go anywhere near it, then Fred, the Skin and Bone NAAFI canteen assistant, flopped onto its back, grabbed its two pectoral fins, held its head to the deck with his head and was screaming "get the hook out"

Everybody moved back and there was Fred, the eighteen year old can man, built like a racing snake on the back of this shark holding it down, brilliant! Eventually after much jocularity about all going down below and leaving Fred the shark wrestler to his fate they moved in to help, and held its head down to the deck with a brush, while they extracted the hook with a pair of pliers. Fine, but what next, the shark was free now but still had Fred on its back. Fred daren't let go unless he finished up as its lunch. Eventually someone got hold of its tail with a cloth round it and someone else held its head down with a long handled brush keeping well clear of the biting parts. They practised once, then one … , two … ., three … . "roll Fred, roll". Fred rolled off and the stoker on the tail end heaved it into the air and over the side.

He tried to get it to land in the Sea boat below and put the shits up the deck apes (able seamen) down there, to get our own back for the snakes, but missed and the shark was away, freedom. There was one big cheer as Fred was lifted aloft and paraded around the quarterdeck as the shark wrestling hero of H. M. S. Eskimo 1965. Talk about making your own entertainment. Pencil thin Fred, all 8 stone of him was now the ships and middle East shark wrestling champion, he loved that, and all the ballyhoo that went with it.

We were back alongside in Bahrain for Christmas 65. I was twenty two the previous August 8th, it's now a couple of days before Christmas and I'm having a Christmas drink with half a dozen of the leckies from my old mess. I'd been invited down the mess for a drink but there was no way I would enter that mess again, not with that spineless brown hatter now in charge, so here we are, guests in the Army Social Club early Saturday afternoon, after our tot and lunch onboard. We were all sitting around a table, enjoying having a drink together for the first time since the trouble, and having a really good time, reminiscing etc. It just so happened that Nutty Bar, the stroppy Killick stoker, was on the next table having a Christmas drink with his stokers. It all went well for the first couple of hours then the stokers started getting a bit boisterous.

I noticed the Army guys down by the bar were whispering and nodding towards us. They obviously didn't approve of what was going on, and I got Nuttie's attention, and said "Keep it down a bit, it's a bit too much for the Pongo's and they don't like it".

He just said, "Fuck off, fucking greenies" and they started building a large pyramid on the table, with all the empty Tenants Anne beer cans. I thought 'Oh no, there's going to be trouble here', the tension was growing and you could cut the atmosphere with a knife. The Pongo's were all watching, my lads have now gone all quiet and are looking at me for inspiration, and are right behind me and ready for anything I say. I said "Pack it in, Nutty, we're guests here, plus we want to use the club over Christmas. "

He shouted "Oh yeah Green, and what the fuck are you going to do about it?"

All my lads are quiet, all his lads are quiet, all the pongo's are looking on. He leaned back on his chair put his foot under the rim of the table top, shouted "Green!" and then kicked the table over. There was the table and fifty or sixty full and empty beer cans, flying everywhere all over the highly polished floor, and making one hell of a racket and mess. I wasn't angry, I just felt that everything had been thrown away, what a prick, we won't be able to come here for Christmas after this. The whole Ships company will be barred from now on. Then he shouted , "Green what are you going to do about that", I said "There's no point, the damage is done. " He obviously took that as a weakness on my part, wrong. He leapt over to where I was sitting and said, "Outside or I'll hammer you where you are".

My emotions went from being just little a bit concerned to such an abnormal fury, so quickly. I went absolutely berserk. "Right Barr, get your fucking arse outside now. "

I was away in front, "Come on you fucking twat, I'm going to rip your fucking head off. Now move, outside" I was through the foyer and past the toilets and through the entrance door, where there was a two foot wall supporting a raised flower bed. My brain was going like the clappers. How had it come to this, we didn't want to be in the shit all over Christmas onboard, we could both get stuffed. As he came through the door, I tried to calm the situation.

I said "Sit down here Nutty, lets sort this out. " "O. K. " then he gave me a big Glasgow kiss, a vicious head butt. My nose broke, split and burst like a ripe plum. I brought my right arm up as hard as I could. My fist clenched and caught him a beauty hammer blow to the left hand side of his face. His whole head seemed to burst. He went backwards on to this small wall. I had spun round and my second blow, a big punch to the same side of his face, instantaneously followed by another two. Bang! Bang! He had gone from the sitting position to lying back in the flowerbed, blood pumping everywhere he was unconscious lying on his back chorkling, his teeth were showing through the side of his face, he couldn't breath properly with that amount of blood running to the back of his throat, I looked up and saw this armed Pongo running towards me. I took off down the side of the club, he's lifting his rifle up and shouting "Halt!" I dived in behind a big fuel tank before he could opened fire, I undid my flies, and then came walking out back towards the Pongo with the .303 rifle. "He went that way" I said, fastening my flies and the Pongo went galloping off over the playing fields looking for me.

There was an Army landrover just arrived to sort out the situation. I leaned over to see how Nutty was, they were administering first aid, and not before time. He was unconscious and choking on all the blood.

The Army Captain said "Did you do this?"

I said, "You're joking, he's my mate it was one of your lot, quick get him to hospital, he can't breathe".

I said, "The guy's run over the playing fields, one of your blokes is after him. "

I could see Nuttie's teeth and white jaw bone through the Port side of his face, the flesh was just hanging his teeth had done the job they had evolved for, slicing meat. They lifted him up and put him in the landrover and away. I rushed into the toilets. I was covered in blood. My snoring organ was pumping claret.

I washed my arms and face the best I could and grabbed a load of toilet paper to stem the bleeding of my broken nose and legged it. I had to get back onboard cleaned up, and turned in before the shit hit the fan, as I knew it was going to. I was thinking it was an amazing run ashore, although it all happened so quickly. I wondered what the outcome would be.

I didn't see anyone from inside the club. They just let us get on with it, but the Pongos must have phoned for assistance which was why the landrover had arrived. I arrived down the gunners mess without any questions being asked. Everyone turned a blind eye and said now't. (the three wise monkey's, hear no evil, see no evil, speak no evil) I was up to the bathroom rapid, quick shower, wash the blood out of my white uniform and leave it to soak in bleach over night in my dhobi bucket, then ease my nose into a better position, pull the gash together and fix it as best I could with a plaster, and got turned in. See what tomorrow brings, I'm imagining all hell is going to break loose, never mind we'll find out soon enough.

I awoke first thing in the morning, my hooter was pulsating like a Victualled members knob on ladies day, it was all scabbed up like a syphilitic Bollock. I kept a low profile and went for my shower – no-one was saying anything. They were all looking in every direction but mine. Its no good, I've got to find out how nutty Barr is, the silence is deafening the Turkey could be dead. I got dressed and I am on my way down to the Stokers Mess, I'm really worried about what I'm going to find out, but its got to be done. I'm descending the ladder into their mess when Mickey Quinn, who was an Irish boxer with a great sense of humour and a right piss head, as soon as he realised it was me coming down the ladder into their mess, he shouts "Jimmy" and when he saw the minor damage to my face, he roared with laughter.

"Sue him Jimmy, sue the bastard. "

By now all the mess members were smiling and taking the piss. To my left at the bottom of the ladder I saw Nutty, the Killick of the Stokers Mess but not that well liked. He was looking into the mirror and all I could see was the right hand side of his face. Thank Christ it was alright.

I said, "How are you Nutty?"

He turned around and I couldn't believe what I was seeing. His left eye had disappeared under the swelling. It looked like a pig's head, almost as though he had another head on the left side. He had stitches from his mouth to just under his ear.

He hadn't been back on board long and it had taken them all night to stitch him up. Apparently, they had to stitch the inside of his swollen mouth, first, and then the outside. They asked him who did it, he said he didn't know "Some fucking Pongo". and that was plausible as that was the general name of the game. All the stokers were giving me the thumbs up. I had never been so relieved since the old King died.

There was an enquiry going on onboard ship, and ashore in the Pongo's Barracks, but miraculously no one had seen a thing, Amazing wasn't it! – – - bloody marvellous I'd say. About a week later I was going for a shower after work. I had my towel on soap bag and dhobi'ing in my Dhobi bucket, when one of the officers was walking past the top of our mess. He saw it was me coming up the ladder sported a hint of a smile, winked and gave me the thumbs up. Brilliant everybody was satisfied a good job done well. Confirmation everyone knew but nobody knew, a nods as good as a wink to a blind man with piles.

Nutty was a completely different bloke after that he didn't upset anyone again for the rest of the commission. The incident just happened to do everyone a favour. Christmas Day came and about twenty of us from the Gunners Mess and the Marine Barracks had our tots then went to the Army Social Club for a couple of hours. We'd had a good laugh with all the squaddies, now it was time to go back onboard for Christmas dinner. We were starving we could have eaten a horse between two bread vans.

We got back onboard only to find the galley closed and to be told, "you're too late, you've missed it. " We couldn't have been more pissed off.

We were down the mess having a can of beer when for some reason I had to go up to the Bridge. On my way I passed the wardroom whose door was open and the curtain slightly open. I peered inside and couldn't believe what I saw. The big wardroom table was set for what looked like a banquet. All the food was in a big heated trolley all the wine de-cantered in giraffes. I looked everywhere but there wasn't an officer to be seen. They were obviously all ashore somewhere (probably illegally). I was down the mess in a flash and said "I've found our dinner". Quite a lot came up to the wardroom, the rest couldn't believe we were about to demolish the Officers Christmas dinner. Surely they'd just about hang us for it. It was like a feast for the conquerors.

We were starving and we sure were enjoying this, plenty of wine the turkey was being ripped apart, quite evenly as it happened by one of the bootnecks, all our feet on the table and were having a sing song, about a dozen matelots really going for it. We had our fill and then it was time to thin out before the return of the swine. As we left I looked back, what a sight, I would have loved to have been a fly on the wall when the pigs arrived back for their Christmas dinner. – Too fucking late.

As it was we were down our own messes turned in, sleeping it off getting ready for the evening. Unbelievably nothing was said by the Grunters. They had obviously returned and it must have been considered bad form to create a storm, especially as they would all have been three parts pissed anyway, and we might just have decided Roast Pork was our next feast.

They would just keep it in mind and make us pay for it as soon as the opportunity arose. (small'y apples, little acorns.) We had a quite run ashore over at the Army camp without any obvious occurrences which made a change. Boxing Day, the cox'n came down the mess just to show his face. He'd had a few wets already in the other mess's. We had already had our tots, (so we couldn't ply him with rum) so he joined in with us, polishing off what beer we did have, and after about an hour he's laughing like a drain. He was well on the way burbling like a rock ape, and saying what a mistake it was to have put Halliwell in charge of the Greenies Mess, and he shouldn't have moved us, "but" he said, it came from above, and he couldn't do a thing about it. Just as I thought it was a conspiracy. Big Ron was too big a character for those wardroom minnows to control, and now he'd been drafted they were after being seen to have got some form of authority back, slimy bastards. I said "we would offer you another beer but we're running out". (the big hook).

I said, "Can we purchase a crate of beer?" (We knew there was no way legally as it's all issued formally, mess by mess in the Forenoon with the Officer of the Day present overseeing it.)

He said "No way. "

Then I started on him. "Are you telling us that you're the cox'n (Head policeman) and you can't even organise a crate of beer on your own ship. "

"I'm not saying that".

I kept on at him for about half an hour, while we're still feeding him beer.

"Ok just one case".

"Brilliant, I've cracked it. "

I paid him for a case and he said "come with me, bring a big bucket and a cloth to hide it in. "

It was late afternoon and the ship was dead. Everyone was turned in sleeping it off. I followed him up the ladders.

Wondering where we were going.

I couldn't believe it, we went onto the bridge, just beside the Captain's chair, where he navigates the ship from, there was a semi. concealed wooden hatch in the deck. When lifted, low and behold another floor three feet below, with lots of pigeon holes where all the signalling flags, pennants etc were stored. He pulled the most difficult wooden structure aside, then fuck a rat, there were about three dozen cases of beer stowed behind the flags, right under the Captain's arse! Brilliant! I know where the illegal stash is now, and I'm not telling anybody. Were going to be laughing kit bags from now on, and they can't do a fucking thing about it. It's the Chief's mess's contraband, and I'm going to be dipping my fucking bread in, – – – – – - Deep. – – – -Ace. We drank the case of beer and sent the cox'n off on his way wondering what the flying fucking hell had happened. There are more ways of killing a pig than choking it to death with strawberries.

Shortly afterwards there was a film being shown in the dining hall just above our mess. It was in the afternoon and it could well have been New Year's Eve. Well it was well after tot time and it sounds as if there was a riot going on up above. I went up to have a look and all hell was going on. The officer of the day turned up at the far side of the dining hall, shouting and trying to take charge of the situation. He had no chance and so disappeared for about half an hour, he was sent down again by his superiors but still did not have a cat in hells chance of calming this lot down. I hadn't a clue what had kicked them all off but they weren't half going some.

Next news they sent the supply officer down with the Great Big Book of Words. I had never heard it for real, either before or since. He started to read the riot act. He's supposed to have an armed guard with him at this point. He's shouting "disperse, disperse". The poor, four eyed twat was shaking in his boots. The lad's reply was a shower of beer cans. He promptly topped up his trollies and legged it back from whence he had emerged, the wardroom or more likely the bridge, with his Big Book of Words tucked securely under his arm and his spindly legs having great difficulty supporting the now even more terrified specimen making its way to some form of refuge up above somewhere. I thought fuck this and thinned out back down the mess. Don't get involved in this one.

I think the wardroom thought better of it and kept their heads down. As soon as it went quiet, all the troops dispersed to their own messes so as not to be implicated. After all had gone quiet the duty watch was detailed off to clean up the dining hall, as though the recent events hadn't taken place, all ready for the following day's breakfast, which was train smash, shit on a raft and cackle berries. All well ... . . that's life in a blue suit.

We were well into the New Year by now, early 1966, the year we won the football world cup. I decided it was time to move on (advancement) and so I requested the paperwork I needed to prepare for my P. P. E. for Petty Officer Electrician. As it happened one of the other LEM's Fred Baines, who was a couple of years older than me and also fancied his chances in the P. O. 's mess, said he'd boff up with me. I soon found out why. Fred was a good bloke but he wasn't the brightest light on the tree, so to put it in a slightly more direct perspective, he was as thick as fucking pigshit. Which from my viewing made him an ideal candidate for the Wardroom. Where most of them had had there heads blown anyway, but which didn't stop them from strutting about full of Piss and self importance.

Well we worked through the curriculum over the next few months, and we were just about as ready as we were going to be, so we both put in a request form to be allowed to sit the written part of the examination. Our requests were handed in to our divisional office.

From that moment on, we were assuming they would be granted and were waiting to be given the date of our written. Fred was panicking and I was saying "don't worry it's a piece of piss. "

Fred got his request form back, granted, to sit the written exam in two days time. I got mine back, not granted, I couldn't believe it, the Bastards. They had watched me revising and swatting up all the new stuff for months, the fucking arseholes, talk about little acorns. They had watched me flog up and worry about it for months then hit me with this. To say I was gutted was a master of under statement. Fred took the written and they passed him, he then took the oral and they passed him.

Then three weeks later, He was rated up to Acting Local, Petty Officer now to really rub the salt in, they gave him a job change to head of the domestic section, which I had been running for months, thus making him my boss. He was so embarrassed and kept saying sorry. I said "Give over Fred, it's those bastards sticking the knife in. " I did feel as though I was on my own. Well if I am, fuck em all I'll show them.

Slinger and the two bootnecks were ship's divers, frogmen in the old parlance. The idea of having ships divers was to enhance the safety of the ship in many ways. One of them was to be able to search the hull of the ship for limpet mines, or any other form of explosives the enemy may have been able to plant on the ship. It was a voluntary job secondary to your own professional job onboard. To qualify as a ships diver required initially, an aptitude test to see if you were capable, you had to prove physically, mentally and be ok medically, and if all that was positive, some time in the future, you would be booked into a four week course at the Royal Naval Diving School, down in the West country at HMS Drake, Plymouth. It was a tough old course apparently, but not without good cause as people's lives were constantly on the line.

The people deemed suitable for the job had to be top line. There was no room for indecisive, 'look at me' wimps. It was one serious job. There were plenty of good times, Ban Yans, barbecues, spear fishing. I fancied having a go at that. Later, we were hearing some right old stories from the lads who had been up in the Radfan Mountains up from Aden. They had photographs of the enemy beheading their captives. There was one I saw, the victim was kneeling down in the unshipping of head position, the sword had gone through the neck and the head was half way to the ground. There was one thing for sure, you didn't have time to hesitate with these bastards. Do them, before they do you.

There was another story they told, one of the Arabs in Crater city had badly abused and slaughtered his wife, and then had committed the unforgivable sin – – – – – he got caught. The only saving grace for him, and the thing that kept his head fixed securely to his body was, it was only a woman, so he wouldn't be facing the death sentence. He was being held in a big deep pit in the ground, fully chained up but mobile. He could walk around his pit. Well apparently his situation had been passed onto the soldiers who had been asked if they could rescue him (in these situations all sorts of deals are dealt). A message was got to him. A helicopter will rescue him soon, be ready, grab the rope. The chopper flew in with knotted rope dangling into the pit. The prisoner hangs on, up, and away they go, a piece of piss.

The crew hauled him up into the cab, shut the doors, then up and really away. So the story goes, they keep on ascending and travelling until they are way up above the Radfan Mountains where our boys are being killed, and they don't know why, for that answer you would have to wake up the politicians from their well earned sleep, and ask them why they sent the troops.

They flew over the enemy position and said goodbye to the murderer. They opened the door and gave him the bums rush, still chained, I suppose there must have been a message there, Somewhere, for someone.

Everyone onboard has had more than enough of this poxed up place. The Persian Gulf is definitely the arsehole of the world, and fuck our luck were bollocks deep right up it. I think I've only got another couple of months to do onboard before the first phase of the Third Commission fly out to relieve us. Thank Fuck.

A memo came out asking for volunteers for ship's divers, I thought Ace, 'I'll have some of that'. I put in a request to take the aptitude test, and if successful go on the Diver's Course, if and when I could be spared. I was sent for by the ship's diving officer only to be told, you're a habitual drinker, "Sorry, we don't want you". That was a laugh for a start, royal navy divers had the envied reputation of being big drinking, roughy toughy Punchy, don't give a fuck, work hard, play hard, there's a good chance we won't be here tomorrow sort of guys, who drank rum by the bucket full. So that was just more bullshit engineered by the lame brains up in the pig sty.

These arseholes are really getting up my nose and way past the bridge

"Because you are a habitual drinker. " Excuse me.

"For Fuck's sake, do me a favour, we were all issued with a third of a pint of two and one, hundred proof rum, and three cans of beer every day, so that was minimum. Just having your ration would qualify everybody for that pathetic title. "

I'm sick to the back teeth now with these clowns performing. They've got it in for me and I'm going nowhere, all this and just since big Ron went on draft, I can't wait for my relief to arrive so I can go home on a bit of leave then start afresh on a new ship.

I do know one thing for sure, as how hard they try, these fucking Morons won't crack me. Because I know I'm better than they are, and that's good enough for me.

The next time we came alongside, Slinger was on duty but I just wanted to get off the ship for a while, so as soon as leave was piped, I was off. I used to like going off on my own in the UK doing just what I wanted to do, but it wasn't such a good idea abroad as you could so easily finish up with your throat cut and your tripes hanging out. I'd had a good run on my own. I had a good curry early, a few wets in the town and finished off in the Pongo's Club having a laugh with them. I walked back to the ship, it must have been about midnight.

I walked up the gangway and asked for my station card, when out of the shadows jumped the officer of the watch, sub Lieutenant Sheppey, my Divisional Officer the 'Poisoned Dwarf'. He was about my age but a high flying radio bod. Straight away, he said "Your speech is slurred and your eyes are glazed, you're drunk. Get your head down and report to the coxn's office first thing in the morning.

This was a set up if ever I've seen one. I started thinking seriously. These bastards are after busting me, if they win, they will not just have stopped my promotion to senior rate, but taken away my leading rate, which in effect would have finished me in the navy. I get turned in but I can't sleep, it's just going over and over in my mind. It seemed more and more obvious Sheppey had been told to nail me.

It was a set up, definitely, I'm shaking and absolutely furious. Somehow I managed to fall asleep. As soon as Call the Hands was piped in the morning, I was up like a cock on pay night, it all came flooding back. Right I'm not having this. I got dressed and legged it up to Sheppey's cabin. This is going to be all or nothing. I burst into his cabin, he was just getting dressed, I said "you were waiting for me last night it was a set up?" "No, It wasn't. " I could tell he was lying.

"Yes, you were, its a conspiracy, and I'm being victimised. " "No, it's not, and your not". My face by now is blood red and nearly bursting, I've stuck my face right into his and I'm screaming "Right, if you don't admit it, I'm going down to the main switchboard and I'm going to parallel two steam turbo generators, one hundred and eighty degrees out of synch. I have written a letter with the reasons for my actions and your name is there at the top of the list. "

I turned to leave in very great hurry. I have never seen terror like that in a bloke's face before. (I would have cleared machinery spaces first.)

"Stop, Stop, Okay what the hell do you expect. "

I turned back to him and screamed, "Right Cox'ns office, now, I want this in writing. "

He saw right away he was stuffed. I can't remember exactly how he went about it, but he dropped it on condition I didn't carry out my objective. I must have agreed, from now on it was an enforced truce. From now on if I put a foot wrong I'm as good as dead. Well one things for certain, I wont be getting anywhere with this shower of shit. I shall have too keep my nose exceptionally clean from now on. Unbeknown to me it was already to late, as I was soon to find out. Roll on my draft. A couple of weeks later we had an invite up to RAF Muharaque, the Air Base in Bahrain to play the RAF Police (Red Caps), at rugby.

We were all going, anything to get off the ship and not have to breathe the same air as those childish hooray fucking Henry's. It will be a big piss up at least. We arrived there and a couple of the troops were showing us around the air base. They had asked if one of the fighter pilots would take us up for a spin. I was right in there. This would be the "A" ride to beat all "A" rides, They would let us know the details later. We met another one of the lads on duty doing security perimeter rounds, they were all dog handlers with Alsations which had a particular penchant for Arab blood, As we approached the main gate, the Arab taxi drivers were voicing abuse through the security fence. The handler started whispering under his breath to his dog, "Wogs. Wogs. "

The transformation in the dog was amazing, he bared his teeth, accompanied by a low vicious growl. The making of his day would have been to sink his big canine molars into their abusive black arses. The wogs soon backed off the fence. It was easy to see who was in charge here, and it certainly wasn't the fudge packers. It was time to get changed for the game. There was a lot of good hearted banter going on and as it turned out was a good game, but being as we were the guests we let them win.

Much jocularity, everyone's taking the piss out of each other, situation normal.

We got cleaned up and with much exited anticipation went down to the conning tower, where we met the pilot for our promised flight in a R. A. F. Jet fighter plane, but unfortunately the trip had to be cancelled. There was a Vulcan 'V' Bomber on the runway, surrounded by countless bodies going about their business, loading with what looked like a gigantic silver beer barrel glistening in the hot afternoon sun, but was in fact, about twenty sizes bigger. Everywhere was cordoned off. When I enquired as to what it was, I was told a "hydrogen bomb". If at first you don't succeed, pull your foreskin over your heed, drop the bomb, and kiss your arse goodbye. Fair enough, I was really chokker at not getting to fly in the fighter and apparently so was the pilot. He had been looking forward to frightening the shit out of us matelots, as apparently he was going to fly so fast, spinning, looping, diving at the ground determined to empty us out from both ends, making us honk and follow through.

Still, it wasn't to be so the coppers went ahead with the only thing left, to get us as pissed as newts and they sure did that.

They were a great bunch, there was this one guy who recited this poem he'd written during his many hours of boredom, whiling away the hours and days in the desert swatting sandflies and roasting his nuts off, we only heard it a couple of times and that was forty two years ago.

> *I once took a plunge in a bucket of thunge*
> *I dived from the pelmet, in my anti-thunge helmet,*
> *I sank to the top, with a crinkling plop*
> *And the inglescarb zoobed on the groot, tra la la*
> *And the inglescarb zoobed on the groot.*

Amazing, remembering a bit of nonsensical rhyme after all these years. It was a cracking run ashore. I awoke in the morning in my bunk and I was starving hungry and it was a bit late and breakfast had just about finished, so I legged it to the dining hall with just a towel around me, hoping to grab a handful of scran before the shutters came down. Hard cheese, too late. The shutter was down but with a three inch gap at the bottom. I looked underneath and all the breakfast trays were gone, but there was a chipolata sausage on the inside of the counter, good I'll have that. I stuck my arm under the shutter, reached and got hold of the greasy snorker and pulled it. It didn't move but a big pair of goldfish bowl eyes came up from the other side of the counter. It was the Goanese cook's middle finger. He was bending down on the other side, and when he arose to see what the fuck had got a grip of his finger, his eyes were bulging out like bulldogs bollocks God only knows what he thought was hanging from his finger probably one of the faggots they were doing for dinner, anyway, bad luck, fresh out, roll on lunch.

It's mid-afternoon now, and I'm checking the upper deck lighting an hour before sunset. This is done so any faults can be rectified before sunset, when all the upper deck lighting is switched on and the flags come down at the Ceremonial Sunset each evening. The main steaming light hasn't come on and that is situated at the top of the main mast. There's quite a storm blowing up at the moment, so I needed a safety harness, my tools and a spare lamp before I can go aloft. I have to let the Officer of the Watch know of my intentions, together we have got to get permission from the Captain to stop all revolving radar aerials and switch off any other dangerous transmitters up the various masts. The fuses have to be removed and signed for to make sure someone doesn't inadvertently switch on an aerial and knock me off the mast or start transmitting on one of the powerful radars, which would fry my nuts and eyeballs, with the least worrying consequences of sterilising me. I'm about fifty feet up the mast and shackled to the yardarm with the safety belt, but safe is not what I'm feeling. The ship is rocking and a rolling as the storm is blowing up. The top of the mast is way over the crashing waves on the port side then swinging all the way over to the starboard side.

I'm hanging on for dear life and trying to undo the seized bolts holding the light fitting together, whilst trying not to drop any tools. I've got a big, dry rag down my waterproof jacket to dry out the rain from inside the light fitting. I'm absolutely frozen and wet through but it's got to be done plus a lot down below will be enjoying giving me a hard time, but I will definitely do it. After a good hour, the job is complete and I make my way down to the Upper Deck, where I again seek permission to test all Upper Deck and navigation lighting.

On completion, I report to the officer of the day, all upper deck lighting tested and correct, and then proceed to make sure all radar and radios are restored to their serviceable conditions. Time for a hot shower to warm my bones up, then dinner and a couple of cans, unless I can get any more.

We've just been told that the first phase ship's compliment of the commission is to be flown home in a couple of weeks. That's brilliant news. Thirsty first of March 66 to be precise. We just hoped it wasn't an April Fool's gag. It wasn't, we had an RAF flight from Muharaque, Bahrain in a VC10, RAF transport. Talk about a well used plane. I was sitting by the door on the port side and we were taking off in a tropical storm and I couldn't believe it, the rain was pissing in through the closed door. I complained to the RAF stewardess and she brought a bucket. She said it would stop when we rose above the clouds, which it obviously did marvellous the wonders of modern technology.

CHAPTER 15

A spell ashore and reminiscing

I received a good welcome home again. I was bronzy, bronzy at the beginning of April, always an advantage when we're out on the razzle, which I was with a vengeance. It was good being on leave with bags of money. I remember waking up in some strange places all over Rochdale and the surrounding area's. I can recall making small talk with Miss Rochdale, one of the girls I'd always fancied from the Tech. (school). The next thing it was early in the morning, I was looking out over Rochdale from the top floor of a brand new block of flats. Quite impressive at the time.

Father was working at Birch Hill Hospital as a stoker in the boiler house, about a mile up the road from our house. He was about five foot six tall, wiry and fifty seven years of age. He didn't get on with his opposite number in the boiler house. He was telling me this other stoker was a big bloke and about forty years old. They had had an argument and had jnfuriated this fellow who then lifted pater up against a wall with hands round his neck and was strangling Father. Well he couldn't breathe and was turning blue and about to flake out, so the bloke released his grip and Father, being the annoying so and so he could be, said "What did you stop for, are you frightened?"

He was enough to make a Saint swear, then he says to him "You wait till my lad comes home from the Navy, he will make you pay for that". Just you wait you'll be sorry. Cheers Dad, just what I needed. He's told me this, but he just wont leave it, and he keeps on, "When are going to see him?"

I asked him when was the best time and he said "Saturday lunch time. He comes off duty at twelve noon and has a couple of pints in the pub just down the hill from the hospital the Ox and Plough. "

"Okay, I'll see you in the Ox at twelve on Saturday. "

This is going to be good, I don't even know the guy. Were sitting in the pub Saturday lunch time with a pint apiece waiting for this fellah to show up. Sure enough just after mid day he comes in, Father always told us kids not to point, but he's got himself worked up and keeps poking my leg to my annoyance.

"There he is, there he is".

I said, "Leave it, I'll bide my time".

"What are you waiting for?"

He's beginning to get on my goat now. We're playing dominoes (5's and 3's) and I'm keeping my eye on the big stoker. He'd had a couple of pints, then he stood up and went out to the toilet to water his donkey. This is it, I let him get in there and then I was up and after him. He was standing at a big continuous urinal and the place was empty, so as I went in, I walked over and stood right next to him.

He must have thought "this isn't right". He probably thought I was a hat rack,

I bumped into him with my left side. He just looked at me, I said "My name's Harry Green (the same as Dads). He said "Oh, fucking hell, – – no. " He'd just finished the night shift. I said "I want to see you outside, around the back now. "

"Oh no, no, I'm sorry let me buy you a beer". He was shaking like a leaf and I said, "If you ever touch him again, you're fucking dead".

"I wont!, I swear!, I swear!. "

I left him there, went back to finish our domino's and said to Father "Don't mention it again, it's sorted. " And so it was.

Father was strutting around like a dog with two dicks. I walked home with him then caught the bus into town to see all the lads and have a proper dinner time session.

It's hard to believe these days, just how good it was to be home, and among your own kind. I'm glad I enjoyed it then. We didn't realize these were the dying years of the beautiful England we all grew up in, it was about to be swamped by all the thieving, lying, criminal parasites from all over the World, and the land our forefathers had fought and died for, for over a thousand years, would be surrendered to our enemies, who would then slither into places of power ie. Unions, schools, colleges, Councils, Parliament. Then bring out directives to be issued to our schools, who then taught re-written history to the detriment of England, who by the way was giving succour to these thankless scavengers, to such an extent that now, the school teachers from that ilk haven't a clue about anything, including reading, writing, arithmetic or any private personal use of their own brains, so what can they pass onto the next generation? It seems as though they just have to apply for and pay for their papers of qualifications which aren't worth the paper they are written on, and the poor University graduates haven't had their brains developed enough to realise they've been conned into massive debts by the lying, thieving, parasitic imbeciles who now line their pockets with our money and call themselves members of Parliament.

If any of them lived in Saudi Arabia, they wouldn't have a hand left to either wipe their arse or eat with. To try and put a fair label on these arseholes is virtually impossible. The words that come to mind are incompetent of knowing their own incompetence, but that can't be right because to be incompetent of something, surely implies that you should know something to be incompetent about. But, alas, after listening to the verbal diarrhoea excreted from the holes in their faces, with their incessant diatribe, these pathetic miscreants are not capable of knowing. Well that's enough of those Motherfuckers for now, although they're bound to resurface again shortly, floundering around in the filth of their own making. It's just too much to hope they drown in it.

That reminds me of Mountbatten, the Queen's cousin, Noel Coward's 'Bosun' as he used to call him. He was Captain of HMS Kelly during the war. It was a small escort destroyer. The bloke, by his own admission disobeyed Admiralty orders to position his ship in a certain location, he decided he knew better and went looking for the enemy ship off France, off his own bat. As it happened he located the German battleship but any other person, Captain etc. would have been Court Marshaled for direct disobedience of orders. He didn't know what the Admiralty plan was, the point being his ship was engaged (came under fire) by the enemy and sunk.

Among all the wreckage and oil floating on the surface, was Mountbatten with the rest of the oil covered survivors. He recognised one of the P. O. stokers from the boiler room. "Ah, Petty Officer Stokes, I see you managed to survive".

"Yes, sir, as you can see, all the shit gets to the top in the end. "

As with all officers of a certain background, with all its associated perks and privileges, he was promoted on the fast track until he was the biggest shit of all. The Last Viceroy of India, you couldn't make it up.

When I joined HMS Sheffield, some time ago, I was given the task of repairing and returning to serviceability, the Mountbatten steering indication system. (A system of indicating lights, connecting the bridge wheel house to the tiller flat, the after steering position.) The idea was to give an illuminated indication of the position of the rudder to various steering positions around the ship. It was merely a doubling up of the rudder indication system that was already in place.

As I learned, it was a really costly exercise to have this system fitted to all ships but the orders came from the one who had to be obeyed, Admiral of the Fleet, Lord Mountbatten. It was so time consuming and ineffective. Everyone wanted rid of it. Eventually, when the man was retired from active service, the systems were removed from all ships. A right bloody joke! One bloke can cause so much chaos and be publicly revered for it. Well he was eventually blown up by the I. R. A. kippers, in his small weekend cruiser, while fishing off the north west coast of Ireland. That was Prince Charles' dear old Uncle Dickie and Noel Cowards bosun gone for a burton. To join the rest of the Hooray Henry Hat racks, in the great Ball room in the sky. What bits they could find of him were given one of the best funerals this country has ever seen, together with all the bullshit that goes with it. Just after I joined HMS Eskimo, the ship was on a courtesy visit to Glasgow. We had sailed up the West Coast of England and the ships company were looking forward to a run ashore in Glasgow that night. We were supposed to arrive at about 1800. It was in the middle of Winter and it was blowing a right bastard as we made our way through the small Islets on our way.

It couldn't have been easy for the young navigating officer, as the approaches to the Clyde are just a maze of small islands and inlets. Well, in his confusion he had taken us up the wrong channel, so now we could not make anywhere near our ETA (Estimated time of arrival) so a signal would have been sent saying we had been delayed. The Captain would have made the decision to ask permission to anchor in Lamlash Bay, on the Isle of Arran. Permission granted, we anchored in the bay a few hundred yards out from Lamlash. By now, all the usual alkies were straining at the leash asking if shore leave was to be granted. The officers couldn't believe anyone would want to risk an open seaboat journey in such weather just for a few pints ashore. Well they submitted saying the last boat back would be at 2330. "Don't be adrift".

So they lowered the seaboat at piped 'privileged leave' which meant only people who had never been adrift 'late' before, were granted leave. I was the second into the boat and it was an evolution just getting in it. Big waves lifting us right up and banging against the ship's side. We all had life jackets on. There were about a dozen of us in what now seemed like an expedition. All aboard were beginning to nearly regret taking the leave, as it was turning into a life threatening evolution by the minuet. We set off for the just visible lights in the harbour, the freezing waves were coming right over us and we were soaking and frozen. If this had been compulsory, there would have been a near mutiny, but as we were going for some beer, it was sweet, alright!.

We arrived alongside the stone steps on the jetty. The cox'n of the boat did well to control the boat, saving it from being smashed to smithereens on the jetty. We all managed to disembark, and get up the steps out of the way of the breaking waves. We found out later the cox'n had a hell of a job getting the boat out of the harbour and then finding the ship, as it was by now blowing a full gale. We managed to find the only pub no problem. The landlord was over the moon with all this unexpected custom. He lit a big fire in the snug and we were all drying out on the outside, and drowning on the inside while singing our fucking heads off without a care in the world.

The cox'n had arrived back alongside and the boat was being swamped so the duty watch were called to hoist and stow the seaboat. It was now far too dangerous for any more evolutions, so re'launching the Liberty boat was out of the question.

"Fuck them ashore". Leave them, they'll survive.

Come eleven o' clock, we had last orders which included a couple of Wood's rum, to keep out the cold, "Oh Yeah!" We got ourselves wrapped up and left the hostelry singing our bollocks off. God knows what the locals and their kids thought of this, on a barely inhabited island, mid-week, near midnight in the middle of a snow storm, in the middle of Winter.

We arrived down at the wharf and it was blowing a real hooligan, the waves crashing over the mole. It was obvious there wasn't going to be an open whaler (sea boat) coming to pick us up. We've got to find somewhere dry out and get our head's down until morning. Someone had spotted a small church with a vicarage next door. Good idea. We proceeded to knock the vicar up, (not literally). The poor bloke must have thought there had been a shipwreck. He opened his door In the teeth of frantic gale and snow storm, in his jim jams and dressing gown, to be confronted by a dozen bedraggled matelots seeking shelter from the storm and many gallons of sustenance he might just manage to have to hand.

He soon sussed the situation and to be fair to him, he opened the small church hall next door. "You can stay in there until morning. At least you'll be dry and out of the weather"

He shut the door on the way out. We were all weighing up our situation. The place was empty, dirty and had an old, threadbare, moth eaten old carpet on the floor. First things first, we wanted a piss. We opened the door and evacuated twelve bladders all at once. When we finally got the door shut, we were in a right old state, covered from head to toe in dust, sleet and snow and the steaming remains of the landlord's finest were frozen to our bell bottoms. We needed some cover – under the carpet – great idea! That's got to be warmer. Twelve bodies under the carpet and our breath and farts would soon warm us up. We could not have dreamt how much dirt and grit was under that carpet as well as in it, that was now coming through and covering the lot of us.

We had to keep still so the dust settled and we could just about breathe, with some difficulty, but it was getting warmer so we put up with it. I was just about nodding off when I awoke with a start, or was it a fart Oh, no, the bands flashing up. First was the harmonious euphonium, "bhummmmmuh", then an inkling of the flute. The sax was next in, followed by the big trombone, fucking hell they're all at it. It's sure warming up now, and I hope to fuck nobody goes to light a fag. I could just imaging it, a right old mixture of oxygen, lots of dust particles for fuel and copious amounts of methane gas. A right explosive mixture if ever there was one ... ...

"Have you got a light Smudge?" Bang! The windows blown out, there's twelve ex. hairy arsed matelots on fire, running up and down outside the vicarage. All this commotion wakes up the Bish, who automatically thinks he's having a visitation from hell. With my imagination running riot, I must have slowly drifted off into a semi comatose sleep, not realizing I was being slowly gassed.

I awoke with a start, my head was splitting. I could hardly breathe and my mouth and nostrils were full of detritus. 'Where the fuck am I?' It smelt like a bear pit, it sounded like two, It wasn't far off. Everyone was waking up for a piss and what a fucking state we were in, all under this threadbare carpet. It's freezing, but at least the storms blown itself out, like most of the toe rags under the carpet waking up, we hang our bell ends out through the Bish's door, then retrieve them rapidly before frost bite sets in. We wake up the Bish. next door and say thanks, then make our way down to the jetty, to await the arrival of the liberty boat. Thank Christ, here it comes. We took the rope off the bowman, whilst the cox'n manoeuvred it alongside.

The look on the faces of the cox'n , the stoker and the bowman, they couldn't believe their eyes. The state of us, our uniforms, wet through, creased to hell and black as the ace of arseholes. They found it funny but there was no jocularity left in us. We arrived back onboard to the usual insults but after a shit, shower, shave, shampoo and a belly full of the chef's best fry up we were full of the joys of spring again and warm as toast. Roll on tot time 1145. We've got a big run ashore tonight in Glasgow, Sochihall Street. The rumour is, to keep your eye out for the girls on the strip. They've been around the block more times than a tramp's dog and most of them are carrying a damn sight more than their handbags, or the latter.

We left the ship after a few cans and a bite to eat at about half past six. We were berthed out of town down the river at Greenock, so we had to get a fast black up into town, we had a few wets up and down the strip to pass the time until the clubs started to open, and the growlers began to surface. It was a bit rough in this area, a lot of the neanderthal's roaming the streets, carried cut throat razors, and I don't think late night shaving was on the agenda, so long as we were aware what to watch out for we would be okay. They used to say, "see you ya bastard what yu like at sewing, well stitch that bastard" leaving the victim with his face opened like a ripe tomato or two.

We'd had a skinful by about eleven and found ourselves in this club. It was very dark, more or less just dim red lighting. I had been dancing with some bird, and the next thing I knew I was outside, behind the club bollocks deep, steaming through a knee trembler up to my nuts in Jock guts. The old kidney wiper was going like a train. I fancied it was the Flying Scotsman on its way from London to Glasgow. We must just be passing Fleetwood and Morecombe Bay as I just caught a whiff of the sea, with the faint aroma of the fishing trawlers coming home with their catch.

'That's it fireman, keep stoking the boiler, we're picking up speed, Carlisle approaching but we're not stopping. It's an express, over the points, ... over the points ... . over the points ... . over the points. We ain't half going some now, the piston has developed a mind of its own. ... . over the points ... over the points. I just realize I haven't had a good look at the dial as yet. I glimpse down, fucking hell … . Captain Hook must have been here before me. She's got a big raw scar going from her forehead across her left eye, which was piercing me. In between whirling and oscillating like a marble in a tumble drier. Every time it stopped, it reminded me of Moby Dick eyeballing Captain Ahab. I slammed on the brakes … over the points … over points. I'm coming up to the vinegar strokes. No chance of stopping, the pistons red hot – into the tunnel … bang … bang … champagne corks are a popping. I'm flooding her guts, out of the tunnel over the points … . over the points into the station, lifting the safeties, releasing a full head of steam. We slowly grind to a halt. There's enough lubrication around to launch the QE II.

I slowly disembark and Popeye is trembling like a jelly on a spin drier, she's trying to walk but is having as much luck as new born foal on a tight rope, and she's got a backbone like a string of conkers, all over the place. I manage to straighten her up a bit and manoeuvre her into a taxi, so now Isiah's (one eye's higher than the other) off home rejoicing, and I'm off rejoicing too. looking for the rest of the troops and some more ale.

That reminds me, after we'd made our discreet exit from Santander, it was chins up lads, we're on our way to Lisboa (Lisbon) in Southern Portugal to spread our good will around another part of Europe. It's a game! It's a game! Well some people thought it was. We sailed up the harbour at high tide and berthed on the wharf just off a large bare earthen square and within sight of the town and its large international football stadium, to be seen over the tops of the local pan tiled dwellings.

It was a Saturday morning and a beautiful sunny day. All necessary work had to be completed before lunchtime so the ship could be left in the capable hands of the duty watch, whilst the rest of the crew would be let loose on Lisbon, to create whatever sort of havoc would be deemed appropriate, in whatever particular circumstances they happen to find themselves.

Unfortunately, I was in the sin bin, so I wouldn't be taking part in these forays. Whoever's game we were involved in, I must have fallen foul of a rule or two because I now found myself under punishment, namely stoppage of leave, so I would have observe the rest of the ships company's antics discreetly, soberly and just enjoy the drama as it unfolded, as it was bound to.

"All divers to the diving store". As we were berthing on a tidal river and in not very deep water, when the tide went out there wouldn't be sufficient water left for the ship to float in, so it would sit quite comfortably on the muddy bottom, but before this could happen, all underwater spying equipment, sonars etc. had to be lifted and stowed away in their appropriate housings safely, so as when the ship's bottom made contact with the river bed no damage would be incurred. After departmental reports to HQ1 that all under water equipment had been stowed correctly, to be absolutely sure no damage would ensue, the divers would carry out a bottom search of the ship, checking all the relevant equipment was stowed, and the hull was in good nick with no other problems, ie. foreign bodies caught up, wires, fishing nets – – -foreign bodies.

On completion, a report is made to HQ1, all external under water equipment is stowed and correct, all machinery space suction pumps stopped, so the divers don't get sucked up the intakes, to arrive in the engine room as a thick red porridge all concerned can now relax, and the tide will carry on doing what it always does regardless. The diving officer took this opportunity to let whichever of the lads were short on this months diving minutes, to make them up now and thus qualify for their diving pay. (nothing is given away in the forces. Unlike the civil service where it seems everything is given away or stolen). I was sitting with the bubble heads with a mug of tea, and listening to what they were up to. Two of the marines and Slingsby were only betting a tot of rum each as to who would be last to escape from under the ship, as the tide went out and it settled on the bottom.

"Fucking hell, the mad bastards. " I can imagine what it would be like if they got stuck, being impressed into the mud with a ship on your back and just no way of escape. "Life in a blue suit". I'm going to be watching this and no other Mother will realize what they're up to.

The three of them are over the side, outboard. They can make their air last just over an hour. The First Lieutenant has got his watch of seaman, with all the ship's mooring ropes loose, so as they don't restrain the ship as she drops with the tide, then eventually settles on the bottom, when all the securing ropes can finally be made fast to the bollards and everything made secure, gangway etc. The deck apes have got a lead line over the side to check the depth.

"About a foot to go, sir".

Wont be long now, I'm watching down the outboard side. The diver's air bubbles are still rising up the ship's side, the diving officer is relaxing on the Upper deck with the standby diver, dressed and ready for any unforeseen emergencies, that everyone hopes will never occur. I'm really getting into it now. Little did the rest know what was going on about thirty feet below, they were relaxing on the upper deck goofing over the side enjoying the lovely sunny morning just before tot and lunchtime.

"Must be settling now sir" says the dabtoe with the leadline. I'm getting worried now. Those mad bastards are playing chicken on the bottom, they won't even be able to see with the mud being disturbed. The bowman shouts "settled forward sir". The tides running out fast now.

"Midships settling sir". Fucking hell, where are the crazy fuckers, The bubbles are still there.

"Stern settling sir". I don't believe this. Come up for fuck's sake. Diving officer receives four pulls (permission to surface), diving officer four pulls reply (permission granted). Lots of bubbles about six foot out from the hull. The're surfacing ... ... they break the surface – – bollocks there's only two of them ... . shit ... . who is it? Pete Hanley and Slinger. They're looking at each other and gesturing. What's happened? Where's Sam?

The Diving Officer wants to know where the third diver is. He's about to send in the standby diver. The two give the OK sign, but do they realise that there's no sign of Jelbert. Fucking hell! First Lieutenant "Ships settled". "Make fast all securing ropes. " "Make gangway safe and secure". "Post rat guards forward and aft. When all secured, muster on quarterdeck for de-briefing. "

The Diving officer sees who's surfaced and says "Where's Marine Jelbert ?"

"Shit. He was with us leaving the bottom. "

Everyone is beginning to realise something is wrong.

"What's that?"

Everyone looks, it's the third diver. He's surfaced around the arse end of the ship. He's got a big smile on his face – the bastards been having us on. Well thank fuck they're all safe. It'll be a big wash up around the rum fanny shortly. Still, all's well and they're all raring to get ashore. That's it. Nearly all the pissheads are ashore,

Sampling the Delights of Lisboa. It was a beautiful afternoon and I had got myself a good viewpoint on one of the highest decks. I could see over the top of most of the red-tiled roof tops and I could just see the top of Lisbon's very famous football stadium, whose name I can't quite remember at the moment, some of the clubs players were taking part at that time in the play offs for the 1966 world cup.

Which by the way England won by beating the runners up Germany at Wembly in the summer of 66. Just for the record. There was a party of about a coachload going off the ship on a visit there, answering a very welcomed invite from the club's organisation. I would have loved to have gone and met Portugals world cup players Eusabio etc., but alas, life in the sin bin isn't all its cracked up to be. I was looking across the quiet road at the bottom of the gangway where we are berthed, and there was a rough square of common type land, about the size of a football pitch and something had just caught my eye, which looked as if it was going to be of some interest. I thought this type of thing only still happened in America. I didn't realise that the canny practice was still operated in Europe. Good on them, at least there are still some places left that haven't been indoctrinated by the pathetic liberal bilge that's about to cause the ruination of a once great Europe. There was a chain gang arriving from the local sing sing, armed with pick axes and shovels, ready to start the task of cleaning up and improving the local area. Brilliant. This should be part of every teacher training course. A couple of weeks on the chain gang would show them how to get real results, sharpish and at minimal expense to the law abiding public, who were lumbered with the expense of feeding these lawless toe rags. There were five instructors, four with automatic rifles, and one with a big ring of keys. The four armed instructors took up high positions with a good view from all corners of the arena. whilst the pacifist with the keys released all the toe rags from their shackles.

This is the best sin bin imaginable. I'm going to get a mug of tea and some sandwiches. I've got a ringside seat, a pair of shorts on, so I'll be sunbathing whilst I peruse the educational entertainment. The miscreants are working their nuts off with the picks and shovels in the baking heat. After a couple of hours it had become blatantly obvious that the students were fucking choking, superb. That will concentrate their priorities in the future. I think their mentor was beginning to appreciate the fact, and was contemplating letting their eager criminal hides rehydrate themselves, with the warm water available from the water butt they had dragged behind them from their hostel of incarceration. Sheer waste full extravagance, when the suck of a lemon skin would suffice for at least another couple of hours, spoiled bastards.

The whingeing bastards had no sense of gratitude what so ever, their guardians had been gratious enough to bring them on an outing in the mid day sun, and all they do is whine, I reckoned they could have persevered for at least another couple of hours before refreshment, to concentrate their minds on the progressive educational technique, which was achieving phenomenally good results. I was still waiting for one of the murderers to make a break for it, but the boring fuckers were having none of it. Their good behaviour must have had something to do with the fact that their guardians, had four automatic weapons trained on them, and were only to eager to use them for instructional purposes. It's amazing what a little bit of gentle positive persuasion can do. There was one thing for sure, they all knew exactly which side their bread was buttered on, and acted accordingly.

As good as the show was, it was beginning to dawn on me that this particular exercise was probably staged for our benefit. Britain was beginning to be known around the world as the British Bull Dog that had lost its teeth. Imagine the effect that this had on the hundreds and thousands of British troops serving their country all over the world, knowing that the country is gradually falling into the hands of these pathetically inept, useless, parasitic, lying, thieving, deceiving, yellow bellied, perverted cock suckers and rug munchers who get up to all their scheming and plotting and terrifyingly , frighteningly supposed planning for their own ends and are so unashamedly amateur at it, that they don't recognise that the rest of the world is looking on laughing and taking the piss out of them and that was forty years ago. The state of affairs in this country is in a state of collapse. The rest of the world was sure taking note and absorbing all the information before setting about sucking the life blood out of our once great nation and reducing it to the last refuge for all the mobile scum of the world, who deserted their own countries and left their own countrymen, usually defenceless women and their own kids behind to starve in poverty, whilst they joined our MPs.

I've got to stop, the truth is making me sick again. There's got to be more later about the so called 'New Labour's ' great ten year millennium's sickening 'gravy train heist' to the cost of all true Labour people in this country, who fell for all their slimy con tricks, which left this country in the massive debt it's in and caused so much devastation in the Middle East, before filling their blood soaked pockets and running, leaving the World to try to clear up their premeditated looting of our economy, whilst they have jailed an Englishman for making a false declaration on a passport.

Don't make me laugh! Roll on justice, I don't go a bundle on this sin bin lark (punishment) apart from the extra work and out of hours musters, it's the stoppage of leave that really draws my balls.

Seeing all the excitement and anticipation of everyone preparing for a good run ashore in a new foreign city, and to have them all returning pissed up in the middle of the night, with whatever scran (food) they've been able to gather, and then having them have a wash up in the mess square over a can of beer, discussing all the main events of the day's escapades. Still, it's got to be done. It makes you appreciate your freedom all the more when you've got it.

We returned to Portsmouth for a short maintenance period and we had to enter dry dock for a much needed bottom scrape, that reminds me I'll have to chase up Eileen at the weekend, she's got to be due for a good overhaul and bottom scrape, just to check for barnacles and the dreaded gribble worm.

Friday night came, and we had our usual brilliant night out. First a trip around the strip, to see all the girls and get some real funny stories, then off down Southsea for the business. It was fairly quiet down Southsea for spare, so I was off to see if Eileen was still working (barmaid). Brilliant, she was. So it was last orders and big smiles, plus those telling looks, her old man's baby sitting, and she's out for the night, staying over at her mate's house in Pompey. I said let your pal know what's going on, and we'll get a room for the night. Ace. All sorted. I'm looking forward to this, a nice cosy bed and a plethora of bedroom sports. I hope the attic rooms available, that way we wont have any eager listeners tuning in. Not that we would give a fuck anyway. I'm over the moon knowing I wont be scraping my elbows and bollocks up and down Southsea common or the beach, again! And Again! And again and again!

We had to be out by half ten Saturday morning, and we'd wake up starving with not a cat in hell's chance of any breakfast, so I'd slip Eileen a crippler just to start the day off right, and then it was time to see her into a cab, then off home not quite rejoicing as it wasn't a place she wanted to be.

I had to get back onboard before 1200 otherwise I would miss my tot, and no way was that ever going to happen. I arrived back about 1100 to the usual "Where the fuck have you been?" all around the mess square. I donned my towel, grabbed my soap bag, and I'm off for a de-scale. Fred Baines, my mate, says" there's been some bloke phoning, asking for you. I told him to phone back just before 1200 and that He'd catch you then, as you would definitely be back by then for your tot, as you never missed it".

"What was his name?"

"Mr Whoppity-Wop Wop. "

"Fucking hell, that's her husband. "

Hoots of laughter, "Wha Hayee, Jimmy's for it. He's right in the shit. "

All the troops are chuffed to fuck, just because they didn't get their end away. Where did he get my name and ship from. I'm in the shower all lathered up thinking of all the implications of this bloke knowing who I am. I've got my nuts in a right old lather. Still, I can't do anything about it but play it by ear. Forget it, cheer up it's Saturday lunch time, my tot, a morsel to eat and I'll be laughing kit bags again, then it's off down the strip on a scrumpy run, see all the whores and pick up the gossip, from last night up and down the strip, then back onboard for 1500 and head down. Up for supper 1800, a can of beer and then off again. Southsea here we come!

I contacted Eileen to make sure she was ok, everything was sorted, nice one. Her old man had called her mate in the forenoon to see where she was, silly cow spilled the beans. Still, we'll laugh at this for years to come. I couldn't work out what he was bothered about, he was as bent as an Arab's dagger and didn't give a toss for Eileen anyway. Well so be it, I had finished my time on Eskimo and I was only to pleased to be going on leave and draft.

It was good to be home for a couple of weeks and see my family and all the lads in the town. They were really keen to find out what I'd been up to in the last couple of years since I had seen them last. It seemed unbelievable that they hadn't done anything or been anywhere in all that time, and the life I'd lived over the same period.

Now here I am waiting to take off to God knows where again and have another basin full, shipping the kidney wiper left right and Chelsea. We always waited in great anticipation for our draft orders, bringing news of our next ship, employment and place of abode, it could be going anywhere in the World, so the sense of anticipation was enormous. I had often volunteered for the Antarctic survey ship HMS Protector, whose station was S. A. and S. A. (South Africa and South Atlantic).

I fancied all the wild life implication, and so I always lived in hope when I was due a draft order. Therefore, I was nearly always let down when I received news of my new position. That makes it sound rather like a posting that I had some sort of input in, whilst in actual fact draftee couldn't give a monkey's fuck what happened to us or where we went, just so long as all the positions were filled.

We were all just part of the general rabble, who weren't exactly pigs, but were to be treated as such (that is what the officer cadets were taught in there basic training in those days), fucking twats! I received my draft order and low and behold, where was I going? HMS Collingwood, the perpetual home for out of work and destitute leckies, or for a short break in between sea going ships. still, I'm quite chuffed really, as I've always had a good time in my home establishment.

I know the ropes. There are some pretty good jobs to be had as ship's company, (staff) what I was looking forward to and hoping to get, was Killick in charge of the dust cart, early start in the morning, finish the job, every afternoon off (on the piss), but if not. Buffers party, camp maintenance, pig farm, special duties etc. etc., but the icing on the cake being billeted in a shore establishment, was the access to as much willing fanny as anyone could possibly want or handle, and as it was only just Easter time, I would have all the summer to enjoy every outdoor sport available to my imagination, and that sure would be going some. The more I thought about it, the more I couldn't wait to join. I was by now just hoping for a good job. Well at least I knew I was going to have a good time, and laugh to boot, as always.

CHAPTER 16

A job at the rum tub

Well I joined HMS Collingwood on the first of April, 1966. I presented myself at the joining section of the RCO (Regulating Control Office) situated in this one big wooden hut, several huts connected together were lots of small sections which had control of every aspect of camp life. The most important of all and the first one everyone joining or leaving the massive camp encountered, the most busy, hardest job to learn (so much involved) was the Joining Section. There was a big cheer.

"Here he is. My relief. " My stomach hit the deck. I said "you're joking".

"Are you LEM H. Green?" "Yes".

"Then believe us, we're not joking. Welcome to the 'A' team".

"Bollocks". I've got such a knot in my stomach.

"Okay Jimmy, here's your joining routine. Go and do that, then report back here, and I'll start showing you the job, I'm away on draft in two weeks so you haven't got much time, and there's a hell of a lot for you to learn, and when you take over its all yours, you're the boss, handle it and the best of British, because your going to need it" the job itself was special duties, meaning that the hours were long and involved, with many irregularities, and the job was exempt from the ships companies duty watch roster, which was a plus.

The next two weeks were hell. The only consolation was our last job of the day, which was to issue the rum ration at five o'clock, which in total lasted about forty minutes. We had to mix between ten and twenty gallons of neat rum of between ninety six and one hundred and four proof. I was soon in introduced on how to issue the rum by our rules. By the time we had finished issuing the rum, we could be left with upwards of fifty tots which hadn't been drawn. This had to be disposed of under the watchful eye of the officer of the day, who by the way was usually some greenhorn Hooray Henry, who happened to be duty watch, and hadn't a clue what was going on and didn't know his arse from his elbow and generally just wanted the whole procedure over with, after he had supervised all the mixed rum going down the drain. (sacrilege), or so he thought, by various means of now you see it now you don't, and some skilled maneuvering of the results on the ticking off boards.

The results were perfect, all the numbers tallied, all ticking off boards correct, all excess mixed rum legally disposed of, all unmixed neat rum sealed up for return to the Spirit room, Officer of the watch pleased with himself for having completed his ordeal without a hitch, and all the movers and shakers all three parts pissed laughing like drains, ready for a bite to eat, bath and dhobi and down the Collingwood club for a few more wets and much jocularity with the wrns, to the utmost envy of the rest of the crew. Therefore, this part of the job compensated for the ordeal endured during the rest of the day, and was certainly the pinnacle of our day.

After two weeks of intensive training in the job, with the obnoxious Petty Officer perched on my shoulder, and haranguing and humiliating me at every opportunity, I was getting the hang of it. Later on, I began to enjoy it. Everybody, except officers, who were coming and going from the camp, had to be processed by this office, and there were over three thousand ratings on the camp. We had our fingers on every pulse and were highly respected for our contributions to running the camp, from the Captain down, in that respect, we had the full backing for what ever we did.

With no questions asked from the Captain down. (carte blanche). Therefore, what we said, went. Sweet as a nut.

One day, Tab Hunter joined, a big Yorkshire bloke I knew from a previous time somewhere. We were good mates and always had a laugh. "Fucking hell, Jimmy, how did you land this job?" He was still an able rate, he hadn't gone for advancement.

"Any good jobs going on the bins?" I said, "no, but I've been waiting for you (I dealt with all incoming and out going draft orders) and I've fixed you up as messman in No 2 Chief's Mess. Good job. Plus plenty of rum" "Fucking hell, cheers Jim. "

I said, "we issue the rum I'll see you at tot time, Rodney Dining Hall 1700, come round to my board three or four times but don't be conspicuous as you get more pissed or you will drop someone in the shit". "Cheers Jim, see you then. "

"Report to the President No 2 Chief's mess, tell him you're the new messman. "

After tot time, Tab was well pissed. I said "I'll take the boards back to the office and I'll see you in the dining hall for supper (dinner) in half an hour. "

I had a quick bath and dhobi, on civvies and met Tab for dinner. We were laughing our nuts off and pissed as rats.

"How the fuck did you land this job. As much rum as you can drink, then have some more and ditch the rest, heaven maaan. "

We finished supper then off down the bar for the night, going over old times. It was a great night. The best thing was, every morning it was the norm for us all to start work hung over. It was the perk of the job, and we gradually got better as the forenoon progressed. Lunchtime a quick babies head chips and peas, into the bar for a couple of liveners, then it was roll on 1700, tot time, start again. That was the routine every day, seven days a week, permanent. No wonder our kidneys used to ache.

It was a hot summer and HMS Collingwood is out in the Hampshire countryside. One Friday night a few of us were invited to a house party on the massive local married patch, with a group of WRNS (sailors with tits) from the camp. The married patch was hotter than Peyton Place, thousands of newly married couples and about a good twenty percent of the matelots away at sea. We had a great night and we were all tanked up. I finished up with a WRN I didn't know, but we got on well. I think I was in a spare bedroom with her, giving her an extra large portion, which she was obviously enjoying. All of a sudden she started howling like the old proverbial, howwwwwwwwllllllllll. fucking hell, howwwwwwwwllllllllll.

What the fuck!, there's me going like a train, then I can't help it, I start giggling. She must have woken everyone up plus half the fucking estate. It wasn't half sexy the piston was pumped right up, Fuck it, I wasn't stopping. Laughing like drain and still going like a train and her pitch was getting higher and higher, we're deep in the tunnel and really going for it. Fuck the neighbours, I can see the light at the end of the tunnel, I just hope its not another train coming the other way, I'm definitely not stopping, anyway they don't know me. Fuck it, – – – – – I am doing.

"You'd better be ready girl, the pressures building, howwwwwwwwllllllll hold onto your ears or I'll blow your fucking head off. BANG a full load delivered on a head of steam pushed along by copious amounts one hundred proof Pussars Rum. The howling mellowed to kind of yodeling, fucking brilliant. We'll have to call out the duty hands with a submersible pump as her guts are flooding. " There's another eruption in the hallway, a loud roar as the rest of the revelers showed their appreciation for our well entertaining effort. Well that put a smile on everyone's faces. Lets have some more pop. Fuck a stoat.

We awoke about nine o'clock on the Saturday morning, I said "Let's get back onboard for the golden nectar, drink of the gods. It's tot time at twelve o'clock. " I can't miss that, Sacrilege.

We were walking through the country lanes, it was a beautiful hot summer forenoon, the sun was beating down as we were passing this ripe cornfield blowing in the morning breeze. I started thinking of earlier on, and in no time at all I was hard as a chocolate frog again. Into the cornfield we go and I laid some corn down for a bed and away we went.

She said "What's that sticking in my bum?" – – -waaaaaaait for it, wait for it,

I had a look and said "don't worry, its a sharp piece of corn (as if.), I'll move it". So I pulled off this monster big black beetle which was biting her arse, I told it to fuck off and find your own, she was no wiser, and proceeded to dispense yet another large portion as big as a horses face, and sure enough here came the vocals again, which just did all the more to spur me on. "Howwwwwllllll!"

I'll bet all the wildlife were running for cover. We're all finished again and we're sweating like a pair of rampant hogs, and the perfumes about right as well. I'm thinking I can't wait to get back onboard for a quick shower as things are getting a bit ripe by now, all this on top of last nights delicate aroma. Talk about whiffy, it reminded me of portsea fish market on a Monday morning. I hope there's no fucking crabs involved.

After a good shit shave and shampoo, Tot and a bit of dinner and then down the bar to see the lads for a livener, and a sitrep on last night's events. We were in stitches.

"Fucking hell Jim, what was you giving the hyena. The fucking windows were rattling. "

"What did you call her?"

"She's known on the other camps as the laughing hyena. "

We were rolling about. I said "I don't care, she was one hell of a go'er. " She had me laughing alright.

I was in the Rodeo and loving it, that's what it was like every week. Thursday night was dance night at the Colllingwood Club. At the side of the parade ground, there were four big wooden huts joined up and laid out as a junior rates social club. We were down there one Thursday night when we trapped these two stunning Maltese birds. It comes closing time and I've asked her where she lives.

"Near Gosport".

Well I've got to find out if I'm going to get my end away. I'm thinking I'm not getting a cab out of the camp, going all the way to Gosport then having to get another one back, not for the benefit of my health anyway, so I said to her "Shall I get us a cab back to yours?"

"Yes, for a night cap" "Good, but you wait here for five minutes while nip to my cabin and get my alarm clock, I just can't be late in the morning. "

"No need, don't you worry, I've got one. "

Well shiver me timbers, Brilliant. All night in sorted, and breakfast to boot. She had a lovely detatched house in Gosport, immaculate in every way inside and out!, and cooked a full English breakfast which was champion, to set me up for the busy weekend which was soon to be starting. So roll on, let's get busy, there's plenty more where that came from.

It must have been about a Tuesday afternoon mid July, when Tab rolled up at my desk in the RCO.

"Jimmy, there's a big summer ball at the chief's mess this Friday evening. The pres. Needs half a dozen lads, collecting glasses etc. Free beer plus a few quid. Come on we'll have a right laugh. "

"I can't, I'm a leading rate. "

"Fuck that, take your hook off, no one will know. "

I said "Rubbish, if I get caught they'll say "so you don't want to be a leading rate and disrate me. " Then its, sing, "Hooks and badges fly away, fly away, fly, fly, fly, away.

"Come on, who's going to know?"

For some reason, I started giving it some serious thought. A good laugh, free beer and pay to boot.

"Ok, I'm in. "

I got a phone call from Tab at about ten thirty the following morning. He said, "The pres. wants to see you up here, no. 2 chiefs mess, in the Pres's office at 1200, " "OK" "I'll see you then, and don't forget to take your hook off. "

I arrived at the kitchen mess room and Tab phoned the Pres. To let him know I was present. He turned up and Tab said this is the new messman. I thought, he's lost his marbles. The Pres. Says "Pleased to meet you, Jimmy, have you had your tot?"

"No". Off he go's, I can hardly believe what's happening here, If were rumbled, I'm right in the shit, not just in it, but deep deep in it.

The chief returns with a good two tots of neat rum. Fuck it in for a penny, I start drinking it. He fills us in on what he wants to happen on Friday night and says "Be good, I'll see you both Friday night. "

We both roared and had some dinner, by this time we're both burbling like rock apes again. "I'll see you tonight. "

We had a wash up down the bar and planned Friday night. Friday I did the rum issue at 1700 and didn't go over the top myself. I had a bit to eat and then went and got ready. Half blues uniform (no hook) then off to the Chief's mess. They had a couple of WRN stewards setting it all up, laying the tables and doing this massive buffet. Everything was a lot grander than I had been expecting. The guests started to arrive in full dress uniform, Chiefs and their wives from all the establishments in the area, plus from ships in the harbour.

After about an hour, it was going really well. You could see the objective was to have a really good time dancing, and as much booze as possible. We were clearing and washing up the empties as quick as possible, whilst keeping a good flow of draught

Guiness lubricating our necks The mess was packed and the atmosphere jovial to say the least, .

Around about ten o'clock, everyone was well on the way, as is the way of all Royal Naval get-togethers. The queue at the bar was solid, and the seated don't want to join the queue. This Chief flags me over. Can I get them a round. Two chiefs, two wives and I say "I'm sorry, I'm only collecting glasses. "

"Here's a fiver, okay?"

"Okay". I took the fiver, plus the money for the round, and got served at the side of the bar and the chief serving wouldn't take the money. Brilliant! I delivered the round, he says "well done, son, keep the change".

"Yee Haugh". Pennies from heaven. Surely it can't get any better than this.

That's it, they're all pissed and I'm now taking orders at a price. Every time I catch a glimpse of Tab we roll up. He's doing the same, the best of it is everyone's happy. We're having a great time. It's coming up to finish, all the taxis are arriving.

We start clearing up, and I go into the small room at the end of the bar, where the sink is, and start washing up. There's piles of it and we're getting through it champion. I've noticed above my head is a very large shelf full of bottles of spirits ready to supplement the bar. The Woods Rum is standing out like a sore thumb, there's three or four bottles of each spirit there, We finish the job fairly late on and we've got a good burble on. The Pres. Comes over, thanks us and says "You've done a great job lads that was marvelous under such pressure, here's seven quid each. Get a last pint and a double Woods rum. " Thanks again lads.

We finish, say goodnight and we leave by the back door galley entrance. We both go "Yeah!" we've both had a skinfull and are laughing like drains,

Tab says, "Look at this". He puts his hand under the mess foundations and pulls out a bottle of Woods Rum. "Dah Dah!" he says "We're all right for the weekend, yeah!"

I say "Come here. " I put my hand somewhere else and say "Dah Dah! Another bottle of Woods Rum. Yeah! We really will be okay for the weekend. "

We still had our rum ration Saturday and Sunday plus the sessions down the bar AND polished off these two bottles in between. It's a good job the camp is quiet over the weekends, two thirds of the crew had gone home. Come Monday I was rougher than squadron of badger's arses. My God I'm never going to recover, I don't know how I got through the day. Still 1700 eventually arrived, tot time, nectar of the Gods, and that livened me up. A few pints down the club, and an early night. Tuesday forenoon, I'm at work in the RCO (Rating Control Office) still feeling dog rough, mouth like the bottom of a Parrots cage, when the phone rang, It was Tab.

"The President of the mess wants to see us both in his office at 1200". "What does he want, " "I'm fucked if I know". "Bollocks, I bet they've missed the Woods rum, God we're right in the shit. "

Fuck, I'll be up for a court marshal. (A requirement to disrate a confirmed Leading Rate, or above)

Tab's been keeping a low profile, everything's going through my mind, some one's recognised I'm the leading hand from the joining section, and the rum tub, which are both high profile jobs. I'm crapping myself. Well nowt for it, but to go and face the music. So hard and long to get my hook and now I'm going to lose it and just for that. Well I can't say I didn't know. That's life in a blue suit.

I make my way up to No 2 Chief's mess and go to the mess room. Tab's looking all forlorn.

"What is it?"

"Fucked if I know. "

"We shouldn't have had that rum. The trouble was we were three parts pissed, it was above our heads and it seemed like a fucking good idea at the time. "

Tab called the Pres. Here he comes, Oh no, fucking hell!

"Hello Jimmy, how are you? Still hung over? We've had reports from all over the fleet – the night could not have gone any better, and you two lads were fucking brilliant. Wait here, I'll get you a couple of tots. I can't tell you how pleased the mess is. We were all a bit worried about it, and we couldn't have expected such results, really well done and thanks a bundle, . Here's another fiver each, you were the tops. Have some lunch. " Phew, what a relief. We had a pint as well with our lunch. The pair of us are going to celebrate tonight, starting at the Rum tub. We had one hell of a night down the canteen bar for a Tuesday night. We couldn't believe it. What a life. The following week a memo went around, 'Volunteers required for ship's divers. Names to the Buffer. ' Brilliant, just what I've been waiting for. I got my name down.

He said "clear it with your Head of Section to take next Wednesday afternoon off, we're doing the aptitude tests in the lake on Horsea Island, if you're free, muster at the transport garage 1300 Wednesday with your swimming gear and plenty of stomach. "

"I'll be there". I was there, alright, this was my chance. I'll show the bastards, whatever they say I'll do it. There were about twenty of us who turned up, and they certainly put us through it, jumping off high buildings, with a dry suit and metal neck sealing ring into the water, putting faulty breathing gear on us. It was all designed to weed out the none but dedicated, There were four of us left in the end. The rest had rapped their hands in for numerous reasons, or been given the bums rush by the instructors. I got what I wanted, I had passed the aptitude test for ships diver. Evidence stored with my service documents, to be entered to do the one month's course at HMS Drake Diving School in Plymouth at some future date to be determined.

I knew it was a very severe and demanding course, both mentally and physically, and the pass rate was very low for good reason – about 20% – that is because they only do either four, six or at the most eight in a class, pairing up (buddies) to work together when down below. That's coming later.

I'm well chuffed. It was approaching the end of July and the ships company sports day was approaching. Everone was hoping for a fine summers day, as it was a very big local event for a lot of the population of Fareham and Gosport, as well as the Ships company and families. There's a huge sports field situated opposite the camp just over the main road, where every imaginable sports event's would take place, having been dreamt up by a committee of ne'r do wells and couch potatoes. (Wind the fuckers up.) The main gate is open for the afternoon and there is limited access to the camp and further attractions, plus the four senior rates mess's and bars, two Pos, two CPOs and the Collingwood Club for the Junior rates and their guests. The Friday arrived and it was a really hot sunny day and the attendance was marvellous.

We'd had a couple of beers lunchtime and were watching the events with half an eye, and talent spotting with the remainder. The fanny was about in abundance and whatever could be on show was. A push chair suddenly tapped the back of my leg. I looked around and saw the young sprog then looked up. I nearly had a coronary, the shock on my face must have been a picture. It was Eileen from over Southsea nights, I hadn't serviced her for ages. She started laughing, "don't worry, he's not one of yours".

We had a good laugh and we made arrangements to meet just down the road in Fareham the following night for a meal and a few drinks, and get down to some serious reminiscing in this quiet little hotel I used to frequent on the outskirts of Fareham. An olde worlde type country pub, whose landlord was a very jovial and understanding ex CPO, who catered for the needy, not the bloody greedy, but who also was very glad of the off the cuff mid. week custom to bolster his takings, and was therefore very discreet, every time I turned up out of the blue, he would be smiling like a Cheshire cat, for some reason.

Well that was us back in touch. After Eileen had left the sports field for home, we latched onto these four Jenny Wrens. They were a good laugh so we finished up in the bar of the Collingwood Club, having a sing song, getting pissed and trying to find the quickest way into their drawers! By way of the very convenient air raid shelters. We split up at about six and went back to our messes, bath and dhobi, change into civvies. We all met up again at the club, a couple of wets then down the road into Fareham for a rip-roaring Friday night.

Unbeknown to me, the WRN I was trying to seduce eventually turned out to be my wife. Be warned youngsters, tread carefully, in more ways than one. All the time you are devising a way into their knickers, if you are any sort of a catch for them, they will be planning a permanent way into your wallets and all your future finances. Females are the human equivalent of the praying mantis, totally inscrutable and part of the biggest thieving conspiracy on earth and haven't got a grain of conscience between the lot of them. So cheer up my boys, out piece, use it well then scarper, well out of the reach of the predatory Venus fly traps and devouring sundews. I was well chuffed to have bumped into Eileen the other day. We really got on well together. Again.

It was sweet as a nut being back inside her after so long. We'll keep well in touch from now on.

Tab was back in touch the following week. The Chief's mess were hosting a major summer ball the following week, and the Pres. wanted to see the 'A' team. I was up the mess room lunchtime Tuesday. The Pres. turned up with a large tot each for us, "right lads, are you up for it Fri. night?"

"Too right Chief, just bring them on. " "Good lads, Good lads, that's what I like to hear. " "This is the biggest summer ball we've ever put on, and we're having the mess lounge done up as usual and we're closing the road in front of the mess and having a really big marquee. We're having a Royal Marine band doing a concert, big time, and dignitaries from all over Hampshire and the home fleet. We've really got to make this work. Double your last pay with bonus if all goes well. Free beer again, but don't get too pissed until it's all over. Are you up for it?

"Too right, Chief, can't wait. " "Good you're the best". "We will be Chief, you watch". When he'd gone Tab said "Great, but let's not drop ourselves in the shit. No more bottles of rum. "

"I couldn't agree more. We don't want any unnecessary worry".

Friday night of the big summer ball is here. I help with the tot issue at 1700, a quick bath and dhobi, a bite to eat and I can't wait to get going. I'm up the Chief's mess at about 1930 having a good nose around. Tab's been helping set it up all day being the messman. The wardroom cooks and stewards had been utilized to prepare and set up the buffet and table decorations. It's all laid out in the marquee with an extra large bar set up in there. It was fit for the Queen. " The Royal one" They certainly didn't do things by halves.

The Royal Marine Band were playing soft music on the far side of the dance floor and the guests were beginning to arrive at about 2000. The President was all set to receive his main guests at 2030. The Captain of HMS Collingwood and the Admiral of the Home Fleet who duly arrived spot on time in the large limousine. The introductions were done, the drinks are poured, the band struck up with the dance music. Everyone was relaxed. That's it, they're off, all on the piss, big time. It doesn't take long, not with about four hundred hardened drinkers on the go, the place was soon buzzing. The dance floor is leaping. This is going to be some end of term hop, roll on, There's going to be enough going in tonight to put a guardrail around the moon, and I suspect a handrail on the ladder too.

Unfortunately, I won't be contributing, not tonight anyway, but I'll make up for it over the weekend. All of a sudden we're really busy, they've all started finishing their drinks at the same time. The Guinness is going down well. I've noticed quite a few Chiefs that have half recognized me. They seem to be thinking "I'm sure that's Jimmy Green, but he's a hookey, he must have lost his rate, what a player".   "Can you get me a round?"

Yippee!, it's started, here we go. Be prepared pockets, you're going to be overflowing. It's been going for about an hour and a half and it is really throbbing. The officers are really diplomatic, and they all leave about an hour before the end, so their hosts can let their hair down and perform and really give it what for, and they're not there to witness and spoil it.

I've brought so many rounds to the tables, they all seem to think that's my job. I'm not complaining. One chief flags me over, it's Chief Mech. Loader. He was my last instructor on Killick's course. He pinged me alright, "Jimmy, two pints, and two G and T's. "

I said, "Drink up quick and I'll get it. "

His guests were empty, but he still had a good half a pint. I said "Drink up". He didn't, so I picked up his drink and saw it off. His jaw dropped, his guests rolled up and I went to the bar to top them up. That's when I realized I was getting quite pissed. I delivered their round and managed to squeeze a huge tip out of him with much jocularity.

It was going great, Tab was well on the way. We were going to have some clearing up to do after this lot. There was so much it was decided to stack it all up tidy and it would be washed and stored in the forenoon the following day. The band were all well pissed and having a right old blow. The last waltz was going and all the transport was arriving. By the look of it, it had been a roaring success. The place looked as if a bomb had hit it.

We were having a couple more pints with rum chasers as we we're tidying up, when the Pres. bimbled over, and burbling like a rock ape he thanked us ever so much, he said what we already knew, what a success and paid us big whacks. We were well pissed by now and laughing our nuts off. We left by the rear galley door and Tab says, "You didn't get one did you" "As if" "good come here" ... . His hand disappears under the mess and from behind a supporting pillar ?

"Boom, boom"! A bottle of Woods. I said, "you twat, we weren't going to do it. "

He laughs "yeah! But it's only one for the weekend. They're not going to miss that are they?"

I said, "Come here", I stick my hand behind the mess the bins.

"Boom boom"! Another bottle of Woods – well that was it. We couldn't bollock each other, we just rolled up in fits of laughter, bellies full of Guiness, Woods rum, Volovants, Lobster, crab, ham sandwiches and you've guessed it, yes, Caviar, pockets bulging with well earned cash. What a night, roll on tomorrow were looking forward to some time off – – – after we've done the rum tub.

We set off for our mess, going over the night's events. We sat on the mess steps for a good hour, marmalising one of the bottles. We'll save the other one until after our Sunday dinner time session down the bar. What a life! Roll on death, and rest at last.

The President sent for us again on Tuesday lunch. He gave us a large tot apiece and an extra fiver. He said they had had the best reports from the Admiral down and they were all so impressed with everything and he couldn't thank us enough for our contributions. So we thought it best not to mention the Woods Rum. Good memories It'll never happen that way again.

I found myself on a date with the WRN I had met on the sports field, Janet, this was a first for me, I'd never actually taken a WRN out before. I'd boned quite a few over the years but not anything serious. That reminds me of one occasion when I was on the reserve fleet moored off the back of 'Whale Island'. I was at the Thursday night hop at the NAAFI club opposite the main WRNS barracks on the border of Portsmouth and Southsea. I was dancing with this WRN who was in uniform (the stockings and suspenders were always a winner, stocking tops, hot flesh! Nearly there), I asked her "Why the rig?" She said she was a driver and had to go to Whale Island (HMS Excellent) to pick up the Admiral from a wardroom reception at midnight. I was in like Flynn, "I'm on H. M. S. Sheffield, Reserve Fleet, part of H. M. S. Bellerophon, Whale Island, any chance of a lift back later on?"

"Oh! Okay then , but we'll have to go via the back streets, ie follow the dockyard wall around so we won't be seen. "

That's my kind of girl. We arrived on a back street near Whale Island at about 2315, plenty of time to waste. It wasn't long before we were in the back seat of the Admiral's limo, lights out, and even shorter time still before I was filleting the Admiral's driver on the back seat. The time of the vinegar strokes had come and gone, we had a good giggle while straightening ourselves off, saying Admiral So and So will be sitting here in ten minutes time, probably opening the window and thinking 'Someone's had a bag of scallops in the boot of this car'. Close!. More like a handful of sprats, I said "thanks for the lift, as well" and carried on my way rejoicing. I was still tickled pink as I was slinging my hammock in the darkened mess on the Sheffield up the trot. Fucking good run ashore, again. "I'll be up your flue in a minute or two, or my name's not Jack me Tickler. "

I was thinking, she could have had the good manners to ask my name, fucking slapper, we could have met up again. It was quite a turn on bagging off in the back of the Admiral's limo. Wondering what the old fucker would be thinking about as he eyed up his driver with his nostrils twitching on his way home.

Well for our date I met Janet by the WRN'RY gate which was part of the large wire fence surrounding their accommodation, which I personally couldn't see the point of, I was sure the three thousand or so matelots on camp were quite capable of looking after themselves and hadn't really got anything to worry about from the two hundred odd feeds of fanny in there, but there you go, you never know.

Well we went for a couple of bevies in the Collingwood Club and then took a stroll down into Fareham. It was a sunny evening and by the time we'd got half way down the high street, she made a comment on how many people I knew. Since we left the club, everyone had been saying "Okay Jimmy".

I hadn't noticed myself, because I knew nearly everybody. Well she seemed impressed but I didn't know why. Poor lonely souls I suppose. Well we had a pub meal and an alright night out but it wasn't my style at all. We didn't make any further arrangements and I couldn't wait for tomorrow night and my usual good night out. I knew what I was doing the next day. A few wets and then over to the Green Dragon on the married patch for leg over and all night in, which happened and went down well.

My time in Collingwood was drawing to a close as I had received my draft order informing me of my next ship, which was always an exciting time, finding out the history of the ship and its commitment for the next couple of years of so, which would involve my own future.

CHAPTER 17

Ships Divers course

I was to join HMS Decoy, a daring class destroyer in Portsmouth Dockyard on 16th August 1966 which I was quite apprehensively looking forward to, because you never quite knew whether you would fit in or not. As it happened the Decoy was undergoing a refit and was in dry dock in Portsmouth Dockyard. The Ship's company were accommodated in the Royal Naval Barracks, HMS Victory, which was adjacent to the dock yard, the wall of which was the dividing line between the two, with a big dock yard gate, policed, separating the two.

Well it couldn't be more handy, as it was situated right in the middle of Portsmouth, and the Red Light district which had grown up all around the barracks, since the first sailors had arrived with their wanton tackle, eons before Nelsons Tars. All we had to do to have a good run ashore was exit the main gate and we were right in the middle of all the action, at the end of the run ashore we would cautiously manoeuvre ourselves through the barracks gate to try and not draw attention to ourselves, and the accommodation was right there, Bobs your uncle perfect. I can't actually remember leaving Collingwood so it must have been some leaving do, probably lasting a week or so. I don't think I ever bumped into Tab again after that. I do remember seeing him in an advertising magazine. He was selling fire extinguishers in the North East. Well there you go! There's a job out there for all if you look.

I joined the ship in dry dock. The ship's company at that particular time was only a quarter strength, as the ship was undergoing a refit and much of the updating work to ship and equipment was being carried out by dock yard personnel. Our main task the ships company, was predominantly safety, fire watching over all the red hot noisy riveters working with nearly white hot rivets, and welders constantly causing fires on the other side of bulkheads where they were working. At this time of relative inactivity, it was seen as an opportune moment to get some ship's divers qualified, so my time had come. I sure wasn't going to blow it. They sent four volunteers down to HMS Drake in Plymouth to attempt the diving course. Everyone knew how tough it was going to be, so here we go.

We arrived at HMS Drake a shore establishment adjacent to Plymouth dock yard on the Sunday, we got ourselves victualled in, all ready for the kick off on Monday morning. Little did we know what we were letting ourselves in for. We assembled in one of the classrooms at the diving school, which was situated at the far side of the dockyard on the warf, overlooking the estuary where the river Tamar flowed under the big road and rail bridges, which gave the road and rail transport access to Cornwall from Devon, because of the narrow entrance to the massive harbour, the river then formed a big tidal estuary with thick, glutinous, smelly mud for a Seabed which was uncovered when the tide was out, where, over the next month we would be whiling away the lovely Autumn days, fighting for our lives underwater in the black, fast flowing water of the tidal estuary.

We were sitting to attention awaiting the entrance and introduction to the most hideous, grotesque, sadistic, disfigured little bastard, whose total power stopped at nothing, with seemingly no redress to anyone else, except his senior, who we now believe must be at least as perverted as this little rat faced twat, for any of his actions. I remember several times being underwater thinking I was drawing my last breath, but being too distressed to surface or show alarm.

However I couldn't stop my brain planning the demise of this fucking poison dwarf, from forcing my arm down its throat, securing a firm grip on its bollocks and removing them via the upper foresaid orifice.

He strutted to the front of the class and stood there for a couple of minutes, while we took in what was before us. His wizened little face, with a turned up snot locker that sported a pair of nostrils that a big boar warthog would have been envious of, which by the way were aiming straight at us, and on top of that he had not long before been propelled straight through a car windscreen, which had rendered his face a mass of newly healed red ugly scars and lacerations, which were now standing out red raw. It didn't do much for his poise.

I had just read *The Lord of the Rings* on my previous ship, and this abomination before me, reminded me of my brain's interpretation of the slimy little shit of a misfit, – -Gollum. Then this fucking cretin opened its mouth.

"I will start the process of elimination shortly and come Friday, I will be left with at the most, eight, but more likely four to six of you pathetic individuals, who for some strange reason are under the delusion that you are even good enough to be considered for undertaking the Ship's Divers Course. "

At this, someone muttered "You won't get rid of me".

"Who was that? Who hasn't got the guts to identify himself?" "It was me".

"Sir!" "It was me, Sir". "What's your name?" "Goddard, Sir".

"Well, Goddard, remove yourself from my instruction and report yourself back to the ship you crawled off A. S. A. P., and never let me clap eyes on your malformed carcass ever again. Now MOVE!"

One down, twenty seven to go. That really made me dig my heels in. I'll show you, I will qualify. The cards are on the table. All the staff had to be called "Sir", even the Able Seaman Divers, the leading rates of which I was one, and the Petty Officers didn't like that, especially when the AB's told them to make the tea. They were dropping like flies, there was only going to be one way through this – to keep your mouth shut, ignore the obscenities and do exactly as you're told.

The following morning, we all mustered at the Diving School. We were given a brief explanation on the workings of the SABA (Self contained Air Breathing Apparatus), the signals used from diver to tender on the surface, emergency signals, emergency surfacing etc. Etc. then a demonstration by two of the AB divers on how to get ones body with the help of a buddy diver, through the neck of a dry suit, which was quite an evolution, then to fit neck rings to make it waterproof. On completion, to reverse the procedure to extricate yourself from this second skin. These procedures have to be practised to get the time down to an acceptable level, time being crucial, before entering the water in an emergency, ie. bomb scare, to locate and mark any bomb found, and to clear the water before detonation, to keep ones body intact and in good working order, all ready for tot time.

We were all paired off with a buddy ready to dive. We dressed each other then donned a pair of lead soled calf length boots. We had a securing life line attached to our shoulder harness, which your buddy held on to, whilst on the jetty. Your life was now in his hands. The order: all divers enter the water, once in the water you were held on the surface by your buddy, then it was necessary to holds ones arm aloft holding the wrist seal open, while at the same time squatting while floating, thus expelling all excess air from your diving suit, making yourself less buoyant and easier to leave the surface, then a written record of the time the diver's left surface. All divers are to report arrival on the sea bed with a signal to his buddy via his life line.

The order to leave the surface would be given, our buddies gave us slack rope and we plummeted thirty feet to the bottom. It was an awful feeling, being pulled down by your boots and you couldn't do anything about it. Everything went pitch black as you sank into glutinous mud on the bottom. As we weren't used to breathing from a set, and not quite getting the normal air supply as usual, there was a tendency to want to pull your face mask off to get more air, but there wasn't any. Our breathing set consisted of two bottles (Pongos run about in tanks) one being closed off while breathing down the other.

We were told to walk about until the air was exhausted to get ourselves used to it when we gasped for air, put our arm behind us, find the stop cock for the second bottle, open it. The pressure equalises between the two bottles, then close it again as this is our last air supply and we've got to keep enough in reserve to get to the surface. You breathe that bottle down again until you run out, then equalise again. You have now got to surface, one pull on my buddy line to gain his attention, one pull reply. Now four pulls (I wasn't to surface). By this time, you're hoping like fuck, we've got it all right, because I can't leave the bottom on my own. The buddy line received four pulls, letting me know what message he received from me, the line tightens to take my weight and I start leaving the bottom. Thank Christ he's pulling me up. I break the surface, make my way to the iron ladder in the jetty wall, climb out and I am assisted onto the jetty by my buddy. I removed my face mask and draw in fresh air, as much as I want. What a feeling.

I am informed that I have breathed down my set in just under half an hour, to qualify that has to last just over an hour, so I've got to learn to regulate breathing, big breath, hold it, hold it, breathe out slowly and repeat until I can stay under for an hour. This is going to be frightening and not easy. After my debrief it was my turn to tend my buddy. In he went and then down. My suit's leaked and I'm now freezing and we're going to be spending all day everyday like this. I'd better get used to it. I was concentrating so much on taking care of my buddy on the sea bed, I hadn't noticed how many people were left. There were six of us, standing on the jetty tending buddies. It hadn't dawned on me that all the rest had either rapped their hands in or been given the bum's rush by Gollum.

We had the de-brief in a classroom after we had all charged our sets up ready for morning. There were twelve of us left and we couldn't even remember what any of the bums looked like. It was bath and dhobi time, get changed into night clothing then yippee, what we'd been waking up for all day – tot time – because it was a separate issue for the diving school and they knew what we'd been through, we got a lot stronger mix, one and one, instead of two water and one rum, a big dinner straight afterwards, then down the bar for a wash up. We had a really good laugh, all these people you didn't know but were all in the same boat. After going over the days events, it hit us just how tired we were after stomping around on the sea bed all afternoon with lead soled boots on.

It's only about nine o'clock but it's bedtime, got to get some sleep and be as fit as a butcher's dog in the morning and be ready for that little slimy fucker. We awoke to a howling gale and were aching in places I didn't know we had places. We muster at the diving school, get dressed and shit face informs us we are going to attempt some tasks on the sea bed. WE are going to be working off a shot rope. Basically, a thick rope secured to the jetty with a large, round, flat steel weight (shot) secured at the other end and lowered to the bottom of the jetty wall, down about thirty foot depending on the tide. This was to be used to assist you in your tasks (work it out for yourself how, when you get down there!).

I'm in the water being held on the surface by my buddy, keeping taut my buddy line, just to really get up our noses and give us the screaming shits, Bollock Brains has had our visor's masking taped up, so we can't see a fucking thing. He hand me two objects, one I can feel is a hacksaw, the other feel like about twelve inches of angle iron, like a side support of a Pussar's bed.

Down you go and cut five small pieces of that and don't surface until complete". I worked out how to hold the angle iron stillish, I had to secure it about four foot from the sea bed to the shot rope. By signals, I got my buddy to give me slack on the shot rope, which I then formed a knot by making two loops passing the angle iron through, then getting him to tighten the rope again. Now I could hold with my left hand and saw with my right. It took me all my air but I did it, storing each piece down my boot so as not to lose them, evidence. By now, it must have been about ten thirty and was I pleased to get out of the water. Gollum came over to me, he had a piece of paper in his hand.

"Green, you've got visitors at the main gate. " I didn't know anyone in Devon. "Who is it?" "It's your Mother and sister Beryl. "

I couldn't believe it, the only two people in the world I loved and they're at the main gate. I thought my Mother was in Rochdale, Lancashire and I hadn't seen her since last Christmas and Beryl separated from her husband about five years previous, and we hadn't heard from her and didn't know where she was or even if she was still alive. You can imagine my elation. All my birthdays and Christmases had come at once.

"Is it okay if I nip down to the main gate and make arrangements to see them tonight?" "Of course it is, away you go". "Cheers, sir". I couldn't get the set off my back quick enough. I was so excited. "Thanks a lot, sir". "That's okay, don't come back". I stopped in my tracks, my heart felt as though it had fallen through my boots … … the fucking arsehole. "If you leave here, don't come back. "

My mind went blank. I all of sudden felt empty, as though I had just been wrung out.

"Can I send them a message?" "Yes, chop, chop, give it to the runner then get on your buddy line and get him in the water". I sent the message '*catch the bus outside the*

gate and get off in Plymouth Bus Station, I will catch the same bus tonight and I'll meet
you at the bus stop a. s. a. p. after six thirty. Love you, can't wait. '

I went to tending my buddy while he went about the same task as I had just completed. The thoughts going through my mind for the next forty minutes while I stood there soaking and freezing inside the so called dry suit. I couldn't even look at the sick little bastard, I could have done more than kill him, the pathetic little piece of pig shit. When my buddy had finished his task, the next job was to charge our sets ready for the afternoon. After lunch I was the first in the water, face mask still blacked out. He handed me three objects, feeling them it was a heavy hammer, a cold chisel (steel chisel) and about a foot of heavy linked mild steeel chain.

"Down you go and cut off three links as quick as you can. "

What a job, trying to hold the chain still on the metal hot, which was buried in mud, position the blunt chisel on the last link, then hit the chisel hard enough to make some sort of cut, and all this in total blackness. After about half an hour, I was so pissed off. Every time I positioned the chisel on the chain link, in my mind's eye, this was Gollum's scrotum and when I wellied the chisel I was chopping off the dwarf's bollocks. Well the incentive was good because I completed the task, gave four pulls, was acknowledged and then hauled to the surface, as we were wearing heavy leaded boots to root us to the seabed and couldn't surface on our own, my job complete and was well pleased to be back on the surface.

By the time my buddy had done, it was clean up and recharged our sets ready for the following morning, then secure, tot time, bath and dhob's then change for shore. Can't wait.

I arrived in town at about seven o'clock. We were all so pleased to see each other, I hadn't seen Mother for nearly a year, and it was about ten years since I'd seen our Beryl. We went for a quiet drink and catch up but they couldn't stay much longer after hanging around all day in the bad weather. They had to get back to St Austell in Cornwall, about a fifty mile bus journey. I told them what had happened and they agreed the last thing they wanted was for me to be thrown off course.

We had a good hour and we wouldn't lose touch again. This made me more determined to finish the course and rejoin my ship as a qualified ship's diver and muff diver. My CV just keeps growing we got dressed the following morning (Thursday) of the first week and there were only six of us left. We were so busy we didn't notice what else was going on. I thought, they can't really get rid of any more.

Wrong that afternoon, we were fully charged after lunch and my buddy was told to enter the water first, all the time improving on making our air last sixty minutes (the target). He surfaced after about forty five minutes, knackered, wet through, and frozen as the dry suits were punctured, and looking forward to not having to do much for the next hour but tend me. As he took off his set on the jetty with great relief, Gollum appeared and said to me, "take your set off and put it on your buddy, he's going straight back down again. " "I've just done my stint, it's his turn now. " His face was a picture of disbelief incredulility, shock and misery "Put the set on him". Get him dressed, chop chop. "No way, I'm an Englishman, I want a break and a cup of tea before I go down again. " "Ok, go have yourself a cup of tea, then pack your bags, collect your travel warrant and report back to your parent ship, Bye. "

Well, swallow my knob, that was a fucking surprise. What's going to happen now? I haven't got a buddy. Gollum takes my line and puts me in the water. He's got me walking about here, there and everywhere, learning to obey signals received on my buddy line. I was thinking I must be the next one to go to even things up, but the longer I was there, the more my face seemed to fit.

All of a sudden things changed. The atmosphere was now good and they were all showing interest in showing us the ropes, unbeknown to us, at the time we were now the selected class to be taken through the course. Although they never let on, we always thought one wrong move and we're off down the road.

We've just been informed that there's no shore leave tonight as we're going to do a midnight deep dive at the entrance to Plymouth harbour. We're informed that we will be diving off the Diving Quipped MFV (Motor Fishing Vessel) which had been converted to be the school's permanent diving boat.

It was a big wooden sea going fishing vessel, of which there used to be thousands operating around the coast of Britain. There is a marker buoy to which the vessel will be moored and it is one hundred and twenty feet to the sea bed, the maximum safe depth to which a diver can descend to, using compressed air. (S. A. B. A. the set were using). Our task is, wearing the heavy leaded boots, to descend down the shot rope 120' slowly to the bottom, one pull on arrival, take the small rope secured at the bottom and walk around the main shot rope for fifteen minutes, when four pulls will be received from your buddy on the boat then slowly ascend below your smallest bubbles (which you can't see), incorporating two decompression stops on the way up to avoid the bends, one at sixty feet and the last at thirty feet, to be indicated to you by your buddy.

Sounds straightforward enough. I didn't realise the next twenty minutes were to be the most terrifying of my whole life. I was to be so close to nearly instant death for all of that time. I was told to be ready, do my checks, my buddy to check me out then I'm ready to go.

It certainly didn't look inviting. It was high tide which had just turned, the water was beginning to race out of the narrow harbour entrance, with all the water stored in the massive estuary, plus the river water which was constantly flowing into it, the total trying to make its escape to the sea as the resistance against it dropped with the fall of the tide. There was a searchlight shining on the buoy and the water was frothing as it sped past the securing rope. It appeared to be ebbing at about ten knots, it looked terrifying.

"Okay, diver enter the water". Keep a tight grip on that shot rope otherwise you'll be gone.

Not good. I jumped in, grabbed hold of the shot rope, emptied the air out of my suit, signalled okay, then left the surface. I was gripping the rope as tight as possible, because the speed of the water rushing past was nearly pulling me off the shot rope. I kept descending, pitch black, freezing, then I started getting a salt water spray in my mouth as I was breathing. This was frightening but I thought this must be what happens at this depth. Our instruction up to this point had been minimal, to say the least. they had been concentrating on getting rid of the would be film stars.

I eventually planted my boots on the sea bed, 120' foot down with no escape. The water was by now moving so fast, there was no way I was letting go of that rope I would have disappeared off out to sea and down into Davy Jones's locker, where my bones would have been picked clean by King Neptune's scavengers resident down there, it was my only physical contact with which to escape to the surface from this living hell. By this time I was absolutely terrified, the most frightened I'd ever been in my life, with no way I could see of me ever reaching the surface again alive, The spray of water had got heavier and the only way I could get rid of it was to swallow it. This isn't easy as it's making me want to vomit but I can't or I'll drown.

My fingers are gripping the rope now so tight now, because my natural reaction was to pull my face mask to get more air, but I know I'm dead if I do this. Fifteen minutes seems like a life time away, the lead boots are holding me prisoner, making sure I can't escape from the sea bed, I don't feel as I can stop myself from retching, its looking more and more likely this is going to be the place of my demise, my knuckles are hurting I'm gripping the rope so tightly. I have now slowed my breathing right down and I'm holding my breath for as long as possible, then swallowing the sea water and rebreathing as slowly as possible, as I feel even more spray passing my teeth.

I am really forcing myself to keep hold of the rope and not pull off my mask, which is unbelievably hard when you can't breathe properly. After what seemed like all night, I received four pulls, heaven sent I replied, then my buddy started pulling me up. I still can't find adequate words to explain the relief I was beginning to feel at not being imprisoned on the bottom and rising towards the surface, plus feeling someone else on the end of my lifeline. As I ascended the water pressure was getting less, and the spray lightened, a little more air for my bursting lungs. He stopped me for decompression at 60' for five minutes then again at 30'. I couldn't believe I was nearly out of this nightmare. I broke the surface, I ripped off my inadequate face mask and took the biggest sweetest lung full of the good Lords fresh air imaginable. This was heaven sent. I struggled up the rope ladder and onto the boat, I couldn't get this fucking death trap of a set off my back quick enough.

As soon as my face mask was off, I was gasping down this fresh air. Gollum looked concerned. "Are you all right?" At this, all the sea water in my gut made a dash for freedom, it came out in a rapid torrent I splattered his boots but I couldn't speak. All I wanted, needed, was fresh air.

I just said, "Yes, I'm ok and sat on a bollard to recover whilst the rest of the troops carried out their tasks. I slowly recovered and began to respect how precious this fresh air is, and how lucky I was to be still alive, and so thankful for it.

We returned to base to recharge our sets, ready for an early start in the morning. It doesn't matter what time it is or how tired you are, sets are never left empty. No one knows when the next emergency may arise. and the diving gear has always to be ready to go. We arrived at the diving school first thing in the morning, and as we were getting dressed we were informed that we were about to do a half neckless bottom search of H. M. S. Lion, which was berthed along side the jetty opposite the diving school. I was detailed off to be the lead swimmer, starting off at the bows, I was to swim the keel, For'd to aft. Aft to For'd.

With the rest of the divers buddied up at six foot intervals, stretching all the way across the bottom of the ship from the keel of this big cruiser outwards, then up the side to the surface, feeling for mines as they swim down one side around the stern then back down the other side. On this first job in the forenoon, I entered the water and was holding on to the bows of the ship all ready to go. Gollom gave the order to go ahead and I began to swim straight down the keel, I left the surface and my first gulp wasn't air but neat sea water which I had taken into my lungs. Everything after that was automatic. My head broke the surface. I ripped off my mask, coughed and spluttered out the sea water and gasped in some fresh air. Gollum went absolutely banzaie, shouting and screaming "on the jetty, on the jetty! Mud run, mud run!"

We'd heard of this lung searing punishment and dreamt that we'd never get it, but it was all part of the training and he had been waiting for an opportune moment to inflict his sadistic pleasure upon us, which was fair enough as I could have drowned and that wouldn't have looked to good on his CV as an instructor.

If they had taught us properly in the first place, we would have known to check our sets correctly. I found out my breathing tube, coming from the air bottle had worked loose, and that was the reason for the spray and torture last night. By now the tube was just about hanging off and this took in neat seawater. This made me realise just what a close call it was last night – 120' down, so close! Still, that's one thing for certain, I'll always doubly check all connections in the future.

The tide was on its way out and there was about 30' of thick mud exposed at the shoreline in the estuary. We were in our dry suits and Bollock chops says "Start there and get the one hundred yards to that sewage outfall as quickly as possible. I'm timing you. Now, away you go"

We sank into the stinking mud, up to our knees, and couldn't move. He's in the Gemini (rubber boat) about twenty feet away in the water, screaming his head off. I soon extricated my legs from the gunge and found the only way to move was to belly flop across the surface of the mud, propelling myself forward with my elbows. I was first to finish, my lungs were bursting. I bellied down to the water's edge and into the water. Heaven. Just to float weightless and get rid of all the slime.

The next thing, I had this searing pain in my head. Gollum, the bastard, had sneaked up behind me in the rubber boat and smacked me over the top of my head with the oar, then started screaming "Get back! Get back!" "What the fuck's up with this degenerate prick"?

"On the mud, On the mud, back to the fucking start. You're a Team! You're a Team! Your supposed to be a fucking team!, now get back and get that useless piece of shit!"

The youngest diver, he was just about eighteen, he had been struggling at the start and was now buried down to his bollocks in the mud and couldn't get out, the more he struggled the deeper he got. The rest of us had to belly crawl all the way back to the start, pull the little bastard free, then escort the little fucker back to the finish, where I thought my lungs were bursting. It couldn't have gone any better for Bollock Chops. He was screaming with glee. "That took you shower of pathetic twats the longest ever. Round again tomorrow night before you finish" and if its no better, Round again, and again until it fucking well is.

'Oh goody, goody, something for us to really look forward to all day tomorrow, you motherfucking little cunt. I hope your ear holes turn into arseholes and shit all over your shoulders. 'That's the end of the first week and the last of the lead soled boots, thank fuck. Apparently they've served their purpose separated the wheat from the chaff, and I managed to get through it without the dreaded DD entered on to my service documents (discharged dead). Now to see if I can get through the next three weeks, clocking up the necessary one hundred hours underwater to qualify and still avoid the DD.

We've been having a laugh while on the piss on Sunday, we're all looking forward to Monday when we get to wear fins (flippers) for the first time. It's hard to imagine the luxury of being able to swim free and not be shackled to the bottom by those heavily weighted boots. Roll on, we're on our way. We budded up in the water, left arm connected to your buddy's right arm by a three foot buddy line each, when swimming your buddy is no more than six foot maximum away from you. In poor visibility you couldn't see him but you always knew he was there somewhere close. it was ace free swimming with fins, feeling weightless.

Our first task was to master our signalling skills while navigating ourselves around a 150' jackstay on the seabed, this being a large thick rope secured to the seabed, and arranged in the shape of a large unilateral triangle. We were told to navigate our way around it, and on completion they would indicate to us by means of our safety line rising up to the rubber boat (Gemini). .

We couldn't see anything on the seabed for all the thick black mud we were stirring up and fouling the water with, therefore it was an evolution trying to work out where the rope was going just to keep hold and follow it, I was holding on to the jackstay "rope" with one hand trying my best not to lose it, with my buddy accidently swimming into me every so often, we didn't have a clue where the hell we were navigating ourselves through thick black mud, when we came to the first angle, we had to work out where it went and then how to turn back on ourselves without finishing up in a right bunch of bastards (knots).

We were fumbling our way around the sharp corner when all of a sudden something grabbed my facemask. Fucking hell my eyeballs shot out and were nearly touching my visor, I involuntarily called for a damp and nearly followed through, that would have been a nice surprise for my buddy at the end of the day when he came to extricate me from the diving bag I'd been wallowing about in all day. Somewhat of a powerful aroma to bring him back to reality and clear his sinus's, a lot more effective than Vic.

"What the fuck's going on"? The next news, we're in the biggest bunch of bastards in seven navies (a snarl up). We were trying to work out what was happening while at the same time trying to make sure our facemasks weren't ripped off.

There were arms and legs everywhere, we worked it out. The lacerated, pig faced, piece of horse shit had only sent another pair of divers around the circuit in the opposite direction. We were now all snagged and tangled up in the biggest bunch of twats ever, plus we couldn't see a thing being covered in slimy shit. We gave four pulls, we'll have to surface to untangle the human knots. As soon as our heads broke the surface they received an onslaught of blows from the boat's paddle, wielded by the mentally deranged, lunatic who had conned everybody and was hoodwinked us all into thinking that he was a fucking diving instructor.

I swear if he whacks my skull again I'll ram that paddle so far up his fucking arse he'll think he's a toffee apple. That was the way of our instruction during the second week. Breaking the ice, getting to know one another, developing a bit of trust It may not seem conventional these days but it did wonders to concentrate the mind. I don't think I had ever had so much physical exercise and pressure inflicted on me in such a short time in my whole life. I do know one thing, after securing at the end of the day, bath and dhobi, tot, supper, a couple of pints and that was it, bed time and sleep, the sleep of the dead but we were getting very fit, very fast and by mid morning as the days went by, we felt like a million dollars, especially on the lovely sunny days.

We were beginning to see how this activity could eventually become almost enjoyable. After we had gone through all that shit underwater we had learnt so much about the preciousness of life – that it was truly magnificent just to be alive and to be able to breathe this sweet, life supporting fresh air and know that through our maniacally driven efforts, we were gradually becoming increasingly more competent in the water, and well on the way to achieving our goals, to becoming members of that much admired and respected brotherhood of bombed out fuckers. (Bubble Heads).

Half way through the third week, we had come on well doing lots of different evolutions in Plymouth Sound (Estuary) and we were enjoying it as much as possible. Gollum decided to give us a bit of a sporting break on the Thursday afternoon and let us have a go at fishing in the Sound. Our fishing tool was a two foot length of camp bed iron sharpened at one end, so a piece of round sprung steel was our weapon. The idea was to see the mince pies of the flatfish buried in the gravel or sand on the sea bed, approach from behind and stab them between the eyes. Hopefully, plaice, flounder or dabs for supper! At the same time picking up any available scallops on the way, We'll see.

I was buddied up with a petty officer marine engineer (PO Stoker Submarines), we're in the water with our high tech fishing gear, we do our checks then leave the surface. We arrive on the bottom, about 60' down, the visibility isn't very good, he's 6' away, at the end of our buddy line, but I can't see him. The tides on the turn and lifting all the debris off the bottom. I swim around some 6' rocks and there's something swaying on the bottom with the changing tide. I do a quick examination and decide it's a body wrapped in chicken wire, and weighted down. There are the remnants of what appeared to be a sacking cloth underneath the wire, I withdraw my knife to open it up and have a butchers hook just to confirm it was a 'stiff', before taking it to the surface to have it investigated.

I called over my buddy just to witness my actions, as this was probably be the handy work of a London mob, and dumped by the all too eager hard up local fishermen for a few shekles My buddy came over, weighed up the situation as I was about to start opening it up, shook his head indicating the negative, started paddling himself in the upright position and saluting. Fucking prick. What a waste of space. We should have at least put a marker on it.

We left it to decompose in peace and feed the fish. We carried on searching the sea bed and after about ten minutes, I was on a gravel bottom and hadn't even had a glimpse of what we'd been told to look for, so this is going to be a first.

I saw what appeared to be two evenly spaced medium sized marbles about two inches apart. I observed for a short while then I noticed one of them move. Brilliant, they are eyes. Keeping as still as possible, I slid my spear along its backbone and positioned the point just astern of its 'mincer's, then effected a quick lunge down through the fish. Shit Shoot. The sea bed erupted. What the flying fucking hell is it?

I went from calm to near panic, whatever it was didn't go fuck all on having a camp bed iron stuck right through it, between its eyes at that, and it was going mental berserk even. There was a big long tail with lots of spikes running down it which was threatening to do me some real damage. The inconsiderate, smelly bastard. My buddy swam straight over to see what all the commotion was about. He couldn't believe his eyes seeing me with what appeared an open umbrella on the end of my arm doing a frantic death dance just clear of the seabed, arms and legs all over the place. He signalled to the boat up top 'we're surfacing'.

We broke the surface and Gollum was there waiting to start performing with his paddle. He suddenly started shouting "leave the surface, get down, get down below, you fucking morons. "

That's when I let the twat have it, I flicked the irate monster from the deep off the end of my spear and into his lap. I've never seen anyone so shocked and move so quickly. It's well armed tail was giving Gollum some real grief. He couldn't get away from it, where ever he jumped to in his panic It was there flapping around the boat after him, it was as though it was determined to give him a few more well deserved lacerations, hopefully to his nuts to add to his already horrendous trophies on his boat race, laugh, I couldn't take my mask off as I was going to have to dive below very quickly, very shortly. I was laughing so much I was pissing myself jam tarting and nearly fucking choking in the now not so very dry, dry suit. It was going to be a bit ripe and minty when my buddy came to extricate me out of it later on.

We found out later that the 'Devil from the Deep' was a Thorn Back Ray. It had two rows of what appeared rose bush thorns all the way down its dangerous tail. At least it gave Gollum what for. I'm swimming along the bottom, catching scallops, chuffed to ten and laughing my nuts off. "Gollum", serves him right. We're getting the measure of the little sadistic bastard in the end.

We're into the last week and we've spent so many hours in the water we feel as though we belong there. It's a great feeling of weightlessness. As soon as we're in the water, we're flying, the breathing now comes naturally and we're getting 60 minutes breathing out of our sets no problem. We've set off across Plymouth Sound on a beautiful morning, we've got enough air for the day and plenty of food on the vessel (A sea going M. F. V. motor fishing vessel) for lunch.

We don't know what's in store for us but we're all so confident now, we're looking forward to whatever he can throw at us. Knob Head, Shit for Brains, takes the boat into the shallows about 40 feet in depth in a small cove on the opposite side of the Estuary, then goes on to say "You're going to carry out a snag line search of the sea bed, designed to locate any piece of equipment dropped over the side by accident, ie. an outboard motor ... . A dead Gollam" Sounds good, we can't wait.

Gollam, we probably wouldn't find the latter, what a shame. We laid out the dan buoys in a large rectangle with thick ropes along the sea bed about 50 foot by 100 foot. Hopefully, with the missing item within its boundaries where the two divers, one on each boundary rope, would start swimming from one end.

Dragging a lightly weighted lead line (rope) along the sea bed, where hopefully it would snag on the missing object. The diver would tie the two ropes together then swim along the lead line to the centre and see what the line's caught on. If rock, lift over, swim back, untie and carry on. Got it, good, before I descended I had two handfuls of the relevant ropes in my hands. We were just about to dive when Fuck Knuckle lowered me a camp bed iron spear and said "Fish as well".

I dived down the dan buoy anchor rope, the start, and reached the bottom about 40', the visibility was about six foot and I started sorting all these ropes out. I check, re-check, oh no I haven't got the snag line. It must have slipped out of my hand on the way down. I can't find it. We'll have to start again. I must have let it go when he gave me the spear. Here we go, one pull, attention, followed by four pulls. I want to come up. Reply, four pulls. Come up. I break the surface, look up the side of the diving boat and there's Gollum hanging over the side. It looks as though he's having a coronary, his purple road mapped head looks as if it's about to burst. His ranting doesn't bother me. We get all the ropes sorted out and get back on with the job. We complete the task without any more trauma. With the days work complete, he granted us the luxury of spending the last half hour fishing.

I was swimming past this large rock about 8 feet tall, when something moving to my right hand side caught my eye, instinctively I let fly with the spear in my right hand, with so much force the point went through the fish and struck the rock. There was so much force expended, the sprung steel camp bed iron bent (permanently). You would normally have to put it in a vice and lever to do that, but there you are, I couldn't believe it. I had impaled a wrasse a free swimming fish like a trout or salmon, and not a stationary bottom feeder like a plaice or flounder.

When we surfaced and Gollum saw the fish he was over the moon, it was the first time we had seen him smile. It's the kind of fish you could only normally catch with a spring loaded spear gun. He was most impressed.

"How the hell did you catch that?"

I thought, I'll show him. I swam after it, envious looks from the rest of the crew, yeah alright, no way. It was mid-afternoon and time to stow all remaining equipment and set off back to the diving school a couple of miles away on the other side of the estuary.

By the time we'd cheesed all the ropes down, stowed the dan buoys and secured everything else on the boat, to say we were absolutely knackered was the master of all understatements. We flaked out in the wheelhouse while Gollum got the engine going, powered up the capstan and retrieved the anchor. We were all so exhausted we were nearly asleep and looking forward to a nice relaxing journey back across the harbour, for some reason the engine cut out.

He went to restart the engine and turned the ignition key ... uuurrrggghh ... ... uuuurrrgghh ... . uuurrrggghh. Nothing. Uuurrrgghh – – -uuurrrrggghh – – -uuurrrgghh still nothing, by this time our sphyncters are beginning to twitch, we can smell a rat. Uuurrrgghh – – uuurrrrggghh, we can not only smell a rat, but we can see the fucking thing. Gollum, you bastard.

"Okay, you lot get your gear back on and in the water, the batteries flat, your going to have to tow us back. "

He must be off his fucking head, this is a 30 – 50 ton sea going motor fishing vessel.

"Come on, chop, chop, we haven't got all night. Get a tow rope over the bows, you five in the water, rope under the left arm, right arm alternate. On your backs and start paddling. " Our sphyncters have now gone into overdrive, but I couldn't follow through there was nothing left inside me.

After about five minutes they shouted over the bows, "That's it, keep going, we're moving. " I thought, yeah and so are my bowels. After about half an hour I was in so much pain all over, it was unbelievable. I was retching but there was nothing only the salt water I had been swallowing. This is impossible. "Okay you tossers, back on the boat" My head is beginning to clear, is it?, is it?, yes it is! It's fucking Gollum!. Somehow we're back onboard and in the wheelhouse and spread eagled all over the deck. My whole body is convulsing. Gollum says, "I'll try again. " He turns the ignition switch. The main engine bursts into life. It sounds like all the angels in heaven have just burst into song, and they are singing to us. Gollum says "You wouldn't believe it, I had forgotten to turn on the isolating switch!"

We couldn't have killed him, we just couldn't give a fuck any more. None of us had the energy. It was suffice to lie there on the deck with our eyes closed heart beat gradually slowing down to something near normal, and listen to the heaven sent throb of the boats diesel engine propelling us nearer and ever nearer to the lifesaving amber nectar which was patently waiting for us ashore. We tied up on the diving school jetty, unloaded the boat, charged up our sets, then retired to the mess, to revel in a Bath and dhobi and the unbelievable life saving sustenance of the Gods, our tots. (Rum issue).

It couldn't have felt any better to have been one of the ancient Gods. I just made it to my bunk and I slept the sleep of the dead, all evening, all night. I awoke in the morning feeling as though I had just spent the night in a cement mixer. It was the most strenuous day ever. I even had aches and pains in my piss. Fuck knows what's in my jobby.

We had Saturday afternoon and Sunday off, with just some relevant diving and safety information to learn and inwardly digest, but we had time for a couple of good sessions ashore, which was really useful and beneficial in bonding. The best fun of all was the amount of shit we were giving Gollum the more pissed we got. The five of us were by now as thick as thieves. The conversations covering the last three weeks were something else, reminiscing on all that had happened in the recent past, and looking forward with trepidation to our fourth and final week. We knew it was going to be mostly about bottom searches, to the uninitiated that's the ship's bottom, and not rummaging around in each others trolleys, discovering duck runs, stench trenches, blow holes, brown hatters glory holes, farting clappers etc. We mustered at the diving school first thing Monday morning, which consisted basically of a single storey brick building with a corrugated iron roof, a makeshift classroom at one end, and the diving store and air compressors to charge the sets at the other and the whole being on the side of the quay, about thirty feet away from the sea wall and tidal estuary, all very sparse considering what was achieved from there, with so little investment.

George Francis, our Petty Officer Clearance Diver (bomb squad) instructor (Gollam) was now appearing to be surrounded by a mysterious glow as he stood in front of the blackboard, instructing us on the basics of carrying out a ship's bottom search, looking for limpet mines, which are about 12" round, magnetic mines placed on the ship's bottom in strategic places, such as on the outside of the ship's ammunition magazines, fuel tanks, engine rooms, boiler rooms, steering gear, propellers etc, where they would cause as much damage to personnel and ship as possible. The shortest known fuse for these was about twenty minutes, giving the enemy diver time to swim clear and save his own skin before detonation, therefore, if a suspicious event was taking place and if it was spotted, a pipe (broadcast) would be made over the ship's tannoy, "Awkward state one, all divers to the diving store.

The ship would close down to action stations, all watertight doors closed, ship's company closed up expecting the ship to blow up any minute. The divers are getting dressed and being given all information available, which side etc. Time is ticking by, probably about ten minutes gone and they're just entering the water if they manage to find a limpet, they are booby trapped. If you lift one off the ship's side, they are equipped with a number of spring loaded plungers which will be released, engaging internal contacts, which in turn, detonates the explosives, at which stage, it is just too late to put your head between your legs and kiss your arse goodbye. You will already be a mush of offal, being the next big eats for the local sea life. Still, we get an extra 75 pence a day in our pay packet to make it worth our while!

Really good of the politicians to let this amount of money out their grasp, when, with a little bit more thought and application, they could have secured it for themselves to boost their expenses and give them a better life and leave their purloined wages secure for when they are forced, by hook or by crook off the big fat gravy train, making off with the hard workers of this country's cash. Chop their fucking hands off. No wonder they're all against Sharia law. They would all have their thieving hands chopped off. For them to agree would be like turkeys voting for Christmas.

Monday morning and we're about to do our first half necklace bottom search and we're going onto HMS Lion, a cruiser, which has recently been put in mothballs (not literally). It's a big ship with two massive propellers suspended in a couple of giant 'A' frames hanging from the bottom of the ship below the steering gear compartment and the quarterdeck. Everything is going to be black, so we have got to make sure we don't go through the 'A' frame and tie ourselves in knots as we don't want to drown through a cock up. Well here we go, Gollum's detailed me off to be keel swimmer again. That's not exactly the most sought after job, which entailed me swimming vertically down the bows of the ship, searching all the way until I reach the bottom and then swim the whole length of the ship along the keel at the centre of the ship with everything above me over 25, 000 tons. Of armoured warship, and in the middle half way along below the engine room and boiler room with at least 30ft. of solid metal either side of me which I would have to negotiate in an emergency before I could even think about ascending, pretty thought provoking to say the least. The rest of the team are all buddied together stretching up to the surface on one side.

I swim along the keel of the ship, get to the stern, we carry out a manoeuvre to search the stern, two 'A' frames and all the machinery inlets along the bottom of the ship. We reach the stern then all of a sudden I'm held fast by my buddy line. It's pitch black,

I'm guessing we're at the stern. I reckon someone's gone through an 'A' frame while searching the propellers. We're there for ages trying to free ourselves and all the time, we're breathing our air supply down when we only had enough to complete the job quickly in the first place. We free ourselves in the end complete the manoeuvre turning around to swim back up the opposite side and continue to swim forward.

Then I run out of air. I equalise with the second bottle and that is it. The next time I equalise I have to surface, dangerously low on air. I run out again, I've never been this low before and I thought it would last a lot longer. We've nearly completed the job so to try and finish I equalise again and carry on. Wrong. I run out again and equalise again and run out of air completely this time. There's nothing left I've got both valves open this is it, to the surface A. S. A. P. or dead. I've got to get from the middle of the engine room underneath the ship to the surface with one lung full of air. I had to let the rest know, I didn't know how I managed it but I must have. Just. My   lungs   were bursting, I was dizzy I was starting to feel relaxed when I broke the surface just starting to pass out, I ripped off my mask, gasping for air. Gollum had already sussed out what was happening and was waiting for us, The state he was in, it was as if we hadn't seen him flustered before, he knew he'd nearly lost me. Alls well that ends well. Treating us to another special mud run. This time we took a barrel of sand with us. Painful was nowhere near the word. We spent the rest of the week practising bottom searches, of the type ships! interspersed with a drop of fishing, there being no sprats available it had to be scallops, which were coming up by the bucket load, proper treading medicine, sadly mid week, with nothing to tread.

It was really good now, everyone knew and could do their jobs well. We just had the big test on Thursday. The instructional divers were going to lay an unknown amount of magnetic mines on the Lion's hull, plus plastic explosives pushed into the machinery intake grills and our task was to find and mark them and be clear of the water within twenty minutes, before the first explosions took place. We completed the job to everyone's satisfaction which was also the end of course, we were elated, so now there were going to be celebrations all round.

We were presented with our diving manuals, log books and badges, a Diver's helmet (bubble head) to be worn on the wrist sleeve of our uniform and would always be perused with much envy. Especially by those who didn't have the bollocks to finish the course when they had the chance in the first place, Poor Darlings, join the rest of the nearly was's and has been's, vote Liberal and help to lower every fuckers standards!. Until the Country arrives at the point where no one is capable of doing anything constructive anymore, and that point is frighteningly close. Then it was big eats, tot and a massive end of course piss up with our instructors down the Plymouth divers local pub. We're really looking forward to this. Our first Bubble heads run ashore. One to remember.

What a night that was. At first we were waiting for our hero, the instigator of all our pain and worry over the last twenty eight days which seemed more like six months, fucking Gollum, the poxed up poison dwarf. It turned out in the end that he was a great bloke. All the early bollocks was all part of the instruction. Find the best as quickly as possible in the limited time available, discard the rubbish and get on with the job to produce the best results with what you were given in the first place. that's the only way.

Gollum got the best reception of the lot, because he was our Course Instructor, and he had made it all happen, getting us all well qualified. Everyone was getting pissed and performing but that's what divers do while they can, the landlord was a retired clearance diver (bomb squad) and not one of them was mentally stable.

We awoke on Friday morning in a right state. We returned all our temporary loan equipment bedding etc., said our last goodbyes and carried on our way, long weekend en route back to our ships as newly qualified ship's divers. "Yeah, I'll fucking show 'em". Thursday night at our do, pretty late on when we'd all had a right skinful, I noticed this very good looking young woman eyeballing me. I went and had a word while we had a drink, we got on really well, good conversation and she had a terrific sense of humour, she said she would love for me to take her home. She seemed quite popular in the Diver's pub. Well I'm up for it. That's when I noticed she was in a wheelchair, no problems, she was a good laugh and was up for whatever was going on by the look of it, I asked her where she lived. "Not far, just past the dockyard and opposite the park. " She says "I'm sorry you can't come in when we get home, Mum and Dad are waiting up for me, but we can go into the park for a bit if you're game. "I can't believe my ears, game I'll give you bloody game, set and match to boot.

I thought I'd finished diving for the week never mind, maybe just a touch more schnorkeling to finish off the course proper, put the icing on the cake so to speak plus I'd eaten enough scallops to keep me treading for a good month, Ideal, I won't forget this one in a hurry.

We were sitting on a park bench practising local manoeuvres when she got me in an upside down pin fall, whispering sweet nothings down my voice pipe, as it was going really well I cautiously enquired about the second round and she said, "Hang me on the park railings by the collar and shoulder pads of my overcoat. Where there's a will there's a way" "Fucking hell, – – hang gliding, I can't wait, unbelievable, getting my wings as well. – – Flying tonight" Ace to base, Ace to base unexpected manoeuver's ahead no parachute, all safety's secondary, Yeeha!.

She was a natural, I soon had the necessary lagging removed, then out piece and the kidney wiper was well and truly buried. That made short work of her hiccoughs, she was nearly choking instead. She had her legs wrapped around me for safety's sake and we weren't half going some. She just had time to brace herself as the Armada was coming. Oops, too late for the sand bags, barricades and life boat, her guts were flooded. I got her back in her chariot before the need of a submersible pump arose, we proceeded home across the main road with much rejoicing, contentment and jovial hilarity. She was a right good egg, well now she was. Her Mother opened the front door and displayed a wonderful big homely smile, "Meet Harry, Mum, he's brought me home from the pub. " At this point I was beginning to nearly feel a little bit of a twinge of embarrassment and a suggestion of being a bit of a heel, but no that won't do.

We shook hands and she said "Thank you very much for bringing her home. " At that she turned and shouted "Dad, come and meet Harry, he's brought our Amy home from the pub. " Shaking hands, "Pleased to meet you, Harry, it's always a real pleasure to meet a Portsmouth rating. " I thanked Amy for a very pleasant and entertaining evening and was saying goodnight to Ma and Pa when my curiosity got the better of me, "Excuse me sir, but something is puzzling me. – – – Just how did you know I was a Portsmouth rating?" "Because my friend, the miserable, ungrateful Plymouth ratings leave her hanging up on the railings, miserable bastards, and I've got to don my Jim jams and go to the park and effect a rescue before word gets about and all the growlers plus the seven dwarfs turn up hoping for a share in the hairy pie. " Thanks again "H" for taking good care of our Aimz and being such a Gentleman.

"Portsmouth ratings, salt of the earth … … … … . . salt of the earth.

CHAPTER 18

Frolocks in the Windies

I rejoined my ship in Pompey dockyard, the short refit was just about complete and so all the living accommodation was being made habitable. It was up to the leading hands and Presidents of Messes to organise the best they could with what ever they could lay their hands on to make their respective messes as liveable and homely as possible. My Mess, the Leckies was right up forward No 4, Mess 3 Decks down, below Nos. 1, 2, and 3 messes on No 2 deck, which was the thro' ship deck, in which the Burma road was situated, the For'd to Aft main thoroughfare, on which all the crews main amenities were situated, NAAFI, main offices, galley, bathrooms, heads (toilets), scab lifters abode, Pox doctors retreat, Jaunties Caboose (police office). From this deck all along its length, were ladders going up to the upper deck, other mess decks, ops. rm. Bridge etc., and down to machinery spaces, engine rooms, boiler rooms, auxiliary machinery spaces, store rooms, magazines (for ammunition, not porno! I can imagine how your minds are working.) and various other mess decks, and the steering gear right down aft.

I've just remembered the decoy was built before dining halls were a fitted luxury. The hot food was brought from the galley to a main servery on the Burma Road. The food trays were kept in big heaters under the counter. When the "Pipe" (broadcast) was made "Hands to dinner" the servery shutters would go up and the scran (food) would be dished up to the long queue of junior ratings, starving, waiting for dinner after tot. There would be two junior Chefs behind the counter to dish out your ration onto your tin plate (prisoner style). I was in the queue about six from the front, just waiting for hands to dinner, when they would start dishing up. One of the chefs, a young nineteen year old Scouser was telling his mates about his experience over the last week. His Mother had had a stroke and was in a coma in a Liverpool hospital. He had been given compassionate leave to go and visit her.

I was looking and listening to this lad, thinking he must have some sort of death wish. I had never seen anything like it in the Andrew (Navy) before. He was standing there brazen as anything with dyed blonde hair, more than a hint of make up, and finger nails for pricking the sausages with. He was obviously going for it, big time. He would be getting right up the noses of all the regulating staff, who at that moment would have been working out how to give him the bum's rush big time A. S. A. P., as soon as the powers that be took in what he was up to. A dishonourable discharge after 90 days in detention quarters (sailor's jail). Shirt lifting Hat racks were just not allowed. All discovered perverts were tried, found guilty, gaoled for 90, then slung out in disgrace, and this wasn't so very long ago. Just before the shirt lifters weedled their way into political power and changed the fucking rules. – Typical. Sodem and Gemorra, they never learn.

Apparently, he had gone on leave to see his Mum in hospital, who was still in a coma, he had gone out on the town in Liverpool with all his dodgy mates who had got him well pissed, and then taken him for a make over, which was unheard of in those days for women, let alone blokes !. – – Using the term very loosely.

The next day he was visiting his Mum and talking to her, which brought her out of the coma. She couldn't make out who it was in front of her with the dyed green/blonde hair, make up and finger nails "Who is it?" With a heavy lisp "It's me Mum, Richard but I prefer Dick. I've come home from the Navy to see you and Oh by the way Mum, I've turned queer "a right raving mincer.

(He carried on explaining this to his mates with an exaggerated lithp)

"Fucking hell, she took one look, a big gasp and flaked out into another coma. The rest of the family were fuming. They told me to pack my bags and fuck off back down the poncey south and don't dare to show my face up here ever again".

"So, here I am, I've come back to look after all my lovely thailors". "Hands to Dinner, Ok Jack, what do you want?"

The queue started moving, I had fish and chips on my tray and said "Can I have some peas please Chef".

"I'd like to pee up your dish".

"Fuck off, you fucking knobber. " "M M M H! – – , get you thailor. "

He was poncing around for another few days then just disappeared, never to be seen again. He probably finished up on the game in Soho, servicing all the queer theatrical types who congregated around all the cinemas and theatres, and especially the fudge packers rallying point the ever famous Shaftsbury Avenue. They got the name right there that's for sure. The place was apparently crawling with them, still there you go. I don't know where they all keep coming from because the fuckers don't breed. We used to say it won't be long before they are making it compulsory and by the cringe they've done it. They made their plans in the universities then put them into action at the end of the nineties, perverted and bankrupt the country faster than a hatter could shave his legs.

We were still settling in to our new mess No 4. It was right in the bows of the ship on No 3 deck. It was situated just above the waterline and our kit lockers were fitted to the periphery of the mess following the contours of the ship's bows as that was where we were. My bunk was the best as I got the pick, being Killick of the mess. I had chosen the one furthest from the ladder going up to the mess deck above and occupying three kit locker tops with a mattress on top. There were three port holes (scuttles) on either side of the ship situated in our mess, one of which was level with my pillow, which was the absolute dog's bollocks brilliant I was able to lie on my bunk and look through the port hole, wherever the ship was or what it was doing.

On a fine, calm day, the ship could be steaming along at anything up to 33 knots max and if the bow wave wasn't too high, I could open the scuttle, getting all the fresh air and stick my head out admiring the great sensation of rushing along at "N" knots with my head just above the bow wave. Every now and then I would get caught out if the ship took a dip in a big swell, the scuttle would disappear beneath the waves and we would ship a big green bastard, which would enter the mess with a 12" circumference and start flooding the mess via my bunk, causing a mad panic to try and force the scuttle shut against the huge water pressure. Multiply this by the six scuttles and we never knew where it might come from. All good fun in a blue suit. A laugh a minute, until it drenched you in the middle of the night, when it was, What the fuck!.

We had transformed our mess deck from a rough grey painted iron and steel box to something a bit more homely for us to proudly call our mess, all the different departments wanted there mess to be envied and be the best on the ship, a bit of inter departmental rivalry always lifted the moral of the ships company to the benefit of the whole ship. I had made good use of all my carpentry skills, and had also purloined enough 12 inch square linoleum deck tiles, to cover the bare metal deck and make it more acceptable and warmer etc on the bare feet, and create a more friendly atmosphere for those of us who could tell the difference and of course for everyone's benefit.

When all the dockyard work was complete and all the dockyard mateys were gone, the ship was back under the command of the Captain and his ship's company proper.

The following week was always shake down, every day at sea off Portsmouth and Portland, putting every piece of machinery through its paces and acquainting every member and new member of the ship's company with their jobs etc and testing all equipment onboard from the temperature settings on the deep fat fryer (chip pan) up to the three twin 4. 5" big automatic gun turrets plus anti submarine equipment. When all was tested and correct the ship would be sent down to Portland in Dorset for a six week work up at the war school in the Seas off Portland, to train and gel the ships company into a fighting unit, and hone them up as an efficient, reliable unit, ready for war and any unforeseen piss ups and revelry we might find ourselves having to deal with, any where in the World, and believe me, we got in some real hard practise during our time down in Dorset, especially our runs ashore in Weymouth.

In the June and July hot summer weekends, dishing out extra large portions to all the young fillies who had travelled down from all over the country with nothing but the highest expectations on there minds, and disappointment for them just wasn't an option.

Once a week, usually on a Saturday forenoon, the Captain would conduct mess deck rounds, different days for the rest of the ship. which was the Navy's way of keeping on top of everything in the living quarters. Each mess would delegate about four rating to act as mess cooks to get the mess spick and span for inspection under the instruction of the Killick of the mess, who would report for inspection at midday to the Captain. Who on completion would then name the best mess, and present them with the cake, baked in the galley, thus killing many birds with one stone (practise for Junior Cooks). It was always a good tot time Saturday lunch after rounds, normally followed by the Chief Chef's special lunch, because the galley and associated compartments were also part of the Captains rounds, so an extra special effort was always made to impress the man with the big hat.

With every one satisfied it was then off ashore for the rest of the day and night. To carry out our onshore duties to the best of our abilities, thus ensuring the young ladies went home from their holidays with something good to remember, and an even better reason to return the following year, for little more of what did them good, or find the bastard who left her with a bun in her oven.

On top of all the usual fire exercises etc, which usually involved the whole ships' company. There were extra exercises for the ships diving team of which I was now a member. We all had to learn to work together efficiently as a team as we were now the only way the ship had of dealing with any mines or bombs that might be planted under water on the ship's hull, during our circumnavigation of where ever the fucking hell we were going to. The trouble with the magnetic limpet mines was they had hidden plungers behind the face plate, which would be released if you pulled the device off the hull, thus allowing the device to explode. Not good, and on top of that the longest fuse (timing device) known was only 20 minutes, so not much time after detection to muster, get dressed, get in the water, search the hull, find and mark any suspect, then clear the water quick, before putting your head between your legs and kissing your arse goodbye.

Having found and marked a mine with a float up to the surface. Onboard, they would isolate the watertight compartment behind the mine so that after the explosion and consequent hole in the side only that compartment would flood thus containing the damage, and saving the ship. Tall order. Still, it had to be done. We would practise freeing mooring ropes and wires, tangled around the propellers, pulling bloated drowned bodies out of the sea after disasters, caused by whatever reason. Anything that could happen underwater or even in the water, the twelve strong diving team would be expected to cope with and usually did.

On a Saturday morning, at the end of the six weeks, the staff diving inspectors were setting tasks and examining us on the results. Our team, 4 divers two in the water (buddies) doing the job, the other standby diver ready to come to our assistance on the bottom if we got into difficulties and the fourth driving the boat. (Pinn'ace, cutter or Gemini) with all the equipment in it. This particular task they had set us was to find a vessel on the seabed which had been sunk there about sixty years previous and was in about 50ft of water just inside the mole (breakwater) of Portland harbour.

They gave us the area to search. Once found, that was the big obstacle, they wanted to know the length, breadth, depth, how many propellers, what it was used for. All measurements to be taken using your body length, approximately 6 foot, both arm span approximately same as body length, forearm 18", hand span 4". They said, "Whilst your examining the vessel, under no circumstances are you to venture into the holds. " By saying that, straight away we want to know why not.

The two of us had finished the business and were swimming along the upper deck, gathering any further information we could. The tide was beginning to turn and the visibility was dropping from about 20' . I happened to look up and saw the standby diver had been exercised and was on his way down looking for uslooking for us. I pointed him out to my buddy and we dived into a hold out of view, held our breath (no bubbles). He was only a young lad about seventeen, he swam over the hold we were in and was very warily swimming along the upper deck. We came out of the hold and swam quickly to catch him up, approaching him from behind, I grabbed his fin (flipper) and shook his leg violently. I have never seen anyone move so quickly.

We were always told that our diver's knife on a belt around our waist, would be difficult to remove in an emergency. He was petrified, in one quick move, he rolled over onto his back having removed his knife en route into an attacking position, to see what was about to devour him. We backed off sharpish before sampling his flashing blade. His eyes were standing out like racing dog's bollocks. I'm sure they were touching the front of his visor. Talk about Popeye, he was petrified, just how much so, we found later when we were undressing. There was a powerful aroma which didn't resemble anything we'd been swimming near! The young un had really emptied out. We passed with flying colours.

The vessel was a First World War barge used for carrying coal out to the ships anchored in Weymouth Bay. From what we could see in the hold, there was about 50 years worth of knives and forks and metal dinner trays that generations of matelots had thrown over the side to save washing up, as there ships had passed unknowingly overhead. We had been doing the work up, for six weeks and our big examination was being carried out on the next Friday afternoon in a big war games scenario off Portland, involving lots of warships, anti-submarine helicopters, submarines, fighter bomber jet planes, the whole shebang!.

The tension is huge, all the multiple scenario's set over the next fourteen hours had to be passed before our work up was deemed complete, and we could be passed out into the fleet to go about our commission as deemed by the Admiralty in any part of the world for the next couple of years, with all the unknown trials and tribulations to come. There was a full team of CPO's, Admiral's staff onboard examining everything we did. If at the end of the day they thought the ship wasn't up to scratch to join the rest of the fleet, they had the power to hold the ship back for another week to get up to standard and nobody wanted that.

It was hell anyway, it just so happened that the Admiral of the Portland Helicopter base was retiring that day and had decided to have a final inspection flight around the fleet as a last farewell at about 1600 hours.

We were all closed up at action stations when there was a frantic pipe over the tannoy system, "All divers to the diving store at the rush. " What's all this about? I stop what I'm doing down the engine room and leg it hot foot to the diving store, Suddenly the ship banks to starboard as it turns sharply and the stokers down below get Full ahead rung on. Which is only done in a real emergency, all four boilers, two in either boiler room, are immediately put on line to feed both engine rooms for the huge acceleration being demanded from the bridge.

"Full steam ahead".

An order only rung up in an emergency. The stern of the ship bites into the water with the huge acceleration of both propellers, creating a huge bow wave up forward. We are now racing to an incident which occurred on the horizon. One of our lookouts has reported a large flash from the helicopter which is patrolling around and observing the active fleet exercise, just before it ditched in the oggin (sea). We were at the store frantically getting dressed. We were soon all dressed, sets on (breathing) tested, awaiting further instruction. We were speeding through the water at 33knots, which is fast. The ship has two engine rooms and two boiler rooms, double normal, which produced such speed. It also had a sharp cut away reinforced bow, which was designed to cut and sink submarines if they were caught on the surface with their periscopes up. We soon arrived on the scene.

There was a bit of debris floating about and a couple of copter wheels. They had pin pointed the wreck with our sonar set, and it was suspended about 200ft down. Probably an air pocket trapped in the cockpit holding it up. Our diving limit with compressed air was 120 feet. They were contemplating sending us down but that was then deemed to be far to dangerous as the air pocket could escape at any time, which it did shortly afterwards, causing the helicopter to plummet to the sea bed, taking the Admiral and his crew to a temporary watery grave.

Talk about a green rub. His last day after all those years, and it was his own decision to have a last fly around.

There was nothing we could do but retrieve the debris in the Gemini (diving boat) and mark its last resting place and depth of the water onto the charts for further investigation with the appropriate equipment, when a deep sea recovery by clearance divers (the bomb squad). at a later date could take place.

We had completed our six weeks work up and passed our rigorous examination by the work up staff and were now deemed ready to carry on with our commission where ever in the world our presence was required, Yeah roll on, lets get amongst it.

There was a great feeling of relief onboard that it was all over. Everything from now is going to be for real. The following morning, Saturday, the Captain decided to have the ship's hull inspected by the diving team just to be certain there wasn't any damage to any of the underwater sonar sets or hull fittings and to be certain none of the Portland staff had left any little farewell presents on the hull to be discovered at a later date, by one of their divers. It was now Saturday morning and suddenly there was a pipe over the tannoy, "Awkward State 3. All divers to the Diving Store. " We all mustered and commenced getting dressed, the diving officer explains "You're going to do a half necklace, bottom search and you Jimmy Green are keel swimmer. " You can't dive if you've got a cold because you can't clear your ears by blowing down your nose onto your nose clip, your ears should pop as the pressure inside your head is equalised with the outside water pressure.

I had the beginnings of a cold but I thought I'll be alright. I didn't want to appear to be trying to get out of it. I have a hole through the wafer thin bone behind my starboard (right) nostril, which was punched through in the infirmary while I had a sinus syringe to see if that was causing my migraines, when I was seventeen years old just before I joined the Navy. It wasn't the cause but the hole is still there. Being keel swimmer I swim down the bows of the ship then the length of the ship in the middle with the whole of the ship on top of me. By the time I'm under the engine and boiler rooms there's no escape, it's pitch black so everything is done by feeley, feeley.

When descending, the first 15 feet are the worse, it's the only time the pressure doubles. 15lbs square inch on the surface and goes up 1lb per foot as you descend ie 15 feet down surface pressure plus 15lb – 30lb square inch.

I left the surface and as how hard I blew onto my nose clip my ears wouldn't pop. The outside pressure was building up and pushing my ear drums in. The pain was now excruciating and it felt like someone was pushing two knitting needles onto my ear drums. Suddenly the pain in my right ear disappeared. I blew on my nose clip and I could feel all this air escaping through my starboard ear drum. It had burst. I surfaced and the diving officer was screaming at me "Get down, get down! "another prick.

I pointed to my ear but he didn't get it, so I blew on my nose clip and a lot of red bubbles came spewing out of my ear.

"Ok, clear the water, next diver, you're now keel swimmer. Jimmy report to the sick bay. "

They stopped all my weekend leaves (if there were any) for the next three months because I had to have a massive shot of penicillin injected three times a day. In no time at all I was completely deaf in that ear. All the blood etc soon blocked my ear passage and it was itching all the time by my ear drum as it was beginning to heal, which unfortunately no one could get to, and the itching in the middle of my head was driving me insane. Then there was a drip drip down my ear lobe for weeks. It was driving me mad. After about six months it did heal up. When the Doc took a shufti (look) he said it had ripped the drum down the middle, but it had healed, but because it had stretched it, it now sagged down instead of being taut, therefore, my hearing is now impaired, slightly mutton Geoff (deaf).

We were now in Pompey (Portsmouth) and it was decided I needed to get my qualifying minutes in as I was now well behind, and my diving pay would be stopped. So here we go, we're going out in the diving boat to the Napoleonic fort, a big round defence fortress out in the Solent. We're going to dive on one of those to see if we can find something of interest. I was wondering if my newly healed ear drum would stand up to the pressure. I needn't have worried, it just took a little bit extra blowing and they both popped so I was ok.

We searched around the base of the forts but unfortunately we didn't find anything of any significance. Onboard the decoy, my job was Leading Electrician seconded to the two engine rooms and two boiler rooms. The four boilers pushed out super heated steam of over four hundred degrees centigrade to power the main engine turbines and the main electrical turbo alternators which in turn fed power at 440v to the ship's main switchboards, which in turn supplied all the ship's electrical needs.

I used to like entering the boiler rooms through their individual air locks, especially in Winter time. We only wore a pair of overalls because of the heat generated, there it seemed like a training period for the fires of hell, but it was something special working down there and got good respect from the rest of the ships company who would cringe if a boiler room airlock door was opened whilst walking past.

It could take there breath away. At secure each evening, the first job was a bath and dhobi. I had my own galvanized dhobi bucket in which I would dhobi first my skidders and socks and then my ovies. Thus we were turned out clean and smart each forenoon if daywork or watch if a watchkeeper. The purpose of the air locks was to maintain the air pressure inside the boiler room. This pressure was developed through large air supply fans. The air pressure outside the boilers had to be higher than inside the boilers, So if there was to be any passage of air it would be from the outside in and not inside to out, as this way it could bring with it a large flame to meet poor old stokes who was nozzle jockey'ing on the boiler front, the nozzles carried the heated F. F. O. furnace fuel oil into the boiler, there were three or four different sized big nozzle's mounted on an eighteen inch circular plate on the front of each boiler, by pushing one in or taking one out the stoker could control the amount of fuel entering the boiler and so the steam pressure.

There were two boilers side by side with a 12" gap between them. The two jockies took their commands from the P. O. Stoker standing behind them controlling the very important mixture of air and water keeping the massive kettle boiling and regulating the steam pressure, if he loses control loss of water for instance the steam pressure will rise instantaneously possibly bursting the boiler tubes causing the boiler to blow filling the boiler room with super heated steam killing all down there instantly, or if the water goes out of the top of the glass water droplets will follow the superheated steam out of the top of the boiler into the engine room hitting the steam turbine blades like bullets and leaving the rest of the ship in deep shit. It was absolutely terrifying when a full Gale was blowing up top, trying to stand up on the boiler front plates was an evolution in itself never mind carrying out all the tricky manoeuvres for four hours at a time, there was one thing for sure there were no big fat bastards down on the boiler front for very long it was all steamed and frightened off them in next to no time.

There were several gaps in the boilers frontage where the big flames would shoot out (a flash back) if someone left both air lock doors open or didn't quite close one before opening the other, thus causing a difference in air pressure, and incorrect balance, and frightening the shit out of the watch keepers on the boiler front, who quite often came out of there wearing a badge of respect, half a head of hair. The other half being singed off by a big boiler flash back, which Stokes would milk for all it was worth whilst spinning the shit on his next run ashore to another kind of old boiler, trying to convince her she would be better off if he could remove her dung hampers and keep them to be used as an emergency fire blanket when next on watch down the boiler room. Any port in a storm. Horny bastard.

There were so many things down there to keep the mind focussed. All steam is invisible, what people see coming out of a kettle is water vapour after the steam has cooled and that's just 100 degrees centigrade. In the boiler room, if a super heated steam leak develops, a pin hole in an internally corroding pipe for instance, no one can see it and if you walk past it, it will cut you in half. The first knowledge of it is a high pitched whistle. Everyone freezes, the only way to find it was to hold a brush handle or equivalent in front of you and walk towards the whistle. When the stick falls in half they'd found it.

The Petty officer stoker who was in charge of the boiler room and controlled the two boilers, had to keep a stable mixture and therefore a steady steam temperature / pressure. He would be frantically adjusting the air pressure going into the boiler to keep things stable if he got the mixture wrong ie. Water, fuel oil, air. If the boilers were short of air they would start pulsating as the fuel burning was fighting for more oxygen. These boilers were each the size of a small living room and were situated about a foot apart when they started pulsating violently, full of super heated steam. It was frightening to say the least.

It happened once when I was returning from behind the boilers after fixing an electrical fault I was in the small gap when both boilers began pulsating and just touching me now and again, if they both came in together I would be squashed. I thought it was curtains, good night nurse. One of the worst jobs for me was fixing a fault on the boiler periscope light fitting. The PO Stoker operating the boiler had a periscope going up the front of the boiler then into the top of the boiler in the gap between the water tubes (now full of super heated steam over 400 deg C.) and the outer boiler casing where the flaming boiler exhaust fumes were heading for the funnel and away to atmosphere, and at the back of the boiler in the same space was a light fitting.

If Stokes could see the light it meant he'd got the mixture correct and wasn't making smoke (with unburned fuel oil) which in itself was a cardinal sin, for which the Captain would soon make his displeasure known. If black smoke was pouring from the funnel, the enemy would pick up your position and send you a few salvo's of high explosive shells to be going on with, which could be good night nurse for the vessel and everyone sailing within her. Not good. It was the sign of an incompetent boiler operator, who would soon be on the Engineer Officer's Report, to have his fucking oriscope read in no pleasant fashion.

In rough weather the whole operation was a terrifying experience, the whole ship up in the air over to Port then Starboard, dropping, lifting, hanging on sliding across the front of the boiler spilling hot oil, water, all over the place while still operating all the red hot controls for the boiler, at the same time sweating your bollocks off, thinking just another three and a half hours to go, to watch change then we'll get to fuck out of here. Our reliefs can have some.

This particular forenoon, the lamp had gone out and I was called to repair the same. I was behind the boiler where there was little room and little light all the pipes are asbestos lagged and carrying steam they are in a twenty inch gap behind the boiler and the bulkhead. I had to manoeuvre myself in between the obstacles up to the top of the boiler being burnt through my overalls all the way. It was like hell. With asbestos gloves I would remove the light fitting (getting burnt everywhere) then block the hole with a big wet towel to stop the boiler fumes, which were now coming out of the hole and burning plus choking me. I had just completed the task and couldn't wait to get out when I had the most frightening experience of my life.

All of a sudden there was the loudest noise in a confined space, imaginable. It sounded like a boiling Niagara Falls was bursting all around the place. I thought the other boiler had burst at the top about fifteen feet away from me. There was red hot water vapour screaming out from behind the other boiler, cooling from somewhere between 500 and 600 deg. C. I couldn't move. I was bouncing between red hot pipes and my whole body was shaking violently I honestly thought that I was a goner plus the ship. It didn't stop it seemed to go on for ever. My bones were vibrating. Just as quickly as it had started, it stopped, apparently about ten minutes later after the steam pressure had dropped back its to normal safe working level. I made my way between the boilers to the front. When the stokers on the boiler front (throttle jockey's) saw me coming out from between the boilers, burned, soot black, greasy, sweating and shaking uncontrollably, they couldn't believe their eyes literally someone returning from hell. What had happened was, every so often a safety test had to be done on the boilers to check that they wouldn't heat up to bursting point if something went badly wrong. Unbeknown to me they had commenced this evolution, I also didn't know there was a large safety valve situated at the top and back of each boiler. The PO Stoker was so busy he'd forgotten I was working behind the boiler. They had been building up the steam temperature and pressure by putting more burners on and watching the temperature gauge slowly rising, every ones nerves were on tenterhooks, all the time hoping that there would be no faults and none of the internal tubes would fracture, because if there was a major failure inside the boiler, the boiler could and probably would burst and the following explosions would be the death of the boiler room and everyone in it.

Eventually I think between five and six hundred degrees centigrade which the top temperature-pressure the safety valve was set at was reached, the safety valve lifted releasing the excess pressure, and that's when my hell began. We didn't even have ear defenders in those days. I wasn't even checked over afterwards, but why should I have been. I went for a shower, tended my burns and started to tell the story around the mess deck tot table. My it was so good to be there and out of that hell hole. Happy days! Musn't crumble, there wasn't a major failure inside the boiler after all so "The Queen – God Bless Her". Alls well that ends well.

We were in Pompey and it was coming up for Christmas 1966, and we were going on 17 days leave on the coming Friday, so we decided on a mid week Christmas run ashore. A belly full of rough cider and finish up with an Indian rat curry, at that time the local authorities were finding dustbins, boxes, plastic bags full of empty cat and dog food cans at the rear of the Chinese, Indian eateries, no wonder they had their own personal flavours to choose from. they called it chicken but we knew better. We were on our way of this shit hole, when the biggest moth I'd ever seen landed on Dickie Dyke's shoulder (one of my electrical mechanics) as he was walking out in front of me. I grabbed it in the palm of my hand, Dickie turned round and I said "Nice hot curry?" "Too right. " There were six of us and when we got outside I said, I'll give anybody my tot tomorrow who will eat what I've got in my hand. " Straight away Dickie said "I will." As I keep saying a full tot was gold dust.

I got hold of its wings and its body was like half a finger with big running legs. Straight away he was sorry he'd volunteered but he couldn't lose face now. He had to do it. After umming and ahhing and pulling faces for about five minutes, he closed his eyes and opened his mouth. I slipped the struggling furry little fucker with its big hairy legs going like the clappers as far down the scousers throat as possible, and said "shut your trap and watch it with your molars". (this is going to be good), but young Dykes was a bit of a squeamish type and was jumping up and down pissing about trying to swallow the fucking thing. Bloody Fairy.

After about 20 seconds and three or four gulps attempting to swallow afters, the moth made a partial escape on a tidal wave of rat curry and fermenting rough cider, at that moment it was a six legged large bodied hang gliding refugee heading at speed for the Southsea pavement. Young Dykes, with his eyes watering, was perusing his Christmas ruby (curry) all over the pavement, with the behe'moth making its way out of the big pile of steaming vomit with its big strong legs dragging its minty body onto the dry runway, wondering what the fucks going on, no doubt. Its wings were well coated and sticking to the pavement as was its big fur coat, and try as it might, it couldn't take off. We were in uncontrollable fits of laughter, rolled up. I retrieved it and said, " anybody else, they were diving in all directions, no takers, fucking sprogs, I will down it for a tot apiece". They couldn't believe it and said "too right, You're on".

I began mustering as much saliva as I could, but as much as I tried for some reason to no avail. I shipped it into the old north and south head first and tried to swallow, but my mouth was dry as a nuns cunt, its struggling legs soaked up my saliva and the bastard got itself stuck at the back of my throat. I could feel all of its powerful legs going like the clappers. Luckily it was running in the right direction down my throat, the extra long way out. It took me about ten minutes of continual swallowing, and mustering more and more saliva before I eventually manoeuvred it passed my tonsils and down into the void, to join my by now fermenting rat curry. To say my lads were pissed off was a massive under statement. All Christmas leave to mourn the tot they had just lost. "That's it, you owe me a tot apiece, I'll savour them after leave. " Rub it in.

We'd had a brilliant run ashore and were making out way back to the dockyard. Dykes was now bellyaching that he was hungry after mustering his kit all over the pavement down Southsea. . We stopped at the chippy outside the dockyard gate while he got some replenishments. We were well taking the piss as he munched his way through his supper once again.

It's Friday morning now and we're going on Christmas leave "1966" after tot time at midday. We're not allowed in the mess until 11. 45 as the cooks are having a good old huck out leaving the grot immaculate to come back too and less of a fire risk while most of us are away. and no one feels like doing any work, so there's four of us skulking down in the small electrical workshop in the bowels of the ship. For a bit of fun we knock up a Ouija board.

We upturned a tot glass and turn all the lights off which just leaves us with a red night light on. It was all very eerie, ask it a question, someone asked "Who's going to have a bad Christmas leave?" We had a finger each hardly touching the glass, then it took off. ' JIM. W. ' At this point, the hair on my neck was up, Dickie Dyke's scream shattering the silence, that put the fear of God up the lot of us, and we all nearly shit ourselves. Dykes and Smudge were off up the ladder jam tarting as they went and were gone. The remains of the rat curry manifesting itself, the two of us left were as white as ghosts. We put the lights back on and binned the Ouija board. We didn't try that again.

We had something to look forward to after Christmas leave. HMS Decoy and HMS Juno were sailing for a six month tour of duty around the West Indies. It's going to be good, we're going to be diving all over the Caribbean, countless beautiful tropical islands which we'll visit. Christmas leave went well. I met up with one of the girls from the tech who I had always fancied, she had been in the year above me at school so I hadn't had a chance of meeting her. She was as fit as a butchers dog and she'd just won the Miss Rochdale competition and had turned out to be a real cracker. . So we whiled away Christmas and New Year together at our leisure. A truly out of the blue bonus. (Dip your bread in H. – – – – - As well)

After leave and after I'd collected my due's, we set sail from Pompey on our way to the West Indie's, our first port of call was to be Punta de Garda in the Azores. We arrived a few days later in the afternoon. The weather had been improving each day as we journeyed south until now, we were basking in the sub tropical sunshine dressed only in shorts and flip flops. Our run ashore on the first night, which we'd been looking forward to was dramatically cancelled. "All divers to the diving store, " we were informed that HMS Ottis, a diesel electric submarine, which was accompanying us, had clipped a reef on the way in with one of her propellers and had broken off an eighteen inch by four inch chunk from the phosphor bronze propeller, which was now causing it to make a hell of a noise as it rotated, the higher the revs. The louder the noise (cavitation).

This was unacceptable as the sub. is supposed to run silent and be unobserved, and whenever a British fleet left the UK, it was always followed a Russian, supposedly fishing vessel, which was always bristling with radar antennae and under water sonar, listening devices (Cold War, hide and seek). The Subs sonar equipment had picked up the cavitation, and its divers when alongside had found the problem, and rigged up an underwater platform and staging arrangement to stand on and work off, built around the propeller.

After initial inspection all divers were informed of the damage to the starboard screw.

There was an 18 inch semi-circle which had been clipped out of one of the three blades on one propeller.

The rest of the blades on the propellers were razor sharp to cut through the water. Our job was to file the damaged blade down to a razor edge, from a max. Phospher bronze 2 inch thickness. With underwater lights rigged, we set about our task. Three teams of divers, one from each ship taking it in turns, breathing our sets down, filing away, returning to the ship to recharge and wait our next turn and so on. Just after midnight, we were charged up again, and standing by the gangway on the quarterdeck of our ship H. M. S. Decoy which was moored outboard of H. M. S. Juno awaiting further instructions, when a taxi pulled up on the jetty and out fell half a dozen stokers. They couldn't walk and so crawled up Juno's gangway past their officer of the day, across their flight deck, then down our gangway, where the bosun's mate put each of the lads station cards in their mouths, whereupon one by one they crawled over the hatch combing, and down the ladder to the Burma road, then off to their mess. It was hilarious. I'd never seen the spectacle before, because I would always have been with them.

The Officer Of the day of Juno was fuming, (he didn't go fuck all on it at all) our ship, being an old fashioned world war two designed big gunned twin engine / boiler roomed very fast destroyer with submarine chopping bows, which really looked the part and with a Captain and crew to match and Juno being brand new, sporting a tiny looking one barrel 4. 5" gun, feeble looking and with a right Tosser for a Captain plus a crew to match. (I'm in charge, and without a clue, situation normal!) There was much envy for our ship and plenty of rivalry to go with it. We had the comradeship, Juno was being run strictly by the book (never a good thing, it just shows those in charge havn't got a grasp of the changing situations thus rendering their brains useless). The OOW . shouting to Decoys Bosun's mate, who was in charge of the gangway "What are you going to do about that lot?"

Not quite understanding he replied, "What do you mean, – – -Sir?" "just look at them" "They're always like that – – - Sir, ".

We worked on the propeller all night and by 0900 it was as good as it was ever going to be until she could have another propeller fitted. We managed to get a run ashore in that night before we sailed for Bermuda in the morning, which was about the first island as we arrived on station, sweating our cobblers off, we docked in Hamilton for a courtesy call and enjoyed swimming in the fine blue waters with the silver sands on their beautiful beaches. It was a quiet place really but we had a couple of good runs ashore. After visiting a few more stunning islands as we were sailing through the idyllic waters, being captivated by the sight of the dolphins, rays, sharks, flying fish which I didn't actually believe existed before seeing them skimming over the wave tops for myself, lying on my stomach with my head protruding over the bows observing the dolphins playing in our bow wave, just brilliant. We had the good fortune to visit Curacao and berth in Willemstad, the capital after we had crossed the Caribbean for the first of many times to come in the next few months.

Everything was particularly good here from day one. We had two RFA's with us (Royal Fleet Auxiliaries) supply ships to replenish our stores when required. One was a tanker to supply us with our fuel and fresh water, the other dry stores, to supply everything else, food, beer, rum, clothing, spare parts all we would need, except fanny, and that's why we were in Curacao, there was absolutely bucket, bucket and even more bucket loads just waiting for us ashore. – – Bastard!.

The second day was being spent unloading supplies from the RFA's and topping up the warships. HMS Decoy was berthed directly astern of the dry stores vessel, which was unloading hundreds of cases of beer with her crane and the cases were being shipped ashore in very large cargo nets.

As the crane's jib was moving over the gap between the ship and the jetty, the cargo net broke and about a hundred cases of beer fell into the sea, – – disaster?, wait one. – – – "For who?".

The first we knew about it was a pipe over the main broadcast "All Divers to the diving store". The diving officer explained what had happened and we were to retrieve as much beer as possible. Hip Hip – Hooray, H. M. S. Decoy to the rescue. He then told us that on the following day Saturday, we were going on a private diving expedition fishing etc., with the local diving fraternity, to be concluded with a ban yan (beach Barbi party) for the rest of the day. (Things are really getting good.)

He said, "The plan is, we'll lower the Gemini into the water and diver / cox'n. to keep the boat between ship and jetty, where its not very visible from above, then cover most of it with a tarpaulin, onboard will be two pairs of divers. The first pair's job is to take cases of beer from the sea bed to surface and place on the pontoon (large floating platform to stop ship banging against the jetty), where part of the RFA's crew will retrieve it. The second pair, you Jimmy, and Knocker, will bring a case each, back to the Gemini, keeping out of sight under the RFA, then under the Decoy to the Gemini. Surface under the tarpaulin where the Cox'n. will relieve you of your re-cycled/contraband until we have about twenty or so cases, then assist the first pair to completion". This is just what the doctor ordered!

I'd never been so eager since I turned up to drink the four tots, brilliant.

All this going on right under their noses. We completed our task, explaining that the rest of the beer was lost due to the cardboard cases collapsing. Horse shit ten bob a bag, Bull shit – – free. They were so grateful to us for saving what we did, they rewarded us with another four cases as a big thank you (stick around kids, you may learn something). just like talking to yourself – – a piece of piss.

We were up and raring to go the following morning. We loaded up the Landover which the local diving club had sent around, with all our equipment plus victuals for the B. B. Q. and plenty of beer, plus our rum rations, there was plenty for everyone in the Fanny. We met the club president who was a retired lieutenant commander Diving officer, from the Dutch Navy, who had emigrated to Dutch Curacao and started the Paradise Diving Club. (I'm pretty sure around about this time we were due our pay rise.) it can't be bad.

We arrived at a beautiful secluded tropical beach with the forest of palms behind us, and were informed this was the best private diving beach on the island. Our dive officer told us "It's a totally free dive, no buddies look after your own lives, have a good one. Big barbecue and piss up on completion be careful".

As we were walking down the beach all dressed, I said to Cloggy (Dutch "bossman") who was carrying a spear gun, "What is the routine if sharks appear?"

"I'm hoping they will, so keep still, hold your breath and don't move, otherwise they'll go away, and I want to spear them for the B-B-Q. "– – – fair enough".

We entered the water, swam out about 30 yards when suddenly the seabed dropped away a mountainside dropping down into the Abyss. . I was following Cloggy down with a couple of our lads. There was all kinds of tropical wildlife it was superb. I looked up and I could no longer see the surface, just an azure blue, where divers above me were getting smaller and smaller the deeper we went, I couldn't understand why they weren't coming with us. Our diving limit was 120 foot max. but I had no idea how deep I was, the navy didn't provide depth gauges, I was just following Cloggy down the mountainside. I looked up and the rest had stopped way above us. We seemed to be in a small forest of 3 to 4 foot long sponges growing out of the side of the ravine where we were swimming.

All of a sudden Cloggy stopped signalled me to do the same, then slowly aimed his spear gun from his right shoulder and started clicking his left finger and thumb. I couldn't see the object of his attention as yet but it was very exciting, I was just hoping it wasn't a matlot's head eating shark which was the centre of his attention. Fortunately a small school of barracuda appeared from within the sponges, they had teeth like Alsatians and I wasn't fancy'ing having those clamped around my nuts no thanks. One came swimming slowly towards his clicking fingers, very inquisitive, then 'Pop!' he shot it, right through the head. Perfect, the rest beat a hasty retreat into the cover of the sponges from whence they came, thank fuck.

My hair roots suddenly started tingling, and all my body nerves started to feel raw and exposed, I also felt sick. My brain was racing, what could it be, I twigged 'this is nitrogen narcosis; I've come down too deep for my compressed air. ' I'm up for the bends on ascent if I'm not careful I rose about six feet and that was enough, I was okay again. I tapped Cloggy on the shoulder and pointed to his depth gauge 180 foot. I was 60 foot deeper than I should have been, that was obviously the safety margin I'd found, well I'm okay, so far anyway. It would have been handy if we had depth and visable air gauges but we didn't. We started ascending up the side of the ravine slowly, slowly keeping well below our smallest bubbles, that way we could avoid stops and not get the bends, fingers crossed.

There were very few de'compression chambers around in the early 1960's, and certainly none as yet in the unspoiled, soon to be developed and ruined West Indies.

Which was why anything went in paradise, in those halcyon days, and boy weren't we just up for it all, dipping our bread in where ever and when ever possible. We eventually surfaced and thanked them for a brilliant dive, one we'll never forget. We piled all our stuff together ready to be picked up later, and proceeded to light the B. B. Q, a 50 gallon oil drum, cut in half lengthways with one inch holes punched in it for ventilation, and a thick metal mesh on top for the grill.

We had barbecued barracuda steak, beef steak, sausages, potatoes and chicken all washed down with excessive amounts of beer and Nelsons blood, and any other fuckers blood for that matter, whilst singing all the old matelots songs, ditties and sea shanties, to the accompaniment of a guitar the lads were passing around and playing. Absolutely superb, it couldn't have been any better. The dogs bollocks to say the least.

Well after sunset our transport turned up. We extinguished the fire, picked up the rubbish, tidied the beach and boarded our transport for a sing song all the way back to the ship where we unloaded, said thanks to our hosts, stowed all our gear, had a shower then re-grouped down the mess for a terrific wash up and night cap around the mess table, which was a major source of envy for the rest of the troops who couldn't help ear wigging, wishing they were divers, but they weren't, tough shit.

If you want something at least have the balls to put yourself out and go and get it. What a brilliant day. What's coming tomorrow? Bring it on.

The troops that had been ashore the night before in Willestad, and had had a really good time and had been given some flyers advertising a really lively night club on the other side of the Island, 'The Raging Bull', "The Rampant Bull", "The Horny Bullock", "The Bulls Bollocks", "Beever Creek", or something similar. Plenty of girls, that's the place for us. Hot Horny Steaming Sweaty Fanny. Yeah !. That's for us, lets get among'st it

We were going ashore after tot time to the nearest beach for a swim and bronzy bronzy, then back onboard for supper, a clean up, bath and dhobi, then we're off to see what they have to offer at the ' Rampant, Raging, Horny, Bulls Bollocks'. Or whatever its called.

We arrived in a fast black (taxi) to see the place was elevated, with chalets at the top, beautiful garden paths winding up and down, small pools with fountains, dim coloured lighting with a focal point of a large circular bar with a thatched tropical roof, all filling our nostrils with a hot musky perfume giving more of a hint of the delights of things to come. At the first glance it appeared to be almost Heaven. There were two or three skimpily clad good looking young women by the bar, but after about an hour when the rest of the horny brigade arrived the place was throbbing in unison with all the crew's members, the scantily clad lovely young females all about our age were spread about all over the place. I was sitting at the bar and shouted across to my oppo "What do you think of these then?"

I was weighing up in my hands the most gorgeous pair of tits I think I'd ever seen, nipples like rotten oranges topping milky cream wobbly mountains, (sorry did I say almost heaven.) It goes without saying that the blood transfusion had already taken place. She was licking and kissing my ear while at the same time whispering "Jiggy-jig Jack – are you up for it – – ". "What do you think this is a fucking periscope" "come on you can whisper sweet nothings down my voice pipe".

Too fucking right, let's go. I've got the breaking strain of a Kit-Kat when it comes to munching Fanny. It had taken a while for the penny to drop but this was brilliant, a one-stop brothel crawling with good looking Flange. We were in our element, the chalets were busy the bar throbbing the dance floor full and everything else pulsating – dancing and shagging to the HOT – - Latin American bongo and steel drums. (Hark ! I think I can hear them now – – Bollocks its the binmen.)

A big daisy chain doing the conga was making its way meandering up and down the paths past gloriously scented and inviting bushes, the night air was intoxicating, superb, the shrubs had a spectacular scented aroma as well, double loungers around the bar and pool with feather lined throws would have been the dogs bollocks, but lets not get greedy. Contortionism and indoor sports in the chalets will do for now, fuck the chandeliers, Good work if you can get it. We stayed for about five days then reluctantly well drained and hung over we sailed, totally Fucked. What a run ashore, it had to be one of the best. Certainly a good yardstick to try to improve on over the next few months, but with not much chance of topping, but we'll have a ball trying.

CHAPTER 19

Unwanted lodgers from carnival

It was about two days later, we were having a game of cards on the mess deck table, which was situated at the bottom of our mess ladder leading up to the deck apes mess, when I saw something land on the table near my hand. I thought it was some ones tame flea trying to get a shufty at my hand. I put my finger on it and picked it up between finger and thumb and took a look (butcher's hook). I couldn't believe it mobile shellfish, I was holding a crab. Being Killick in charge, cleanliness of the mess, I'm not so sure about Godliness, is my responsibility. I didn't let on what I was up to, but stood up and said "I'll be back shortly, no one is to leave the mess. Stinky ! (LEM Humm), you're in charge while I'm gone. Make sure no one leaves the mess". "What is it Jim what's wrong?, " "Stay put you'll find out soon enough!"

I reported to the sick bay. I saw the doc. and said "We need a short arm inspection down 4 mess, someone's brought mobile dandruff into the mess. The crabs are coming down and landing without parachutes. "

The doc said "OK, I'll be down in 5 minutes, get em lined up no one is to leave the mess. "

"OK, Doc. " I'll see to that.

The pox doctor arrived with his apprentice, (Nurse) and he sat on the end of the table's bench seat with a torch in his left hand, and a long pencil in his right hand. The SBA (Sick Berth Attendant, nurse) said "OK, drop your trousers and file past the doc. There were over twenty mess members, this is when all the giggling, joviality and harsh humour started, situation normal. The first lad stood in front of the doc. who shone his torch on the young fella's tackle, he started his immediate task, fishing for crabs without a creel, the whole mess was watching and totally engrossed in the whole delicate procedure, after an initial perusal of his immediate pubic area and chopper, he cautiously lifted his piece with the pencil to peruse his nuts. Ok. turn around, bend over and a quick shufty up his duck run, shit locker, Flue, he couldn't see much up there for the lads own personal fur lagging, it was more like looking up a Bears arse than a matlots, the black hole of Calcutta had fuck all on Bungy's ring piece, he would have had trouble finding Lobsters let alone crabs, still he persevered, if they were up there they sure would have been cosy. Crabs 1 – Doc 0. "OK next!"

The comments were now coming thick and fast.

The chief Elec. has arrived on the scene to oversee and try to keep some sort of discipline, while having a good chuckle to himself. Fucking hell "Look at the size of that I bet there's not many of them in a pound, I wonder what he feeds it on. All that meat and only two potatoes, I wonder if he's got enough blood to fill it. Now we know why he keeps going pale, he's not anaemic after all. " It must severely drain his system when he gets a lob on.

"shave a dogs head, chopper Harris", now we know how he got his name, and the poor guy at the other end of the queue, was getting well pissed off keep being asked when the maggot would be hatching. "

"You wouldn't like it on the end of your nose for a fucking wart that's for sure, now go fuck yourself with the blunt end of a rag mans trumpet you tosser. " Okay calm down, calm down, was the chief's input.

The Doc soon found the culprit who was harbouring a whole arse hole full of stow away's. The Pox Doctor then said "Everyone to the bathroom, Dhobi all the lagging you're wearing, then all of you shave off down there, and don't forget the crab ladder going up past your belly button, get that off, .

You don't want them making there way up to your chest then having a sexual field day under your arm pits, you'll be sorry. The killick of the mess will come down to the sick bay and pick up the medication, " crab powder about a bucket full", he will make sure that when you've all shaved off and showered, you all get a good coating of the shellfish repellent and make sure you get it right up your chuff, plum, you don't want them re appearing out of your duck run in a weeks time, douse your bunks as well. The little fuckers get everywhere. " Take no chances. You don't want to be transporting your arsehole about whilst being eaten alive, like a mobile live fish mongers.

Apparantly to lay their eggs, they go down the hair follicle and lay their eggs under the skin, so woe betide any crabby little fucker who doesn't get rid of them before they get established, once hatched scratching will be to no avail as they will be partying under the skin driving the host absolutely mental. A lot is to be learned living on a pussars mess deck, some one will have been there.

What a pantomime that was going on in the bathroom. Pubic hair everywhere, it looked like Christmas at a chicken plucking factory with a few wild turkeys thrown in for good measure. The crab powder was like flour we looked like 20 plus snowmen it was hilarious, then the real fun started we had to make our way back to our mess, out of the bathroom and down the Burma road past the main galley serving hatch with the rest of the ship's company roaring with laughter and taking the piss. Flour graders, graded grains make finer flour.

"You crabby bastards was the cry from all on route back to the mess deck (privacy! As if), no wonder matelots developed thick skins over the years. "

When all the piss taking had quietened down a bit, we started to wonder what the hell else might be lurking in our tackle. One things for sure we'd find out soon enough, whenever whoever had a dose of V. D. and was rotten reported it to the sick bay, their tot would be stopped and all would be revealed, then the wrath of the mess deck players would descend upon him like the biggest cartload of horse shit in seven counties. Dirty little infested fucker, serve's himself right for dipping his wick in unclean whores and spreading it about. Just what the pox doctor ordered, a job at last.

A couple of weeks later the chief sent for me down the office, " Ah! Come in Jimmy I've got some really bad news for your mess". "What's that then chief ""Young Smiths mum and dad have had an accident on their motorbike, in fact they've been killed. I want you to take him to one side and break it to him gently, in proper Naval style, I think it will be better coming from you, I know you get on well with all the troops and I think they will really appreciate that". "Bloody hell Chief, Ok I'll do my best", back down the mess I said. "Pay attention I've got some particularly bad news so if you could be prepared while I break it to you, I will be most greatful for your understanding and support as I've never had to do anything like this before and I'm sorry. If you could all stand up, right – all mess members who have their mum and dad waiting for them back home, muster over this side of the mess – – – – – – – – – – – – – -Whe're you going Smith? "

"All MP's are arseholes"

"I resent that remark"

"Why, are you an MP. "

"No, I'm a Arsehole".

Our next Port of call was to be Trinidad and Tobago, we anchored off in the harbour really looking forward to getting ashore at the weekend as the annual Ma de gras was to take place that weekend, a really non stop ball wrenching West Indian Carnival, really famous for being a weekend to be lost in the joys of total obliteration immersed in Old Oak rum and unbelievable debauchery, and fuck our luck we've just arrived in time for the party. All day Thursday as we toiled in the breezy air and Caribbean sunshine we got the waft of the steel drums drifting across the sun kissed paradise bay, as the locals were preparing for the weekend and dreaming up all sorts of stunts to pull on a warship full of horny matlots just arrived in the bay bearing all sorts of gifts and gold from God knows where, to exchange for all sorts of clap from where we all know where.

Shore leave starts after tot time Friday, the air of excitement onboard is electric. We raised anchor Fri. Morning and sailed to our allocated berth which wasn't next to the town but a couple of miles around the island in a beautiful secluded bay, on to a rickety old jetty which looked like tropical paradise. The local taxis soon found out where we were and turned up in droves to transport us all to the action. We were in our seventh heaven, Port o Spain was absolutely heaving with Fanny, p. s. (Not the American type). It had been winking at us from ashore for the last couple of days, now its tine for the satisfaction action by the bucket load, – – magic. Some say we occasionally ventured back on board over the next couple of days, on that I couldn't comment. What a weekend that was heaven

We were working Tropical routine while visiting, turn too at 0600 and secure at 1300 then off ashore for the rest of the day to do what had to be done. I think it might have had something to do with the burying of multitudes of bones, thank Christ. I was part of the ships cricket team, a pace bowler I always considered myself pretty good, I got results, the first three balls at the batsman, put the fear of God up him, then the second three at the wicket. It had always worked pretty well in my life up to now, was I in for a shock. We were Invited to play the Trinidad Police team during the week, we were looking forward to a good game. This was 1967 and the West Indies had just Marmalised the M. C. C. (England) at Lords a few weeks earlier. They had an exceptional team in those days, always world champs, no one could touch them, their team W. I's. was made up from players from all the different islands, I never gave it a thought, I didn't even connect the two.

Well anyway we won the toss and put them in to bat. I was opening bowler, the batsman's protection was pads and gloves the girlies attire of today wasn't even remotely considered not even worthy of mentioning in the established world of the noble art. . I was as fit as a butchers dog, I took my usual sixteen pace run up and let fly, the ball whistled past his starboard lug hole and they all whistled and cheered, funny I thought, but bowled him another couple similar which he just managed to evade, I came down with the fourth hoping for a real good one to send him on his way, but by the cringe did he give it some welly, lost ball, bastard, I'll have him next ball, bollocks out of the ground again.

Last ball of the over and they're all smiling now, we've got the measure of this geezer, smack another four, and so it went on, and on, and on. We finished the twenty over's or so, now it was our turn to smack them all over Trinidad, some fucking hope. I was seventh man, they let the openers etc. get a few so as not to totally demoralise everybody, my turn, I wandered out one pad one glove as usual, all the fielders erupted. Here he is, by now I was beginning to think my Goose was well and true'ly cooked. I took up my guard middle and leg. that was a waist of time, I looked up but couldn't see the bowler, perusing the field I noticed they had two long stops.   One   behind me where he should be on the boundary waiting for the hurricane and another on the boundary in front of me, but where's the bowler. The umpire says take up your guard, what the hell, that was when I noticed this Giant has moved off the boundary in front or me and, and, bollocks, he's coming towards me like a big black tornado, picking up speed as well, I don't believe this, Goliath is now going like an express train and still coming towards me, shit shoot, he is the fucking bowler, I notice his wild eyes and nostrils flaring like a runaway nigrescent mustang (what colours blood, thank fuck for that, I've shit myself) the behemoth let fly, I heard something whistle past my scull like a thousand angry hornets, I didn't see it, too fast, it sounded leather'ish with a seam, so I took it to be the ball.

I weighed up the situation and thought "this bloke means business". The faces on the rest of the fielders were a picture, for them anyway. I blocked the next two canon shots which nearly snapped my bat and rattled my skeleton, I'm sure the vertebrae and discs in my back were suddenly loosened, I was beginning to picture my head bursting like a ripe water melon on a cocoa nut shy when the inevitable sound of leather on bone was bound to connect shortly, then relief at last, my middle stump left the wicket, then the pitch, then out of the ground heading at speed for Tobago the neighbouring island, I retreated from the pitch to a tumultuous applause, my sphincter still twitching and going like a football rattle, fuck em all I thought, the piss taking bastards. I'll bet they're glad there's not a second innings. Anyway we came second, time for the wash up in the Pavilion, a wooden hut full of Old Oak rum with a few tables and chairs outside. I don't know who the giant bowler was but I've got more than a sneaking suspicion he wasn't a Trinidadian bobby. Joel Garner or similar rings a bell, Stretch – - he was certainly to long for a short time.

Our introduction to the bevy was their captain bringing out of the clubhouse a tray with a dozen bottles of Old Oak rum with the tops off. He said if anyone wants coke to go with it, its on sale inside, the rum was made local for next to nothing, while the cola had to be shipped in and was therefore expensive. We'll manage with the gallon and half of the nectar thank you very much. You're not going to believe this but after about an hour the whole team was waisted. Even pissed.

Our transport turned up a single decker bus, there was only two junior rates in the team myself and Jackie Yarwood, a killick stoker. All the rest were Grunters plus two trainee pigs, snotties (midshipman) consequently we got detailed off to carry the big cricket bag back onboard. On mustering the Bods it was noticed that one was missing, after a quick search I found the offender, a snotty, comatose under a far table. No matter how we tried we couldn't get him to come round, so myself and Jackie flaked him over the top of the cricket bag took a handle apiece and manhandled the total to the bus, to the delighted cheers of the rest of the inebriates, on arrival back at the ship it was something else trying to negotiate the big heavy cricket bag up the steep gangway, while at the same time trying to give the appearance of normality to the rest of the rubber necking crew who were loafing on the upper deck, especially with the precariously balanced snotty still on the bag and still quite oblivious to anything that was going on in the West Indies in general, let alone from the top of the cricket bag. There was one bonus to our struggle back, we had been off the ship all day and consequently missed the rum issue, therefore myself and Jackie were victualled in for a late tot, just what the undertaker ordered. We stowed all the gear swallowed our tots had some scran then flaked out for the night. Completely – – -tired out. – – – -fucked even. We had spent our six days break in Trinidad and it had been superb, but now it was time to leave and get back on patrol, we were all so exhausted we couldn't wait to get back out to sea and get settled into the daily routine.

We're sailing in half an hour so the usual Pipe was made over the main broadcast "Special sea dutymen close up, all machinery being run up and tested, we still haven't sailed after a further hour. Special sea dutymen fall out, something's obviously wrong speculation is rife as to what it is. The buzz is Sabotage, we can't believe this, on our ship, who the hell would do, or even want to do that. Sure enough someone had destroyed the steering motor bearings, we weren't going anywhere without them. The big problem now is that everyone is under suspicion, just who is the toerag of a mutineer who could in future put all our lives at risk. The traitor has to be found, in the old days he would have been dancing on thin air after being run up the yardarm by his shipmates with his head in a noose before sunset.

We're a bit more Liberal these days if the deckapes get hold of him before the Joss mans henchmen, he'll be wearing his cock as a necktie and bollocks a dickie bow, have his hands chopped off and be wiping his arse with a pair of stumps. Well maybe not quite so liberal. As is now obvious it's imperative the crushers get hold of the culprit before anyone else susses him out. The heinous crime had been committed in a main machinery space and so the culprit would most probably be in the engineering department as these area's are closed to everyone else. They chose two leading rates of which I was one, as I was the departments electrician, to keep watches 24/7 patrolling all the ships machinery spaces to attempt to deter any future attack until the felon was apprehended.

The outcome of all this was the ship would stay alongside in Trinidad until spare parts could be flown out from the U. K. and fitted on arrival. All the engineering departments shore leave was cancelled but the rest of the ships company could carry on as normal much to their amusement. After about four days of 4 hrs. On 4hrs off. Watchkeeping the pair of us could hardly keep our eyes open, and were so knackered up and down ladders all day and all night we would have strung the bastard up ourselves given half a chance. The system worked, a chief mechanician (Eng. Dept.) was apprehended, Balls intact, and locked up in a secure compartment to be flown home for a Court marshal A. S. A. P. on my rounds during the previous days I had been having a laugh with the same when he was on watch down the Eng. Rm. He seemed to find it quite amusing when I explained what I would like to do to the offender if I got my hands on him. Well that's life in a blue suit, you just don't know what's coming next. Spare parts arrived fitted and tested all correct, 0400 special sea dutymen close up, were sailing at last, 0500 special sea duty men stand down. "All divers muster at the diving store, At the rush" What the fuck. The ship was starb'd side too and our Port side was open to the incoming rising tide arriving through the beautiful lagoon entrance where we were berthed. Unfortunately the tide had brought with it hundreds of thousands of cricket ball sized jellyfish which were now backing up on our port side and blocking the main engine cooling water intakes about 20ft. Below the surface water line, stopping the engines from starting up. It was a revolting sight like Giant frogspawn, Tapioca or Sago pudding which I found particularly abhorrent.

The plan was for a couple of divers to enter the water make thier way down to the intake grills remove the offending said jelly fish and all would be Tikkerty Boo. Myself and Jackie Yarwood were mysteriously chosen for this nauseating problematic evolution, probably as a reward for coming back pissed from the cricket, bastards. We jumped in to the seemingly boiling cauldron of sickly white pulsating mess and Buddied up, it was weird as we left the surface and couldn't see a thing, we felt our way down to the intakes and started dislodging hundreds of slimy opaque throbbing stinging little bastards out that were clogging the cooling water intake grills, sucked in at the first attempt to start main engines.

The task was impossible as they were all around us and there were innumerable replacements, as we pulled them out the tide forced in more. The task was postponed until high tide when there was no high water pressure forcing them against the ships side. So down again after high tide when they had dispersed around the lagoon at slack water and we cleared the intakes of the gruesome mess left behind jammed in and clogging the grills with buckets full of what seemed like Gorilla snot . All clear "empty all strainers! Flash up, and away we go, thank fuck" .

We've done most of the tour of the Windies and its approaching time to be leaving for the U. K. There's a visit to Grand Bahama in the Virgin Islands and Bermuda Planned so were looking forward to those, then last stop to get some rabbits and duty free's at Gibraltar. Once at sea the whole ships company move into the three or four watch system (shift work), so that all aspects of shipboard life is kept running smoothly, the watches are, the Dogs 1600 till 2000, first, middle, morning, forenoon and afternoon. All four hour watches except the split dogs, 1600 – 1800, 1800 –2000, to allow to change watches so Jacks not keeping the same hours all the time, so consequently there are always some watchkeepers asleep in the messdecks especially the stokers mess. A shakes system was run from the bridge with the Bosuns mate being responsible for carrying them out. Consequently a notice had to be put on the relevant bunks so he could find the right ones in the dark, there was always some wag about to bring a smile to our faces ie. J Smith shake 0340. Shake Hard, If Hard Shake till soft.

About a week later we docked in Freeport Grand Bahamas for a few days, it was really expensive and way out of our league, so it would have to be ashore in tiddly uniform, not forgetting the golden Lanyard, to strangle the wallets out of the local Brown Hatters. We would be seeing the top sights, top shows, swimming from tropical beaches and drinking some of the best bevy on the Island. You can't beat Matlot's at quantative easing, the pressure from the millionaires wallets just falls away, and they love it, a little bit of sophistication after Ma di Gras in Trinidad was just what we needed, after buying a few rabbits (presents) for home in the duty free area we slipped our berth and slung our hook, to head out for our last port of call in the Carribean (this trip, more to come) Bermuda which we were getting to know quite well as it was usually the first and last Port of call on visits to that area including Florida and the keys. Excuse me what job was this. That's right, one of the best and didn't we love it and make the most of our misfortune. Bollocks! Dream on.

Bermuda was good but not as good, some people had to work here, peons, we had to spend our own money, but the diving and B. B. Q's were excellent and the Crayfish plus Lobsters nearly made up for it. The local Fanny put on a big dinner dance for us, they couldn't help it really. An immaculate Royal Naval Destroyer berthed in one of the top locations, Floodlit at night and bursting at the gunnels with oodles of unexplored fresh cock, no one could blame them it was amazing how they lost all inhibitions when a British warship arrived, it was every ones chance to carry out their fantasies to the extreme if that is what suited them, and no one would be the wiser. After a few days the ship would up anchor and disappear over the horizon and out of their lives for ever (or until next time) leaving them with their treasured memories of the time they spent with little Jack Hornier than most. I was shaking a wicked leg around the dance floor, when the spotlight stopped on the pair of us, I hadn't been paying attention (not to them anyway) when we were presented with a huge beer stein with a flip top lid, brilliant my lucks come in by the bucket full especially with the doll I'm stuck to like a limpet, and as it turned out for the rest of the night as well. – – -Somebody's got to do it. – – Yee Hah.

The last day was spent decking the ship out in bunting and fairy lights extra awnings etc. as the wardroom were throwing a cock and tail party for all the stiffs who managed to

Purloin an invite, as usual it was pretty formal and fulfilled an obligation to the Island. On completion the duty watch were required to dismantle all the party gear and stow it, all ready for sailing the following morning. We were to join a big N., A. T. O. exercise for the following week off Key West. Florida. Our last big commitment before leaving the station for home waters.

We were fully flashed up during the morning watch, four boilers on line when we let go for'd. let go aft. at 0800 and true to form the jetty was pulsating and throbbing as we were leaving behind in our wake most of the spare Fanny on the Island plus lots more of the not so spare, sobbing into their hankies and waving goodbye, farewell, adieu, au revoir, God bless and Bon Voyage and quite a few Piss Off's from the cuckolds as well, from the jetty as Decoy and ships company slowly slipped our berth gradually increasing speed heading for the horizon, giving the crew ample time to recharge their weapons making sure all armament was fully loaded and ready for action at our next Port of call no matter where the eventuality. "England Expects Every Man To Do His Duty" and by gum we were certainly up for that.

A life on the ocean waves, de dum, dah, dah, de dum. Bring em on the more the merrier, in with it out with it don't fuck about with it knob glorious knob.

As soon as the fleet was assembled for the war games which included tens of surface warships with their attendant supply vessels carrying food, dry supplies, furnace fuel oil, diesel oil, ammunition, spare parts, helicopters, jet fighters, bombers, submarines the whole shebang, the sea's in that area were teeming with war vessels straining at the lease to blow each other out of the water, anything to eliminate the opposition A. S. A. P. This was at the height of the cold war and we could find ourselves doing this for real at very short notice at anytime in the not too distant future. (The Cuban Missile Crisis was in full swing at the time and we were right in the middle of it).

When as if to order over the horizon comes smokey Joe. A Russian trawler bristling with wireless antennae for information gathering , equipment and radar aerials to spy on the activities of the enemy fleet, plus asdic sets to track our submarines. Their information was always spot on, it was obvious to us the Russians had spies by the cart load in our headquarters, but obviously not so obvious to the well paid personnel who's job it was to maintain our secrets. Trouble was they were nearly all as bent as Arabs daggers, so what chance did secrecy have, practically none. On completion of the exercise Smokey Joe would relay all the top secret information gathered back to a Russian mother ship, which in turn would transmit back to headquarters in Russia. then deploy off over the horizon to await details of the next N. A. T. O. exercise ready to gather even more of our so called top secret information. You couldn't make it up.

To save all the expense of the armed forces why not just post all the info., too them. I guess its because its all just one big Ludicrous front, and were the dummies paying for it. The information put out was that the games were a complete success, well fucking Hoorah, although they didn't say who for. We were now sailing North for Gibraltar to take over as Guard ship for six weeks, to stop the Generalissimo Franco from moving in and claiming the rock as his own, Spains. Can you believe the cheek of the man, Gibraltar being less than a mile away from Spain and directly connected by a causeway, its obvious to any M. P. it truly belongs to the U. K. over a thousand miles away, and if anybody disputes that fact we'll send in our troops and blast them out of the water.

It doesn't matter how many of our own mum's and dad's children, off spring get killed and maimed. So long as we are doing it in the name of Democracy and freedom for the people. We were there to fuck him and his deigo's off for the British Government, should they try. The rock is British, got it and its staying that way. He keeps a little smoking tub (smoky Joe) of what he considers to be a warship on guard just outside the harbour ready to nip in and stake a claim if we give it a chance, our M. P. 's aren't daft, that's why they've stationed us there, ready to blast their nuts off if they have the Gall to try. no hope. We're not sure if that's the only one he's got, but to be fair its doing its job by keeping us in attendance, which isn't a bad job at all, for us, cheers Franky me old son.

We spent the next six weeks in Gib. Just wishing it away so we could get home for a while before our next trip. The diving was ok around the rock but a little disappointing after where we had just been, The fanny was always scarce on the rock, the locals had union Flags flying and painted everywhere to give the impression they were pro British, but that was swallowed only by the bone domes in Westminster. The truth being they were milking the British tax payer of millions for allowing the troops to be based there, supposedly controlling the entrance to the Med. When they didn't want to be under the control of the dictator Franco of Spain, and had no way of maintaining themselves financially, they took the better of the two evils and faked a love affair with Britain while ripping off all the troops at every opportunity on the rock.

Typically one Pongo's wife was in the checkout queue of the grocers store behind the gibbering locals, when a R. A. F. type's wife behind her said "excuse me, but the woman in front of you hasn't got enough money to pay for her shopping and has told the cashier to put the rest of her on bill on the foreigners tab behind her, which she did as it was the standard practice, little did the diego's know the R. A. F. type two behind spoke Spanish, thieving two faced bastards.

fter a couple of weeks we met some Brits. Living on the Rock, they had a good life style and their own properties, as there wasn't that many of them in the social group they tended to have some pretty wild parties. We couldn't believe our luck at our first invite when after a few of their cocktail specials the lagging started to come off. Fucking hell Smudge were in like Flynn here. We soon found out the life was pretty boring living there permanently, when any new blood arrived it was roped in A. S. A. P. to take part in the Toga parties which to say the least were fast and furious and physically draining, bastard, fuck our luck. I'm sure if we persevere we'll survive. I had kept in touch with Janet the jenny wren from H. M. S. Collingwood by airmail and we'd exchanged a couple of letters, which was a first for me, the usual routine being find em. Fuck em then forget em.

That always seemed the best and only policy to keep their thieving hands out of your pockets and relieving any bulk you may have acquired from your wallets. We had received an arrival date for the U. K. so I wrote home within about three weeks giving the mail good time to arrive there, and let them know we were soon to be on our way. We slipped our berth and departed after our six weeks tour as guard ship when our relief arrived, the queue outside the sickbay tiff's door was growing longer and earlier every morning as the social players began squeezing up, an occupation hazard after visiting the local poxed up whores, and my didn't they have some exotic diseases to export to the U. K., there were some long faces onboard from the troops who were by now pumped full of penicillin and their liberty curtailed.

YEt the hardest thing of all for them to cope with was the stoppage of their tot until they were all clear, and the dreaded Gonococi bird was on its back and well and truly dead. By then they would be fully rejuvenated pumped up and ready for action on the circuit once more doing with zeal the performances totally expected of them. Good lads, that's it, don't let the side down, keep a humping and a pumping, believe me, no matter what they all say in public, that's exactly what all the lot of them want in private. So keep your mouths shut and save embarrassing yourselves because we know what your really thinking, we've laid too big a percentage for you to be any different.

CHAPTER 20

Homeward Bounders

On the way home the ships mechanical and electrical defect list was submitted to our home port (Portsmouth) for programming in and work to commence on our arrival, part of the work included the underwater Asdic equipment, and shaft alignment checks which required a dry dock for us to berth down in. Unfortunately all docks in Portsmouth were taken and the next nearest available one was down in Janner land, where the oggies grow on tree's, Plymouth. That suited all the victualed members fine, mostly single men who lived onboard permanently., but really pissed off the whining R. A. 's. Married members who lived ashore with their families in married quarters, or the switched on kiddies who had bought their own homes for their families in the ships home port.

Now instead of being able to go home nearly every night the poor darlings would have to make the three hundred odd mile return journey to Portsmouth from Plymouth every weekend, while during the week have to put up with the earache every night when they queued up to phone their wives only to hear "I know what your up to, so and so's old man says you've been out on the town. No thanks that's definitely not for me. We're the free spirits, the wandering Toms. Yeah!. Out enjoying the nightlife, every night where ever we happen to find ourselves. Work hard play twice as hard, have been doing for years, the light weights couldn't understand how we did it, practice me old sons practise.

I gave the Jenny Wren a bell, Janet, and low and behold she wants to come down to Plymouth to see me. I'm not so sure I want this, I never make arrangements if at all possible, that way the worlds your oyster and nobody gets let down, I hate some one else tying up my life. I play everything off the cuff all for today fuck tomorrow, it may never come. It looks like I've been Shanghai'd though, she's only booked into the wrens quarters of the sailors fleet club for the following weekend, it looks like I've been well and truly goosed. I got myself a weekend pass and booked myself a room around the corner in the same club. I met her in town after tot Saturday Lunchtime, I thought this a bit weird she had her bessi oppo with her from Collingwood with my superb vision the only thing that I could see In my minds eye was me filleting the pair of them. Not the case as it turned out, she disappeared from view so I left it at that. We had a dinner time sesh in one of the Matlot's pub's then made our way back to the fleet club for head down to recuperate for the evening, as I was leaving her by the wrens quarters as you do, the sap was not only rising but an incredible rate.

Now the ambition of just about every matlot since for ever was to manage to get laid in the wrns. Quarters. I some how convinced her we should give it a go, fuck the consequences, we crept in Tom and Jerry style unhindered I couldn't believe my luck. The accommodation was a bit sparse to say the least. There were two rows of ten cubicles either side reminiscent of large toilet traps with partition walls about six feet six high, we let our selves into the room which sported a tiny single bed, beggars can't be choosers, they sure had supplied the women with the accommodation they deserved, it was so quiet you could hear a pin drop. I think that was the last moment I cared about the noise, after a while when I had to surface for air a strange noise caught my attention, I cocked the good ear, and hark it was the sound of two more birds giggling, your going to have to wait your turn ladies, this is turning into a dockyard job, I'm Never going to get any sleep. Typical, life in a blue suit. We had a good Sat. night on the town and finished up back in the wrens quarters for the night.

All the rest of the minge occupying the quarters that night proved to be good old sports, as there were no adverse enquiries or complaints from the orifice in the morning, so, low and behold, the same again Sunday. It turned out to be a good weekend, and I saw her onto the train back early that night and made arrangements to keep in contact. I met up with the rest of the lads in a very popular spit and sawdust scrumpy house, bursting at the seams with hilarious whores down the strip in Plymouth. I caught up with what I'd missed over the weekend, and not the Dose's that are always quite prevalent in such establishments We finished up devouring a giant oggie apiece before boarding a fast black back onboard. As it was now, we had another five weeks on the loose in Plymouth before returning to Portsmouth for Easter leave, plenty of work onboard during the daytime, too much really as the dockyard had turned a lot down, which would now have to be completed by the ships company, on top of their own, planned in programme.

Still it had its compensations Plymouth was noted for its ball and body draining runs ashore, which I was sure we would be tentatively looking into and exploring, but only in as much as the human body could be expected to endure, and definitely no more "Fucking Roll on", Oggie, Oggie, Ogvgie, Hump, Hump, Hump!.

For everybody out there thinking of running down Jolly Jack Tar for his envied, but well deserved, lascivious conduct, where ever he was fulfilling his natural obligation to his intrinsically acquired duties, there were always at least twice as many females queue'ing up to participate in any such eccentricities, so before you start, put that in your envious dried up pipe and smoke it, and get over the time when you threw Your hat in the ring only to find out you didn't come up to Par!. so thin out, your reading the wrong book, "Go forth and multiply. "and take your prejudiced opinions elsewhere with you, preferably to Growlers anonymous.

The Decoy being in the last generation of riveted hulled ships deployed in the Royal Navy, made it practically unbearable to live on whilst undergoing repairs or modifications to the hull, especially when in dry dock. When the cacophony of noise was amplified out of all proportion as the sounds reverberated round and round the amphitheatre of the massive granite terraced hole in the ground, where resting in the middle and in the bowels of the dry dock was Decoy.

Especially when the dockyard matey's were cutting off the heads of old one inch diameter rivets, with a windy chisel located inside a steel compressed air driven handgun, your eardrums took such a battering they could be ringing for days to come, yet this wasn't as noisy as when replacing one inch sheet steel plate to the ships side, having hundreds of holes drilled at six inch intervals to accommodate the hundreds of white hot rivets to be hammered over with a windy hammer far exceeding the decibels of the previous.

It could be very quiet when you entered a compartment, when all of a sudden some lunatic without warning would start riveting, this could literally be another case of, "what colours blood" – – -"thank fuck for that I've shit myself". All this before the introduction of ear defenders, no wonder they used to say we had cloth ears, "Pardon – – Half past six" "NO – - for fucks sake, what's for dinner" "half past eleven" "Fuck Off you mutton eared Twat". "Steak and Kidney Pudding". Chief, – – – I give up.

I paid a visit to the diving school one forenoon and invited "Gollom" round for Gulpers of my tot, that lead on to a spine shattering run ashore down the strip, where we bumped into a couple of bootnecks off the Eskimo, that turned out to be a great laugh reminiscing on the Middle East and East Africa. and trick or treating in Iraq.

Fred the pencil thin can man shark wrestling off Bahrain. Gun running patrol up the Gulf, Devouring the Grunters Christmas dinners, Brilliant never to be forgotten. r time down in Guz. (Plymouth) I decided to put any spare time I had to good use, and study for my next, hopefull advancement to Petty Officer, petty meaning small, Officer meaning Pig. Hence small pig. The change in life style was the biggest jump in the "Andrew" (R. N.) Moving up from a broadside mess being a leading hand and taking all the shit for the mis-demeanor's of all the irks and morons below you, who couldn't give a shit for any rules or regulations and just wanted out and into civvy street at any cost, the main attraction on top of money, was escaping from the boiling pot of the sometimes unfathomable aspirations of the members of the open mess, to the closed and trusted environment inside the P. O's. Mess. Where all were treated as roughly equal, and if any trouble was spotted on the horizon and thought to be coming their way, they all stuck together like shit to a kaki blanket making sure if possible none of their members went down and to contain any problems to the inside boundaries of the mess, to be dealt with by the mess president accordingly.

Also a major plus being they were issued with a neat tot, that would nearly take the skin off the back of your throat, but although being highly illegal, at between 96, and 104, proof spirit it would keep and not go flat, and so be the basis of many Senior rates social events, or" monster piss ups". Where if alongside, shore side's fanny would be allowed to be invited onboard and into the P. O's Mess for social intercourse, Have You got cloth ears? I said social! Social, Fucking hell!. As can be seen, the advantages were enormous and very much revered to be safeguarded and treasured but jealously envied by the cretins below. You getting my drift!.

sat the written paper onboard, passed, and was then given the opportunity to take the much feared oral section, in the instructional area of the dockyard. Three senior Electrical Officers from different locations would chair the examining board to ensure any favouritism for whatever reason at all, couldn't be brought into the proceedings, after roughly a two hour grilling on any subject that took their fancy, I was invited to await their decision in an adjacent room while they discussed the why's and wherefore's of my merits or lack of them. In conclusion I would be given the verdict of their deliberations which was always final. Thank my lucky stars and all the hard work I'd put in, I passed, Brilliant.

A good reason for a celebratory run ashore, as if any were ever needed. I could now relax and patiently await my turn to be up rated to acting Petty Officer at the whim of the powers that be, or not, as the case may be. All depending on the continuation of my good conduct and Character. I don't know who the fuck dreamed that one up. If that really was the case all the fucking navy would still be A. B's. After completion of the maintenance period we had a few days shake down off Plymouth testing all equipment to make sure we were top line again and ready to take our place in the fleet to continue defending our shores so the general population could sleep safe and soundly in their beds at night.

We had time to admire the Eddystone Lighthouse ten miles out to sea off Plymouth Hoe and marvel at the brave men who first prepared the deadly rocks for construction when they were only uncovered and visable after high tide as the water level dropped, they rowed the massive blocks of Portland stone already dove tailed to fit together on arrival, all the way out there only to get lost in the fog on arrival, and left floundering deep in the channel wondering if that was their lot, but no, with unbelievable faith determination and perseverance after rowing for ever, arrived and then unloaded the tons of Portland stone before the tide turned, then rowed the ten plus miles back to the safety of Plymouth harbour.

To think that after hundreds of such horrendous journeys they eventually erected a masterpiece of engineering excellence, to eventually save countless thousands of lives up to date. Thanks, you fantastic long gone heroes. All main machinery trials completed we deployed hotfoot to assist a sinking trawler mid channel off Torquay, the boat was stabilised portable pumps installed and towed into Portland harbour, on completion we received a signal detailing us off to proceed with all haste to the north of Scotland some emergency requiring our presence, so we proceeded past Portsmouth to the consternation of the R. A's and the wrath of their wives and snotty screaming kids say no more.

We refuel'd from a tanker off Pompy just South of the Isle of Wight on completion the throttle jocky's punched in the big black burners (max. F. F. O. into the boilers.) and proceed at a great rate of knots for Jockland to find out what the problem was. We were later informed that a top secret American fighter bomber had ditched in the vicinity the Shetland Isles and all available vessels are to participate in a massive co-ordinated search for it, and hopefully find and secure it before the Russians do. The weather was horrendous at the time so it was going to be fun until it was found. As is often the case when operating in such extreme weather conditions accidents will developed rotor problems, maybe ice forming while she was searching the seabed in her designated quadrant of the search area and ditched, we were despatched to find her but to no avail as she must have sunk to the bottom like a stone, alas taking all her crew members down with her to a cold watery grave.

That's life in a blue suit, so just get on with it. The missing aircraft was located after about ten days, a marker buoy was fixed, a guard ship positioned to await the arrival of the recovery vessels to complete the evolution. In the mean time a few ships were sent into Lerwick the main town on Shetland for the weekend for a short break. A very cold and bleak place this time of the year, there are no tree's on the Island I suppose the constant arctic wind has got something to do with that, that said it didn't have a detrimental effect on our run ashore, which was good having a few bevies with the other ships company's. We were detailed to patrol the area until the salvage was complete, so the following weekend we headed down to the Orkney Isles and a visit to Scapa Flow where it all happened during W. W. 2. .

The place is a graveyard for untold warships, it was decided for us, we were to dive on various wrecks while in the area. We set off for H. M. S. Royal Oak, torpedoed and sunk whilst at anchor by a German U. Boat, but unfortunately the strong swirling currents put a block on that. We persevered and dived on an unknown Battle Cruiser in calmer waters, it proved to be an eerie experience, first when leaving the surface in the dark foreboding fjord knowing of the hundreds of dead sailors bones lying at rest below us, and then about ninety feet down the two of us swimming along the dark desolate upper deck with the steep sides of the fjord looming overhead, it made us all the more conscious of the fact that we still had to get back to the surface and in these conditions anything can happen and usually does nothing is for certain or taken for granted, at the same time thinking about the fate of our predecessors and their bones in the giant metal coffin just below us.

How just before the last time this ship saw daylight there were massive explosions lighting up the night sky's as the magazines were hit and all the ammunition went up, raging fires, splintered thick metal bulkheads and six inch armour plating from around the machinery spaces opened up like tin cans and shrapnel flying about in all directions, then even more explosions as the 400 degree plus super heated steam boilers blew up.

The poor unfortunate crew who hadn't been blown to pieces or instantly vaporised, were sailors burning, broken and limbless screaming for help but to no avail as everyone was in the same boat, only to be put out of their agony shortly by the thankful release of drowning, hell on Earth, and for what, for the country they died for to give succour to hundreds of thousands of foreigners in so called distress, who were then allowed full citizenship without even knowing who the hell they were or their true intentions, who then went on to weadle their way into positions of authority and power and eventually Parliament to consequently pass laws which are in no way beneficial to this country, thus ruining the land internally and making it possible to neutralise our once great country without declaring war on us, without giving any thought for the men or the reasons they were given who fought for Our freedom, criminal. We saluted them said a short prayer and thanked them all before leaving them in peace and departing for the surface. God Bless you all.

It left us with plenty of food for thought of the terrors experienced in that very place and really not that long ago. – – – – LEST WE FORGET.

On completion of the salvage operation we sailed from the immediate area down for a run ashore on the Mainland of Scotland. We anchored off Ayr South of Glasgow, we ended up in a bar on the seafront with about half a dozen chief's and the same no. P. O's. the place was deserted, later on we managed to find a Chinese restaurant using the term very loosely. I was one of the first to order and after what seemed like days the first apology for a meal arrived. God only knows who was cobbling the food together, but it certainly wasn't a cook, probably sew sew or tap tap or maybe even dhobi I was so hungry I could have downed a scabby dog, I managed to get most of it down my neck to the astonishment of the rest. I was now sitting there waiting for the others and beginning to feel sick when Cass Clay ups and goes to the toilet, when he came out I could smell a rat, (I'd probably just eaten one.) the way he was hanging about and not returning to his seat.

When the chokey disappeared out the back that was it, Cass grabbed his coat and was out of the door and going for it for all he was worth. Well I thought I'm not getting collard to pay for his meal, and mine was near poison so I'm up and running too, I grabbed my burbery of the hook as I sped through the door. That was it, the trigger had been pulled, just like the keystone cops the other ten are up and panicking and not wanting to get panhandled for paying the lot, two minuets later there's a dozen Chuff's and Puff's high tailing it down Ayr seafront going a good gallop in the pissing rain freezing their cobblers off and moaning that they were so hungry, they are going to castrate Cass Clay for causing all the panic and eruptions. The senior chief had got a right twat on, he was saying his meal had just arrived and he was so hungry he was actually enjoying it, he'd only had a few rushed mouthfuls as he watched the rest of the troops disappearing in increasing numbers and so, totally against his dignity and much against his better judgement had to join the hurdlers as they scrambled over the tables and chairs in a mad dash for the exit, he said he was fucked if he was going to be paying for twelve so called meals and where's Clay, "I'm going to read his fucking horoscope, he'll wish he'd never been born by the time I'm finished with him. " By now it was midnight and were all standing on the end of some God forsaken jetty wet through, waiting for the arrival of the open topped Liberty boat (a bloody whaler) to get us back onboard and away. Thank Fuck.

We arrived back in Portsmouth about three weeks later than originally scheduled, which finally put an end to the R. A's wingeing and whining. It was now time to face the music and see just what fate and the future had stored up and waiting for me.

CHAPTER 21

Torpedoed

I got in touch with Janet over in Collingwood and made arrangements for the weekend. We had already booked ourselves a holiday away together during the summer leave period, mid August in a boarding house on the Isle of Man. Neither of us had been there before and had heard good reports, so providing the bed was comfy we would enjoy ourselves. I was duty watch on the Friday, so we met up in Portsmouth early Sat. evening for a short weekend together. It was a beautiful summer evening and we were walking into Southsea, I was trying to cheer her up, as for some reason unknown to me at the time, she was sporting a right old face on her, like a slapped arse, which I must say I hadn't seen before, I kept asking what's wrong but to no avail, then in the end she broke down, crying her heart out.

What is it, I can't help if I don't know, it can't be that bad. I'm pregnant!. Fucking hell it was worse, like a knife going in. From out of nowhere I heard myself saying, we'll get married then. at that she cheered up no end. Me, after thinking about it for while, Bollocks I've been fucking torpedoed, welland truly sunk. My Goose is really cooked this time. This was really not on the agenda for me, at all, ever. Now it looks like I'm well and truly right up shit creek without a paddle. I never thought that I'd get caught, I'd fallen into the great big sticky web passed down from mother to daughter from time memorable, what should have been the good weekend I'd been looking forward to was rapidly turning into a mental nightmare. The usual option when Jolly Jack Tar found himself in this situation was to report the problem to the powers that be, onboard, who had the solution to all the females wielding a golden lanyard looking for life on easy street with their hands firmly entrenched deep in a sailors pockets.

The problem was so serious in those days that the Navy had developed its own solutions to the problem, to keep their numbers up and their sailors misery to a minimum, they would draft the would be host to the parasite off to a ship in the Far East with no forwarding address for anything up to a three year stint. Problem solved, the would be predatory vampires would be left to stew in the juices of their own making looking for another unsuspecting host to visit their dishonourable intentions upon, and the Navy could carry on enjoying the fruits of the labour of their near press ganged fleets of Sailors with minimum hassle. Thinking of my experiences in the far East, Monsoons, Singapore ear, prickly heat, girls looking like lotus flowers, but in reality poxed up to the eyeballs, more like deadly nightshade or poison ivy, vicious Chinese pimps to contend with. For some reason I didn't take that route. I'll take my chances and do the best I can for the three of us.

I'll have to go down to Sussex and meet her parents, "Good evening, my name is Harry I've come to ask for Janet's hand in Marriage" "Oh! That's nice , when" " Next month", "Oh! Oh! Why so soon". "Well Granddad, she's got a belly full of arms and legs so the sooner the better". I thought it better to keep it short and sweet. Succinct, less of a shock maybe. A quick movement!, I didn't think he was suddenly clutching his wallet, I was just hoping it wasn't a serious heart attack!. I'd just fucked up their annual holiday, was I really making his weekend!, I wasn't sure, I didn't like the angle his jaw was hanging at, and surely his eyeballs shouldn't be revolving like that, perhaps its just his way, they say these civvies can be a bit weird at times. I said we would finalise the details quite soon, thanked him for listening so patiently and I left wondering about the state of his health, he was hanging on to the front door jam and seemed to be having trouble breathing, his knees were definitely buckling.

He should see the Doc. for a good check up before we move in I think that will truly put the cat amongst the pigeons. He should be alright though with a regular supply of sedatives, especially when the shit machine arrives. God bless him!, God help him might be more appropriate, and throw a bit our way while your at it

Back onboard I asked Bob Burdis a run ashore oppo. of mine if he would be my best man, after about twenty minuets when he was gradually regaining control of his body and starting to get his breath back, (Bastard) He said he would. True to form the news instigated so much mirth and extracting of the urine, which was only to be expected when the main player took a dive.

My mind started to wander, wondering what the weather was like at the moment out the far flung, monsoon or baking humidity, nothing out there held anything remotely pleasant for me, just one big syphilitic shit hole as near to hell on Earth as anywhere could be. If I disappeared that would wipe the smile off Burdis's face he would have to take my place and marry her. I could just see the pair of them walking down the Isle, Bob dressed up like a Chinese money lender, with Janet in tow looking like she'd swallowed a space hopper, that would give him pause for thought especially when he was on gas alert for the first time.

Janet's Mother "Patience Fanny" some supreme monogram is that, has taken over thank God and is organising the wedding ceremony in Sussex, just as well because we'll be sailing soon for a couple of months patrolling the Med. again for a while.

Another obstacle is figuring out the best way to effect her departure from the W. R. N. S., being as we didn't have any money at all we would have to take advantage of any such aid as was available. For her to resign would deliver no coinage whatsoever, but to apply for, and accept the shame that goes with Discharged Pregnant, but carried a sum of a hundred pounds or so with it, went some way towards making the enduring ignominy of the situation somewhat palatable, for a short while anyway, our monitory needs came first no competition.

So the ball was rolling and gathering speed fast. By the time May arrived as quick as a flash, Janet had effected her discharge and was now living at home again with mum and dad, younger sister and even younger brother, they were to say the least back living on top of one another again, the two girls sharing a room together once more, with Whisky the black mongrel dog quite happy for the present!. Little did he know, he soon wouldn't be the only shit machine in residence, and that wasn't going to be the only surprise for him, he was also going to be bottom of the pile.

Looking ahead slightly and preparing the way for the inevitable day of surrender, I've applied for a married quarter in or around Portsmouth, we will have to take our chances with what comes up, they are fairly plentiful in that area so it shouldn't be too long at the latest we should be housed long before the screaming shit machine arrives just prior to Christmas 1967.

The ships immediate programme has just been published we are back in Pompey the last two weeks in July and the first two in August so that gives her mum some dates to aim for unless she can organise the wedding while I'm still at sea, no such luck I suspect I'll just have to be there. We decided to keep the holiday on the Isle of man and just update its title, now to be called a honeymoon the only difference being we would have a lot less money to spend after the expense of the wedding.

We sailed from Portsmouth to do another stint in Gibraltar, to relieve the ship having completed its tour of duty there. It was now getting more like home from home, tot and a few wets onboard lunchtime then ashore down the main Street one of the first bars en route we called in was the "Black Watch" Bar, named after the Scottish Pongo's Regiment (smelly old man of the jungle), that was about right.

It might even have been called the Tartan bar because it was decorated with all the different Tartans Of the Old Scottish regiments, (we used to call them scotch, just to get the heathen Bastards going), below the bar level and all around the walls, it held some fantastic memories for us. Winding up the smelly's, then the punch ups that followed, some we won some we lost all part of keeping our hand in at fighting. After all that's what the Government paid us for to do their dirty work for them. Pity some of them didn't show their Chicken lily livered faces, we could have smacked some sense into the self centred bent moronic buffoons and we wouldn't have charged them a penny for the privilege!. Early evening sneaked up on us and we were burbling like rock apes, that's it time for a laugh round to sugars bar before we got too pissed to enjoy the banter. Oooh!

This Is my lucky day, its my sailors come to see me, in from the sea with all the rest of the flotsam and jetsam at high tide, up you to Sugar we've missed you, you fucking Brown owl, get your laughing tackle round this bastard and mind your fucking tonsils. OOoooh! Fuck off you lot, I'm here for the needy not the bloody greedy. At that he pulled out the biggest lipstick cock from his hold all removed the cap, rotated the piece and out popped the most enormous reddest bell end ever seen in seven navies, he proceeded to touch up his ever pouting lips while fluttering his eyelids, which was all the time egging everyone on to multitudinous cheering. "another round please you bent bastard" Oooh I'll swing for you one day (hang), not For me, From me, you fucking knobber, at the same time transferring all the money from Jacks pocket to the till. Sugar wasn't daft, far from it, he had the market collard living the life of Riley, also when there were no ships in and it was quiet, he would be off sailing around the Med.

In his luxury yacht, munching his way in and out of all the small Islands trying to set up some sort of record, it takes all sorts. The Raving Queen of all the Rock, or maybe "Muncher Extra'ordiniare" "Fancy eating You here! Jack" He had certainly set himself up with a Munchers Emporium, a brown hatters haven, a hat rack's heaven. Certainly a Perverts paradise. We'd all had a good giggle and run ashore, it was now back onboard and head down, we had an early start in the morning, the team were going diving off the end of the Airport runway, some vital equipment had dropped off an Airliner and into the oggin, it needed to be retrieved in order to prove the incompetence of some bull shitter and string the bastard up giving the rest of his like, some reason to get their act together concentrate their minds on the job in hand, and bring the rest of their jobs up to Par ie

There are no such things as accidents only incompetence on somebody's part which should not be tolerated especially when commercial airliners are involved, the message being if you don't want to find yourself dancing on thin air, do your job properly. After retrieving the said vital piece of missing equipment we went fishing, Cray fish by the basket full, we were going to cook them on a secluded beach we knew beautiful fresh lobbies and crayfish, gives you the horn something cronic, enough to drain the blood from your eyeballs (right good treading medicine) Whoohoa! Its gonna go up tonight, its gonna go up tonight get em off girl your on next.

It'll make more than your eyes water believe me, there's enough here to choke a fuckin donkey, Having trouble walking, come here I'll soon have you smiling again, a quick back splint will do the trick. That'll straighten you out while you have a gay day. "I'm innocent your honour, the bed was on fire when I got in it. " One unsuspecting couple took a ferry trip across the Straits to Tangier, Morocco, where at the time, general rules seemed to be non existent, live sex shows abounded during the day and night time, animals included, pigs, dogs, even sodding donkey's.

Instead of complaining they used the old adage, when in Rome do as the Romans do, as they were going about their business trying to ignore the loudly advertised entertainment, a big surly Arab tried to abduct their blond haired blue eyed little boy of about four years, they should have been warned before the start of the journey, as it was a well known fact that young European boys were a prized possession of the Arab traders!, bandits!, fucking arse bandits, it was no fucking joke, us Matlots had to be extra careful on a run ashore over there you could easily end up fighting for your life.

There was always a group of us together watching each others backs (not the only ones.) at all time, things got more dangerous as we relaxed with the bevy inside us, to be careless straying off on your own and getting lost has cost more than one serviceman a lot more than his dignity, It wasn't exactly the day out they'd planned finding themselves abducted and impaled on the front of some dirty Arab, wondering what the fuck Granny would have to say about all this. The whole place was syph'd up to the rooftops, the pox doctors nightmare, that was one thing in our favour though, as in this situation we wouldn't be going bagging off not even using your mates cock so we definitely wouldn't be squeezing up (rotten) thank fuck. To say the least that place wasn't for the faint hearted and not even the not so easily upset.

Whilst making their way back and effecting their escape, they were accosted again and again to sell their little boy to the Arab traders, evil bastards. How many youngsters had they turned into white slaves and then sold on into prostitution over the years was nobodies business, and their still at it. Keep it quiet, nudge, nudge, wink, wink, don't let the general public know. After arriving back A. S. A. P. at the married quarters, they thanked their lucky stars they were still all intact and swore to God they'd never go anywhere near any Arabs ever again, not even on the rock. How to win friends and influence people, some bloody hope. Fucking perverts.

H. M. S. Ottis, a diesel electric submarine came alongside on her way out to the Med. We were looking over the side down on to her conning tower when she berthed.

After she was secured and made fast her state of readiness for sea was relaxed, her watertight integrity breached and the orders were given to open up the main hatch to the upper deck. We were absolutely amazed at what began to unfold before our very eyes, green fumes began emanating from inside the hull followed by the unbelievable stench of what followed shortly afterwards, crawling out of the hatch with dirty long oil soaked hair, skin, sallow and yellow from lack of sunlight, ingrained with the oil and grease from down the dark hole, with overalls that were glistening like a sweat soaked second skin, Submariners, we'd heard of these beings but were never expecting to be swamped by them.

Fucking hell they had been submerged since the U. K. a good couple of weeks and had been breathing the same re-circulated air with minor top ups while re-charging the submarines batteries at periscope depth, since leaving the U. k. no wonder they were minty, being rationed to a pint of water each per day to be used for everything, including all ablutions, any dhoby'ing, wetting the whistle, the chances of any of the precious liquid finding it's way down to their nether regions and dampening down the all too common clag nuts and dangle berries was non existent. They come alongside use our washing facilities, abuse our hospitality to the maximum, fucking Gollams. There motto "We come unseen" the reality was "we come unclean", they all stunk like Polecats with dog breath Alitosis, and now the dirty filthy smelly bastards were pouring onboard and polluting our living space, the bathroom was by now overflowing with minging, wandering fucking Jews, typical, they had no respect or consideration for anyone else at all.

Selfish bastards, and we'll only have to clean up all their shit and pollution right after they've scrubbed themselves down, unbelievable. Never mind, at least their on our side. – – Twats. After they'd cleaned up a tad we had them spread around our messes for a few beers, they turned out to be a great bunch of blokes, they would have to be to put up with that load of bollocks so we made arrangements to carry on for a run ashore together on completion, just as soon as we had unblocked the fucking drains, – – – – Crabby bastards. – – -scaly cunts.

After assisting them with their onboard maintenance for a couple days they slipped quietly away during the middle watch to commence their cloak and dagger surveillance of the Mediterranean sea, playing cat and mouse with the trespassing Russian submarines, carrying out their illegal surveillance of the western hemispheres defence systems to the oblivious satisfaction of the non warring Mediterranean type yokels, who caught the odd mystery submarine in their fishing nets and then went on and on about the monster from the deep which tore free from their shrimping gear.

We completed our stint as guard ship and sailed for home, we called in at Brest for a quick run ashore just to liven the Frogs up, get their bile reacting in the negative which was all too common with them, they hate the Brits as do the rest, but they just can't help showing it, especially when we arrive by the warship full. It doesn't matter which ship visits, they always have a lively weekend with the sickbay working overtime, but with cheap wine and brandy under our belts ready to knock out the bums back home, all we needed now to complete the exercise was to purloin a couple of boxes of the putrefying embalming stuff they make ashore. cheese they call it.

The eruptions that stuff had caused, upsetting the conviviality of the mess deck, especially after a week or two at sea. Embarrassed ! matlot's searched their lockers for a hidden pair of rotten socks or similar because secretly no one knew where it was coming from, and it just might belong to them, all the kit lockers being bolted together with numerous ventilation holes between them, circulated the ripe stench of the unknown offending French culprit freely between every ones personal gear, secretly made everyone feel responsible. As each new morning broke the ever more powerful rancid aroma was reminding me more and more of the beautiful mademoiselle's matted armpits and festering crutch, " (a good enough reason for the use of the copious amounts of perfume they get through), or even that wild Canadian polecats arse that I rescued from its prison under the gangway when we were exploring up in British Columbia. How the hell anybody can actually eat this stuff is unbelievable, this had now gone beyond a joke its got to be found.

Here it is. Fucking hell it Is my locker that's chucking up, I'll never live this down if I'm connected to it, I hadn't bought any ashore so I wasn't really associating myself with it. I had forgotten that when we were storing ship just before we sailed I had re-routed a couple of small boxes that had been on their way to the wardroom, no wonder the pigs had all got faces like lemon sucking Gorgons, devouring that stuff. I managed to secretly manhandle the foul, fetid, excrescent down to the Quarterdeck where I beat the shit out of it before consigning it to the deep, thank fuck, Amen.

We arrived in Pompey where I secured an extended Long Weekend, I took the future wife north to meet my parents, purchase an engagement ring and Sus. out the living, work and housing situation for when I was released from the Mob. in a couple of years time. To say the initial experience was a shock to the system would be the understatement of the century. The beautiful proud old cotton town was absolutely crawling with foreigners mostly Pakistanis, they must have been coming in on a conveyor belt I don't think I'd seen so many in Karachi. I could sense the tension and pressure in the town centre how the hell had this been allowed to happen.

If ever a good reason was needed to string up the incompetent buffoons who set themselves up as politicians from the lamp posts this was it. The Armed Forces had been deployed all over the World to stave off any invasion and look after the countries interests for the indigenous population who worked hard and paid for their protection with their hard earned pennies and with the lives of their precious sons. Then to get invaded behind their backs while the spurious anarchists had purposely had the troops deployed out of the country under the false pretences of their making. Treachery of the highest order, hang the guilty for doing it, and the rest for not stopping them. I cannot express my disdain for these two faced cretins highly enough so I won't even try any more.

I purchased an engagement ring in the high street we dined out with my parents, as for the rest of it totally out of the question. The whole spirit of the community had been destroyed, family firms generations old, carpenters and joiners, plumbers, bricklayers, plasterers, bakers, butchers, fishmongers, cotton mills all the life blood of the community, etc. etc. etc. all gone, once gone, gone forever. Moral, non existent, the whole state of the town deteriorating down out of existence, all my school friends and their families gone to better climes, where the odds weren't stacked against them, as in their own country. A thousand years of history thrown away, down the pan , a thousand years of brave soldiers died for nothing. This will be one of the last times I will visit the town of my childhood before its final criminal transformation, and demise.

The wedding has been set for the end of July, our honeymoon surprise, surprise is booked for the following week on the Isle of Man, I won't tell a lie I'm not looking forward to any of it, at all. There's doing your duty and doing your duty I think this is stretching it a bit far, but as the old saying goes, you made your bed now you lie in it. I think I'm going to find this one a bit lumpy along the way, still that's life in a blue suit mustn't crumble.

We've had a couple of, loss of freedom runs ashore, in Pompey, and that's exactly what they were and felt like. I've travelled down to Sussex mid week in time to prepare for the weekend, its at the stage when I'll just be glad when its all over. I'm on the Sea front discussing the situation with my intended, wondering what time everyone will be arriving and where they'll be staying.

Bob my best man is arriving Friday afternoon, I asked her what time her "besy oppo" was arriving, obviously a sore point, " she's not coming", that seemed damn weird as these two were inseparable. I began to smell a rat, and a fucking big one at that, a Coypu! Cacibara. !. a politician even!. I started wondering if I was a bit thick or something as the penny began to slowly drop, I had never felt so sick in my whole life, I'm ready for off, I would have been gone there and then if it hadn't been for the situation, talk about Hog tied and Ham strung, betrayed wasn't the half of it.

By Friday afternoon I was more than ready for off. I would have been gone but Bob would be arriving shortly, Mum and Dad would be half way down from Lancashire, the rest of the family arriving from all over the country, I can't let everybody down, I'm sick to the stomach, I have to talk to somebody, somehow I end up having a heart to heart with my maybe future sister in law, she's having a hard job convincing me it's just a phase all girls go through, because, as far as I can see it, all the blokes going through the same phase get locked up with a lot more blokes, presumably to get in more practise before being let loose on society again, to reek even more havoc, once again munching their way through the parks, public toilets and cinema's ad infinitum.

Politicians, school teachers, etc. etc. Creating a whole new generation of a grazing society. The whole fucking lot beats me, are they all fucking queer, before I really know what's going on, all the guests have arrived we've said ta ta to all the women, and all us blokes are off down town to start the biggest piss up in seven navies. Fuck em all, fuck em all, the long and the short and the tall, Round the teeth round the gums, watch out stomach yer it comes. This is it, the preparation for the sacrificial slaughter tomorrow has begun. More beer, More beer, More rum, More rum. We took over the rear lounge of the local Railway Terminus Hotel for the evening, it wasn't planned it just happened that way. It was table cloths and waiter service in those days, long before modern governments pooled their expertise and turned everywhere into the shitholes they are today.

We had a really good night considering, It was a Friday night there were about a dozen of us and a big fat jovial French waiter served our tables with the first drinks, when he arrived with the last (forth) tables drinks, I said "same again" and we heard at a later date that was how it went on for the next five hours. The waiter was telling us he didn't get an opportunity to serve anyone else all night. No wonder I needed a livener the next day in the Old Plough with Father and Bob whilst waiting for the Bride to arrive, in the pub Bob was shaking so much the Landlady said to him "never mind it will soon be all over" I said another large whisky please and its me not him. The wedding went to plan (not mine) after the ceremony we were in the vestry signing the book when I first spotted Janet's full name, I had to look a couple of times just to make sure it wasn't my brain still in auto., Janet Fanny Green. I never imagined I'd manage to get it written indelibly into the family name and not even knowing it, it must have been written in the stars.

All the legal business out of the way, we finished up in another church hall for the reception, where the now Mother in Law ran the local cub / scout troupe, Claustrophobic wasn't the word I just wanted out of this strange environment and away. I was thinking, I've gone and bloody well done it now. " Marry in haste, repent at leisure" All the old ones are the best. True that's why. Time to leave for the London train thank Christ. All our luggage was in her uncles car who was going to run us into Town to catch the local train into Brighton. During the course of the afternoon one of the lads had offered to run us all the way into Brighton, brilliant.

We said our goodbye's and made our way through the expectant crowd to uncles car. To everyone's disappointment we opened the boot removed our luggage and deposited it in matey's boot, alighted blew the horn waved and fucked off rapid at an ever increasing rate of knots feeling an immense sense of freedom just to be away out on our own, doing our own thing, I could see why I joined the Navy in the first place now it looks like its all fucked up for no good reason. We left them all staring at uncles car all daubed up with graffiti and tin cans tied to the rear end left now sadly with nowhere to go.

We caught the London train spent the night in a Soho hotel, had a couple of Matlot's wets in the bar, a really heightened anti climax, caught the boat train to Liverpool in the morning, missed the scheduled ferry, arrived on the later one, missed our evening meal, but thankfully the landlady had stowed away a salad for us, which we devoured ravenously, if that's what you can do with a salad, before retiring to our boudoir and marmalising the bottle of Champagne and the rest of the booze I had so carefully stowed away for any such unforeseen emergency. We arose the following morning to a beautiful day and spent the forenoon exploring the mysteries of Douglas. Douglas being the name of the town and not the local Hatrack.

Evening time arrived and we had been promenading ourselves up and down the seafront trying to get used to being Mr. and Mrs. Green no mean feat, we had explored the place to death and were now looking for a drinking establishment with some life in it. We heard a live band playing and decided to give it a whirl. It was packed, being a typical holiday set up with all the tables and chairs in the middle of the huge room with a runway all the way around the outside for the waiters to be able to do their job, and the punters to come and go as and when etc. etc., we had been standing up for ages when a seat became vacant and available at the table next to us where an old couple were sitting, they offered the seat so I sat Janet down there, she looked as if she really needed it, no wonder with a belly full of arms and legs, and having been carting them about up and down the sea front all afternoon. after a further couple of pints my legs were so tired after the previous days hyper activity I just had to sit down. So I sat Fan (name change from now on, of which she didn't go a bundle) on my knee and we started a conversation with this nice old couple who were also on holiday.

Suddenly out of the blue someone shouted in my face, "Hey You" stop that canoodling and left , we all looked at each other and laughed as she was only sitting on my knee and I had my arm around her shoulders. We carried on with our conversation and after about ten minuets the same again, but before I could say anything he was gone, the twat, we looked at each other beginning to feel a bit embarrassed. I was looking the other way talking to the old fella about the navy when I was on the receiving end of this fucking moron poking me violently in my shoulder, "I've told you two, stop that canoodling" that was it I instantly lost my rag. "that's my wife your talking about, I screamed "come here" and just before Fanny landed on her feet , he must have spotted my eyeballs vibrating in and out at a great rate of knots because he was off, going like a hare with a dog up its arse, and I was that dog. Two circuits of the entire floor and I was nearly on him, by now all the Grockles had lost interest in the live band and were cheering me on as we circumnavigated the throbbing floor.

He must have realised his goose was nearly cooked because on the next circuit instead of passing the managers shaky prefabricated office he dived inside and locked the flimsy door. Steam was just about coming out of my ears and the safety's coming up for lifting. " Come out, Come out you yella bellied streak of piss" I was shouting, to the ever growing excitement of the grockles Who were now up and chanting nail him, nail him, nail the bastard, by now I had my left foot up on the door frame and was yanking at the door handle, heave, heave it was coming, another couple of strong pulls and the door would be off. I didn't know why at the time but the roar trebled, I soon found out why, three more bouncers had appeared from nowhere and were molesting and manoeuvring me in the general direction of the main exit door.

For some reason they wouldn't listen to my protestations and I suddenly found myself outside slung onto the pavement, Bastards, there's a first time for everything, this was the proverbial "Bums rush", – – Chicago style, – – cunts, as I was dusting myself down, brushing off and straightening my tie, who appeared on the scene right on cue, that's right, Mrs Fanny fucking Green!. I'm still on a high with the Pop (beer) and the adrenalin coursing through my veins like the driving steam of the Flying Scotsman, its lifeblood. She's looking at me wondering what the fucking hell she's married, and I'm thinking we only went in there for a few quiet wets and all fucking hell breaks loose, I don't know. One thing I do know for sure, somebody's going to get a fucking good shagging tonight and its not going to be me.

I don't know what it is with me and the Isle of Man, but years later I visited again this time as President of the P. O. 's mess on another Pussars warship, also alongside at the time was one of our diesel submarines on which occurred a major incident.

Talk about the shit hitting the fan, everyone was covered, we were knee deep in the fucking stuff. Courts marshal flying about everywhere, left, right and Chelsea. The whole fucking apple cart turned upside down, inside out and to no ones benefit at all but, definitely to my detriment. Bollocks, but that's a story for another time. In the meanwhile we've got more than enough on our plate to occupy our minds trying to deal with our immediate future. Like somewhere to live when we get back would be handy for a start, but that's the beginning of a whole new story.

To be continued.

Harry.

Bye.

Aged 16 in 1959 in 'Tin Town'. On my first motorbike,
a Francis-Barnett 197cc.

My dog Rough, 1960 about six months old.

Rhyl Boating Lake 1959.

1959, Blackpool on my first motorbike, a Francis-Barnett 197cc.

*Lake Windermere,
went on my bike, 1959.*

Me and my dog Rough when he was just six weeks, 1960. He lived in his new kennel that I built under my window.

On Samson, at Drakes Farm, Barnsdale, just before Adrian whipped his back end and sent us galloping up the field. First time on a horse, August 1957, aged 13 years.

Outward Bound from HMS Collingwood, in the New Forest, 1961.

Harry and a Junior Stoker, HMS Collingwood, Defiance Division, 1961.

Top of the Rock – Gibralter, Killick of mess Eskimo.

Red Rider, 'Bungi' Williamson and me on the 4.5 inch gun,
on arrival in troubled Aden.

HMS Eskimo, just before the bomb blast. Aden.

The Three Wise Monkeys, *me (hear no evil), Bungi (see no evil) and Red Rider (speak no evil).*

Bagsy Baker, me and Malcolm Pyrah (who was killed), China Fleet Club, Hong Kong, 1962.

General Salute Present Arms – The Captain of Collingwood taking our Passing Out Division, August, 1961. We are the Gaurd of Honour – we are at The Salute and the Captain is returning Salute. Harry five along from left.

Me and Brum Faulkener, drinking draught Tiger Beer in the Fleet Club (United Services) Singapore, 1962.

Been in a couple of weeks. Harry second from left, front row. Rough blue serge suit, highly 'spit and polished' boots.

The 'Big One', HMS Hartland Point, Harry Green, 1962, Singapore.
Dockyard in the background.

1966–1968, HMS Decoy leaving Portsmouth, Gosport in the backgound. She had two engine
rooms and two boiler rooms and was the last 3-turret (twin 4.5 ins) ship in the Royal Navy.
We did two 3 month tours of the West Indies, before any modern building work. They were
nearly all unspoilt tropical islands (brilliant).

August, 1961, just completed New Entry Training and our Passing Out Division. Marching off the parade ground, HMS Collingwood, to await a sea going ship.

HMS Eskimo, 1964–1966, Middle East, East Africa, Spain, Portugal, Gibralter, ports around England, Scotland, all Channel Islands, Orkney, Hebrides, Norway, Sweden and Germany.

New Entry Training 20 February–8 August 1961, HMS Collingwood.
Harry second from right, back row.

'Sir Francis,' I said, 'there's Armada,' I said. Well, not really, but Factory Supervisor Gladys
Wilkinson was in great form showing some of the HMS Eskimo visitors around Cleethorpes Factory.